The Seventy
Great Mysteries
of the Ancient
World

UNLOCKING THE SECRETS OF PAST CIVILIZATIONS

With 431 illustrations, 177 in color

 Thames & Hudson

The Seventy
Great Mysteries of the
Ancient World

UNLOCKING THE SECRETS OF PAST CIVILIZATIONS

EDITED BY BRIAN M. FAGAN

Contents

Myths & Legends: Hidden Truths?

Mysteries of the Stone Age

Ancient Civilizations

Tombs & Lost Treasures

Ancient & Undeciphered Scripts

The Fall of Civilizations

List of Contributors

BRIAN M. FAGAN is Professor of Anthropology at the University of California, Santa Barbara, and a leading archaeological writer. He has written major studies of climate change, Egypt and the history of archaeological discovery, as well as the standard textbook *Ancient North America* (3rd ed., 2000). **22, 45, 48, 65, 67, 68, 70**

CHRISTOPHER CHIPPINDALE, a curator in the Cambridge University Museum of Archaeology and Anthropology, is author of *Stonehenge Complete* (2nd ed., 1994). One of his fields of research is the archaeology of rock art in Aboriginal north Australia. **16, 25, 26, 29**

RICHARD A. DIEHL is Professor of Anthropology and Director of the Alabama Museum of Natural History at the University of Alabama. He has specialized in the archaeological study of ancient Mesoamerican civilizations for forty years. He is author of *Tula: the Toltec Capital of Ancient Mexico* (1983) and co-author with Michael D. Coe of *In the Land of the Olmec* (1980). **37**

AIDAN DODSON is a Visiting Fellow in the Department of Archaeology at the University of Bristol. He has written extensively on Egyptian history and funerary archaeology, and among his recent publications are *The Mummy in Ancient Egypt*, with Salima Ikram (1998), and *After the Pyramids* (London, 2000). **35, 50**

ESTHER EIDINOW is researching aspects of uncertainty among the ancient Greeks for a D.Phil. in Ancient Greek history at Magdalen College, Oxford. **39**

CAROL J. ELLICK is founding director of the public programmes department at Statistical Research Inc., an archaeological and historical consulting company in Tucson, Arizona. She specializes in the development of archaeological education materials for the pre-collegiate classroom and the interpretation of the human past for the public. **69**

KENNETH L. FEDER is an archaeologist in the Department of Anthropology at Central Connecticut State University in New Britain, Connecticut. He is the founder and director of the Farmington River Archaeological Project, a fellow of the Committee for the Scientific Investigation of Claims of the Paranormal, and the author of several books, including *The Past in Perspective* (2000) and *Frauds, Myths, and Mysteries: Science and Pseudoscience in Archaeology* (4th ed., 2001). **5, 6, 7, 8**

ROBERTA HARRIS lectures on the archaeology of the Ancient Near East, specializing in the biblical period. She was for many years the Honorary Secretary of the Anglo-Israel Society and the Founding Editor of its annual *Bulletin*. She is the author of *Exploring the World of the Bible Lands* (1995). **1, 2, 3, 9, 10, 53, 54**

JOHN HAYWOOD is an Honorary Teaching Fellow in the Department of History at the University of Lancaster and a Fellow of the Royal Historical Society of Great Britain. He is the author of several books, including *Encyclopaedia of the Viking Age* (2000) and *The Historical Atlas of the Celtic World* (2001). **40**

CHARLES HIGHAM is Professor of Anthropology at the University of Otago, New Zealand. He has been undertaking research in Thailand and Cambodia for the past 31 years, and has written several books on aspects of Southeast Asian archaeology, including *The Archaeology of Mainland Southeast Asia* (1989), *The Bronze Age of Southeast Asia* (1996) and *The Civilization of Angkor* (2001). A Fellow of the British Academy, Professor Higham is currently directing a major research programme in Cambodia, on the origins of the civilization of Angkor. **52**

MARK HUMPHRIES is a lecturer in the Department of Ancient Classics at the National University of Ireland, Maynooth, and is a specialist in the history and archaeology of the later Roman empire and early Christianity. He is the author of *Communities of the Blessed* (1999), a new appraisal of early Christian expansion in western Europe. **66**

LAWRENCE KEPPIE, who is a professor based at the Hunterian Museum, University of Glasgow, has written extensively on the Roman legions, Latin inscriptions and Roman remains in Scotland. His many books include *The Making of the Roman Army: From Republic to Empire* (1998). **42**

DAVID LEWIS-WILLIAMS is Professor Emeritus and Senior Mentor in the Rock Art Research Institute, University of Witwatersrand, Johannesburg. His publications include *Believing and Seeing: Symbolic Meanings in Southern San Rock Paintings* (1981), *Stories that Float from Afar: Nineteenth-century/Xam San Folklore* (2000) and, with Jean Clottes, *The Shamans of Prehistory: Trance and Magic in the Painted Caves* (1998). **20**

J.P. MALLORY is Professor of Prehistoric Archaeology at the Queen's University, Belfast, and specializes in the early prehistory of the Indo-European-speaking peoples. He is author of *In Search of the Indo-Europeans* (1989) and co-author of both *Encyclopedia of Indo-European Culture* (1997) and *The Tarim Mummies* (2000). **30, 36**

SIMON MARTIN is a graduate of the Royal College of Art and is currently an Honorary Research Fellow at the Institute of Archaeology, University College London. For the past six years he has been doing epigraphic fieldwork at Calakmul. He is co-author (with Nikolai Grube) of *Chronicle of the Maya Kings and Queens* (2000). **14, 44**

STEVEN MITHEN is Professor of Early Prehistory at the University of Reading. His research interests include the evolution of the human mind, prehistoric hunter-gatherers and the use of computer simulation in archaeology. His current field project is based in Wadi Faynan, Jordan. His publications include *Thoughtful Foragers: A Study of Human Decision Making* (1990) and *The Prehistory of the Mind* (1996). **17, 18, 19, 23, 24**

MICHAEL R. MOLNAR is an astronomer and a specialist on astral symbolism on ancient coins. He is the author of *The Star of Bethlehem: The Legacy of the Magi* (1999). **11**

COLIN PARDOE is a consultant in archaeology and biological anthropology. He has written on the relationship between biology and culture. **21**

KONSTANTINOS POLITIS is a special assistant curator in the Department of Medieval and Modern Europe at the British Museum, specializing in the archaeology of the Dead Sea region. He directed the Sanctuary of Lot excavation and restoration project, and now directs excavations at ancient Zoar in Safi, Jordan. **4**

ANDREW ROBINSON is the author of *The Story of Writing: Alphabets, Hieroglyphs and Pictograms* (1995) and *Lost Languages: The Riddle of the World's Undeciphered Scripts* (forthcoming). He is Literary Editor of *The Times Higher Education Supplement*. **55, 56, 57, 58, 59, 60, 61, 62, 63, 64**

CHRIS SCARRE is Deputy Director of the McDonald Institute for Archaeological Research and editor of the *Cambridge Archaeological Journal*. He was editor and principal author of *Past Worlds: The Times Atlas of Archaeology* (1988), and *Timelines of the Ancient World* (1993). He has also written *Chronicle of the Roman Emperors* (1995) and co-authored *World Civilizations* (1997). **27, 28, 41**

IAN SHAW is Lecturer in Egyptian Archaeology at the University of Liverpool. He is the author of *Egyptian Warfare and Weapons* (1991), co-author of the *British Museum Dictionary of Ancient Egypt* (1995), editor of the *Oxford History of Ancient Egypt* (2000) and co-editor of *Ancient Egyptian Materials and Technology* (2000). **31, 32, 33, 34**

CHRISTOPHER SNYDER is Associate Professor of European History and Chair of the Department of History and Politics at Marymount University in Arlington, Virginia. He is the author of *An Age of Tyrants: Britain and the Britons, AD 400–600* (1998) and *Exploring the World of King Arthur* (2000). **12**

CHARLES STANISH is Associate Professor of Anthropology at the University of California, Los Angeles. He has conducted surveys and excavations in the Lake Titicaca Basin of Peru and Bolivia, specializing in the origins of complex political and economic organization. He is the co-author (with Brian Bauer) of *Ritual and Pilgrimage in the Ancient Andes* (2001). **46, 47**

JAMES F. STRANGE is Professor of Religious Studies at the University of South Florida, Tampa. He specializes in New Testament Studies, and the archaeology of the Roman and Byzantine periods in the eastern Mediterranean. He is the author of several books and many articles on archaeology. **13**

JO ANNE VAN TILBURG is Director of the on-going Easter Island Statue Project. She is a Research Associate of the Cotsen Institute of Archaeology, University of California, Los Angeles, where she is Director of the Rock Art Archive. Among her publications are *Easter Island. Archaeology, Ecology and Culture* (1994) and the Easter Island entry in the *Encyclopedia of Prehistory for Human Relations Area Files*. She is currently writing the biography of Katherine Routledge, co-leader of the Mana Expedition to Easter Island. **49**

RICHARD F. TOWNSEND is Curator of the Department of African and Amerindian Art at The Art Institute of Chicago. He has written about Aztec art, architecture and ritual landscape. His publications include *The Aztecs* (2000) and the major exhibition catalogues *The Ancient Americas* (1992) and *Ancient West Mexico* (1998). **15**

ROGER WILSON is Professor of Archaeology in the Department of Archaeology, University of Nottingham, where he is also Head of Department. He specializes in the Greek and Roman archaeology of Sicily and the central Mediterranean. He is the author of several books, including *Sicily under the Roman Empire* (1990). **38, 43, 51**

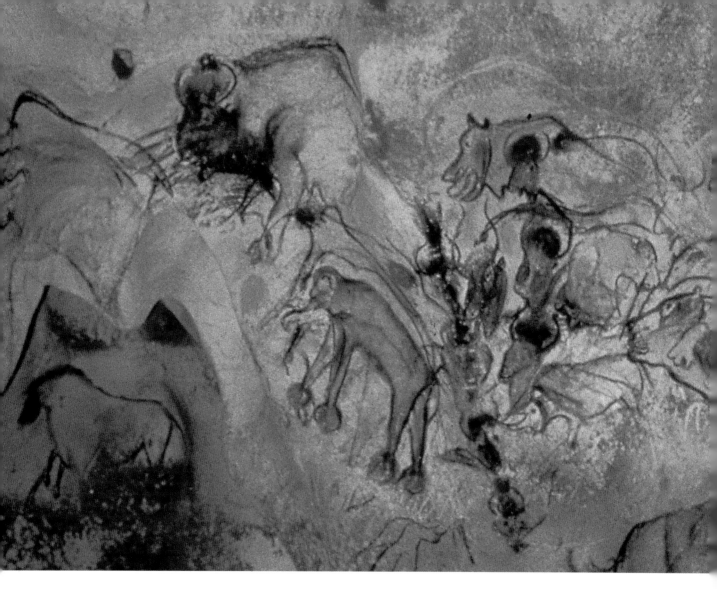

Preface

THE HUMAN PAST, with its unsolved mysteries, surrounds us on every side. Archaeologists are concerned with uncovering the story of humanity, in all its diversity, spanning an immense period of more than two-and-a-half million years. In this pursuit, they frequently investigate the mysteries of the past, and it is perhaps this aspect of their work that most readily captures the popular imagination.

We search for people, places and events recounted in myths and legends which have disappeared – or which perhaps never existed except in the human imagination, where they are so deeply rooted that they have become potent symbols or strongly held beliefs. We feel a desire to understand our own past, yet the distance of time often adds to the air of mystery. Where did our remote ancestors come from

and how did we evolve and develop? We wonder what happened to successful and apparently invincible ancient empires which seem suddenly to have collapsed and disappeared; and we cannot conceive how our own predecessors created some of the world's greatest monuments, or why.

Here we examine a wide range of mysteries from what we call the 'ancient world', a term which defies precise definition. A century ago, we would have equated it with the ancient Mediterranean world, with Egypt, Greece, the Near East, Mesopotamia and Rome. The mysteries of the past then encompassed Classical legend and such questions as the location of the Garden of Eden.

Today, the 'ancient world' encompasses everything from African hominids to early maize farmers in Mexico and Chinese royal burials. The 'ancient world' of a hundred years ago was a village compared with the 'global' archaeological world of today. Our stage is the world, so we content ourselves with the

broadest of definitions. Our 'ancient world' covers all periods of human history and all parts of the world, up to the voyages of Europeans to the 'new world' beginning five centuries or so ago.

The 20th century abounded with books on some of the world's best-known mysteries, but few people are aware of the astounding range of controversies and unsolved puzzles from the ancient world. *The Seventy Great Mysteries of the Ancient World* aims to fill this gap. No one will agree with all our choices, but they are spread widely enough in time and space to reflect the remarkable diversity of human societies in the past, and they include mysteries unimagined a century ago. To mention only a few: Who were the first Americans? Was there once a Mother Goddess cult? Why did Maya civilization collapse so suddenly? And did comets and asteroids devastate the earth and early civilizations?

Many ancient mysteries arouse passions so violent that laypeople and scholars take sides with the fervour of religious believers. The articles in *The Seventy Great Mysteries of the Ancient World* are authoritative and, above all, dispassionate, thanks to the expertise of the 28 distinguished authors who have contributed to the volume. They provide a balanced perspective on some of the most hotly contested debates about the past. Some of our contributors readily admit that they cannot provide definitive answers to abiding mysteries of the past. There is a refreshing scientific honesty in these pages.

This is a fascinating, provocative journey through the most enthralling mysteries of the past, written by some of the best experts in the business. As such, this book has enduring value.

BRIAN M. FAGAN

Above **The brilliant paintings of Chauvet Cave in France have been dated to 30,000 years ago, making them the earliest representational paintings known.**

Introduction:
A Scientific Pursuit

The most beautiful thing we can experience is the mysterious. It is the source of all true art and science.

ALBERT EINSTEIN, 1930

THE BIBLICAL FLOOD, ATLANTIS, enigmas of the Stone Age, undeciphered scripts and lost civilizations wrapped in swirling mists: this book is a journey through some of the major mysteries of the human past, from all corners of the world. Many of them are enduring conundra, which may never be resolved by science. Others are fundamental questions about ancient human societies that have puzzled scientists for more than a century.

The Seventy Great Mysteries of the Ancient World is divided into six parts. We begin with 'Myths and Legends: Hidden Truths?', some of the more celebrated mysteries of the past, which have passed into popular culture over many centuries. Science and myth are uneasy bedfellows, for the former requires concrete proof, while the latter often demands belief. Our perspective here is one of science, a search for the historical grounding of enduring legends. We examine the evidence for the existence of the Garden of Eden and the Exodus, and we also discuss the persistent controversies about the lost continent of Atlantis and the Trojan War, which have engaged the attention of respected scholars since Victorian times.

The key word here is 'evidence'. For example, what solid historical evidence exists for the Holy Grail or for the whereabouts of Aztlán, the mythical birthplace of the Aztecs? Does the story of Jason and the Argonauts have a basis in actual ancient Greek voyages to the Black Sea? Is the quest for the Ark of the Covenant a fruitless one? Do the Australian Aborigines preserve a memory in the so-called Dreamtime of the first human colonization of Australia tens of thousands of years ago? And does the Turin Shroud really hold an image of the dead Christ?

'Mysteries of the Stone Age' ranges widely over earlier prehistory, tackling some of the major issues that still puzzle archaeologists and scientists. We explore the origins of modern humanity and the controversies surrounding our beginnings in tropical Africa, the origins of speech, and the enigma posed by the world's first artistic traditions of some 30,000

Left **Theseus kills the Minotaur in this black-figure Greek vase painting, c. 540 BC. The legend may preserve a memory of the Minoans of Crete, who practised a religion in which bulls appear to have played a significant role.**

Right **Lindow Man, as found in a peat bog in northern England. Other bodies have been discovered across northern Europe – were they religious sacrifices, executed criminals or murder victims?**

Below **The enigmatic stone figures of Easter Island have intrigued visitors since the 18th century. The giant statues, known as *moai*, are thought to depict high-ranking ancestors; their red topknots represent the feather headdresses common in Polynesia.**

years ago. Who were the first Americans? How did humans first cross into Australia and how long ago? What wiped out such big game animals as the woolly mammoth and the sabre-toothed tiger at the end of the Ice Age? Another intriguing debate surrounds the origins of farming in southwestern Asia some 12,000 years ago, which triggered fundamental changes in human societies that endure today. Many suppose the first farmers to have had a matriarchal

A hunter with bow and arrow depicted in a rock painting from the Drakensberg Mountains, South Africa. Such rock art is found all over the world and is a direct record of how ancient people experienced their world.

over the age of the Egyptian Sphinx. Then there are issues still unresolved by modern science, such as the cause of pharaoh Tutankhamun's death and the mysteries of the Nazca Lines in southern Peru. Human sacrifice and mummification are persistent themes in many ancient civilizations, leaving us to wonder why people like the Incas and the Carthaginians sacrificed children to appease the gods, and to ponder the close links between fertility of the soil and the continuity of human life. The mummified bodies found in China's Tarim Basin were not sacrifices – but who were these mysterious people, with their tattoos and tartan clothes? Ancient Rome, so familiar in many respects from archaeology and the Classical authors, nevertheless still retains some mysteries, from the secret cult of Mithraism to the puzzle of the lost legions.

'Tombs and Lost Treasures' reviews some of archaeology's most spectacular discoveries and the many questions they pose. The Copper Scroll from the Dead Sea, while closely studied and translated, remains enigmatic and has not yet yielded up the secrets of its contents. Others, like the terracotta regiments of the Chinese emperor Shihuangdi, offer tantalizing hints of the extraordinary wealth that may still remain buried in the unexcavated tomb of the emperor. But all these finds remind us that spectacular artifacts are only part of the excitement of discovery. Far more important are the questions which they pose about the societies they came from, and the religious beliefs behind them.

society built around a cult of the mother goddess. We examine the evidence for this belief. And who was Ötzi the now-famous Iceman, who lost his life and was miraculously preserved in the Alps over 5000 years ago? Other questions asked are where did the Indo-Europeans come from, and how did ancient peoples build Stonehenge?

'Ancient Civilizations' covers many controversial issues, among them Afrocentrism and the identity of ancient Egyptian civilization and the alleged African origins of the Olmec people of Mesoamerica. These controversies fan violent passions, as do debates

Left **Archaeologist Johan Reinhard reveals the frozen mummy of a child, sacrificed by the Incas on the top of a high peak in the Andes. Such sacrifices were thought to appease the powerful deity of creation, whose realm was high mountains.**

Opposite **The Aedicule in the Church of the Holy Sepulchre in Jerusalem is believed by many to have been built over the tomb of Christ.**

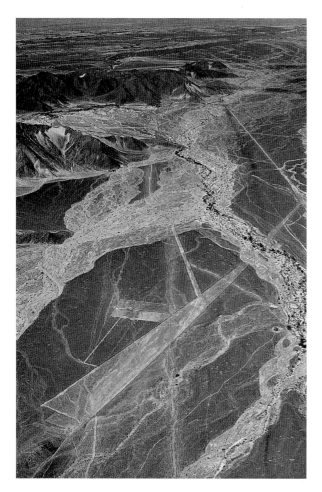

'Ancient and Undeciphered Scripts' delves into some of archaeology's greatest unsolved enigmas. Decipherment requires remarkable scholarly skills and often involves dedicated teamwork – or sometimes fierce competition – between scholars who combine a passion for detail with the imaginative ability to make inspired leaps of faith. The triumphant decipherment of Egyptian hieroglyphs, Assyrian cuneiform and Maya script are well known. Here we describe some of the scripts that are still undeciphered, and artifacts that have defied expert scrutiny for generations, among them the Indus script, Cretan Linear A, the Phaistos disc and some early scripts of highland Mexico.

'The Fall of Civilizations' looks at some of the ways in which ancient civilizations collapsed, a surprisingly neglected subject. The fall of Rome and the collapse of ancient Maya civilization have been the subject of controversy for generations. Ecology, social stress, warfare and many other causes have often been invoked to explain collapse,

Opposite left **The mysterious Nazca Lines of Peru's south coast, revealed in this airview, date from 100 BC to AD 700. Some researchers believe that the lines were ceremonial pathways, others that they were linked to ancient watercourses.**

Left **The magnificent ruins of the Maya city of Palenque in Mexico. The question of why complex and successful civilizations, such as the Maya, suddenly collapsed is perhaps one of the most compelling mysteries of the human past.**

Left **The strange symbolism and arcane rituals of the Roman cult of Mithraism have long intrigued scholars. This sculpture from the Roman fort of Housesteads, northern England, depicts the birth of Mithras from an egg.**

Right **A cup with an inscription in Etruscan. The language of the Etruscans remains a mystery, even though we know what individual letters signify.**

but catastrophic climate change is assuming new importance, thanks to remarkable progress in deciphering short-term climatic shifts, especially over the past few thousand years. We show how new information on strong El Niño events is changing our perception of the collapse of Moche civilization in northern coastal Peru, and how severe drought cycles contributed to the much-discussed ancestral pueblo (Anasazi) collapse in the American Southwest. Even more dramatic are a new generation of controversial explanations which involve catastrophic cometary encounters and other severe astronomical phenomena as a leading cause of collapse and devastation.

Over three-quarters of a century after the discovery of the tomb of Tutankhamun, the pace of archaeological discovery has not slowed. There remain many fascinating mysteries of the past to engage both scholar and layperson alike. Herein lies the abiding joy of archaeology, a celebration of human diversity in all its bewildering complexity and mystery.

Myths & Legends: Hidden Truths?

'ALL RIGHT, I will take you to the world of legend. You know that time, that place well, where animals talked and walked as men, untamed, unchanged, real people still....' The Northwest Indian story of the creation is one of countless such myths, a way of explaining the world order, the beginnings of existence. The ancient Egyptians told of the god Atum, who emerged from the watery chaos and raised a primordial earthen mound over the waters. Genesis, Chapter 1, recounts how God created the world and humanity in six days. We humans have a unique capacity for spiritual and symbolic thought, for defining the boundaries of existence, the relationship between the individual, the group and the cosmos in song and recitation. We are also intensely curious about the past, which is why so many of us have a preoccupation with the historical veracity of myths and legends.

Some of the greatest literature of the Western world – the Scriptures, Homer's *Iliad*, the *Epic of Gilgamesh* and the Norse Sagas, to mention only a few – began as oral epics, which were later set down in writing and have been cherished, studied and analysed exhaustively to this day. They contain some of our best-loved stories of adventure and bravery – Jason seeking the Golden Fleece or Theseus battling the monstrous Minotaur in the Labyrinth. Inevitably, inquisitive science asks the question of questions: are the legends true? Did Moses actually flee Egypt at a time of plague and pestilence? Were the cities of Sodom and Gomorrah destroyed by fire and brimstone? Is the Trojan War historical fact and was King Arthur a living person who quested for a Holy Grail? Definitive answers

Jean-François Detroy, *The Capture of the Golden Fleece*, 1743: what truth lies behind the story of Jason and the Argonauts?

often seem to elude us, for legends are not readily susceptible to definitive proof, as demanded by sceptical science.

The search is demanding. The quest for the Garden of Eden involves researches into Sumerian literature as well as archaeology. Sir Leonard Woolley believed (wrongly) that he had found evidence for the biblical Flood in a deep trench at Ur in southern Iraq. Today, there are claims that the sudden flooding of the Euxine Lake and the creation of the Black Sea caused folk memories of the Flood. Atlantis has generated an enormous speculative and scholarly literature. One of the most durable theories is that the Greek philosopher Plato recorded dim memories of the highly advanced Bronze Age civilization on Crete. Navigating through such controversies is to journey through shark-infested academic waters under constant attack from those who do not question the historical existence of, say, the Ark of the Covenant, the Ten Lost Tribes of Israel or the Star of Bethlehem. Epic tales and spectacular disasters may offer adventurous scenarios and simplistic explanations for the past, but often science proves that historical reality was much more complicated.

All early civilizations created powerful ideologies, by which they explained their origins or vindicated the rule of divine kings and imperial rulers. Ancient Maya mythology was an elaborate fabrication, which placed powerful lords at the heart of a mythic world. Their priests maintained the celebrated Long Count calendar, which some people believe predicts the end of the world in AD 2012. But can one apply ancient Maya teachings to the 21st-century world? The Aztecs of the Mexican highlands created for themselves a glorious imperial past in the early 15th century AD, designed to justify their military campaigns and conquests. Their manufactured history placed their ancestral homeland to the northwest of the Basin of Mexico, at a lake called Aztlán. Can we now locate Aztlán and the original homeland of the Aztecs? The scientific jury is still out.

The Maya and Aztecs thought of the living and spiritual worlds as a continuum, where men and women of unusual spiritual power had the ability to cross into the supernatural realm, to communicate with the ancestors and the forces of the spiritual world. In such cultures, the question of whether creation legends or epic tales are true or susceptible to scientific proof never arises. They are part of the fabric of human existence. The Australian Dreamtime is such a symbolic world, which surrounds every band member and pervades all life.

The Shroud of Turin is among the most famous and controversial of all relics of Christ, a cloth with the back and front images of a man, said to be Jesus himself. Radiocarbon dates place the Shroud in the 13th or 14th centuries, but there are serious anomalies and questions surrounding both the dating and the way in which the image was produced, or appeared on the fabric. The questions over the Shroud are a classic example of some of the limitations of science in unravelling mysteries of the past.

Some of the greatest challenges for science lie in the verification of long-established myths and legends. To search for answers is harmless enough, provided one remembers that, to many people, they constitute either historical truth or the core of human history and existence as a matter of legitimate and deeply held faith. And science is powerless in the face of fervent belief.

The Holy Grail appears before Lancelot and the other knights of the Round Table. The question of whether King Arthur and his fabled court actually existed arouses great controversy and debate.

The Garden of Eden

Time: mythical
Location: possibly southern Iraq

Eden is a unique place on earth, but no creature is permitted to know its exact location. In the time to come … God will reveal the path to Eden.

A RABBINIC PARABLE

N O ONE HAS ever known where the biblical Garden of Eden lies, with a great, life-giving river flowing through it. The book of Genesis tells us 'God planted a garden eastward in Eden' (Genesis 2: 8), which is taken to indicate an area of southern Iraq anciently called the Land of Sumer and Akkad. Over the centuries many people have looked for this fabled garden, but it has never been found. Similar legends are known from Sumer also, although they lack the sense of sin and punishment present in the Hebrew account. Later theologians, from St Paul on, thought of the Garden of Eden as a place of heavenly reward rather than an earthly paradise (2 Corinthians 12: 3).

The biblical image of the Garden of Eden as an earthly Paradise or Garden of Delight, with God, the Father and the King, blessing Adam and Eve from the heavens. The planets in their spheres divide heaven from earth.

Left **A picnic in a garden, from a Persian manuscript of the early 16th century AD. The Persians gave the world the idea of Paradise, from a word meaning 'park'.** *Above* **A pool in the garden of Nebamun, from his 18th-dynasty Egyptian tomb. The pool is surrounded by trees, providing welcome shade.**

Egypt, contrast starkly with the dust of the dry plains and sandy desert beyond. Without fresh water nothing can survive – plant, animal or human. And along the sea coasts the land cannot be tilled unless there are springs or clear running streams for the crops. Where rain does fall it is never completely predictable; even irrigation agriculture is at the mercy of the water supply. In the Nile Valley Pharaoh's dream of seven years of abundance then famine for seven more (Genesis 41: 1–4), reflects a very real situation in Egypt that persisted until the mid-20th century when the Aswan dam was built.

Thus the idea of a garden has been precious in the Near East for millennia. The very name 'Eden' is linked either to an Akkadian word *edinu* meaning 'a plain' or, more probably, to a Hebrew root meaning 'delight' or 'pleasure'; from earliest times it was linked to the idea of Paradise. Our word 'paradise' originates in the Old Persian *apiri-daeza* – a park – which became *pardes* in Hebrew and then *paradeiseos* in Greek. In Greek translations of the Bible the word was first used of the Garden of Eden and then for all gardens and pleasure parks, such as the great complex of palaces set in well-watered gardens with swimming pools and water features that King Herod created at Jericho in the 1st century BC.

Gardens in Egypt and the Near East

The idea of a garden is deeply rooted in the Semitic psyche – probably as an antithesis to the parched landscapes that lie all around the cultivated areas where people live. It is hard labour to bring food out of the unwilling earth of much of the Near East. This huge region has always been an area of immense contrasts: well-watered, highly fertile oases, carefully nurtured by their inhabitants, exist in the middle of arid deserts. The immensely rich river valleys such as the Tigris and Euphrates, flowing through Turkey, Syria and Iraq, and the Nile in

In pharaonic Egypt kings and aristocrats surrounded their homes with irrigated gardens that produced fruit and vegetables; fish for the table came from pools, beside which people relaxed in the heat of the day. Such a garden is mentioned in the Hebrew Bible in the area between the double walls that guarded Jerusalem (2 Kings 25: 4). This may well be the same as the garden of King Uzziah noted in 2 Kings 21: 18. Elsewhere in the ancient Near East royalty created paradise gardens, such as those of the palaces of Assyria and Babylon. Some kings also created vast parks for wildlife, not so much for conservation as for hunting all kinds of imported and specially bred game – the most famous being the lions hunted by Assurbanipal (668–627 BC) depicted on the reliefs from his palace at Nineveh. Another relief shows this same king and his wife feasting in a bower of vines amid the luxurious trees of their palace gardens. A garden, probably created by Sennacherib (704–681 BC), is depicted in yet another Nineveh relief, criss-crossed by irrigation canals fed from an aqueduct built by the king to bring water to the vegetable plots, orchards and parks of the city, from the Zagros mountains some 80 km (50 miles) to the east.

The Hanging Gardens of Babylon

The most famous gardens of all – the Hanging Gardens of Babylon – were renowned even in ancient times. These 'gardens of delight' (a good way to translate 'Garden of Eden') were one of the Seven Wonders of the ancient world. In legend they were

Above **Assurbanipal, king of Assyria, feasting in the palace gardens. Relief from the palace at Nineveh, 7th century BC.**
Below **Reconstructed façade from Nebuchadnezzar's throne room, Babylon, with palm trees and shrubs, 6th century BC.**

Above **A Mesopotamian cylinder seal, with two figures seated on either side of a sacred tree – on the right is a goddess, as shown by her horned headdress. Behind each rears a serpent, prefiguring the story of the Garden of Eden?** *Left* **Adam and Eve, by Masolino and Masaccio, 15th century. Note the snake's head in the shape of an obviously female head.**

all sorts of plants. More recent archaeological investigation has identified an area north of the royal palace where massive irrigated terraces may well have been planted with trees and flowers for the use of the king and his family and followers. Interestingly, this area lay between the walls of the palace proper at the extreme northwest corner of Babylon and the outwork walls to the north. It is possible then that the classic location for a royal garden was in the area between the double defensive walls of a city, close to its palace, as in Jerusalem.

The idea of Eden

The royal gardens of the ancient Near East are practical evocations of a mythical dream. The image of the biblical Garden of Eden itself is of an earthly or a heavenly paradise to which human beings aspire as a place of rest. In Western civilization it relates to notions of a 'Golden Age', 'the Happy Isles', 'the Islands of the Blessed' and 'the Elysian fields', and others like them. The concept of Arcadian innocence has proved very persistent.

In the Bible, Eden is a place of innocence, belonging in an age of innocence, when people could speak with God as with a friend. Then we grew up. As the fruit of the Tree of Knowledge opened our eyes to the reality of our condition we became fully human. We knew that we must work to live, that disease, evil, poverty and death stalk the world. The truth of a parable is very profound and works on the level of the human heart. Today we are more ready to recognize that the Garden of Eden has its place only in our souls, where the meaning of a symbolic myth is more powerful than any concrete fact.

created by the Babylonian king Nebuchadnezzar (604–562 BC) for his Median wife, Amyitis, who pined for the wooded mountains of her native land. Early in the 20th century, the German archaeologist Robert Koldewey thought that he might have identified the foundations of this structure, which he imagined as a kind of terraced ziggurat covered with

The Biblical Flood & Noah's Ark

2

Time: mythical/mid-6th millennium BC
Location: southwestern Turkey/Black Sea?

So God said to Noah, 'The end of all flesh has come before me, for the earth is filled with violence because of them. And now I am going to destroy them [and] the earth. Make yourself an Ark of gopher wood ... I am now going to bring about the Flood – water to cover the earth destroying all living things on it.'

GENESIS 6: 13, 17

THE BIBLICAL STORY of the great Flood that drowned the whole world is recounted in the book of Genesis, chapters 6–9. When God decided to destroy His Creation due to the sins of humankind, Noah alone was saved because he was a righteous man. God gave him detailed instructions on how to build a ship (usually called the Ark), which would have looked much like a long house with a gabled roof and many small rooms. When the rains started Noah led his family on board, together with representatives of all living creatures in pairs.

The rains continued until the entire surface of the land was submerged; but eventually they ceased and the floodwaters began to recede. The Ark came to rest on the mountains of Ararat and Noah sent out birds to see if it was safe to leave the Ark. First he sent a raven and then three more times he sent a dove. When the last one did not return, Noah knew that the earth was drying out and they could all disembark. Once on dry land his first action was to offer sacrifice. God approved of it and decided never again to doom the world for the sins of humankind. He established a covenant with Noah and bade him 'Go forth and multiply and fill the earth' (Genesis 9: 1). Humans would have in their care all the creatures of the earth and, as a sign of this covenant, God placed the rainbow in the sky.

The quest for Noah's Ark

From ancient times people have looked to one mountain peak or another as the place where Noah's Ark came to rest. In recent times many expeditions have set out to find its remains and there are numerous mountains to choose from in the Near East. One is Pir Omar Gudrun, called Mount Nisir in the past, which lies near Kirkuk in Iraq (ancient Mesopotamia), east of the old Assyrian homeland in the Zagros Mountains. Another favoured area is in the Taurus Mountains east of Lake Van in Armenia. At the time of the Assyrian Empire (roughly 9th–7th centuries BC) this was the kingdom of Urartu (note

Below **Noah's Ark resting on Mount Ararat: a dove returns, carrying a leafy twig to Noah, the first sign that the waters of the Flood are receding.**

Left **Tablet 11 of the famous Epic of Gilgamesh from ancient Babylonia. It recounts the flood story of Ut-Napishtim, the Mesopotamian equivalent of Noah (c. 2000–1800 BC).** *Opposite* **Mosaic from San Marco, Venice, showing Noah and his family in the Ark. Noah is releasing all the animals of the earth, in pairs, from the Ark.**

and from the Mediterranean to Mesopotamia. The Greek Flood hero was called Deucalion. Like Noah, he and his wife built an Ark and, loading animals on board, set sail to avoid destruction. In ancient Mesopotamia the Flood hero was at different periods called Ziusudra, Atrahasis and Ut-Napishtim.

It is this Mesopotamian legend that most closely resembles the story of Noah in the Hebrew Bible. In 1873 George Smith of the British Museum published the Epic of Gilgamesh, a mythical king of Uruk who, with his close companion Enkidu, had many adventures. When Enkidu died, Gilgamesh was distraught, and set out to find the secret of eternal life from his ancestor Ut-Napishtim, who had survived the Flood, and to whom, together with his wife, the gods had granted immortality. Ut-Napishtim's story is told in some detail and it is very like the biblical tale of Noah and the Ark, except for its multitude of gods.

In the 1920s the English archaeologist Leonard Woolley excavated at Ur, the city in southern Mesopotamia that was the birthplace of the biblical patriarch Abraham. Woolley caused an enormous stir by telegraphing to London that he had found evidence for the Flood at Ur. Unfortunately he had not, and neither have later archaeologists excavating at other sites on the southern Mesopotamian plain. What they did find were deep layers of water-laid silt, interrupting evidence of habitation in the form of pottery, graves and buildings, that were present both below and above the 'Flood' levels. These silty layers are in fact restricted to particular areas of the settlements and never encompass a whole site. They may not be the Flood, but they are certainly evidence for localized flooding by the Tigris and the Euphrates, the great rivers of the Land of Sumer and Akkad.

All the cities of Mesopotamia are perforce situated on one or other of these rivers or their tributaries; the rivers gave life to the settlements but also brought the danger of flooding. If, far upstream in Turkey or Syria, there was an unusually heavy deluge, or perhaps the winter snows melted too fast in the mountains, then the great rivers quickly became torrential, breaking their banks and causing enormous damage over relatively small areas. This would happen all the more easily where, in their

the similarity of the name to the biblical Ararat). Occasionally Mount Massis, the highest peak of this range, has been the object of expeditions to locate Noah's Ark. So too have the Kurdish mountains southeast of Lake Van but, despite sporadic flurries of optimism, the Ark has never come to light. This is hardly surprising, since the story of Noah in the Book of Genesis is not couched in historical terms at all. Rather it is mythological in form. It preserves an early and unsophisticated image of a God who still speaks directly with his worshippers. He is indeed depicted as One and All-powerful, but somehow also human in character, not really all that different from the gods of other Near Eastern peoples at the time.

Searching for signs of the Flood

It has often been pointed out that the legend of a great Flood, and of the hero who survives it to bring new life to the world, is paralleled in many ancient mythologies, from South America to Australasia,

Left **The Great Flood Pit excavated by Sir Leonard Woolley at Ur in southern Mesopotamia in the 1920s. Woolley believed he had found evidence of the biblical Flood, but the thick band of water-laid silt that divides two habitation layers is only evidence for very localized flooding that did not even affect the entire site of Ur, let alone the whole ancient Near East.**

Opposite above **On board the research vessel that is exploring the submerged ancient shoreline of the Black Sea. The team led by Robert Ballard are using remote-controlled submersibles which send pictures back that can be monitored.** *Opposite below* **The Black Sea flood, mid-6th millennium BC. There would have been a total rise in sea level of about 150 m (500 ft) and a change from a freshwater to a saltwater environment.**

lower reaches, the rivers flowed slowly across the alluvial plains in levees (raised beds) far above the rich fields they watered. Evidence of flooding is only to be expected in such circumstances. Today, in the south, many of the ancient sites are now located in the desert, for the rivers have cut and recut their courses again and again in the delta region with the passage of time.

Archaeologists and historians have for many years assumed that Noah's Flood is a folk memory of one such flooding event, even perhaps of an especially catastrophic one. The memory may have been carried with Abraham's clan on the long journey from Ur to Canaan, and given a fresh and monotheistic flavour in their new homeland. The oral traditions that underlie the written narrative in Genesis could easily have persisted in the hands of skilled story-tellers over many centuries, and it is clear from

inconsistencies in the biblical text itself that these sources did not agree in every detail.

The Black Sea flood?

There is, however, a new and fascinating theory proposed by two American scholars, William Ryan and Walter Pitman, both geophysicists who are particularly interested in the Black Sea. They see the Great Flood as a truly cataclysmic event that occurred in the Black Sea around the middle of the 6th millennium BC. The Black Sea was then a freshwater lake, called the New Euxine Lake by modern geologists. At that time its surface was some 150 m (500 ft) below sea level. The melting of the glaciers at the end of the Ice Age had caused a rise in worldwide sea levels. The Mediterranean Sea (itself fed from the Atlantic via the Straits of Gibraltar) poured its salt water through the Dardanelles into the Sea of

about two years, downcutting its bed and carrying all before it. Even so it would have raised the level of the whole of the Black Sea by only about 15 cm (6 in) each day and the flat land around the lake shore would have disappeared at the rate of perhaps a mile a day.

There were almost certainly people living in farming villages around the lake at that time, just as there were elsewhere in the Near East. Mostly they would have been able to escape the rising waters, with their animals, by boat, on donkey or even on foot if necessary. The groups, fleeing in all directions, would have taken horrific memories of the Flood with them. These memories would have gradually altered into folklore and myth as they were recounted in story and song in the mouths of generations of bards and ordinary people.

This was the theory – and it is now being tested by an expedition using remotely operated submersibles with cameras to explore the bed of the Black Sea. The pictures sent back by the cameras can be viewed on board the expedition ship. Amazingly, early results are very exciting: remains of what could possibly be buildings have been located at a depth of 91 m (300 ft) and will be further investigated.

Marmara. At the eastern end a neck of land blocked the way to the New Euxine, but gradually, as the sea level continued to rise, water flowed across that area, slowly at first and then perhaps with more rapidity. Then, aided possibly by one of the earthquakes that are so common in Turkey, the neck of land split apart and millions of gallons of salt water roared into today's Bosporus and crashed eastwards through it, cascading down with immense violence into the lake far below. Ryan and Pitman have estimated that about 10 cubic miles of water poured west to east through the narrow channel each day for

This then, might well be the origin of the Flood legend in the opinion of the two American scholars. Noah's story could be one memory of it and the hero of the Mesopotamian epics another and even the Deucalion legend in Greece could make a third. Difficult though this idea would undoubtedly be to prove, it is hard to dismiss it out of hand.

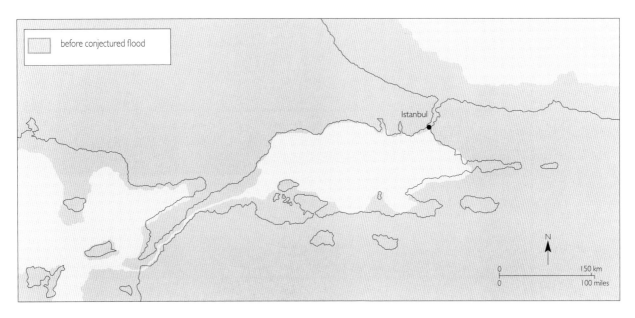

before conjectured flood

Istanbul

N

0   150 km
0   100 miles

Moses & the Exodus: Myth or Reality?

3

Time: 13th century BC?
Location: Egypt/Sinai Peninsula

Thus says the Lord, the God of Israel, 'Let my people go'.

EXODUS 5: 1

THE BOOK OF EXODUS in the Hebrew Bible opens with an account of the oppression of the Israelites in Egypt and their liberation by Moses from slavery. Although the son of an Israelite couple, Moses was brought up by an Egyptian princess. As an adult he killed an Egyptian overseer whom he had caught abusing an Israelite slave. When his deed became known, Moses was forced to flee into the desert, where he received a revelation of God at the Burning Bush. As a result, Moses returned to Egypt and, together with his brother Aaron, demanded that the Israelites should be set free.

Pharaoh refused, thus bringing the ten plagues on his country. The tenth plague, the death of the first-born, struck every Egyptian household, and Pharaoh now urged the Israelites to leave Egypt. In the desert east of Egypt, God caused the Red Sea to open up, allowing the Israelites to cross dryshod, but then the waters returned, drowning the pursuing Egyptians – Pharaoh having changed his mind.

Not all scholars believe either that Moses existed or that the Exodus from Egypt ever took place as it is recorded. Many, however, consider that while the biblical account of the miracles of the ten plagues

Above **The Israelites cross the Red Sea while the pursuing Egyptians drown in its waters; fresco from the synagogue at Dura-Europos, Syria, mid-3rd century AD.**

and the crossing of the Red Sea is mythical as it is presented, there is nevertheless a core of historical information contained in the narratives, as found mainly in the books of Exodus, Numbers and Deuteronomy. The two schools of thought are often called 'minimalist' and 'maximalist', and the controversy over the Exodus story is part of a much larger debate about the use of the Hebrew Bible as a source for the history of Israel.

The minimalists point to a lack of specific evidence in Egypt, Sinai or anywhere else, as well as the miraculous nature of the ten plagues and the parting of the Red Sea. They believe that the biblical narratives were composed very much later than the events they purport to describe, between the late 6th and the 2nd centuries BC, and were designed for didactic, theological purposes. Also, as there was no such thing as the writing of history at that time, the stories in the Hebrew Bible are merely myth and folklore and are unreliable and inaccurate. Archaeological and historical research therefore cannot throw light on the Bible.

The so-called 'maximalists' on the other hand, who comprise the majority view, hold rather different opinions about the nature of the biblical text, though they do recognize that the Hebrew Bible was finalized long after the events it reports. When the

Babylonians under Nebuchadnezzar destroyed the First Temple in 587/6 BC they took the leaders of the people from Jerusalem and Judah into exile in Babylon. And it was there, between 586 and 538 BC, that the final versions of many of the books of the Hebrew Bible were collated from the various oral and written sources that the exiles had to hand. The biblical narrative thus still retains a considerable amount of accurate historical information.

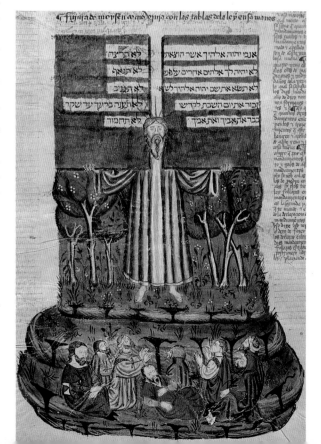

Opposite **An aerial view of Mount Sinai and surrounding peaks.**
Right **Moses holding the tablets of the Ten Commandments, while the Israelites huddle below; the Alba Bible, 1422.**

Such scholars point out that there is a primary narrative concerning the group led by Moses, who received the Law (Torah) at Mount Sinai. In addition to the Exodus under Moses, the biblical account also preserves traces of several journeys in Sinai, so it is at least possible that the ancestral Israelites were coming and going over a long period. While it is impossible to be certain of the route of the Exodus, and of the location of many of the places mentioned by names unknown today in Sinai, these scholars believe that archaeological and historical studies have the potential to throw light on the biblical narratives.

Israelites in Egypt?

The minimalists declare that not a single piece of concrete evidence exists for Moses or the Exodus, nor for the Israelite presence in Canaan, and dismiss this part of the Hebrew Bible as the fabrication of a later age. The maximalists, however, while agreeing that there is no evidence in Egypt, Sinai or elsewhere specifically relating to Moses and the Exodus, nevertheless point to a large body of circumstantial evidence indicating both the presence of Semitic peoples in Egypt, and the arrival of a new population in the central highlands of Judah in the 13th–12th centuries BC. Using the known facts of Egyptian history they demonstrate that from the 19th century BC and perhaps earlier, groups of Semitic nomads were coming to Egypt to trade, buy food and some to settle if they could, usually in the eastern part of the Nile delta. Among these immigrant groups were the ancestors of the Israelites, the patriarchal clans under Jacob's leadership. They came to join Joseph in Egypt and were given the task of herding cattle for Pharaoh, settling by royal command in the land of Goshen, now usually associated with the eastern delta region.

During a subsequent period of Egyptian weakness the descendants of the original settlers established their own rule over the delta region, founding their capital at Avaris. They are known to history as the Hyksos, a name meaning 'chiefs of foreign hill country' – a good description of southern Canaan. Their leaders were chased out of Egypt by a resurgent native dynasty in around the mid-16th century BC. The bulk of the Semitic peasantry remained behind to become part of the agrarian population of the delta. It is these folk who were 'enslaved' in the biblical account by the 'king who did not know Joseph' (Exodus 1: 8). This is probably a reference to the pharaohs of the 19th Dynasty, who came to power *c.* 1307 BC and who seem to have had a family link to

the eastern delta area, for they made it their base. Their capital was at Pi-Ramessu (biblical Raamses, modern Qantir), not far from Avaris.

These pharaohs constructed several other cities, including Pi-Atum (biblical Pithom, modern Tell el-Rataba), and a chain of border fortresses and supply depots in the same area, to prevent incursions from the bedouin of Sinai and others. To achieve this the pharaohs employed the population of the region in a corvée labour system, not unlike that of medieval Europe. Among the Egyptian villagers were descendants of Hyksos groups as well as other immigrants, all of them no doubt eager to escape this unwelcome imposition. Thus the Israelites are said to have left Egypt together with a mixed multitude (Exodus 12: 38). It is therefore believed by many experts that the Exodus fits best into a 13th-century BC setting, during the long reign of Ramesses II (*c.* 1290–1224 BC).

The route of the Exodus

The route by which Moses led the Israelites out of Egypt is, however, certainly a mystery. It is not even known why the Hebrew 'Yam Suf' was translated into English as the 'Red' rather than the 'Reed' Sea. Nor is it known where it was. There is no consensus about the identification of the Israelite camps, but perhaps this is not surprising: the bedouin tribes of Sinai would hardly have perpetuated Hebrew place-names. The route of the Exodus and the desert wanderings, as well as the location of Mount Sinai are untraceable. Kadesh-Barnea, where the Israelites encamped for nearly 40 years before continuing their journey to Canaan, might be identified with the oasis of Ein Qudeirat in northeast Sinai, but there are no remains there dating from the appropriate period.

The Promised Land

Moses died and was buried on Mount Nebo in Moab (Deuteronomy 34: 1, 5) and it was Joshua who led the people across the Jordan and into the hill country of Canaan. There is little proof for the conquest of the land as related in the books of Joshua and Judges, but there is evidence for the establishment of small farming villages in these hills for the first time. They date to between the 13th and the 11th centuries BC, at the same time as the lands bordering the east Mediterranean were under attack by migrants from the Aegean world. In Egyptian texts these groups are referred to as the 'Sea Peoples'. Among them were the Philistines who settled in the area now known as the Gaza Strip. Refugees from the disruption on the coastal plain made new lives for themselves in villages in the hill country inland, where they met up with Israelites coming from the east. There are many signs of technological innovations in the agricultural communities that they established together. One interesting fact is that, in contrast to the contemporaneous coastal settlements, there is no evidence of pig bones among the animal remains

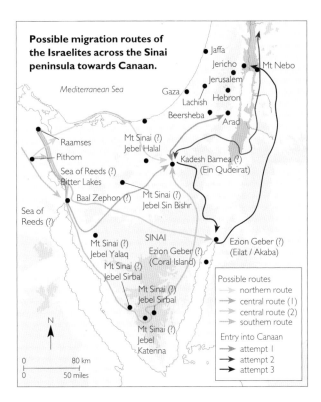

Possible migration routes of the Israelites across the Sinai peninsula towards Canaan.

from the majority of these villages. (In later Judaism pig meat was forbidden by ritual law.) This may well indicate not only the presence of Israelites in the hill villages, but also the fact that it was their religious beliefs that governed these communities.

There is one more piece of evidence that constitutes conclusive proof for the presence of Israel in Canaan by the late 12th and 11th centuries BC. In the fifth year of his reign (*c.* 1219 BC), the Egyptian pharaoh Merneptah campaigned through the area in the hope of re-establishing Egyptian control. In the commemorative monument he later set up at Karnak listing his conquests, he noted that among others in Canaan he had utterly destroyed the people of Israel. It is ironic that the first extra-biblical note of the existence of Israel also lays claim to its total destruction.

So although direct proof for Moses and the Exodus is lacking, there is a considerable body of circumstantial evidence that is hard to ignore. Ultimately it remains a matter of individual conviction, but for those who believe in the essential truth of the events recounted in the Bible, there is a mystery that will always surround the narratives.

Opposite **Sea Peoples depicted on the walls of Medinet Habu, Luxor, Egypt; their helmets show that they are Philistines.**
Left **The Israel Stela of Merneptah, recording his victories in Canaan – including the destruction of the people of Israel.**

The Lost Cities of Sodom & Gomorrah

Time: c. 3150–1550 BC
Location: Jordan

Then the Lord rained upon Sodom and Gomorrah brimstone and fire from the Lord out of heaven; And he overthrew those cities, and all the plain, and all the inhabitants of the cities, and that which grew upon the ground.

GENESIS 19: 24–25

THE DESTRUCTION of the cities of Sodom and Gomorrah is one of the most intriguing stories told in the Old Testament of the Bible, and repeated in the Koran. The main characters are the greatest patriarch, Abraham, and his nephew Lot. They were burdened with the serious moral dilemmas of land rights, homosexuality, succession and incest – all still relevant today. The episode has been regarded simply as an analogy for the study of biblical ethics, but is there any evidence for the existence of these cities and the events described?

The biblical narrative
In the story, Abraham and Lot travelled through the land of Canaan as shepherds, grazing their flocks, until the animals grew so numerous that the land could no longer support them all. Abraham decided that they should separate, and gave Lot the first choice of where to go. Lot chose the well-watered plain of the Jordan Valley and went to live near Sodom, one of five prosperous 'cities of the plain', the others being Adamh, Zeboiim and Zoar. But the men of Sodom were homosexual sinners and God warned them that if they did not repent, He would destroy them. Abraham debated with God regarding the ethics of destroying righteous people along with the guilty, until it was realized that Lot was the only righteous person in Sodom.

Two angels were sent to warn Lot of the impending destruction of Sodom, and when the Sodomites

Left **The destruction of Sodom and Gomorrah: a detail from the Bible Tapestry, German, early 16th century.**

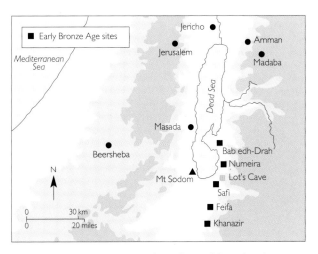

Map of the Dead Sea area to show the position of early Bronze Age sites, possibly the 'cities of the plain'.

heard of Lot's heavenly visitors, they went to his house and demanded to see them. Fearing that the wicked Sodomites would molest the angels, Lot offered the crowd his two virgin daughters instead. Finally the angels blinded the Sodomites at the door and told Lot to flee immediately with his family. As God rained down fire and brimstone on the cities of Sodom and Gomorrah, Lot escaped towards the city of Zoar with his wife and two daughters. But on the way, Lot's wife disobeyed God's instruction not to look back and was turned into a pillar of salt. Lot was afraid to stay in Zoar and instead sought refuge in a cave, along with his daughters. After a long period of isolation, the daughters feared they would never meet a man who could father their children and continue their lineage. So together they agreed to get their father drunk and seduce him when he was unaware of what he was doing. Two sons resulted from these incestuous unions: Moab and Ben-ammi, the forefathers of the Moabite and Ammonite tribes.

So what evidence do we have that any of this story is true? There are in fact certain natural and geological phenomena in the Dead Sea area which seem to corroborate the Sodom and Gomorrah story. In addition, recent archaeological discoveries lend credibility to the biblical account.

Biblical phenomena occurring naturally

Earthquakes occur regularly in the Dead Sea area as a result of two huge land masses sliding apart and subsiding. We know from historical records that whole cities elsewhere have been devastated in the past by earthquakes, and they would be particularly severe

when located on such a geological fault. The same geological processes have also created the lowest point on the earth's surface. The Dead Sea, lying below sea level in this deep rift valley, is a highly saline body of water, and salt formations are common features around its shores. Salt pillars are created which sometimes, by chance, resemble human forms; and if anything falls into the Dead Sea it is rapidly encrusted by salt. It is therefore not hard to imagine how the story of Lot's wife turning into a pillar of salt could have stemmed from such unusual, but natural, processes.

Another peculiar characteristic of the Dead Sea is that it is rich in bitumen, which periodically surfaces as large lumps or oil slicks. This is reminiscent of an episode when the kings of Sodom and Gomorrah got stuck in 'slime pits' as they fled during a battle with the kings of Syria (Genesis 14: 10). Furthermore, fist-sized sulphur nodules are commonly found embedded in the soft marly soils around the Dead Sea shores. The ancient writers of the Old Testament story of Sodom and Gomorrah certainly must have been aware of these flammable balls which they called 'brimstone', and so their description of a burning deluge raining down from heaven and destroying cities may well have been inspired by these strange objects.

Natural erosion of the soft marls around the Dead Sea often produces pillars, reminiscent of the fate of Lot's wife.

Searching for Sodom and Gomorrah

For over a century, biblical scholars and archaeologists have attempted to locate the sites of Sodom and Gomorrah. Initially the debate centred around whether they were located in the northern or southern part of the Dead Sea. In 1851 De Saulcy conducted a survey northwest of the Dead Sea, suggesting that Jericho and Qumran were the lost biblical cities. By the 1920s Father Alexis Mallon's excavations at Teleilat Ghassul on the northeastern shore revealed a large Chalcolithic period settlement (*c.* 3600 BC), which seemed to be a more plausible alternative. The difficulty with this proposal, however, is that there was no occupation of the site during the Bronze Age (3150–1550 BC), the period to which most scholars attribute the Sodom and Gomorrah story.

In 1896 a unique mosaic floor map dating to the 6th to 7th centuries AD was discovered in Madaba, in modern Jordan. On this map Zoar – the city that Lot had initially escaped to – was located at the southeast end of the Dead Sea. This area had been described by the Classical historians Diodorus, Strabo, Josephus and Tacitus, and later by the medieval Arab geographers Yakut, Mas'udi, Mukaddasi and Ibn 'Abbas. In 1924 William F. Albright, Revd Melvin G. Kyle, Father Alexis Mallon and others surveyed the region, hoping to verify the location of Zoar. Its identification with the land of Moab led them to search south of the

Mujib river, identified as the biblical Arnon. After investigating the Lisan peninsula and the nearby valleys, they concluded that the modern town of Safi was ancient Zoar, a theory that had first been put forward much earlier by Sir John Maundevil, during his visit to Safi between 1322 and 1356.

The search for Sodom and Gomorrah was joined in the 1930s by Le P. F. M. Abel, F. Frank and Nelson Glueck, who investigated the shallow basin south of the Dead Sea. This salt-pan area fits the Old Testament description of the 'vale of Siddim' as next to the 'salt sea' (Genesis 14: 3) and a 'wasteland' (Deuteronomy 29: 23). The most recent research by Konstantinos Politis has confirmed that Safi was indeed Zoar – and it is located exactly where depicted on the Madaba map.

Another proposition, that the 'cities of the plain' (Genesis 13: 12) had disappeared below the waters of the Dead Sea, was first mentioned by the 4th-century AD pilgrim Egeria. Then in the late 19th century several small islands were recorded in the north end of the sea by William Lynch, Albright and Kyle, which have since become submerged. The Dead Sea is now being studied from NASA satellite photographs and by submarine investigation of its sea floor, looking for any signs of the lost cities. Although inconclusive, the theory that Sodom and Gomorrah could be found beneath the Dead Sea, rather than along its shorelines, certainly seems plausible.

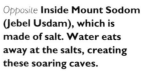

Left **A detail from the 6th–7th century AD mosaic map at Madaba, Jordan, depicting the sanctuary of Lot above the city of Zoar.**

Right **An excavation trench at Bab edh-Drah showing a burnt destruction phase dating to the Early Bronze Age (c. 3000 BC).**

Opposite **Inside Mount Sodom (Jebel Usdam), which is made of salt. Water eats away at the salts, creating these soaring caves.**

Recent archaeological evidence

Recent surveys and excavations on the ancient shorelines and along the geological fault lines of the southern Dead Sea basin have been conducted by Paul Lapp, Walter Rast, Thomas Shaub and Burton MacDonald. In the 1970s and 1980s they discovered large, once-thriving settlements there. Some, such as Bab edh-Drah, ended with fiery destructions during the Early Bronze Age (c. 3000 BC). Could these sites correspond to the legendary 'cities of the plain'? In 1976 these cities were found to be listed on Early Bronze Age tablets discovered at Ebla in Syria. Does this discovery confirm their historical existence?

During the 1990s Konstantinos Politis excavated Deir 'Ain 'Abata near Safi, uncovering a church built over a cave in which early Byzantine Christians believed Lot took refuge after the destruction of Sodom and Gomorrah. Roman-period finds suggest an earlier veneration of the site. The additional discovery of substantial Early and Middle Bronze Age remains indicates that the cave was occupied during the period when, it is thought, the Genesis story occurred. Meanwhile, the latest excavations at nearby sites have uncovered similar Middle Bronze Age artifacts.

While the Old Testament is primarily considered a book of moral guidelines, it is intriguing that modern archaeological and geological discoveries are confirming the physical and historical landscape in which the 'improbable' story of Sodom and Gomorrah really could have taken place.

Atlantis: Fact or Fiction?

Time: unknown (c. 9600 BC?/1520 BC?/mythical)
Location: Mediterranean?/Atlantic?

When you were speaking yesterday about your city and citizens, the tale which I have just been repeating to you came into my mind, and I remarked with astonishment how, by some mysterious coincidence, you agreed in almost every particular with the narrative of Solon.

PLATO, *CRITIAS*, 4TH CENTURY BC

THE IMAGE OF A great and powerful nation, rooted in the deepest strata of human antiquity, whose dominance over the ancient world ended virtually overnight as a result of an unimaginable cataclysm is one that has intrigued people for more than two millennia. We are referring here, of course, to the great island nation of Atlantis.

Atlantis: context of the myth

Though Atlantis is said to have achieved its peak more than 11,000 years ago, it is not until a little more than 2350 years ago – sometime between about 359 and 347 BC – that it surfaces in literature. Its name appears in two dialogues by the Greek philosopher Plato – *Timaeus* and *Critias* – named for the main correspondents in two of Plato's imaginary

A 1st-century AD marble sculpture of Plato (427–347 BC), the original source for the story of Atlantis. Plato introduced Atlantis and described its society in detail in two of his dialogues: *Timaeus* and *Critias*.

conversations between Socrates and his students. At the outset of the *Timaeus* dialogue, Socrates mentions the previous day's discussion of the 'perfect' society. Plato is here referring to his most famous dialogue, the *Republic*, in fact written several years earlier. Plato then has Socrates enumerate the features of the perfect government presented in the *Republic*: artisans and farmers would be separated from the military; soldiers would be merciful, trained in athletics and music, would live communally and would own no gold, silver or any private property.

Socrates despairs of hypothetical discussions and gives his students an assignment in what amounts to applied philosophy. He suggests that they should exemplify the perfection of a society that lives according to the precepts laid out in the *Republic* by engaging them in a just war.

Critias, dutifully carrying out the suggestion of his teacher, volunteers: 'Then listen, Socrates, to a tale which though strange, is certainly true'. Critias says that he heard this story from his grandfather (also named Critias), who in turn maintained that he heard it from his own father, Dropides, who heard it from the Greek sage Solon, who heard it originally from Egyptian priests when he was in Egypt shortly after 600 BC. By Plato's own account, in *Critias* we are reading an indirect version of a story that had originated more than 200 years previously.

The perfect state: Athens, *not* Atlantis

The Egyptian priests told Solon a tale about ancient Athens which was 'the best governed of all cities'. It is this ancient Athens of 9300 years before Plato's time that serves as his model for the perfect state. The priests tell Solon of the most heroic deed of the

ancient Athenians: they defeated in battle 'a mighty power which unprovoked made an expedition against the whole of Europe and Asia'. They describe this expansionist nation as originating beyond the 'Pillars of Hercules', in the Atlantic Ocean. And the name of this great power was Atlantis.

Atlantis had held sway across northern Africa all the way to Egypt. But after this defeat in battle by the Athenians, Critias tells us that Atlantis was totally destroyed by the gods in a tremendous cataclysm of earthquakes and floods.

After outlining the Atlantis story, Critias remarks to Socrates: 'When you were speaking yesterday about your city and citizens, the tale which I have just been repeating to you came into my mind, and I remarked with astonishment how, by some mysterious coincidence, you agreed in almost every particular with the narrative of Solon.' In fact, Critias' description of the society of ancient Athens makes it a perfect, detailed – and not coincidental – match for Plato's hypothetical perfect nation described in his *Republic*.

A historical source for Atlantis?

Did Plato base his description of Atlantis or ancient Athens on actual history, or did he fabricate the entire episode? In fact, there was a significant Mediterranean civilization – Minoan Crete, ancient even from the perspective of the Greeks of Plato's time – that was at least partially destroyed by a major cataclysm. A number of modern scholars have

Above **Memorial of Chairedemos and Lykeas, warriors killed in the Peloponnesian War between Athens and Sparta (431–404 BC). Elements of this conflict, fought during Plato's lifetime, and aspects of both city-states – for example the political structure of Sparta – may have been used by Plato in formulating the conflict between Atlantis and Athens.**

Right **A map of Atlantis by Athanasius Kircher, 1678, situating it, as Plato indicated, beyond the Pillars of Hercules, somewhere in the mid-Atlantic. Note that north is at the bottom.**

Left **The Throne Room at Knossos, Crete, with the throne flanked by painted griffins and plants. Minoan Crete was a significant, early Mediterranean civilization, and was already ancient by Plato's time. Did Plato base his description of Atlantis on this society? Unfortunately, not all the facts fit this theory.**

Below **The Minoan palace or temple of Knossos, dating to the mid-2nd millennium BC. It was a complex building, with numerous rooms, many with fine wall-paintings.**

suggested that, though the size and location of Atlantis were greatly exaggerated or mistaken in *Critias* (perhaps through a mistranslation), Plato's tale is based ultimately on the cataclysmic eruption of the volcano on Thera, an island located to the east of Greece and north of Crete in the Aegean Sea. The volcanic caldera left behind by the Thera eruption in the 17th or 16th century BC (the date is still much debated, see pp. 271–4), is twice the size of that of Krakatoa which, when it erupted in AD 1883 killed tens of thousands of people. The larger eruption on Thera must have had an even more devastating impact and would likely have warranted mention in the historical records of places like Egypt, where the impact was indirect.

For some, Minoan Crete *is* Atlantis and in *Critias* Plato presents a somewhat distorted picture of its destruction as a result of the eruption of Thera. To maintain this, however, one has to ignore the fact that, or at least explain why, Crete is in the wrong location, is the wrong size, flourished at the wrong time, never fought a war with Athens, and was not destroyed cataclysmically. Archaeology has shown that, although Minoan coastal communities were badly damaged by the tsunamis generated by the Theran eruption, the Minoan civilization not only survived but flourished for perhaps two centuries afterwards.

Other authors have asserted that the fabulous Minoan colony on Thera was the model for Atlantis. Certainly, the Minoan settlement there was obliterated by the eruption of the volcano, but equally certainly, Plato was not speaking about the destruction of merely an outpost – impressive though it was – of an ancient civilization. At the same time, Thera is still in the wrong place, clearly the wrong size, and the wrong age to be a direct model for Plato's Atlantis.

Atlantis, the modern fantasy

No discussion about Atlantis would be complete without mention of the truly fantastic claims made about the lost continent in the 19th and 20th centuries. More than anyone else, Minnesota congressman, twice-failed vice-presidential aspirant and amateur historian Ignatius Donnelly revived the myth with the 1881 publication of his book, *Atlantis: The Antediluvian World*. For Donnelly, Plato's Atlantis is the root of all cultural achievement and the source for civilization in Egypt, Mesopotamia, the Indus Valley and Europe, as well as South and

Right **A rock crystal vase from the Minoan palace at Zakros, eastern Crete. The obvious technical sophistication of the Minoans reflected in their art and architecture has led some to search for commonalities between this ancient civilization and the extremely advanced Atlantean society described in Plato's dialogues.**

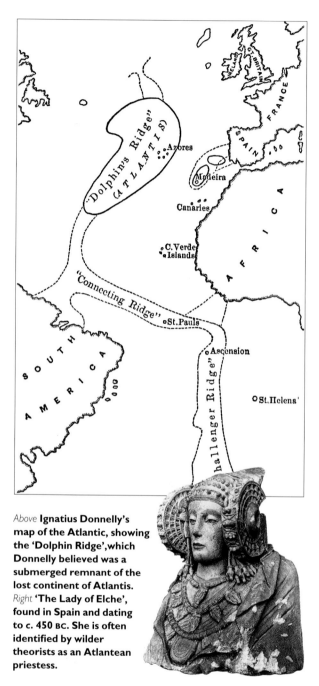

Above **Ignatius Donnelly's map of the Atlantic, showing the 'Dolphin Ridge',which Donnelly believed was a submerged remnant of the lost continent of Atlantis.** *Right* **'The Lady of Elche', found in Spain and dating to *c.* 450 BC. She is often identified by wilder theorists as an Atlantean priestess.**

extraterrestrial aliens. More recently, late-20th-century psychics have claimed to be in touch with spirits from the lost continent, providing all manner of Atlantean advice for denizens of the modern world. Of course, no evidence has been forthcoming to support the validity of any such claims.

Plato's point

It is doubtless the case that Plato used the historical record with which he was familiar to craft his Atlantean dialogues. Perhaps there were traditions of an ancient natural catastrophe that destroyed a powerful nation more than 1000 years before Plato's time, and Plato exploited those stories to convey his message. However, supporters of even a partially literal interpretation of *Critias* recognize that Plato was not intending to write history, but concocted elements of the story intentionally to serve as metaphors for the moral he was attempting to impart. For example, Rodney Castleden in his book, *Atlantis Destroyed*, argues that Plato's Atlantis is a good match of a combination of Minoan Crete and Thera, while at the same time recognizing that part of the story is a retelling of more recent history including the Peloponnesian War which pitted Athens against Sparta. Sparta was victorious, and its political structure appears to have made its way into Plato's description of ancient Athens.

Ultimately, scouring *Critias* for descriptive particulars about Atlantis that closely parallel the details of specific ancient societies is beside Plato's primary point. For Plato, Atlantis is not so much a civilization as a plot device. The details he puts into the mouth of Critias are not intended as history but, instead, serve a more important function to a writer who is, after all, not a historian but a philosopher. To make his point, Plato must make Atlantis a nearly insurmountable adversary. Plato's detailed description of Atlantis was intended necessarily to impress the reader with its material wealth, technological sophistication and military power. That the smaller, materially poorer, technologically less well-endowed, and militarily weaker Athenians could defeat the Atlanteans conveys the essential message of *Critias*: what matters in history is not just wealth or power. What is more important is the way a people govern themselves. For Plato, the intellectual achievement of a perfect government and society is far more important – and is victorious over – material wealth or power. It is to Plato's credit as a teacher that he tells a ripping good tale in making that point.

North America. His thesis does not bear up well under the scrutiny of modern archaeology or geology; there is no evidence that these cultures all owe their evolution to any other primary source, let alone Atlantis. Compared to some other late 19th- and 20th-century thinkers, however, Donnelly is a model of intellectual restraint. The Theosophists led by Helena Blavatsky suggested that Atlanteans flew in aeroplanes and grew crops obtained from

The Trojan War

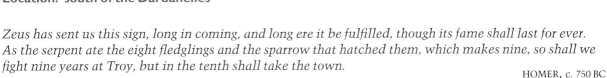

Time: 13th century BC?
Location: south of the Dardanelles

Zeus has sent us this sign, long in coming, and long ere it be fulfilled, though its fame shall last for ever. As the serpent ate the eight fledglings and the sparrow that hatched them, which makes nine, so shall we fight nine years at Troy, but in the tenth shall take the town.

HOMER, *c.* 750 BC

THE LEGEND OF the Trojan War begins as a story of rivalry between three beautiful women: Hera, the wife of Zeus, and their daughters Aphrodite and Athena. Their jealousy erupted at the wedding celebration for the mortal King Peleus and his new wife Thetis, the sea nymph. Eris, the goddess of discord, brought along a golden apple to the ceremony which she announced was a gift to the 'fairest woman' there.

The goddesses Hera, Aphrodite and Athena all laid claim to the apple – and the title. Eris not so innocently suggested that Zeus make the decision as to which of the women in his family was most deserving. Zeus wisely declined and passed the difficult task instead to Paris, who was the son of Priam, king of Troy.

Hera promised Paris unimagined power if she were his choice. Athena offered him historic glory on the field of battle. Aphrodite promised the love of the most beautiful woman on earth. Forsaking the attractions of political power and military glory, Paris presented the golden apple to Aphrodite, a decision which has been immortalized down the centuries as the 'Judgment of Paris'.

The 17th-century Flemish painter Peter Paul Rubens here depicts Paris, son of Priam, the king of Troy, presenting the golden apple to Aphrodite in the famous beauty contest staged at the wedding of Peleus and memorialized in Homer's *Iliad* as the Judgment of Paris.

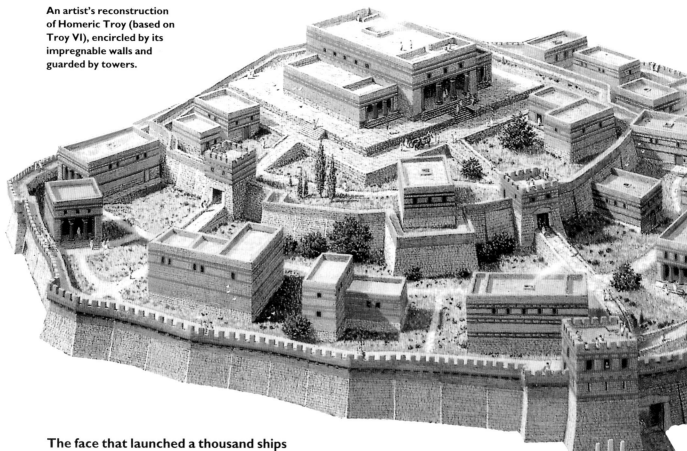

An artist's reconstruction of Homeric Troy (based on Troy VI), encircled by its impregnable walls and guarded by towers.

The face that launched a thousand ships

At the time, the most beautiful woman in the world was Helen, daughter of Zeus and Leda. Unfortunately, Helen was already married to Menelaus, the king of Sparta. To make matters worse, fearful that this marriage to one of her many suitors would provoke bitter fighting among the others, Helen's mortal stepfather Tyndareus had elicited a promise from all the other Greek rulers and warriors to protect Helen's marriage to Menelaus.

Back in Troy, Paris contrived to have himself assigned as the Trojan ambassador to Sparta. On his arrival, Aphrodite used her power to cause Helen to fall in love with Paris. The two lovers then absconded to Troy, together with the better part of Menelaus' wealth. Thus was the stage set for what was to become a decade-long conflict waged by the Greeks who sent 'one thousand ships' against Troy in an attempt to retrieve the wife and wealth of the king of Sparta.

The Trojan War: legend, history, or both?

The story of the Trojan War as set down in Homer's *Iliad* dates from around 750 BC. Greek historians who followed, notably Herodotus and Thucydides, readily accepted Homer's tale and believed that Troy had been an actual city located, just as described in the *Iliad*, near the Hellespont (the narrow strait today called the Dardanelles), and that the Trojan War with the Greeks, united under the Mycenaean ruler Agamemnon, was a historical fact.

Modern writers and scholars have been more sceptical; after all, there are no historical records that verify Homer's tale or that even confirm the existence of Troy. However, the general theme in the *Iliad* of a lengthy campaign into western Asia (in about 1250 BC according to the information in Herodotus) by a united Greek force – perhaps for slaves and natural resources – is plausible.

The Bronze Age context of the *Iliad*

Although the 13th-century BC Mediterranean world was far removed from Homer's time, the *Iliad* contains a number of specific descriptions that we now know are quite accurate. For example, in the Second

Book of the *Iliad*, there is a listing, and even a partial description, of 164 towns that are said to have sent armed contingents to assist in the battle against Troy. Many of the places Homer lists were well known when he was alive; but, as Michael Wood points out in his book, *In Search of the Trojan War*, there are also several places in the list that were long-abandoned by Homer's time and were unknown to Greek geographers. Modern archaeological and historical research has now shown that these were real places and that Homer situated and described them accurately.

Was Troy a real place? Archaeological evidence

What about Troy itself? Archaeologists and historians have long searched south of the Dardanelles in the region historically called the Troad (on the assumption that it was once ruled by ancient Troy) for the ruins of this city. Most interest has focused on the mound at Hisarlik, whose location generally conforms to the geography of Troy as described by Homer. And many of the details Homer provided for the appearance of Troy are a reasonable – though by no means perfect or exclusive – fit for what archaeological research has uncovered at the site.

Heinrich Schliemann is most closely associated with the search for Troy. He excavated at Hisarlik in a series of campaigns between 1870 and 1890, discovering a number of superimposed cities in the

Above **Cross-section of the mound at Hisarlik, showing the complex sequence of superimposed layers.**

Above **Heinrich Schliemann, the man most responsible for the notion that Homer's Troy is located in the mound at Hisarlik, in Turkey.**

Entrance gate and tower at Troy. Homer's description of Troy as a large city with 'fine towers' conforms to the city wall at Hisarlik, though admittedly not uniquely so.

Excavations are on-going at the mound of Hisarlik, more than a century after Schliemann's archaeological work there ended. This is a view of the Sanctuary, looking northwest, in 1997. It is an immensely complex site: Schliemann originally distinguished nine primary occupation levels, but subsequent work has identified multiple sub-phases.

mound and distinguishing nine primary occupations (labelled I–IX). Further work at Hisarlik over the years by archaeologists such as Carl Blegen and more recently Manfred Korfmann has identified multiple sub-phases. Though nothing has ever been found – by Schliemann or anyone else – that proved that this is, in fact, the location of Homer's Troy, archaeological evidence at Hisarlik, particularly the levels Troy VI and VII(a), conforms to some of the details of Homer's description of the time and place.

Homer's description of Troy in the *Iliad* as a large city with 'fine towers' and 'lofty gates' seems to fit

Troy VI, which was large and impressive, though admittedly not uniquely so. More specifically, Homer mentions that the city wall at Troy was a magnificently engineered defensive structure, but that it was poorly built along its western flank. The city wall around Troy VI is over 4 m (13 ft) thick and in places more than 9 m (29 ft) tall, but exhibits inferior construction along its western side. Homer also mentions a great tower located at the main gate of the city; archaeologists have determined that an imposing gate flanked the main entrance of Troy VI.

Clearly, also, the residents of Hisarlik/Troy had been in contact with the Mycenaean world: Bronze Age artifacts from Greece – in particular Mycenaean pottery – were found at the site. Spectacular objects recovered by Schliemann also indicate the presence of a powerful royal family – as would be expected from Homer. The 'Treasure of Priam' included gold rings, bracelets and two breathtaking gold diadems, one of which became known as the 'Jewels of Helen'.

Left **Schliemann's wife, Sophie, wearing the jewels from the 'Treasure of Priam'. Photographs like this inspired tremendous interest in Schliemann's discoveries, but also exposed his excesses and ego.** *Right* **Gold sauceboat from Priam's Treasure. The treasure disappeared from Berlin at the end of the Second World War and its whereabouts were a mystery until it was rediscovered in Moscow.**

A photograph of Schliemann's wife Sophie wearing the jewels has become an icon of Schliemann's large ego and love of notoriety. More recently it has been determined that the hoard actually dates to Troy II (the second city in the nine-level sequence); it therefore dates to about 1000 years *before* the Trojan War. The Treasure itself mysteriously disappeared at the end of the Second World War, but re-emerged in Moscow in the 1990s.

Finally, there is evidence, in the form of traces of fire and fallen masonry, of violent destruction at the end of both Troy VI and VII phases. Troy VI, however, seems to have been destroyed not by military force but by earthquake. Troy VII was more likely damaged in battle and some argue, therefore, that it is Troy VII that more closely corresponds to Homer's Troy.

The Trojan Horse
Homer makes numerous references to the fine breeding of Trojan horses. Archaeological evidence consisting of numerous horse bones and horse-related hardware matches – though again not uniquely so – Homer's Troy. The equine at Troy most people are familiar with is the so-called Trojan Horse. The Greeks constructed an enormous wooden representation of a horse, which they left, ostensibly as a gift to Athena, at the gates of Troy. The Greek army then retreated, appearing finally to have accepted the loss of Helen. Believing themselves the victors, the Trojans brought the enormous

icon into their city. After nightfall, a contingent of Greek soldiers, secreted within the belly of the horse, descended and attacked, opening the city gates to their comrades hidden outside the wall. Unprepared for such an attack, the men of Troy were killed and the women were captured and taken back to Greece as slaves and concubines. Helen too was taken by Greek forces and returned to her husband.

Remarkably, the Trojan Horse described by Homer may have some historical validity. There are written descriptions and artistic representations in the Near East dating from around the 13th century BC of battering rams, used to break through a city's defences, built in the form of horses. Historian Michael Wood suggests that the Trojan Horse in the *Iliad* may have been a transmuted recollection of just such a 'siege machine'.

Troy: reality or myth?
Whether the Trojan War was legend, history, or both cannot be determined definitively. It seems clear that the *Iliad* contains a number of accurate descriptions of Bronze Age geography, politics and material culture, and there is also a stratum of truth in the subtext of the story. But in assessing whether the particulars of the Trojan War legend can be verified, the cautionary conclusion of American Classicist Jeremy B. Rutter is worth quoting: 'Belief or disbelief in the historicity of the Trojan War becomes in the end an act of faith, whichever position one adopts.'

The Trojan Horse depicted on an amphora from Mykonos, dating from the later 7th century BC.

Theseus & the Minotaur 7

Time: mythical/Bronze Age
Location: Crete, the Aegean

So, Minos, moved to cover his disgrace, resolved to hide the monster in a prison, and he built it with intricate design, by Daedalus contrived, an architect of wonderful ability, and famous. This [prison] he planned of mazey wanderings that deceived the eyes, and labyrinthic passages ...

OVID, 1ST CENTURY AD

ACCORDING TO APOLLODORUS of Athens, our 2nd-century BC source for the story of Theseus and the Minotaur (fragments of which can be traced to the late 6th century BC), Theseus was an ancient king of Athens. His ostensible father was the mortal king Aegeus, but it is also asserted that the god Poseidon was Theseus' 'biological father'. The story of Theseus has as one of its central themes a young man's coming of age by overcoming daunting challenges. As is often the case in Greek myth, the path to manhood is littered with vainglory, irony and sorrow. But is there any wider historical truth to the tale?

After Theseus' birth in the country village of Troezen, Aegeus placed his sword and sandals under a large boulder nearby, instructing his wife Aethra to keep the boy in the village until he was old enough and strong enough to recover these items from under the rock. When this comes to pass, Theseus is to join his father in Athens.

In time, Theseus grew up and became a large and powerful young man. He then easily lifted the boulder and recovered his father's belongings. Having accomplished this task, he planned to travel to Athens, just as he had been instructed. Aethra pleaded with him to go by sea but Theseus elected to travel by the more dangerous land route, infested with brigands, highwaymen and wild animals. Predictably enough, he encountered, and overcame, many dangers along the road. Using his enormous strength and great guile, Theseus successfully met each challenge; for example, he threw the outlaw Sciron into the sea, killed the malevolent Procrustes, and also dispatched the ferocious 'wild sow of Crommyon', which must have been far fiercer than it sounds.

The blood-price of Athens: feeding the Minotaur

When Theseus arrived in Athens, he was confronted by a great tragedy that had befallen his country. Several years previously – Apollodorus says it was three generations before the Trojan War – Androgeus, the son of King Minos of Crete, had been killed in a battle against Athens. In his rage and grief, King Minos had demanded a blood payment, which the Athenians elected to honour to avoid a larger conflict with Crete. Each year (in some versions of the myth it is once every nine years), seven young

Though usually depicted as a heartless monster, in this painting by G.F. Watts the Minotaur appears rather wistful.

Left **Theseus prepares to deliver the fatal blow to the Minotaur in the centre of a dazzling labyrinth in this mosaic from a Roman villa near Salzburg, AD 400s.**

Right **After his defeat of the Minotaur, Theseus rests on its lifeless body, in a statue by Antonio Canova, 1781–83.**

Athenian men and seven maidens were taken to Crete where they were given to the horrible chimera, the half-human, half-bull Minotaur, which slaughtered them in its labyrinthine prison.

The origin of the Minotaur can be traced to a vain attempt by King Minos to take advantage of the gods. Minos prayed for a perfect bull to sacrifice, and Poseidon consented. The bull was such a magnificent creature that Minos decided to keep it and sacrifice another, less perfect specimen. Poseidon realized what Minos had done and concocted a malevolent punishment. The angry god cast a spell on Minos' wife, Pasiphae, causing her to fall deeply and hopelessly in love with the heavenly bull. She consummated this love for the bull, became pregnant and gave birth to the Minotaur. Minos had the famous architect Daedalus construct a labyrinth in which the Minotaur was imprisoned, thus protecting the citizens of Crete from its depredations.

Theseus arrived in Athens just as the latest group of sacrificial victims was to board the black-sailed ship that would take them to Crete and their deaths. He volunteered to be one of the chosen, convinced that he could defeat the Minotaur and end the horrible sacrifice. King Aegeus tried to dissuade his son from this, but ultimately agreed, with one proviso: if Theseus was successful in confronting the Minotaur and navigating the labyrinth, upon his triumphant return to Athens in the Cretan ship he must replace the black sails with white so that his father would have a signal that Theseus had prevailed.

On their arrival in Crete, Theseus and the others were led to the labyrinth. King Minos' daughter,

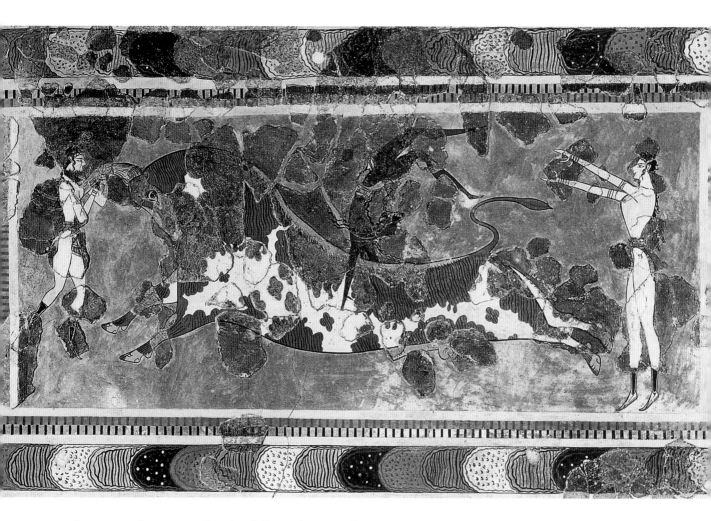

clever Ariadne, immediately fell in love with Theseus and devised a simple strategy to prevent his getting lost in the maze: she provided him with a ball of silk twine which Theseus unwound until he reached the slumbering Minotaur. The Minotaur awoke and after a ferocious struggle Theseus killed the beast. Following the length of twine back to the entrance, Theseus escaped and returned triumphantly to Athens. Unfortunately, he forgot his promise to switch the ship's sails. When Aegeus spied the returning ship with its black sails unfurled, he believed the worst. In his mistaken but inconsolable grief, Aegeus leapt from a high precipice into the sea, ending his own life.

Theseus and the Minotaur: a stratum of truth?

Is there any archaeological evidence for this myth in Crete? Although, certainly, we can rule out the existence of a half-bull, half-man beast, it is interesting that Apollodorus situates King Minos on Crete.

Archaeological work at the site of Knossos on Crete, begun in 1900 by Sir Arthur Evans, revealed the existence of a previously unknown civilization. Evans named it Minoan, after King Minos, and ascertained that it was at its peak between around 1650 and 1420 BC. The ancient Cretans practised a religion in which bulls clearly had a significant role. A well-known fresco found in the enormous Minoan palace of Knossos depicts acrobats somersaulting over a bull in what may be a religious ceremony. Beyond this, the walls of the palace were adorned with giant, stylized, limestone bulls horns. A number of exquisite ritual vessels for liquids – called rhytons – recovered at the palace were made in the naturalistic shape of a bull's head.

In plan, the palace of Knossos exhibits a complex and confusing warren of hundreds and perhaps as many as 1000 rooms, spread out over more than 20,000 sq. m (5 acres). It is, in fact, a labyrinthine structure and people have long made the connection

THESEUS & THE MINOTAUR

Left **Wall-painting from the palace at Knossos depicting a ceremony involving young acrobats and a charging bull. Could such practices be the basis for the story of the sacrifice of Athenian youths to the Minotaur?** *Above* **The obverse of a silver stater from Knossos, c. 500–413 BC, with a running Minotaur, showing the enduring connection with the myth.**

Right **Bull's-head rhyton, a ritual vessel for liquids, from Knossos. The many depictions of bulls in Minoan art and iconography have been interpreted as a reflection of their great religious significance, as well as being a source for the Greek myth of the half-man, half-bull Minotaur.**
Below **A plan of the palace at Knossos – a labyrinth of corridors and storerooms arranged around a large central court.**

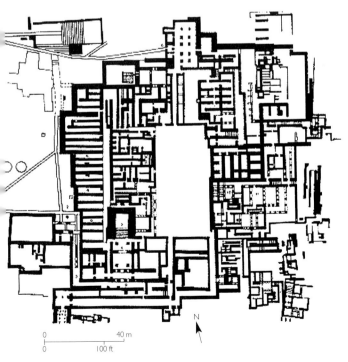

between the temple and the Minotaur's maze. As long ago as 500 BC, long after the temple had been abandoned, Cretans struck coins with the Minotaur displayed on one side and a schematic maze representing the labyrinth on the other.

The myth of Theseus and the Minotaur, therefore, seems to incorporate some actual history viewed through the prism of legend. The story may reflect a period of time during which the Greeks were, perhaps, subservient to the Minoan civilization, and the Minotaur's labyrinth may represent a mythologized interpretation of the complex maze of rooms at the Bronze Age palace-temple at Knossos.

As researchers Rodney Castleden and J. Lesley Fitton separately argue, Theseus' killing of the Minotaur, thereby putting to an end the terrible blood-price paid by the Greeks to the Minoans, may be seen as a mythic metaphor for the historical ascendancy of Greek civilization and their escape from Bronze Age Minoan domination.

Jason & the Argonauts

8

Time: 8th century BC?/mythical
Location: Black Sea area

Taking my start from you, Phoibos, I shall recall the glorious deeds of men long ago who propelled the well-benched Argo through the mouth of the Pontos and between the dark rocks to gain the golden fleece.

APOLLONIUS OF RHODES, 3RD CENTURY BC

T HE LEGEND OF Jason and the Argonauts, whose theme is that of a young hero's rite of passage by a voyage to and return from a distant place, has deep roots in Greece. It is traceable to at least the 5th century BC, when the lyric poet Pindar produced a version, but perhaps the best known rendition was recorded by Apollonius of Rhodes in his work *Argonautika* of the 3rd century BC.

Jason's heritage

The legend begins when Aeson, king of Iolcus in Thessaly, tires of the mantle of power and passes the reigns of government to his brother Pelias, but only until the rightful heir, Aeson's son Jason, reaches

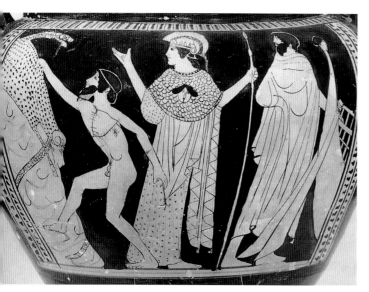

Below **Red-figure vase, c. 470–460 BC, showing Jason grasping the Golden Fleece, with Athena looking on. The stern post of the *Argo* is to the right, its human head a reference to the ship's ability to speak.**

adulthood. Pelias has been warned to beware the man wearing only one sandal and, predictably enough, when Jason becomes a grown man and lays claim to his throne, he arrives at the palace so shod, having lost a sandal on his journey. Fearing Jason and reluctant to step down, Pelias devises a ruse to remove him, perhaps permanently, from Iolcus. He tells Jason that before assuming power he should recover the fabled golden fleece, located in distant Colchis, as it is the rightful property of Jason's family. Intrigued, Jason agrees to set out on this quest. He has a seaworthy vessel constructed, the *Argo*, and amasses a crew of heroes and demigods, including Theseus, Hercules and Orpheus, to help him accomplish his task.

After an arduous voyage through uncharted waters, Jason and his 'Argonauts' arrive in Colchis, where King Aeëtes agrees to Jason's demand for the fleece, but only after Jason submits to a series of trials. Jason is successful, recovers the fleece and, after an equally arduous voyage, returns with the golden prize to his home kingdom.

Assessing the legend of Jason's voyage

No one accepts as accurate the more fantastic elements of this story, filled as it is with golden-fleeced sheep, gods and demigods. Many writers, however, contend that the tale incorporates geographic information gathered in early maritime expeditions by ancient Greek sailors exploring eastwards into the Mediterranean and Black Sea.

As with several other attempts to demonstrate a historical basis for traditions of voyages to distant lands – for example the Chinese story of Fu-sang, or St Brendan's journey to the Land Promised to the Saints – the argument for the historicity of Jason's

voyage is not based on material evidence. Such evidence might consist, for example, of archaeological remains left by the journeyers in the territories they explored (in the *Argonautika*, Jason and his men construct a number of shrines along their route which might be discoverable by archaeologists), or objects left behind by the travellers as they traded with the native people of the areas they encountered, or the presence of exotic materials from the distant places the travellers visited, recovered in archaeological contexts in their home territories.

Instead, the assertion of a historical basis for the story of Jason and the Argonauts is based essentially on geography. Simply stated, readers of Jason's tale have scoured his story for descriptions that are detailed enough to identify the locations mentioned as actual places.

Jason's voyage to the Black Sea?

Using this approach, most scholars of Greek myth believe that the kingdom of Colchis was located just as Apollonius described it, on the eastern margin of the Euxine Sea, the Greek name for the Black Sea, in the modern Republic of Georgia. Historical and archaeological evidence shows that the Greeks explored and colonized the Black Sea's coast in antiquity: Greek colonies there date to the 7th century BC

Above **Tim Severin's replica ship, on his voyage following the route of Jason and the Argonauts.** *Right* **Gold pendant with the head of Athena, from Kul Oba, c. 400–350 BC, an example of Greek goldworking from the Black Sea. Greek knowledge and exploitation of the area's gold deposits may have contributed to the story of the Golden Fleece.**

and initial exploration may have occurred as early as the 8th century BC. From the perspective of the ancient Greeks, the location of Colchis was accurately characterized by Apollonius when he placed it at 'the furthest limits of sea and Earth'.

According to Apollonius, Jason's voyage took him from the ancient Greek port city of Iolcus to the entrance of the Dardanelles and through the perilous passage between the 'Clashing Rocks' (the Symplegades) that guard the entrance to the Black Sea at the Bosporus. From there they sailed east along the north Turkish coast, ultimately reaching Colchis.

Though the various versions of Jason's tale differ, in Apollonius' *Argonautika* on the return trek the Argonauts did not simply backtrack, but instead sailed at a more northerly bearing, reaching a large river Apollonius calls the Istrus, which is almost certainly the Danube, a river known to the ancient Greeks. In this interpretation, Jason and the Argonauts sailed up the Danube, which Apollonius mistakenly believed emptied into the Adriatic Sea. Next, the Argonauts managed to take the *Argo* into a river Apollonius calls Rhodanus, which appears to be the Rhône in France. Jason follows the Rhodanus south where Apollonius understood that it flowed into the Mediterranean. The Argonauts then sailed south along the west coast of Italy, between the

Above **The *Argo* sails through the Symplegades – the Clashing Rocks – by B. Picart, 1730–31.**

Right **The possible routes of Jason and the Argonauts, in decreasing order of credibility. 1. According to Apollonius of Rhodes, the route to Colchis, on the eastern margin of the Black Sea is direct, but the return less so. 2. In this more speculative route, the return voyage takes the *Argo* through northern Europe, Scandinavia and round France and Spain. 3. Henriette Mertz maintained that the Argonauts crossed the Atlantic to South America, based on her interpretation of the landmarks described in various versions of the legend.**

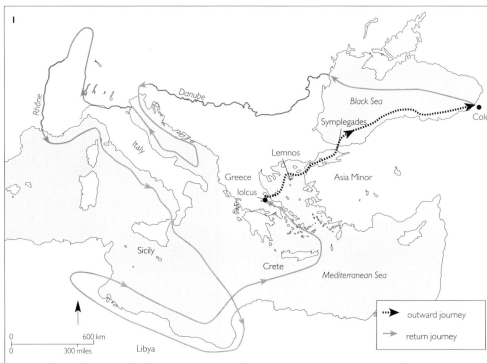

Wandering Rocks marking the strait between Thrinakia (Sicily) and Italy, making landfalls on the North African coast before turning north, passing the eastern margin of Crete and finally arriving back in Iolcus.

Jason's voyage to northern Europe?

In another scenario for the return trip, the Istrus is identified not as the Danube, but as the River Don in Russia, which took the *Argo* into the Volga and ultimately into the Barents Sea where the travellers turned west, following the European coast, eventually turning east through the Strait of Gibraltar into the Mediterranean and home to Iolcus. Moving the *Argo* across the miles of dry land required in this route might seem to have been an insurmountable problem, but we are talking about heroes and demigods here. Even in Apollonius' more reasonable routing, he has the Argonauts carry the *Argo* across miles of Libya's desert before finding the Mediterranean and sailing home.

Jason's voyage to America?

Yet even this ambitious northern route pales in comparison with the fantastic voyage proposed by Henriette Mertz in her book, *The Wine Dark Sea* (1964). According to Mertz, Colchis is not a kingdom

on the Black Sea but a principality located just south of Lake Titicaca in Bolivia, South America. Apollonius' description of the Clashing Rocks represents a natural tidal phenomenon that, according to Mertz, applies nowhere in the Black Sea, but is a perfect match for the strait between Cuba and Haiti. Mertz further claims that the Argonauts eventually sailed northwards, parallel with the coast of North America, before returning home to Greece.

Jason's legend: the verdict

Certainly there is no archaeological evidence of the kind mentioned previously to support any such speculations; there are no archaeological sites in Brazil, or, for that matter, northern Europe, with ancient Greek artifacts, nor are there any known objects from northern Europe or the New World in archaeological contexts in Greece.

Like all such works woven on the fiction writer's loom, there are certainly threads of truth here, but Jason's tale was not intended as history. His is the story of a hero's quest and a young man's coming of age; it is not a memoir. Archaeological evidence of Greek colonies on the Black Sea coast, however, does support the hypothesis that Jason's tale was based on Greek knowledge of the geography at the edges of their known world.

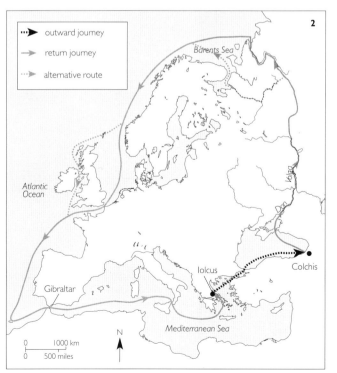

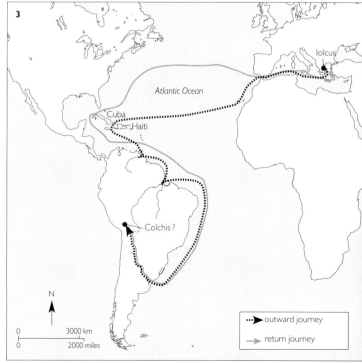

The Ten Lost Tribes
of Israel

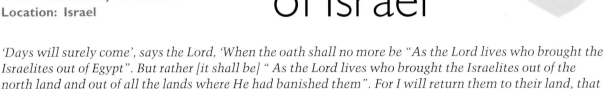

Time: 8th century BC onwards
Location: Israel

'Days will surely come', says the Lord, 'When the oath shall no more be "As the Lord lives who brought the Israelites out of Egypt". But rather [it shall be] " As the Lord lives who brought the Israelites out of the north land and out of all the lands where He had banished them". For I will return them to their land, that I gave to their fathers.'

JEREMIAH 16: 14–15

IN 721 BC THE ASSYRIAN king Sargon the Great marched south with his army through Syria and attacked the kingdom of Israel. Razing its capital, Samaria, the king deported the leaders of the nation, together with their families, to northern Syria, to start new lives as farmers, craftsmen and traders. The people of Israel at that time comprised the tribes of Reuben, Gad, Asher, Ephraim, Manasseh, Dan, Naphtali, Issachar, Simeon and Zebulon; and even though the exiles formed only a minority of this population, they have entered popular folklore as the Ten Lost Tribes of Israel.

What happened to these 'Ten Lost Tribes'? There is very little historical fact, but a great deal of speculation, and traditions and folklore in many parts of the world. The information in the Hebrew Bible is sparse. In 2 Kings 17, verse 6, we are told that some were resettled in northern Syria, in the Habur Valley near Gozan (Tel Halaf) and another unknown town called Halah. The rest of the exiles were sent to towns east of Assyria, in Media. In all probability, the exiles were simply assimilated among the local peoples within a very few generations.

There is, however, one exception. The Jews of Iraqi Kurdistan, who speak a form of neo-Aramaic closely related to the language at the time of the exile, immigrated to the modern state of Israel in the first half of the 20th century. Other Kurdish Jews came from Iran and from Turkey, and today there are approximately 100,000 of them in Israel. Their language, the area of northern Iraq, Syria and eastern Turkey that they came from and, not least, their own traditions, combine to demonstrate convincingly that they are some at least of the true descendants of the Assyrian exile.

Left **The Tribes of Israel, encamped around the Tabernacle in the desert, from a Bible of 1557.** *Right* **Detail of a relief in the palace of Sennacherib, c. 700 BC, of a family being taken into exile from Lachish, Judah, captured by the Assyrians in 701 BC. A family from the kingdom of Israel going into exile 20 years earlier would no doubt have looked very similar.**

This fact has, however, gone largely unnoticed in the deluge of romantic stories that surround the Ten Lost Tribes. Orthodox Jews believe that the tribes still exist beyond the mythical River Sambatyon, and that God will restore them to their homeland in the Messianic Age, in accordance with biblical prophecy (e.g. Jeremiah 31: 7–8). From medieval times down to the 19th century at least, Jews and Christians have searched for this fabled Jewish realm, reputedly in the East or perhaps in Africa, where the lost tribes wait patiently for the millennial kingdom before they can return home. There is an immense literature on the subject. Claims have been made by or on behalf of the Mormons, the Japanese, the Pathans of Pakistan, the Nepalese, the American Indians and even the British and Americans, to name only a few.

Truth behind the claims?

In some cases there may be an element of truth to these claims. In the century after the Assyrian destruction of Israel, many refugees gravitated south to the still autonomous kingdom of Judah, especially its capital, Jerusalem. But seeing the grave threat to their independent existence from Assyria, Babylon and Egypt – the great powers of the day – people were already beginning to migrate from both Israel and Judah. A prophecy of Isaiah, who lived in the reign of Hezekiah of Judah (727–698 BC), speaks of a time when the Lord will restore the diaspora from the lands of Assyria, Patros, Nubia, Elam, Shinar and Hamat (Isaiah 11: 11–12). The earliest overseas colony of Jews for which we have documentary proof was at Yeb, in Egypt, now called Elephantine, the island in the Nile near the First Cataract at Aswan, where there was a Jewish temple for a short while

Above **The Community of Judaism in Burma: Lian Tual, secretary of the Beth Shalom community, Tiddim, 1987.**

during the late 5th century BC. Most of the Jews there were probably serving as mercenaries for the Egyptian king.

During the reign of the last Babylonian king, Nabonidus (555–539 BC), it is likely that groups of Jews accompanied this king on his lengthy journey to Arabia. Probably foreseeing the demise of the Babylonian empire at the hands of the Medes and Persians in 539 BC, they apparently decided to stay on there. It is also known from the Bible that Cyrus the Great, the victorious Persian king, issued a series of edicts in 538 BC, allowing the return of exiled communities to their homelands. But not all the exiled Jews wished to return to Judah (Ezra 1: 4, 6). The majority were comfortably settled and had even colonized other lands, including Persia and Media.

So enclaves of Jewish settlers were already to be found outside their homeland by the 6th and 5th centuries BC. Then during the Hellenistic and Roman periods this diaspora increased until it had spread around the Mediterranean, as a cursory glance at the journeys of St Paul in the New Testament will reveal.

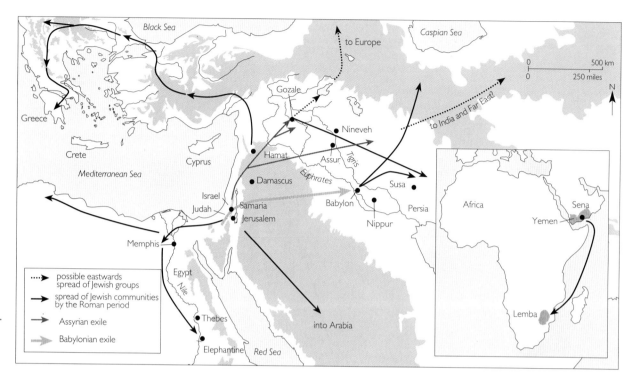

East and West

It would not be surprising, then, if these Jewish migrations moved eastwards as well as westwards. It is known that in comparatively recent times there were Jewish communities in both Arabia and China, just as there are still some groups in India. Among the many who claim Jewish origins, the Pathans are devout Moslems who live in Pakistan, India, Afghanistan and Iran. Although Moslems, they call themselves the Beni Israel (People of Israel) and have retained many Jewish customs such as the Sabbath, which they keep as a day of rest in the Jewish way. The Mizo tribe and the Beni Menashe (Children of Manasseh) in Burma worship Y'wa, a name which is not unlike that of the God of Israel. And in northwest China there are people called the Chiang-min who believe they are descendants of Abraham. They have a special priestly caste who offer sacrifice and place great emphasis on ritual purity.

There are too many examples of such groups to cite them all, but there is nothing inherently impossible about these claims. Jews did wander far and wide and they settled in many remote places. Over the centuries their descendants, very gradually becoming absorbed in the wider community, could easily have lost touch with the mainstream of Judaism, yet still remained dimly aware of their origins.

Lost Tribes in Africa

In Africa, too, there are groups who claim Jewish origin. Of these, the Ethiopian Jews, mostly today in Israel, are the best known. However, there is another group of people, now scattered throughout southern Africa, who may be justified in their claim to be the 'Black Jews of Africa'. These are the Lemba people, whose oral history has recently been documented by Tudor Parfitt of the University of London. They have always asserted that their forebears came from the north, ultimately from a place called Sena, although

There are groups in many parts of the world who claim descent from Israelites. This is a depiction of the 'Supposed order of march of Israelites to Japan, partly taken from ancient pictures', 1877.

58

they did not know where that was. They also believe, although it has not been proven, that they have links with the Jews of Ethiopia. The Lemba observe the Jewish laws of *kashrut* (what foods may and may not be eaten) and may well have introduced the ritual of circumcision into southern Africa.

Dr Parfitt, intrigued by the little he could glean from them of their own history, undertook a journey to trace their origins, which led him from South Africa, through Zimbabwe and ultimately to the Yemen in the southwestern corner of Arabia. Here he found the ancient town of Sena to which he believes the Lemba tradition refers. Many other details seemed to corroborate the Lemba's conviction about their origins, such as family names common both to the Lemba clans and to this region of Arabia.

Evidence in the genes

There is, however, one further piece of evidence – this time based on the latest developments in genetic studies – that lends considerable weight to the Lemba's belief regarding their origins. A genetic study was recently carried out on adult Jewish men in the US, Britain and Israel. It found that more than 70 per cent of *cohanim* (the priestly clan who claim direct descent from Aaron, the brother of Moses, who was charged with the High Priesthood) have a common set of DNA markers on their Y chromosomes. This is a significantly higher percentage than

is found in adult Jewish males who are not *cohanim*. The incidence in non-Jewish male groups is even lower still. This tends to substantiate the claim of the *cohanim* that they may indeed all have had a common ancestor roughly 3000 years ago.

Subsequent tests on men of the Lemba tribe indicated virtually the same occurrence of this DNA marker as is found in Jewish men generally. What is more, the senior Lemba clan, the Bhuba, show a very much higher incidence of this chromosome marker – as high as 53.8 per cent, which is approaching the rate among the Jewish *cohanim* themselves. No non-Jewish group has been found to have anything approaching this incidence of the unique genetic marker.

While this does not definitively prove the Lemba's case, it does add considerable weight to their claim of Jewish ancestry. It would be very rewarding to continue this project among other unified groups of people who claim Jewish descent. While it is unlikely, although not impossible, that these groups do actually stem from Israel's so-called 'Ten Lost Tribes', genetic testing would at least demonstrate conclusively whether they have among their number men whose chromosomes demonstrate a Jewish, perhaps a priestly, lineage. We may never solve the problem of the Lost Tribes themselves, but we may be able to find the families of some lost Jews of the past two millennia.

Opposite above **Map showing the routes of the Exiles from Israel (721 BC) and Judah (701 and 587 BC), and later migrations. These forced and voluntary movements in the ancient period form the background for many traditions concerning the whereabouts of the Lost Tribes of Israel.**

Right **A procession of Lemba in Vendaland, South Africa. The Lemba believe they introduced the worship of the One God, whom they call Mwali, into southern Africa, and also brought the practice of circumcision to the region. There are also strong memories of their association with the site of Great Zimbabwe.**

The Quest for the Ark of the Covenant

10

Time: 13th century BC?
Location: Israel

Whenever the Ark moved forward then Moses said 'Rise up, Lord, and let Your enemies be scattered, let those who hate You flee before You.' And whenever it halted he said 'Return O Lord, to the countless thousands of Israel.'

NUMBERS 10: 35–36

IN THE ANNALS of early Israel the Ark of the Covenant is an enigmatic phenomenon that seems to have fulfilled several roles. Made in the desert just after the Israelites left Egypt, the Ark was to be a carrying box for the Tablets of the Covenant that God had given to Moses on Mount Sinai. The Tablets and the Ark that contained them were thus the testimony to the covenant between God and Israel. Following God's explicit instructions (Exodus 25: 10), the Ark was made of acacia wood and lined

Left **The Ark of the Covenant was traditionally carried into battle, and is shown here by Jean Fouquet (c. 1425–80) being marched around Jericho, helping the Israelites to capture the city during their conquest of the Promised Land.**

Right **A Classical view of the Ark, shown mounted on a wheeled wagon, on a relief from the 4th-century AD synagogue at Capernaum in the Galilee. It is depicted as a Byzantine barrel-vaulted shrine, with panelled doors, a concave, shell-like pediment above and engaged columns along the sides.**

inside and out with pure gold. It had a solid gold cover or lid, on which were set two cherubim whose wings met protectively above the Ark itself. Gold-plated carrying poles were inserted through rings on each side of the Ark, so that it could be carried. It was to be borne before the people whenever they journeyed and was to be installed in their midst in the tented shrine called the Tabernacle, or Tent of Meeting, whenever they encamped.

In Exodus 25, verse 22 God says to Moses, 'I will make myself known to you there, and I will speak with you from above the cover, from between the cherubim, which are above the Ark of Testimony'. For this reason the Ark is sometimes seen as God's footstool and sometimes also as the Mercy Seat. It was the Ark that led Israel into Canaan and once there was instrumental in the fall of Jericho. It could fight for itself as well, on one occasion destroying a false idol when it was captured by the Philistines at the battle of Eben Ezer. It even killed a man of Israel who touched it without permission. Later it was brought to Jerusalem by King David and subsequently installed by Solomon in the Holy of Holies of his new Temple. The Ark was the most precious and central possession of the nation, a potent reminder of Israel's special covenantal relationship with the God of their ancestors.

Fresco from the mid-3rd century AD synagogue at Dura-Europos, Syria, showing the Philistines sending away the Ark.

The fate of the Ark

But that is only the beginning of the mystique that surrounds the Ark of the Covenant. It has captured the imagination of people of many different cultural backgrounds throughout time – the lore of the Ark has developed a life of its own.

Relief from the Arch of Titus in Rome, showing the victorious Roman soldiers carrying away the contents of the Temple in Jerusalem after they sacked the city in AD 70. One recent theory suggests that the Ark was rescued before the Romans burned down the Temple and carried to safety to Qumran, on the shores of the Dead Sea.

Many believe that the Ark was destroyed when the Babylonians captured and devastated Jerusalem in 587/6 BC. In Jewish debates of later times, however, the Rabbis held differing opinions about its fate. It was variously felt that the prophet Jeremiah had concealed it on Mount Nebo; that King Josiah (639–609 BC) had hidden it in a deep cave right on the Temple Mount, below the Holy of Holies of the Temple, long before the Babylonian attack; that it had been taken into exile in Babylon by King Jehoiachin; and, most obscure of all, that it was hidden beneath the woodshed where timber for the altar fire was stored.

There are many other strange traditions as well. It is said, among other things, that the Ark is destined

Small ivory panel showing a sphinx, 9th–8th century BC. This is perhaps what the cherubim guarding the Ark looked like.

to return to the Temple Mount and will be installed in the Holy of Holies of a new Temple that will be built to usher in the Messianic Age. Old Arab chroniclers report that the Ark was taken to safety in Arabia; the Knights Templar searched fruitlessly for it when they held Jerusalem in the Crusader era; alternatively there is a claim that the Ark lies concealed in the vaults of the Vatican; yet others feel that it was captured by the Egyptian Pharaoh Shishak (also known as Shoshenq, 945–924 BC) when he raided deep into Canaan. One recent theory is that when the Romans burned down the Second Temple in AD 70, the Ark was rescued via underground tunnels that led eastwards over 30 km (19 miles) to the neighbourhood of Qumran where it still lies buried.

Yet another persistent legend is that, almost as soon as it was installed in the Temple, the Ark was stolen and taken to Ethiopia by Menelek, son of King Solomon and the Queen of Sheba. There are people from Ethiopia, the Falashas, who claim descent from the Judeans who escorted the Ark on its journey to Ethiopia. One of the traditional titles of the monarch was the 'Lion of Judah' and the old Ethiopian royal family claimed descent from David and Solomon. The Ethiopian Church has asserted for centuries that the Ark has lain concealed among them.

Whatever mysteries are inherent in the numerous legends of the Ark of the Covenant, it seems unlikely that the original could have survived over 3000 years from the time of Moses down to our own day. The likelihood is that the Ark was indeed destroyed when the Babylonians captured Jerusalem and obliterated Solomon's Temple in 587 BC.

The Star of Bethlehem

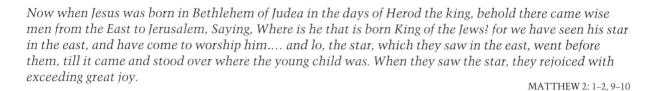

Time: 8–4 BC
Location: Israel

Now when Jesus was born in Bethlehem of Judea in the days of Herod the king, behold there came wise men from the East to Jerusalem, Saying, Where is he that is born King of the Jews? for we have seen his star in the east, and have come to worship him.... and lo, the star, which they saw in the east, went before them, till it came and stood over where the young child was. When they saw the star, they rejoiced with exceeding great joy.

MATTHEW 2: 1–2, 9–10

FEW ANCIENT MYSTERIES are as controversial as the Star of Bethlehem, which according to Christian beliefs announced the birth of Jesus of Nazareth as the Messiah. The description of the star in the Gospel of Matthew is brief. We are told that a star 'in the east' directed Magi (physician-astrologers from the Near East) to find the Messiah in Judea. King Herod of Judea sent them to Bethlehem, the prophesied birthplace of the Messiah. Thus, the Magi's star became known as the Star of Bethlehem.

Some researchers believe that there was no 'star' and that the story may be a myth meant only to convey the message that Jesus had a messianic birth. However, many people believe that there is an historical basis to the story. The quest to find that star has produced many theories.

Determining what may have drawn the Magi to Judea is difficult because no one knows the date of Jesus' birth. Biblical scholars believe that 25 December was not Jesus' birthday, but a Roman holiday for the Unconquerable Sun, which Christians adopted

sometime around AD 354. Furthermore, when Dionysius Exiguus (*c*. AD 533) numbered the years of the calendar, he miscalculated Jesus' birth year. Most biblical scholars consider 8 BC to 4 BC to be the likely timeframe for Jesus' birth because Herod died in early 4 BC and Jesus was born during the 'days of Herod'.

Searching for the mysterious star in and around this timeframe, researchers have proposed several possible celestial objects. Comets, called 'long-haired stars' in ancient times, seem plausible because the star reportedly 'went before' and then 'stood over' the infant Jesus. A comet moves slowly among the stars, which could explain the star's motion. However, a comet's appearance was an omen of a king's death, not his birth. Also, the account in Matthew says that Herod and the people of Jerusalem did not notice the star, which means that the star was not visibly noteworthy.

The same evidence argues against a nova because the appearance of a 'new star' would have been seen by everyone. There is a Chinese record of a nova in 5 BC, but there are no Western astrological records claiming any new star meant a king's birth.

Below **'Severa go with God' says this Roman catacomb tablet which shows the Magi offering gifts to the infant Jesus.**

+SCS BALTHASSAR +SCS MELCHIOR +SCS GASPAR

Left **The three wise men, or Magi, from the East are guided by the Star of Bethlehem: 6th-century mosaic from S. Apollinare Nuovo, Ravenna, Italy.**

Right **Florentine painter Giotto di Bondone was not aware of a comet's foreboding message in ancient times when he painted The Adoration of the Magi (Capella degli Scrovegni, Padua). He may have been inspired by the bright comet of 1304 as he worked on this fresco.**

Left **In the ancient world comets were considered an omen of the death of a king, not his birth. Emperor Augustus Caesar claimed the ominous comet of 44 BC as the wandering soul of the assassinated Julius Caesar, who is shown with the comet on this Roman denarius.**

A clue from a Roman coin

A new perspective about the star's astrological nature came unexpectedly from a Roman coin issued in Antioch close to the time of Jesus' birth. The bronze coin shows the astrological sign, Aries the Ram, under a star. The 'bible of astrology' the *Tetrabiblos* of Claudius Ptolemy (*c.* AD 150) tells us how Aries controls human activity in Judea, Samaria, Idumea, Coele Syria, and Palestine, all of which were in King Herod's realm. The coin may commemorate the AD 6 incorporation of Judea into Roman Syria, where Antioch was the capital city. That is, the star above

Most theories now propose conspicuous planetary conjunctions, but there were countless close passages of planets around the time of Jesus' birth. Visibly striking planetary groupings, however, did not necessarily point to a king's birth. In fact, most astrological conditions for royal births, such as for Roman emperors, were unimpressive by modern standards. That the star was an obscure astrological concept is underscored by the fact that Herod and the people of Jerusalem did not notice it, because Jews did not practise the Magi's astrology.

Left **A Roman coin from c. AD 6 shows Aries the Ram gazing backwards at a star. The inscription reads 'of the people of the Metropolis of Antioch'.**

the ram symbolizes Judea's new fate under Roman Antioch's control. But the coin's importance lies in showing that astrologers would have watched Aries the Ram for a royal birth in Judea.

Not only do the astrological sources tell us where astrologers watched for a new King of the Jews, but they also explain which star announced the king's birth. And that regal star was the 'star of Zeus', namely the planet Jupiter. The optimum time for Jupiter to confer kingships was when the planet was rising as a morning star, which is what 'in the east' means in astrological terms. There were other royal conditions such as when the Moon passed Jupiter in a close conjunction, but few were as important as being 'in the east'.

Examining the likely timeframe of Jesus' birth reveals a unique and extraordinary day. On 17 April 6 BC Jupiter emerged in the east in Aries the Ram. The Moon was also in Aries moving directly towards Jupiter for a close encounter. (Modern calculations

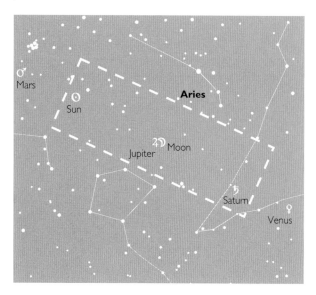

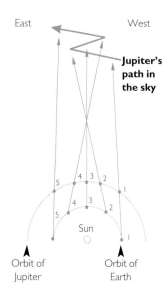

Left **The planets on 17 April 6 BC formed a powerful omen in the astrological sign of Aries the Ram (dashed box) about the birth of the Messiah in Judea. Signs were imaginary zones that loosely coincided with constellations.**

Right **Jupiter is the most likely star which announced Jesus' birth. The planet seemingly reversed its motion among the stars for several days late in 6 BC.**

reveal that the Moon passed before Jupiter.) Moreover, the Sun was in Aries where it was 'exalted', another powerful astrological condition for a king's birth. Even Saturn was present which created an incredible omen for the birth of a *great* king in Judea. A Christian Roman astrologer, Firmicus Maternus (*c.* AD 334) cited these same conditions in Aries as marking the birth of a 'divine and immortal' person – excellent evidence that this inspired the Magi to go to Judea.

Jupiter then did something else that attracted the Magi. The planet left Aries but reversed its motion among the stars ('went before' according to Matthew). Jupiter returned to Aries where it became stationary ('stood over') for several days late in 6 BC.

Modern astronomers refer to Matthew's description as retrograde motion: an optical illusion produced by the earth passing Jupiter in the solar system. The stationing of Jupiter in Aries was another indication pointing to great events in Judea, which made the Magi rejoice, believing they would indeed find the new king in Bethlehem.

There is no proof outside the biblical account that the Magi or anyone else verified Jesus' birthday. But early Christians believed that Jesus was born under a royal star, which fulfilled the Messianic prophecy. In any case, people will have to draw their own conclusions whether he was born under this star in the east.

Right **The Church of the Nativity in Bethlehem is venerated as the birthplace of Jesus.**

King Arthur & the Holy Grail

12

If we could see exactly what happened we should find ourselves in the presence of a theme as well founded, as inspired, and as inalienable from the inheritance of mankind as the Odyssey *or the Old* Testament. *It is all true, or it ought to be; and more and better besides.*

WINSTON CHURCHILL, 1956

A RE THE ARTHURIAN legends 'true'? And do they reflect historical reality? Many modern Arthurian enthusiasts are not comfortable with Churchill's deflecting aphorism, quoted above. We 'ought to be' able to prove Arthur's existence, they believe, given current knowledge of the historical and archaeological evidence. But this is a narrowing of the question. The 'truth' to the mystery of Arthur is informed by history and archaeology, but also by mythology, folklore, literary criticism and other disciplines. In the quest for Camelot, one must be prepared to discover not one Arthur, but many.

An historical Arthur remains a possibility, but good evidence is lacking. The first written accounts of his deeds – the sparse *Annales Cambriae* ('Welsh Annals') and the fabulous *Historia Brittonum* ('History of the Britons') – were produced in the 8th and 9th centuries AD, some 300 years after the date given for Arthur's death (537 in the *Annales Cambriae*). A casual reference to Arthur in the Welsh bardic poem *Y Gododdin* may be older (the poem was probably composed *c.* 600), but it did not appear in written form until the 13th century. There is simply no primary source evidence for Arthur's existence. Gildas, a fellow Briton writing in the early 6th century, does not mention Arthur, nor does Bede, writing his famous history two centuries later but using Gildas and other primary sources. Without contemporary records, historians have not been able to make a very strong case for Arthur.

Arthur and archaeology

In 1191, monks at Glastonbury Abbey excavated their ancient cemetery and uncovered a remarkable grave. Inside a hollowed-out log coffin were the bones of a large man and those of a woman whose golden hair

was still intact. An overturned lead cross near the grave bore the Latin inscription: *Hic iacet sepultus inclitus rex Arturius in insula Avalonia* (Here lies buried the famous King Arthur in the Isle of Avalon).

Had this excavation been without controversy, there would not be much of a mystery about Arthur and Avalon. But the Glastonbury monks knew what they were looking for – a bard had allegedly 'tipped off' their patron, King Henry II – and finding Arthur's bones was guaranteed to bring in revenues from pilgrimage to help pay for rebuilding at the Abbey. The book that had made Arthur famous throughout Europe – Geoffrey of Monmouth's *History of the*

Glastonbury Tor was once surrounded by marsh and was identified in the Middle Ages as the Isle of Avalon.

Kings of Britain (written in 1136) – was by then being roundly criticized by contemporary scholars. Moreover, modern scholars have concluded that the letter forms on the inscribed cross (now lost, along with the bones) are too late to belong to the era in which Arthur allegedly lived, and many now accuse the monks of having pulled off a brilliant hoax.

Devious or not, the Glastonbury monks were the first to look for material evidence for clues to Arthur's existence. The search for Camelot fascinated early antiquarians, who recorded Arthurian associations with sites like South Cadbury. But with the develop-

ment of modern archaeology in the 20th century, new and compelling evidence concerning 'the Age of Arthur' (the 5th and 6th centuries) began to emerge. The first discovery was at Tintagel, in Cornwall, the site of Arthur's birth in Geoffrey's *History*. Ralegh Radford's excavations revealed, beneath the later Norman castle, the remains of several small buildings of stone and slate associated with thousands of pottery sherds. Though the structures were unremarkable,

Right **Aerial view of the rocky promontory called 'Tintagel Island' in Cornwall.** *Below* **A Glasgow University team excavating Site C at Tintagel.**

the sherds were the remains of fine tablewares and amphoras (likely wine and oil containers) imported from North Africa and the eastern Mediterranean from the 5th to the 7th centuries.

Radford interpreted Tintagel as a Celtic monastery whose monks were engaged in active commerce with the Mediterranean world more than a century after Britain ceased to be a province of the Roman empire. More recently, scholars prefer to see Tintagel as the base of a powerful chieftain who used it to receive tribute and distribute gifts to his retainers. Was this chieftain Arthur? The latest excavations at Tintagel unearthed several more small buildings and, covering a drainage ditch, one highly publicized inscribed slate bearing the word ARTOGNOV, which represents the Welsh name *Arthnou*. While this is not

Above **Inscribed slate bearing the name *Artognov*, found during excavations at Tintagel in 1998.** *Below* **The Winchester Round Table: this massive oak table top, created in the 13th or 14th century, was painted early in the reign of Henry VIII (Arthur bears a likeness to the Tudor king).**

Arthur, it is evidence of Latin literacy and organized engineering at Tintagel in the 6th century.

Another excavation that drew much attention was Leslie Alcock's work at South Cadbury in the late 1960s. At the site known locally for centuries as 'Camelot', Alcock excavated a prominent Iron Age hillfort that yielded occupational evidence from the Neolithic to the Late Saxon period. In the 'Arthurian' period (the 5th and 6th centuries), the hillfort was greatly refortified and new structures were built on the enclosed plateau, including a large 'feasting' hall. Dozens of sherds of imported pottery, the same types found at Tintagel, proved that South Cadbury was also involved in the active trade of prestige goods in the later 5th and 6th centuries. Furthermore, the manpower that would have been required to build and guard the new ramparts seemed to suggest a local king of great stature.

The Holy Grail

Like the legends of Myrddin (Merlin) and Tristan and Iseult, that of the Holy Grail may have been an independent tradition later attached to the Arthurian legends. When the Grail first appears, in the French poem *Perceval* written by Chrétien de Troyes *c.* 1190, it is an ornate dish (Old French *graal*) which serves the Mass wafer in the castle of the maimed Fisher King. Because the poem was left unfinished, subsequent authors were given the freedom to depict the Grail in myriad forms. Some reflect pre-Christian Celtic adventure tales of magical cauldrons. Most popular, however, has been

The ornate Ardagh Chalice, made in the 8th century, is the image many modern authors have of the Holy Grail.

that tradition identifying the Grail with the chalice of the Last Supper, the *san graal* or 'holy grail'. This relic, according to medieval apocrypha, passed into the possession of Joseph of Arimathea, whose family brought it to Britain during the founding of the island's first Christian community, at Glastonbury.

Of course, the Glastonbury monks played their part in the shaping of this legend. Still, archaeologists have been curious as to whether there is anything to this tradition of an early Christian community at Glastonbury. Ralegh Radford excavated parts of the Abbey in the late 1950s. He found beneath later Saxon structures slight remains of early wattle buildings, which he interpreted as the founders' church and subsequent monastic oratories. He also found, in the ancient cemetery, proof that the Glastonbury monks had indeed dug where they said and had uncovered early burials. Philip Rahtz conducted excavations of nearby Glastonbury Tor a decade later, uncovering traces of wooden buildings, metalworking debris, and sherds of imported pottery which enabled him to date this occupation to the Arthurian period.

The Once and Future King

Despite this flurry of archaeological activity, nothing has been found which is explicitly identified with an historical Arthur. At the same time, a veritable industry of Arthur books has taken off in Britain and America. These detective-like tales posit candidates for *the* Arthur which include the 2nd-century Roman general Lucius Artorius Castus, the Breton warlord Riothamus, an obscure Welsh king of Gwynedd, and one Artuir, son of the Scottish king Áedán mac Gabráin. Meanwhile local tourist boards watch with interest to see whether Arthur will be declared a Cornishman, a Welshman or a Scot!

This quest to possess a piece of Arthur is nothing new. Richard the Lionheart gave to a crusading companion a sword alleged to be Excalibur, while Henry VIII showed Emperor Charles V the 'real' Round Table hanging in Winchester Castle (though it bore a painted likeness of Henry himself). Both English and Welsh princes used Merlin's prophecies about Arthur to support their own political aims, and latter-day bards like Spenser and Tennyson wrote new tales about Arthur to magnify the glories of reigning monarchs. Since, in most of the medieval legends, Arthur's end is shrouded in mystery, he makes the perfect Once and Future king, to be dug up and debated over by each generation.

The Turin Shroud

Time: AD 33?/AD 1260–1390?
Location: Turin, Italy

And when the Lord had given the linen cloth to the servant of the priest, he went to James and appeared to him.

APOCRYPHA

P UT SIMPLY, the Shroud of Turin is a large linen cloth, 4.3 m (14 ft 3 in) long by 1.1 m (3 ft 7 in) wide, which bears the image – front and back – of a man who apparently died by crucifixion. This fact alone would excite interest, but the claim (not by any church authority) that this is the actual burial cloth of Jesus Christ has become a magnet for controversy. The same claim has provoked detailed scientific examination and international conferences. In 1978 an exhibit of the Shroud at Turin, Italy, attracted three million people; numbers will no doubt be even greater in future exhibitions.

Some think the history of the shroud began in 1357, when Geoffrey II of Charney exhibited it in Lirey, France. Yet earlier mentions of images of Jesus are known. For example, in the 4th century AD one source relates that Thaddaeus or Addai painted an image of Jesus 'with choice pigments' at Edessa in Syria. In the 6th century another source narrates a tale that Christ wiped his face on a towel and thereby imprinted his image on it. Christ gave this towel to an emissary from King Abgar of Edessa. Stories of an image of Christ at Edessa persisted until AD 944, when the Byzantine army moved the image to Constantinople (Istanbul). Here the image rested until AD 1204, when the knights of the Fourth Crusade sacked the city and took its treasures, including the image. This could explain how the Shroud came to be exhibited in France in the 14th century.

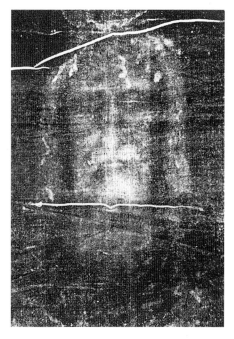

Above **A gold coin of Justinian II, struck between AD 692 and 695 in Constantinople. Such coins were the first to have an image of Jesus, and it is very close to that on the Shroud.** *Right* **A 6th-century AD icon of Jesus from St Katherine's monastery, Mount Sinai.** *Far right* **Negative of the first photograph of the Shroud taken in 1898.**

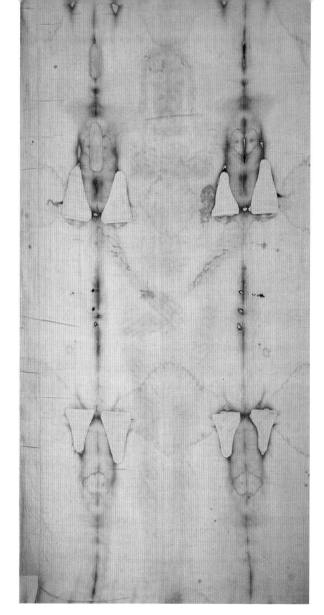

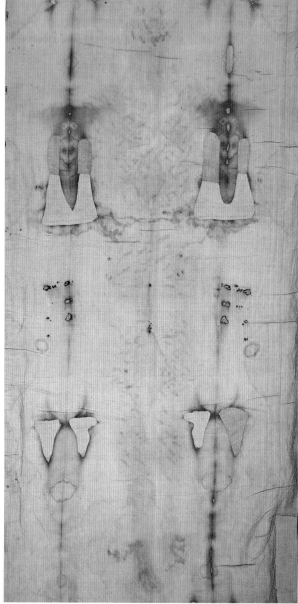

The Shroud and its dating

Many 'burial cloths' of Jesus were exhibited in the Middle Ages, so what is so interesting about the Shroud of Turin?

When viewed, the image on the Shroud is a rather muted, yellowish likeness against a white background. Yet it is best understood as a *negative* image of a crucified man, front and back; strangely, it also contains three-dimensional information. There is also an amazing amount of detail in the image: for example, the human anatomy is depicted with great accuracy, including lesions from scourging, blood flows from nail wounds in the wrists and feet, blood on the scalp, and details of the hair and beard. In addition observers point out a possibly broken nose and even coins on the eyes. The bloodstains have undergone DNA testing and prove to be human, from a male, type AB.

There is also microscopic debris, including specks of dirt, dust and pollen. The pollen comes from numerous plants, with experts claiming to have identified 19 species of plants that grow only in the vicinity of Jerusalem and Jericho.

In 1988 radiocarbon (C14) dating tests of the Shroud were undertaken in laboratories in Zurich, Oxford and Tucson, using the Accelerated Mass Spectrometry (AMS) technique, which allows smaller samples to be radiocarbon dated. A piece of cloth, just 1 cm (⅜ in) by 5.7 cm (2¼ in) was divided between the three laboratories. The results dated the material of the Shroud to AD 1260–1390. Does this not settle the question of its age?

For many, especially in the press, the radiocarbon tests did just that, and in the eyes of numerous scientists the 1988 results were conclusive. Yet others pointed out that the sample was taken from a part of

Opposite **The front (left) and back (right) of the Shroud of Turin. The two vertical lines are burn marks and the triangular patches the result of the fire of 1532.**

Right **Enlargement of the shroud showing the linen weave and particulate matter identified as bloodstains and serum stains.** *Below* **3-D information in the shroud, as depicted by an image analyser showing a full-frontal view.**

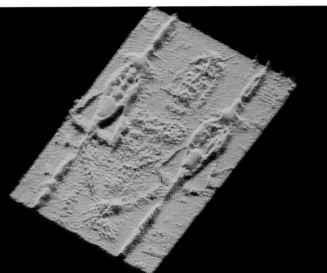

image is a scorch from draping a hot statue. Still others have maintained that the imprint is a kind of 'vapourgraph' in which gases given off from a decomposing human body leave an imprint. And some have sought to prove that it is a natural imprint of a body (the Volkringer effect or dehydration of the linen fibres). There are those who have made a case for radiation theories – the body's natural electro-magnetic field interacting with the cloth. Some have argued for a supernatural burst of electromagnetic radiation at the resurrection of Jesus. There are even those who argue that spiritual energies associated with Christ's resurrection account for the imprint.

So what are we left with in attempting to explain this mysterious linen shroud? Does it really testify to a miracle? There is still room for argument and experiment. Some of the most convincing theories are that the imprint is the result of complex and subtle natural processes that we do not yet fully understand. Experiments with a medical mannikin in an ancient tomb in Jerusalem suggest that heat (from post-mortem fever) and human sweat, which supplies an acid, combined with the alkaline, high-humidity environment of a tomb cut into limestone rock, will produce a subtle image on unbleached linen.

Whatever the actual process might have been, the Shroud of Turin remains a genuine scientific anomaly and resists our best attempts at analysis and classification.

Experiment to reproduce the Turin Shroud image, 1999, using a cloth to which myrrh and aloe have been applied.

the Shroud that has been touched and contaminated by human hands most since it was first exhibited. Furthermore, the Shroud was scorched in a fire in Turin in 1532, and fire introduces new contaminants, a theory confirmed in testing known samples. Others noted that fungi and bacteria grow on ancient linen fibres, and these resist removal by the dating process used for the Shroud. Finally, since the radiocarbon date is 13th or 14th century, the artistic style of the image (if it is a fraud) should be medieval, but it is not.

Explaining the Shroud

So how have people explained the Shroud of Turin? Is it a fraud, an accident, or a miracle? All these explanations have at some time been proposed. For example, although there are no brush strokes on the Shroud from painting, it might have been produced by daubing pigments. Others have suggested that the

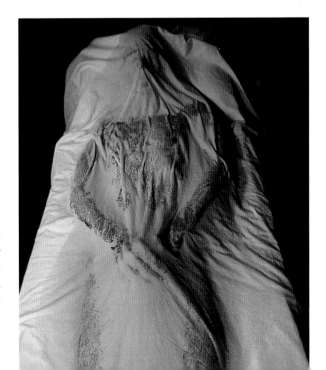

Maya Myth: Will the World End in 2012? 14

Time: AD 250–909
Location: Central America

Again there comes a humiliation, destruction, and demolition.... There came a rain of resin from the sky. There came the one named Gouger of Faces: he gouged out their eyeballs. There came Sudden Bloodletter: he snapped off their heads.

THE POPOL VUH, 16TH CENTURY

COME DECEMBER 2012, the current race of humans is due to be wiped from the face of the earth in a fearful cataclysm, which, to judge from the last destruction by fire, flood and a plague of demons, will come in an unexpected and terrible form. At least, that is what we can expect to be told as we enter the 'final countdown' of the ancient Maya calendar. Give or take a day or so, the 23rd of that fateful month will mark the end of 13 Bak'tuns of the Long Count cycle, completing a journey of 1,872,000 days that began with the last such event in 3114 BC. But what do we actually know about this elaborate system, and what did the Maya think was going to happen in 2012?

The Maya, the most sophisticated and literate of Central America's ancient civilizations, believed in a cyclical universe, one that had experienced recurring creations and annihilations. The best source on these ideas is the Popol Vuh, or 'Book of Council',

This painted vase shows the cigar-smoking lord of the Underworld, God L, as he presides over an important ritual at the dawn of the last creation in 3114 BC. The black background probably alludes to a primeval world before the arrival of light.

a mythological epic produced by the Quiche Maya of highland Guatemala, probably in the late 16th century (though perhaps based on an original written in hieroglyphs). It begins with the parting of sky and earth, which allows the first light into the world. It then describes how the Creator Gods try to populate it with humankind. Their first attempt produces the animals of the earth, but since they cannot speak and praise their makers they are banished to the forest as failures. In the second, people are formed from clay, but they jabber insensibly and their bodies start to crumble. The gods break them up in disgust. For the third creation humans are formed from wood, but they have no souls and forget their creators. To destroy them the gods not only produce the aforementioned flood, fire and demons, they even make their cooking utensils rise up against them, crushing their faces with stones. Finally, the gods try maize dough as the stuff of life and the people of today came into being.

There is much in the greater Popol Vuh myth that we can recognize in the art of Maya civilization's highpoint, the Classic period (AD 250–909), but it is clear that it contains ideas of even deeper antiquity. If the Classic Maya believed in a cyclical universe then its timing, both genesis and armageddon, should be encoded in their Long Count calendar. No one knows exactly where or when this system was invented, but the earliest contemporary date we have falls only in 32 BC. Long Count dates are written in a five-place notation, mostly working in a base of 20 unlike our own base 10. The highest value was normally the Bak'tun – a unit of 144,000 days – but we know that there were 19 higher ones, rarely expressed, all set with the coefficient 13. The

A monolith at the city of Quirigua called Stela C contains the best description of the creation events of 3114 BC. One side records the completion of 13 Bak'tuns (detail). Note the number 13 (highlighted), composed of three dots and two bars, with each dot representing one and the bar representing five.

full Long Count was thus of unimaginable scale, encompassing many trillions of years (far longer than our own universe has existed).

Advances in deciphering the Maya script give some insights into the events of the last 13 Bak'tun date in 3114 BC. These focus not on destruction but creation: there is an 'ordering' of gods, the forming of a central 'hearth' and a 'planting of stones'. Since this was not a true year zero, the inscriptions also tell of mythic episodes long before 3114 BC. Similarly, the Maya calculated dates well into the future, with one royal anniversary projected forward to AD 4772. There can thus be no sense in which 2012 represents the 'end of time'.

Only one inscription, found at the site

This scene from the Dresden Codex, a late hieroglyphic book, appears to show the destruction of the earth by flood. A sky caiman and an aged goddess pour water on to the deity God L.

of Tortuguero, prophetically describes the ending of 13 Bak'tuns in 2012. Sadly, it is damaged and only partially legible. It does refer to *b'olon okte'*, the name of a well-known Maya god, here prefixed by the term *yem* 'descending'. This is rather reminiscent of the image of the Diving God that becomes so popular in Maya art of the Postclassic era (AD 909–1697).

As we know, the Long Count did not survive to see more than a fraction of its vast vision unfold. The last proper date was carved at Tonina, Mexico, in 909. The previous century had seen a social, ecological and demographic crisis sweep the region, bringing Classic civilization to an end (see pp. 282–5). But this disaster pales when compared to the events of the 16th century. The invasion of Europeans was to be a death sentence for untold numbers of Maya, as it was for native peoples throughout the Americas. Decimated by disease, with a new religion imposed on pain of torture and execution, and traditional learning all but eradicated, here was a catastrophe worthy of ancient prophecy.

Aztlán & the Myth of the Aztec Migration 15

Time: 13th–15th centuries BC
Location: Valley of Mexico

These people like the others who populated the country departed from the Seven Caves, in a land where they had lived, called Aztlán. This name means 'Whiteness', or 'Place of the Herons'.

FRAY DIEGO DURAN, 16TH CENTURY

THE AZTECS AND their allies created an empire in central and southern Mexico during the 15th and early 16th centuries AD – barely a hundred years before they were overcome by the Spanish expedition of Hernán Cortés. In the national myth of Mexico today, the Aztecs are idealized in the popular imagination, embodying the heroic, indigenous past and the tragedy of foreign conquest. The conversion of the Aztec capital Tenochtitlan into Spanish colonial Mexico City, and its continuation as the capital of the modern nation, contributes to the elevation of the Aztecs above other Indian peoples as foremost representatives of a 3000-year-old collective pre-Hispanic cultural inheritance.

The origin myth

Where did the Aztecs come from? Early colonial annals and pictorial manuscripts prepared from Aztec sources, as well as archaeological excavations, trace the Aztecs only to the early 13th century in the Valley of Mexico with historical certainty. The ultimate geographical place of their origins remains an unsolved mystery. Aztecs appeared as one of several tribes of nomadic hunter-gatherers and part-time farmers, who, in the 13th century, were migrating into Central Highland Mexico from northern deserts. Myths and legends tell of Aztlán, 'place of cranes', an origin-place far to the north. Aztlán is described as an island-hill rising from a lake. There, the Aztecs emerged from caves and the earth-womb in the time of creation. Eventually they decided to leave. Embarking by canoes to the mainland, they began a long migration. Soon they were joined by another group, the Mexica, 'moon people' (hence the compound name Mexica-Aztecs, by which they are often known). They were led by a chieftain, Huitzilopochtli, 'Hummingbird on the Left', who appears thereafter

Pages from the Codex Boturini depict the Aztec migration from Aztlán, an island in the middle of a lake.

Huitzilopochtli slew the enemy chieftain and had his heart thrown into the lakeshore marshes. The heart landed at the place where the wandering tribe would later found their great pyramid and capital, Tenochtitlan. The place is described as a field of reeds with magically white juniper, cattails and willows. White serpents, frogs and fish swam in a spring. Another version describes twin springs, with dark blue and yellow water. These images were actually borrowed from earlier sources, for they are also depicted in the *Historia Tolteca-Chichimeca*.

Finally the Aztecs saw an eagle perched on a cactus growing on a rocky outcrop – this was a long-sought vision, prophesied by Huitzilopochtli as a mystical sign of the place where the tribe was to settle. This happened in the year '2 house', corresponding to 1325 in the Christian calendar.

Left **The defeated Coyolxauhqui: a sculpture found at the Great Temple of Tenochtitlan.** *Below* **The sign which led the Aztecs to found their capital city of Tenochtitlan: an eagle perched on a cactus on a rock, from the Codex Mendoza.**

as a sacred effigy transported by priests. As the migration continued, priests voiced Huitzilopochtli's oracular directions as to where the tribe was to travel.

The magical birth of Huitzilopochtli had taken place before the migration. The myth tells of an aged priestess, Coatlicue, who was sweeping an earth-shrine atop Coatepetl, 'Serpent Mountain'. Unexpectedly a ball of feathers fell from the sky and impregnated her with Huitzilopochtli. When Coatlicue's sons, the Centzonhuitznaua, 'the four hundred' (i.e. many), and her elder daughter Coyolxauhqui learned of the pregnancy, they were enraged and determined to slay her. The armed host then advanced up the mountain. Suddenly, Huitzilopochtli was born, as a fearsome, supernaturally powerful warrior. Hurling a flaming 'fire serpent' he pierced Coyolxauhqui and cut off her head, sending her body crashing in pieces down the mountain. The Centzonhuitznaua scattered as Huitzilopochtli chased them, slaying without mercy.

Continuing the migration, the tribe moved from place to place, sometimes stopping for years, and at one location a dissident faction split off. They also paused at a mountain, Culhuacan-Chicomoztoc, a feature named in the earlier migration story of the 10th-century Tolteca-Chichimeca. After the Aztecs arrived in the Valley of Mexico, they attempted to settle near the springs of Chapultepec. There another fabled battle took place, when

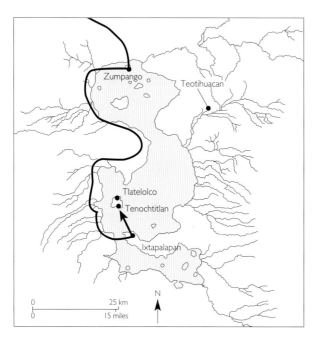

**Map to show the mythical route taken by the Aztecs to their
capital city of Tenochtitlan.**

Separating fact from fiction

What are we to make of these mythic events? In fact,
the early years of the Aztecs in the Valley of Mexico
present a different picture. Despised as barbarians
with no aristocratic ruling lineage, and suffering
humiliating rebuffs and defeats from the older urban
communities, the tribe was forced to flee into the
reedbeds. Yet they proved resilient and enterprising.
By 1428 they had assimilated an urban way of life and
formed an alliance with Tetzcoco and Tlacopan. They
successfully shifted the balance of power to embark
on the conquests that were to make Tenochtitlan the
most feared and richest city of Mexico. The ruler
Itzcóatl soon saw the need to define a new historical
identity. A council assembled to review the obscure
origins, the existing tribal migration accounts, the
humiliations endured and the lack of prestigious
ancestry: all were unacceptable for the new imperial
status. The old records were burned. A new, 'official'
history was prepared, by appropriating well-known
mythic events, and Huitzilopochtli was promoted as
the deified Aztec patron.

Scholars analysing these 'official' texts note that
the story beginning in Aztlán conforms to a pattern
of migration stories distributed south into Guatemala,
in Central Mexico, in Michoacán to the northwest,
and northwards to New Mexico. The sequence begins
in a faraway land or a lake to the north at the onset of
a new era. Often, a people emerge from the earth or
the waters. Departure may be directed by a god or
goddess as a result of dissension or war. The depart-
ing group is joined by others, and a supernatural
leader or messenger points out the route of migration.

Thus the official Aztec migration story reflected
established models, and Aztlán was conceived by the
Aztecs themselves as a mythical place rather than a
specific geographical location, which is why modern
attempts to locate it have ended in speculation.
Huitzilopochtli's 'fatherless' birth and his slaying of
enemies may be seen as an Aztec myth to bypass
their lack of a 'legitimate' aristocratic ancestral
lineage. To commemorate Huitzilopochtli's victory,
the Great Pyramid of Tenochtitlan was designed
as a symbol of the mythic mountain Coatepetl.
Huitzilopochtli's temple stood above, next to that of
Tlaloc, the agricultural Rain God of Mesoamerican
antiquity; below, on the landing, was a sculpture of
the dismembered Coyolxauhqui. The Aztecs thus
created a source of inspiration for their warrior
culture of fierce valour, pride and destruction.

Yet the fact remains that in ancient Mexico there
was a pattern of intermittent connections, from at
least the 1st millennium BC, between urban peoples
of the central highland basins and tribes of the arid
north. It is probable that the Aztecs were from this
vast region, and a people such as the Aztecs were not
likely to forget their beginnings entirely, however
assimilated they became to an urban way of life.

The quest for Aztlán might thus be seen as an
inquiry into a type of culture once found among
many societies living between the southwestern
deserts of the United States and the central highlands of Mexico, and a question of how such peoples
shaped ancient, and modern, Mexican history.

The Great Pyramid of Tenochtitlan, with its twin shrines.

Memories of the
Dreamtime

Time: eternal
Location: Australia

16

The art of Aboriginal Australia is the last great tradition of art in the world to be appreciated by the world at large.

WALLY CARAUNA, 1993

W HEN EUROPEANS took possession of Australia, with the landing of the British First Fleet in Botany Bay in 1788, they shaped the land by their own European values. They mapped it, they divided it into fields and farms, they gave its landmarks English-language names – as if it were an empty land. Archaeologists, within the same cultural tradition, have always had as a central concern the dating of the exact time Aboriginal people settled Australia; their current best estimate is around 60,000 years ago or earlier (see pp. 101–4).

Aboriginal Australians have their own views on these matters. We have, they know and say, always been here, since the Dreaming time when the land was made and put in order, when the creeks and hills were made, when the people were placed each in their own country. The 'Dreamtime', the word used today to express this Aboriginal concept in English, is not a fitting translation. 'Dream' is the wrong word, in hinting at some insubstantial irrational world from which we will wake up to a different and true reality. 'Time' is the wrong word also, for it suggests some distinct period, placed in the past and separate from the present. An essential part of the Dreaming, of the 'always' of the being here, is that things are as they are and must be. Time, measured chronological time, change over time – those central planks in archaeology and Western empirical science – do not come into it.

Art of the Dreamtime

In their ancient rock paintings and rock engravings, Aboriginal Australians have left a pictorial record. Many of the animals and the birds are those in the land today, among them are some such as the brolga and the crocodile, the sulphur-crested cockatoo and

the python, that are creatures important also in the Dreamtime stories. A common motif is a bird-track, sometimes small, the size of a bush-turkey's track, sometimes large, the size of an emu, sometimes even larger. Are these last the over-size images of emu tracks? Or records of a bigger bird? There are images of oversize human feet as well.

Often, but not always, a Dreaming Place is a singular feature of the landscape, such as this naturally occurring great stack of sandstone.

Above **In Australia, rock art is a living tradition. This great frieze in Kakadu National Park was painted in the early 1960s, over traces of earlier paintings.** *Below* **Human tracks cut into a north Australian rock face are worn and crusted with age; some were later outlined in white paint. The celebrated 'dot painting' of recent art in central Australia derives its iconography from ancient rock art.**

In north Australia, the rock paintings of Kakadu National Park and its region go back some thousands of years, certainly 4000 years, probably many more. In its older phases there are many images of Tasmanian tigers, the marsupial carnivore which survived into the 20th century only in Tasmania. On the Australian mainland, the tiger has been extinct since people brought dogs from Southeast Asia – these became the wild dingo, which, as a more efficient medium-sized predator, drove the tiger to extinction. It survived in Tasmania because by the time the dingo arrived in Australia, Tasmania was already separated from the mainland by the rising sea-level of post-glacial times.

Records of the ancient past

We think the dingo came into north Australia some 4000 years ago, so the pictures of Tasmanian tigers are of an extinct creature – but one which has been extinct only that length of time. But a unique painting, high in the remote 'stone country' beyond even the boundary of Kakadu National Park, hints at something older. Well-preserved and well-painted, it seems to depict an adult and juvenile of a singular creature which is certainly not a Tasmanian tiger,

nor any kind of kangaroo or modern marsupial. It has small front legs with front paws rather like hands (as marsupials do), beefy back legs and a broad tail (as marsupials do). It has something odd about its middle, as if it had large and pointed udders or teats hanging below the body (but marsupials have their teats inside the pouches where their young develop). The small, or juvenile one, has something similar. Is this creature one of the megafauna? One identification is of a creature known only from its fossil bones, called *Palorchestes*.

Tantalizingly, we currently know of just the one painting. There may be more in the high stone country, where countless rock-shelters are full of paintings, not much visited and certainly not fully explored for rock art. A central figure in the Dreamtime stories is the Rainbow Serpent, the great Being who moved through the country shaping the land and who has left dramatic sign of her (sometimes his) passing by making the billabongs and pools, the rocks and creeks. Does the Rainbow Serpent preserve some kind of memory of the great snakes, even larger than modern Australian pythons, of past times? Do Aboriginal stories of floods and rising waters also preserve the memory of the end of the Ice Age, when a rising sea-level will have pushed people back from an older sea-shore?

In Kakadu National Park, where that sea-level rise is well dated and rather late in its final stages, a well-dated rock art sequence gives a telling clue: there is a decided increase in paintings which show people fighting at just that era of a rising sea which would have pushed 'people of the shore' into new contact with 'people of the stone' who formerly had been well inland.

Above left **A *churinga* from central Australia. It is thought that the ancestors of the Dreamtime became these sacred objects.** *Above* **This strange creature, its head held up high and to the right, and with its young to the right, may well be one of the long-extinct megafauna.**

Below **Bruce Nabegeyo, *Ngalyod – Rainbow Serpent* (1995). The Rainbow Serpent is a central figure in the Dreamtime stories. In this modern image, Rainbow has the head of that most powerful of creatures, the saltwater crocodile.**

Mysteries of the Stone Age

ALTAMIRA'S POLYCHROME bison, the giant bulls of Lascaux, the rhinoceroses of Chauvet Cave: the Stone Age peoples of the late Ice Age have an enduring fascination, which began with the discoveries of Cro-Magnon art a century ago. We have come a long way from the well-worn stereotypes of those days: skin-wearing cave people armed with clubs hunting sabre-toothed tigers, and brutish Neanderthals shambling across snow-clad Ice Age landscapes. Thanks to archaeology, genetics and a wide array of scientific methods, we know many Stone Age societies in surprisingly intimate detail – their life-ways, their technologies, their complex seasonal movements, even something of their ritual beliefs. Yet, the more we know, the more involved are the controversies.

One of the greatest debates surrounds the origins of *Homo sapiens sapiens* – ourselves. Are the mitochondrial geneticists correct when they argue that we originated in tropical Africa and then spread widely over the Old World and into the Americas during the late Ice Age? Or did modern humans evolve in many different regions, as some scholars fervently believe?

Whatever our origins, we often assume that we are the first hominids capable of logical reasoning and the ability to converse fluently. We point to the sudden appearance of artistic traditions some 30,000 years ago, to newly sophisticated adaptations to arctic environments. The Neanderthals and other archaic humans are often held up as primitive, less-advanced people, but evidence is mounting that they were

The standing stones of Ballochroy with the Paps of Jura, Kintyre, Scotland, behind. Why were such megaliths erected?

tough, intelligent folk, who may have had a form of speech. Nor are we certain what happened to them when modern humans settled in their territories. Recent archaeological discoveries do not necessarily allow us to assume they rapidly became extinct.

As modern humans spread across the world, they encountered formidable barriers and environmental challenges. Recent discoveries have posed intriguing questions as to when Stone Age groups crossed the open sea from Southeast Asia to settle New Guinea, Australia and the Solomon Islands. As with the Americas, the greatest controversies surround first settlement, the date at which humans initially entered virgin, unsettled lands. This issue is especially controversial in North America, where the discovery of Kennewick Man, claimed by some to be Caucasoid, has unleashed a storm of debate over the identity of the first Americans and over the ethics of studying Native American burials. Human impact on the natural environment is another contemporary question. Big game animals – a whole range of megafauna – went extinct in every continent humans spread to. Were humans responsible, or were there other causes?

Some 12,000 years ago, the first farming societies appeared in southwestern Asia at a time of severe drought. Herein lies one of the great mysteries of the Stone Age – why did humans suddenly change from being foragers to farmers? The debate involves a multiplicity of factors, among them sudden climatic change, population growth, sedentary living and technology. But on one point everyone is agreed. The advent of farming and animal domestication changed the rules of human existence altogether and greatly affected our relationships with the environ-ment. The endless round of planting and harvest, life and death, forged a new and close relationship between people and their ancestral lands.

Some of the most intriguing Stone Age mysteries concern ancestors and mother goddesses. The mega-liths of western Europe include stone circles and communal burial places, whose exact function is still discussed, especially their possible role as astronomical observatories for marking the passage of the solstices and other cyclical events. Stonehenge in southern Britain has been likened to a prehistoric cathedral, a complex monument that evolved many times over the centuries. It engenders continuing debate about the manner of its construction and the labour required to build such a stupendous structure.

Most Europeans and large proportion of western and southern Asians have spoken languages belonging to a single linguistic family, which began to spread across Eurasia in the Neolithic or early Bronze Age. Where did this language originate? The question of the home of the Indo-Europeans is one of how language can be tracked through the archaeological record. Archaeology usually deals with such anonymous groups, and not with individuals. Only rarely is the archaeologist fortunate to discover the body of a person, like Ötzi, the Iceman, the frozen and fully clothed corpse found high in the Italian Alps, where he perished, probably of exposure, over 5000 years ago. Modern medicine can tell us more about the Ice Man's health than he knew himself, but the body does not answer the ultimate conundrum: what was he doing so high in the Alps? The solutions to this, and so many other mysteries of the past, take us into the world of the intangible, always hard to decipher from archaeological evidence.

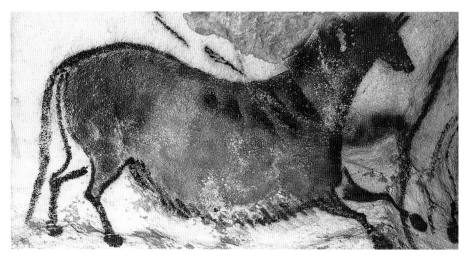

A wild horse cavorts across the walls of Lascaux Cave in France. The significance of such paintings is much debated and there are many differing theories.

The Puzzle of Human Origins

Time: 5–0.1 million years ago
Location: Africa

We are extremely close cousins of other species. And yet we have grown light years away from them.

RICHARD DAWKINS, 1992

THE HARSH, ARID LANDSCAPES of Ethiopia and Kenya hold the fossils of our earliest known relatives, the australopithecines. Dating from as early as around 4.5 million years ago, teeth, fragments of skull and occasionally pieces of leg and arm bones, are found eroding from ancient sediments. When meticulously excavated and pieced together they provide us with a picture of ape-like ancestors about 1 m (3 ft 3 in) tall, with brains the size of chimpanzees at about 450 cu. cm. They walked partially on two legs and had a largely vegetarian diet, with enormous molar teeth designed for grinding dry seeds and stems.

Also from Ethiopia is a fossil skull found in the Omo basin, dating to a mere 130,000 years ago. This has a brain size of about 1400 cu. cm – within the range of people living today. This specimen is

widely regarded as the first modern human, *Homo sapiens*, that has so far been discovered and it most likely had the same ability for language and

Reconstructed skull from Omo Kibish, Ethiopia. Dating to around 130,000 years ago, this is currently the oldest fossil specimen attributed to *Homo sapiens*.

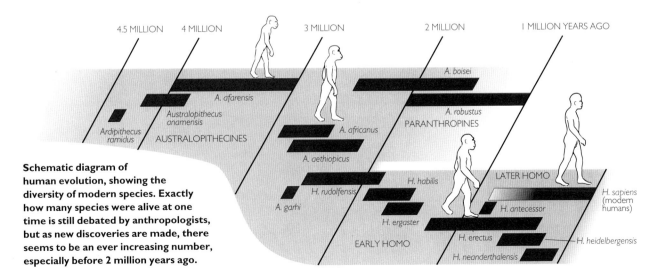

Schematic diagram of human evolution, showing the diversity of modern species. Exactly how many species were alive at one time is still debated by anthropologists, but as new discoveries are made, there seems to be an ever increasing number, especially before 2 million years ago.

4.5 MILLION · 4 MILLION · 3 MILLION · 2 MILLION · 1 MILLION YEARS AGO

Ardipithecus ramidus
Australopithecus anamensis
AUSTRALOPITHECINES
A. afarensis
A. africanus
A. aethiopicus
A. garhi
A. boisei
A. robustus
PARANTHROPINES
H. rudolfensis
H. habilis
H. ergaster
EARLY HOMO
H. antecessor
H. erectus
H. neanderthalensis
LATER HOMO
H. sapiens (modern humans)
H. heidelbergensis

symbolic expression as we do today. The few associated bones show us that it walked fully upright. Quite how we evolved from those ape-like ancestors of 4.5 million years ago to possess our stature, anatomy, intelligence and culture is the puzzle of human origins.

In one respect the answer to this puzzle is extraordinarily simple – biological evolution. Just as all other species evolved under the guiding force of natural selection, so too has our own. Those chance genetic mutations that gave one individual an advantage over others, such as being more adept at making tools, solving problems of finding food or walking on two legs, became fixed within the population and gradually shifted our anatomy, behaviour and intelligence to that which we possess today. But while the processes of biological evolution provide an answer to the puzzle of human origins – as Charles Darwin originally explained – this is not the type of answer that most of us desire. We want a much more detailed solution to this puzzle, one that tells us when and why specific changes in anatomy, behaviour and intelligence occurred.

A multidisciplinary approach

This type of solution is proving much more difficult to find and requires a whole army of different scientists to study the meagre sample of fossil fragments. Actually, the fossils provide just one of several sources of evidence. While anatomy provides some clues to past behaviour, other evidence comes from the stone artifacts, food waste, fire-places and other material residues left by our ancestors, and these are the province of archaeologists. Equally, we must know about the environments within which our ancestors were living, and that requires geologists and ecologists. Various scientific techniques are used to date and extract the maximum information from the remains – so physicists and chemists play a major role in the study of human origins. Moreover, it is not only evidence from the past that must be examined. An understanding of the genetic diversity of living humans is absolutely crucial to determining when and where the very first stages of human evolution took place – the divergence of our lineage from that leading to the chimpanzee – as well as the very final stages when modern humans evolved.

Left **The fossilized remains of 'Lucy',** *Australopithecus afarensis*, **dating to 3.5 million years ago, from Hadar, Ethiopia. Around 50 per cent of the skeleton survived, revealing that this species walked on two legs but also maintained anatomical adaptations for efficient tree climbing.**

Right **The basin of the Omo River in southwest Ethiopia has particularly long sequences of Pliocene and Pleistocene sediments. Fossils found here include those of 3-million-year-old human ancestors.** *Far right* **Dated to 1.6 million years ago, WT-1500, or the Nariokotome Boy, is the most complete skeleton from our evolutionary past. Assigned to** *Homo ergaster***, it shows that fully modern posture and bipedalism had evolved, even though brain size remained at** *c.* **1000 cu. cm, much smaller than that of modern humans.**

A bush not a ladder

Discoveries of fossils and archaeological evidence in the last few decades have in some ways made the puzzle of human origins more difficult to solve – but also far more interesting. It was once thought that human evolution was rather like a ladder, with a single species evolving into another and gradually becoming more like us today. But the new discoveries have shown that this is not the case: human evolution is more like a bush with many different branches, each taking our ancestors and relatives in a slightly different direction – all of which, bar one, proved to be evolutionary dead ends. Consequently it has become difficult to identify which species is ancestral to which, and indeed how many species are represented by the fossil specimens we possess.

We have also become aware that the elements of the package of behavioural and anatomical traits possessed by modern humans do not necessarily always have to go together – many have been shared by other species that have since become extinct. Walking on two legs, for instance, was adopted by several types of australopithecines, who were also likely to have made stone tools – something once thought to have been the attribute of *Homo* alone. During the latter stages of human evolution the Neanderthals had brains the same size as ours, were big-game hunters and probably had complex language, and yet they too were an evolutionary dead end (pp. 92–5).

Homo ergaster

The fossil discoveries have thus allowed us to get rid of simplistic notions about a ladder of evolutionary progress and we now pay more attention to the behavioural ecology of human ancestors and relatives, and the selective pressures for change that came to bear. These pressures often arose from the dramatic environmental changes of the last few million years, which created evolutionary feedback loops so that developments kept piggy-backing on each other. Consider, for example, the shift to habitual walking on two legs, increased meat eating, brains of about 900 cu. cm, and enhanced technical skills at flaking stone, all of which were present by about 1.8 million years ago within a species known as *Homo ergaster*.

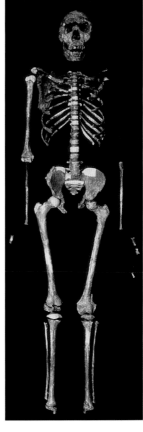

These 3.5 million-year-old footprints of australopithecines were found at Laetoli, Tanzania, by Mary Leakey. The footprints have provided crucial evidence for early bipedalism.

The shift to full bipedalism appears to have occurred around 2 million years ago and to be strongly related to the move to savannah environments caused by a severe reduction in rainfall in equatorial Africa. By adopting an upright posture, our ancestors reduced the amount of solar radiation their bodies received, maintained a lower body temperature and hence could forage when other animals had to rest in the shade. Living in more open environments is also likely to have placed pressures on our ancestors to live in larger social groups as a means of protection from carnivores. Because coping with a large number of social relationships is one of the most intellectually demanding jobs we do, this is thought to have provided the selective pressure for an increase in brain size. This in turn could only have occurred with a high-quality diet including meat-eating, which enabled the length of the gut to be reduced and metabolic energy be released to fuel a larger brain. Meat-eating in turn was made possible by the use of sharp stone tools to cut open carcasses and the possibility of finding these – something requiring the ability to forage when the lions and hyenas had to rest in the shade.

As the brain enlarged, the intellectual powers were provided to make more effective stone tools, to plan foraging trips and to live in ever greater social groups. So it was the feedback between these different developments that was absolutely crucial in the emergence of *Homo ergaster* – a pivotal species in human evolution that was most likely ancestral not only to ourselves but also the Neanderthals.

The rise of modern humans
This example of evolutionary developments at around 2 million years ago shows how the puzzle of human origins is not simply one of finding all the bits, nor just of putting them together in the right order, but of understanding how they interrelate. Precisely the same applies at the most recent end of the puzzle, with the emergence of anatomically modern humans. Here our pieces include the fossil specimens such as the skull from Omo, the fact that all living humans are genetically very similar to each other – much more so than other species even though we live at all ends of the earth and have very different lifestyles – and the absence of any other type of human species alive today. This last fact is at variance with the whole of human evolution up until 28,000 years ago, as several different types of humans had always been alive on the planet at the same time.

Solving this part of the puzzle has proved especially contentious, particularly the questions of how modern humans evolved and spread from Africa. For much of the 20th century many anthropologists believed that the only dispersal from Africa occurred soon after 2 million years ago. They thought that the single species of *Homo sapiens* then evolved from the different ancestral species that had appeared in the old world – from the Neanderthals in Europe and *Homo erectus* in Asia. This became known as the 'Regional Continuity' model. But it has few adherents today. Most anthropologists, geneticists and archaeologists today agree that modern humans evolved about 130,000 years ago in East Africa, most likely during a particularly harsh environmental phase which provided selective pressures for anatomical and – more importantly – cognitive changes. Human population numbers during that time appear to have fallen to as low as 10,000 – so we could easily have gone extinct, leaving the world to the Neanderthals of Europe and *Homo erectus* of Asia. But we survived and in a complex set of dispersals from Africa between 100,000 and 50,000 years ago eventually spread throughout the world and pushed all other human species into extinction. Quite how we were able to do that is another mystery of the stone age.

How Did Language Evolve?

Time: 0.5–0.1 million years ago
Location: Africa

18

Language is not a cultural artifact ... it is a distinct piece of the biological makeup of our brains.

STEPHEN PINKER, 1994

TALKING TO EACH OTHER is both one of the most simple and one of the most complex things that we can do. It is effortless and enjoyable; it is part of being a human being and a participating member of society. As a species we are compulsive communicators, using language to convey our deepest feelings, our advances in knowledge and understanding, and – often – the trivia of our everyday lives. As we communicate we engage in one of the most remarkable products of evolution – the use of language. Many of the utterances we make are likely to be unique; each and every one complies with a complex set of grammatical rules that we are quite unaware of possessing; and they will draw on the 60,000 words that an average member of society has at their disposal. A life without language is almost unimaginable, and when people are prevented from speech they employ sign languages that are every bit as complex as the spoken word.

To someone interested in evolution the particular language spoken is of less interest than the capacity for language itself. Take a child born in China and place her in England, and she will grow up as a fluent English speaker; if Chinese is spoken at home and English at school, the child will become bilingual. This happens because all languages have fundamental similarities. Babies are born with brains pre-programmed to acquire whatever language they are exposed to during the early years of life. By about the age of two, children are learning words at the rate of at least ten a day, and joining them together in structured sentences that often astonish their parents in their complexity and content.

No other system of animal communication is remotely like human language. Bird song, monkey calls and ant pheromones are all highly sophisti-cated but none have the possibility to refer to events either far in the future or in the past, those happening out of immediate experience, or perhaps only ever in the imagination. Chimpanzees, our closest living relatives, communicate by vocalization and gesture, and can learn to manipulate symbols in the laboratory. Scientists have experimented for years to detect any glimmer of human-like language in chimpanzees; most have concluded that they do not exist. Chimpanzees appear quite unable to acquire more than a few hundred 'words', and the 'grammatical' complexity of their own utterances never exceeds the most simple ordering of words.

Our human ancestors of 5 million years ago, who lived in the woodlands of East Africa, are likely to

Sue Savage-Rumbaugh and Panbanisha, a bonobo with substantial understanding of spoken English.

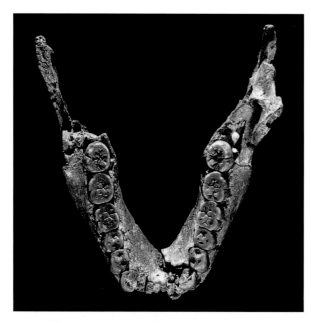

Lower jaw of *Homo ergaster*, showing reduced-size molars in comparison with those of earlier human relatives. The change in dentition was related to diet, and a by-product was an ability to make a large range of sounds.

have had similar 'language' capacities to the chimpanzee – which is effectively none. They would have communicated with each other by vocal calls and gestures. The transformation of this into human language probably happened very gradually, involving not just one transitional step of 'proto-language' but very many small steps culminating with fully complex modern language at about 130,000 years ago with the emergence of our species, *Homo sapiens*.

Pre-conditions for language

The evolution of language was dependent upon the possession of a sufficiently large brain to undertake the neural processing required to understand and generate utterances. But quite how large a brain was necessary remains unclear; that of the chimpanzee and australopithecines at *c.* 450 cu. cm seems inadequate, but *Homo ergaster* of 1.5 million years ago (see p. 88) with a brain of *c.* 900 cu. cm may well have had sufficient brain power – although the appropriate neural connections may still have been absent. *Homo ergaster* also had two other essential pre-conditions for the evolution of language. It was habitually bipedal and ate meat. Running and walking on two legs required a highly controlled breathing system to manage such exertions and this is also essential for producing the large number of

different sounds which is characteristic of spoken language. By relying on meat-eating rather than just consuming large quantities of seeds, stems and roots like its ancestors, *Homo ergaster* also had much smaller teeth. This provided the potential for a wide range of oral sounds as it gave great flexibility for the positioning of tongue, lips and cheeks.

The large brain of *Homo ergaster*, bipedalism and reduced dentition are likely to have evolved for reasons quite unrelated to language. But language could not have evolved until these were in place – they were a necessary pre-condition. Once present, vocal and gestural communications are likely to have gradually increased in frequency and complexity with an ever greater lexicon and more sophisticated grammar. One can readily imagine that those individuals who were able to express information more effectively, such as about the location of game or how to make tools, were at an advantage, as were those who had a more effective understanding of the utterances of others. But early language was also likely to have been used for expressing emotions and especially for building social relationships. Indeed some anthropologists today believe that the origins of language lie in gossip – language provided the 'glue' to prevent ever-larger groups from breaking apart. Others think that language may have been a means for showing off one's intelligence: just as peacocks use bright tail feathers to show off to peahens, so might early men and women have adopted an ever-increasing, and to some extent redundant, vocabulary to show off to the opposite sex. Certainly the skills of oratory are likely to have been important, since one of the key functions of language is to modify the minds of others, often to one's own way of thinking.

The evolution of language

Precisely when these selective pressures for language were most important in human evolution also remains unclear. The key elements of human anatomy that reflect the capacity for spoken language are unfortunately mainly soft tissue or neural circuits within the brain that leave no archaeological trace. So quite when the larynx descended in the throat to differentiate the human vocal tract from that of the chimpanzee, or when the human ability to perceive rapid speech sounds and to split up a continuous audible sequence into discrete words emerged remains unclear. It seems most likely that the enlargement of the human brain between 600,000 and 200,000 years ago, taking it to modern

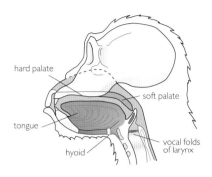

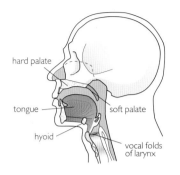

The human voice box, or larynx, is substantially lower in the anatomy of the throat than that of chimpanzees. This constrains the range of sounds that a chimpanzee can make and the descent of the larynx was a critical development for the evolution of language.

Below **In 1963 a well-preserved Neanderthal skeleton was found in a burial pit in Kebara Cave, Israel. This provided the first ever hyoid bone** (*centre*), **which sits in our throats and to which soft tissues relating to our vocal apparatus are attached.**

proportions of *c.* 1200–1500 cu. cm may well have been about building new networks in the brain for language. But the evolution of language is unlikely to have occurred in isolation from other cognitive abilities, such as those of consciousness and creative intelligence – these are likely to have 'piggy-backed' on each other. After all, there seems little point in being able to speak one's mind if one does not know one's mind in the first place.

In the light of evidence of bone harpoons dating to 90,000 years ago and red ochre from caves in South Africa from as much as 120,000 years ago, there seems little doubt that the first *Homo sapiens* had language – it is difficult to imagine people engaging in body painting and making complex tools if they were still unable to talk about what they were doing and why. But other human lineages are also likely to have evolved some language capacities. Anatomical evidence of the Neanderthals suggests that they were sophisticated language users – notably a hyoid bone from Kebara Cave, Israel (*c.* 63,000 years ago) that indicates a vocal tract not significantly different from ours today. But whether Neanderthals evolved a lexicon as large as modern humans and a grammar as complex, remains disputed.

So the evolution of language was a long and gradual process. Its ultimate roots lie in the type of communication systems used by apes today. It needed certain pre-conditions to be put in place, the fortunate product of quite unrelated developments, and then the selective pressures to exist for those individuals who could both produce and compre-hend utterances to be at a reproductive advantage. Those pressures most likely related to living in large social groups, the problems of finding and acquiring food, and communicating about toolmaking. A best guess is that the large-brained humans of at least 250,000 years ago were not only sophisticated hunter-gatherers but also ardent gossipers.

What Happened to the Neanderthals?

Time: 250,000–28,000 years ago
Location: Europe & western Asia

... they were neither 'new and improved' versions of Homo erectus *nor crude prototypes of* Homo sapiens. *They were themselves; they were Neanderthals – one of the most distinctive, successful and intriguing groups of humans that have ever enriched our family history.*

ERICK TRINKAUS & PAT SHIPMAN, 1992

WHAT HAPPENED TO the Neanderthals was the same as what happened to the vast majority of species that have ever lived on earth – they went extinct. There is nothing unusual about that, and as we discover more about human evolution we learn that the Neanderthals were just the most recent of many different types of humans and human ancestors that have suffered the same fate. But what is unusual and so intriguing about the Neanderthals is that they went extinct so very recently, less than 30,000 years ago, and by doing so left our species, *Homo sapiens*, as the only member of our genus alive on the planet. This is certainly very unusual, as all other types of animal including our closest relatives the chimpanzees and gorillas have at least two species alive, while most types of animals have many more. Moreover, Neanderthals seemed to have everything in their favour – they had brains as large as modern humans, a physiology

A drawing of the first identified Neanderthal skull. It was excavated in the Neander Valley in Germany in 1856, hence the name Neanderthal.

extremely well suited to living in their Ice Age environments, they were able to make complex stone tools and were effective big-game hunters. And yet, after having flourished across Europe and western Asia for more than 200,000 years, their population numbers dwindled and they went extinct. Exactly what happened to them remains a key question for archaeologists and anthropologists.

The classic Neanderthals

Homo neanderthalensis evolved from a species, *Homo heidelbergensis*, that colonized Europe soon after 1 million years ago. Quite which fossil specimens are assigned to which species is a matter of some dispute among anthropologists, but it is evident that by 150,000 years ago classic Neanderthal features had evolved. These include a face with a rather large projecting nose and large eyebrow ridges, and a cranium that is flat and sloping when compared with the high and rounded vault of a modern human. Their bodies were stout and robust with large barrel chests and muscular arms and legs. Their bones were thick and heavy, reflecting strenuous lives involving great physical activity. From the remains found in the caves they occupied we know that they were capable big-game hunters, killing horse, deer and bison with stone-tipped spears. Their hunting was often undertaken in rather harsh glacial environments – open tundra-like landscapes. Survival depended upon social co-operation and sharing as much as brute strength. During the time of their existence there were marked environmental changes. At around 125,000 years ago forests spread across Europe, but Neanderthals proved quite able to adapt to the new types of plants and animals that became available for food and as sources of material

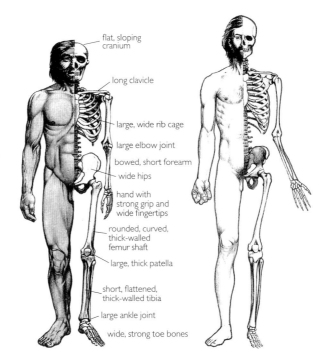

Right **There are anatomical and physiological differences between *Homo sapiens* and Neanderthals which reflect contrasting lifestyles and evolutionary environments. The Neanderthals are generally stouter and more robust, a physique well adapted to living in high latitudes. Modern humans are more gracile, reflecting their equatorial origin. But there is considerable variation in both species – many Neanderthals would not look out of place today.**

flat, sloping cranium

long clavicle

large, wide rib cage

large elbow joint

bowed, short forearm

wide hips

hand with strong grip and wide fingertips

rounded, curved, thick-walled femur shaft

large, thick patella

short, flattened, thick-walled tibia

large ankle joint

wide, strong toe bones

Below **The extent of the Neanderthal world. For much of their existence the far northwest was covered in ice sheets.**

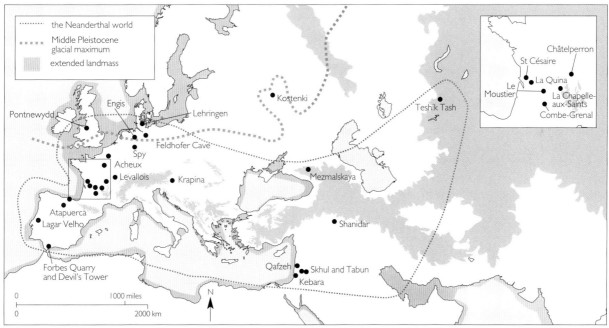

.... the Neanderthal world

- - - - Middle Pleistocene glacial maximum

extended landmass

Châtelperron
St Césaire
Le Moustier
La Quina
La Chapelle-aux-Saints
Combe-Grenal

Pontnewydd
Engis
Lehringen
Kostenki
Teshik Tash
Feldhofer Cave
Spy
Acheux
Levallois
Krapina
Mezmalskaya
Atapuerca
Lagar Velho
Shanidar
Forbes Quarry and Devil's Tower
Qafzeh
Skhul and Tabun
Kebara

0   1000 miles
0   2000 km
N

for making shelters, clothing and tools. All in all, they were a highly successful species, inhabiting some of the most demanding environments humans have ever known, adapting to change, seemingly set to survive into the modern world. So what went wrong?

From an evolutionary point of view nothing went wrong; all that happened was that a new species entered the landscapes in which the Neanderthals hunted and gathered, out-competing them for food, for caves and for sources of stone. A rule of ecology states that two different species cannot share the same 'niche' – and that is exactly what began to happen in western Asia from about 100,000 years ago, and in Europe from 40,000 years ago. The new species was ourselves – *Homo sapiens*.

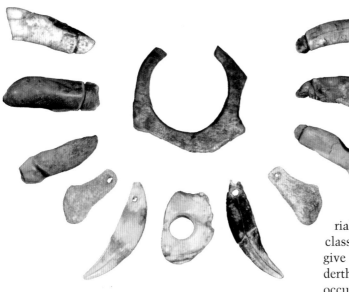

Left **The final Neanderthals in France (33,000–30,000 years ago) began to make ornaments from animal bone and teeth, such as this necklace from Arcy sur Cure.**

Neanderthals vs. modern humans

Having evolved in Africa at *c.* 130,000 years ago, groups of *Homo sapiens* began dispersing into Asia and Europe soon after. Quite why they showed such wanderlust remains unclear, but it is evident that by 60,000 years ago they had spread throughout Southeast Asia and crossed into Australia. Other groups had travelled to Israel by 100,000 years ago, and buried their dead in the caves of Qafzeh and Skhul. And there they may have come face-to-face with Neanderthals – or not. Although Neanderthals were living in precisely the same area at 125,000 and 63,000 years ago, whether they were also there when modern humans arrived, or had all travelled into Europe, remains unclear to archaeologists.

There can be little doubt, however, that once modern humans entered eastern Europe at 40,000 years ago, and then spread rapidly to the west, the two species became aware of each other's presence. There are no archaeological signs of direct contact other than a collection of bone and antler jewelry that some Neanderthals began making in southwest France at around 33,000 years ago. This was a completely novel activity for them, but an established part of modern human culture. The Neanderthals appear to have been copying the modern humans, using their own techniques and choosing their own materials, but inspired by what they saw the modern humans wearing.

Very soon after this, all traces of Neanderthals are lost from Europe – except for within the Iberian peninsula. There are no signs of physical combat having taken place, let alone murder or the type of genocide that happened when Europeans came into contact with the aboriginal peoples of America and Australia. But what we know from the archaeological record is that modern humans had a way of life that was nearly identical to that of the Neanderthals. They also hunted large animals, employed stone as a raw material, required the use of caves for shelter. This is a classic case of niche overlap – and one species had to give way to the other. That it should be the Neanderthals is perhaps surprising. After all they had occupied Europe for many thousands of years and unlike the incoming modern humans had a physiology well suited to the harsh, cold conditions – the modern humans retained a stature and limb proportions much more suitable for equatorial regions, not Arctic-like landscapes. Yet modern humans must have had at least one major advantage, and that seems to have been their culture, which was in turn a consequence of a different type of mind or intelligence.

The most glaring difference between the Neanderthals and modern humans is that the latter made art – carving statuettes and painting cave walls. This may itself have given them an advantage because art can be used to help people to adapt to

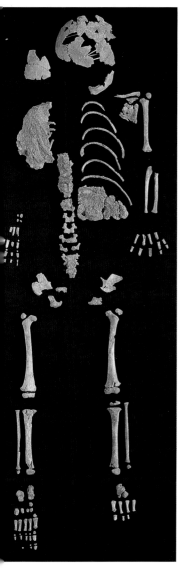

Left **The Lagar Velho child dates to 24,000 years ago – 4000 years after the last known Neanderthal – but is believed by some to show a mix of *Homo sapiens* and Neanderthal traits, the latter reflected in his short, stout limbs. As such, this might be evidence of inter-breeding between the two human species. Other anthropologists suspect that the Lagar Velho child is simply a particularly thick-set *Homo sapiens* boy.**
Right **Ever since the first Neanderthal fossils were found, artists and academics have attempted to reconstruct what they may have looked like. A great deal relies on imagination, such as for hairstyles and clothing. This image (from a TV documentary) is far too uncouth for some.**

Opposite below **The 'Gibraltar man' was one of the earliest Neanderthals found. We now know that he was one of the last Neanderthals, as southern Iberia was a refuge for the Neanderthals after modern humans had spread across the rest of Europe.**

harsh landscapes; it can, for instance be used as a store of information – the tribal encyclopedia – such as concerning animal behaviour, while at the ceremonies associated with the art many people would have gathered and swapped information in a manner that never happened in Neanderthal society. Much of the art, however, appears to have been made after the Neanderthals had disappeared from the European landscape. What it probably reflects is a much greater creativity and ingenuity in the minds of the modern humans – they were just that much better at finding game and gathering plants, they were able to invent tools to exploit a wider range of resources, and began to exploit the landscape at a level of intensity far beyond that which the

Neanderthals had ever achieved. And hence, as the population of the modern humans expanded, that of the Neanderthals dwindled as they had to find the nooks and crannies where modern humans had not yet reached.

Endgame

Iberia is hardly a nook and cranny of Europe, yet it appears to have remained the province of Neanderthals alone for the last few thousand years of their existence. Curiously, modern humans seem to have put a temporary halt on their otherwise relentless global journey and only entered Spain and Portugal at about 28,000 years ago. Some anthropologists claim that a skeleton found at Lagar Velho in Portugal dating to about 24,000 years ago shows that modern humans and Neanderthals had interbred, as this individual's limb proportions are very Neanderthal-like while its skull is very sapiens-like. Mounting evidence, however, suggests that this was not the case and the skeleton is simply that of a rather robust young boy, modern human through and through. Yet the possibility for some hybridization remains – there is a chance that some specifically Neanderthal genes survive within some of us today.

The very last Neanderthals are found at sites in the far south, most notably on Gibraltar. There they not only hunted animals but also gathered shellfish to eat. Those archaeological traces may be of a relict group, unable to expand their numbers due to the dominance of modern humans in the surrounding landscapes. And when the last member of the group died, so too did the species. Just one more to add to the millions that have suffered extinction in the history of the planet.

The Enigma of Palaeolithic Cave Art 20

Time: 40,000–10,000 years ago
Location: western Europe

Thou, silent form, dost tease us out of thought
As doth eternity.

JOHN KEATS, 1819

IN DECEMBER 1994, Jean-Marie Chauvet and two friends were exploring caves in the Ardèche region of France. They were hoping to find evidence for humankind's first art, but had so far enjoyed little success. They were well aware of the magnificent subterranean images of the Upper Palaeolithic period (40,000–10,000 years ago); they knew the art of Lascaux, Niaux and other famous sites. But nothing had prepared them for what they were to find deep in a hill above the Ardèche River.

Scrambling up a slope, they came across a small rockshelter. At the back was a pile of rubble. Carefully, they tested the jumbled stones for evidence of a draught. Yes, they believed that they could detect a movement of air. Excitedly, they removed the fallen debris and discovered a narrow tunnel that led down into the heart of the hill. Eventually, they descended into a vast, glistening, underground chamber. Then they spotted a red imprint of a human hand on the wall: someone had been here a very, very long time ago.

Farther on, they found sophisticated images of horses, lion, bison, rhinoceros, as well as the now-extinct woolly mammoth. Some of the images were painted; others were 'engraved' into the mud walls of the cave. Their lamps pierced the darkness,

revealing the skeletons of cave bears, fire-places and marks made by people who had tapped their flaming torches against the walls, rather as a smoker does with a cigarette on an ashtray. They felt themselves intruders into a lost, perhaps sacred, world.

Tantalizing questions

The discovery of the Chauvet Cave, as it is now known, was one of the greatest archaeological finds of the 20th century. But like so many archaeological discoveries, it raised as many questions as it answered.

How long ago had people, whose bare footprints were still visible in the mud, ventured into these dark chambers? Why did they go so far underground to make images? Was this mysterious kind of subterranean activity the origin of what we today call 'art'? How were these cave images related to those engraved on portable pieces of bone, antler and ivory, and to the small statuettes that had been excavated at Upper Palaeolithic sites? These questions had been asked before, but now they seemed to acquire a new urgency.

The age of the Chauvet images was comparatively easy to establish. Samples of carbon taken from the black paint were analysed by the radiocarbon dating technique. Astonishingly, researchers found that the oldest Chauvet images dated back 32,410 ± 720 years. Despite their sophistication, these are the oldest dated representational images. They were made very near to the first appearance in western Europe of fully modern people, the successors of the more primitive Neanderthals. So a new – and still unanswered – question had to be asked: did 'art' emerge fully formed and sophisticated, without a long period of development? Either way, why were they making images deep underground?

Left **This small human head, carved in mammoth ivory, is about the size of a thumb. It comes from an excavation at Brassempouy (Landes, France), undertaken early in the 20th century when archaeological techniques were not as rigorous as today; as a result, its exact provenance is unknown, and its authenticity is now debated.**

Left **At Pech-Merle (Lot, France), the natural rock formation on the right seems to have suggested a horse's head. Both horses are surrounded by negative handprints made by blowing paint on and around a human hand. A radiocarbon date on the right-hand horse indicates that it is around 24,600 years old.**

Right **The Lion Panel in the Chauvet Cave (Ardèche, France). The site was discovered in 1994. Images here have been dated to more than 30,000 years ago. Remarkably, the soft surface of the cave wall was scraped to prepare for the images, and some painted outlines were made to stand out by further scraping. This panel is in the depths of the cave.**

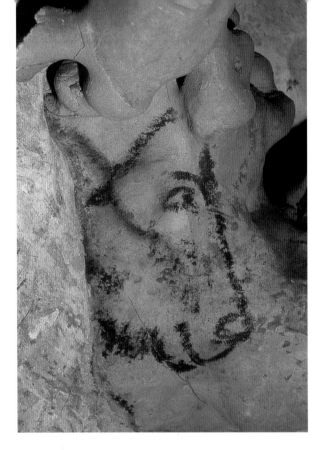

not cover the variety of the art, and it was based on rather tenuous analogies with people living in very different kinds of societies. Nor did it explain features that were still coming to light. For instance, it did not account for the fact that the image-makers so often used the shape of the rock wall to complete the outlines of pictures.

Then, in the 1960s, André Leroi-Gourhan, a former student of the Abbé Breuil, proposed an entirely new explanation. It was based on structuralism, the philosophical position that was developed by the anthropologist Claude Lévi-Strauss. Structuralism argues that all people think in binary oppositions because the human brain is so 'wired'. So our thinking is said to be underlain by oppositions such as culture:nature; hot:cold; light:dark; sacred:profane; raw:cooked; wild:tame; we:they; and male:female.

It was the last of these that Leroi-Gourhan emphasized. To put his views simply, he believed that, for the entire 20,000 years of the Upper Palaeolithic, the

The great 'Why?' question

A century ago, researchers suggested that the comparatively few Upper Palaeolithic images then known were 'simply' *art pour l'art*, art for the sake of art, and that image-making was a pastime that grew out of idle scratching on rock walls. But it was hard to imagine people crawling, squeezing and climbing their way underground just to make pictures of animals that they had seen in the countryside. Then, too, the notion that *art pour l'art* is 'simple' was rightly questioned: indeed, many art historians believe there is no such thing as *art pour l'art*. Art is always set in a social matrix and serves some purpose.

An explanation for the hazardous underground journeys was not long in coming. The French researcher Salomon Reinach argued that 'sympathetic magic' was the reason. People made images, he said, to gain control over the animals they hunted. That such an activity would be shrouded in mystery and would be performed far from human habitation seemed reasonable enough. Later, when images of lions were discovered, the leading French prehistorian of the time, the Abbé Henri Breuil, argued that people made them in order to acquire the power of the predator.

Gradually, researchers began to feel that this sympathetic magic explanation was too simple. It did

Above left **In Rouffignac (Dordogne, France), this horse's head is painted on a flint nodule that juts out from the cave wall. The rest of the animal's body appears to be hidden inside, or behind, the wall.**

Right **Part of the painted ceiling in Rouffignac. In the centre is a large mammoth, an animal that inhabited western Europe in the Ice Age. There are also images of the ibex, a mountain goat that has large, curved horns.**
Far right **The so-called 'sorcerer' that is engraved at the end of the passage cave known as Gabillou (Dordogne, France). The figure has horns and a tail, and appears to be dancing. A line from the mouth joins it to two rectangular grid forms that are similar to ones found in Lascaux.**

caves were organized sanctuaries constructed on the male:female principle. Some animals, such as the horse, stood for 'maleness'; others, such as the bison and the aurochs, stood for 'femaleness'. The 'female' species were, he said, concentrated in the central parts of the caves, while the 'male' species were scattered throughout. Images of lions, bears and other dangerous creatures were said to be located in the depths of the caves.

Researchers now argue that the evidence does not support Leroi-Gourhan's ingenious argument: the images are more randomly situated in the caves. He had not solved the mystery.

A spirit world

Today, there is much debate about another explanation that is also based on the 'wiring' of the human brain, but that does not invoke problematic binary oppositions. Instead, it starts with the observation that most hunting and gathering societies throughout the world have a belief system that, despite its

many variations, can be called shamanism. A shamanistic community believes in a tiered cosmos: the level on which people live, and spiritual realms above and below. The task of the shamans is to transcend these levels so that they can communicate with spirits, heal the sick, control the movements of animals and change the weather. To accomplish this transcendence they enter a state of altered consciousness. Such states range from mild dissociation to deep levels of hallucinations, as well as dreams. In an altered state, they sometimes commune with an animal-helper that gives them power and acts as a guide in the spirit realm.

According to the shamanistic explanation, the Upper Palaeolithic caves were probably seen as routes into the underworld. Physical entry into them may have been virtually indistinguishable from psychological entry into an altered state. In the nether realm, shamans, or would-be shamans, sought spirit animal-helpers and other visions. By sight and touch and in the flickering light of their

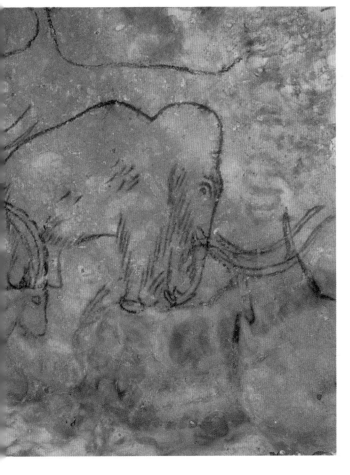

Above **The brilliantly embellished Axial Gallery in Lascaux (Dordogne, France). Horses, aurochs and various 'branched' and grid signs are painted over the ceiling and seem to envelope the viewer.**

lamps and torches, they explored the walls that were, for them, a 'membrane' between them and the awesome spirit realm. When they believed that they had found a spirit-animal, they coaxed it through the membrane and then, using their skills as image-makers, they 'fixed' on the rock what was in essence a vision. This intimate relationship between image and rock face explains why so many images appear to be coming out of, or are part of, the rock surface.

On the other hand, some images are so large and complex that they were probably made by groups rather than individuals. In the presence of these imposing panels, people may have prepared them-selves for the experiences that awaited them in the depths of the caves.

Shamanism is a dynamic belief system and ideol-ogy that people manipulate and change in varying social circumstances. Some of its essentials, such as a belief in entering the underworld, probably stayed

the same throughout the Upper Palaeolithic, but other components doubtless changed as the millen-nia went by.

Some of the great questions posed by the Chauvet Cave and other subterranean 'galleries' are answered by the shamanistic explanation. Others remain. How, for instance, did the meaning of a bison image differ from that of a horse? When a horse was depicted on a piece of portable bone, did it mean something different from a horse in the underworld? We simply do not know. The silent images, like those on Keats's Grecian urn, 'tease us out of thought As doth eternity'. Yet, in Chauvet and other embellished caves, we can reach out and – almost – touch the lost world of the first 'real people'.

Who Were the First Australians?

21

Time: 40,000, 60,000 years ago?
Location: Australia

> *Long time ago …*
> *Before Captain Cook,*
> *We see Macassans*
> *They come with Bärra [northwest wind]*
> *They leave with Bulunu [southeast wind]*

JAMES BARRIPANG, 1994

ACCORDING TO SOME traditional beliefs of Australia's indigenous people, their ancestors were created in the Dreaming (pp. 79–81), the period when both landscape and humans were formed. For them, there is therefore no mystery to their origins. They have always been where they are. Nor is the timing of their origins important. The Dreaming integrates past, present and future in a way that makes chronology a concept of little significance.

For scientists, though, the origins and timing of the arrival of the first Australians have been burning questions for over 200 years. Who were the first Australians? Where did they come from? How did they get here? When did they arrive? What is their place in the global story of human evolution? These questions remain unresolved as each new model is in turn challenged by new theories, evidence and dating techniques.

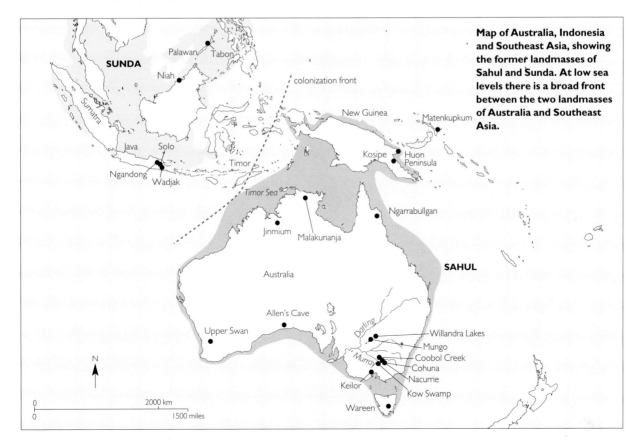

Map of Australia, Indonesia and Southeast Asia, showing the former landmasses of Sahul and Sunda. At low sea levels there is a broad front between the two landmasses of Australia and Southeast Asia.

Where did the first Australians come from?

Australia was colonized from the north, from the Southeast Asian landmass, across what are now Indonesia and Malaysia. Fossils of *Homo erectus* found in Java in the 19th century by Eugene Dubois were proposed as possible ancestors of the first Australians. Research has established that *Homo erectus* was in Java 1.74 million years ago. Skeletons in Southeast Asia less than 100,000 years old are rare. Wadjak from Java, Niah from Sarawak and Tabon from Palawan are all about 10,000 years old.

Aboriginal history is not a history of isolation. James Barripang points to a painting of an Indonesian *prau* (boat).

As sea levels have changed over the millennia in response to global glaciation, Australia was at times joined with Tasmania and New Guinea in a unit known as Sahul. Even at the lowest sea levels, however, Sahul was separated from Southeast Asia. The only way to get to Australia was therefore by boat or canoe, and it is not hard to imagine anatomically modern humans, just like us in thought and ability, constructing bamboo rafts powered by sails woven from leaves. The currents and winds of the region almost guarantee landfall at the end of a trip, and the evidence of land just over the horizon is to be seen in the flight paths of migratory birds and in the columns of smoke from dry-season fires.

The early settlement of Australia is likely to have been undertaken by organized expeditions of whole groups, perhaps maritime fishing villages who eventually made permanent bases on the southern shores of the Timor Sea. Given the length of shoreline available, dozens of groups could have made their homes at roughly the same time without intruding on established property. If so, the first Australians might have numbered in the thousands. And the final sea-level rise around 10,000 years ago probably did not result in the total isolation of the early settlers, even though at European contact indigenous Australians were not seafarers. Fishing voyages of Macassans in the last few hundred years are well documented and the arrival of the dingo, a domestic dog, about 4000 years ago, is another instance of continuous traffic.

When did people first arrive in Australia?

Until the middle of the 20th century, archaeologists assumed that the first migration into Australia took place during the last glaciation, now dated between 25,000 and 13,000 years ago, when sea levels were last low. By the early 1970s, however, it was clear that the first Australians had arrived well before this. Investigation of the peopling of Australia has proceeded hand in hand with the development of ever more innovative dating methods. From radiocarbon dates of 9000 years ago in 1961 to 38,000 in 1981, the pace of discovery has pushed back the earliest evidence of occupation. Dates from localities including Malakunanja, Jinmium and Mungo have now led a number of archaeologists to argue for colonization at 60,000 years, or even earlier.

There is, however, also considerable debate about the dating methods and the interpretation of the results. While some argue that there is no convincing evidence of occupation before 40,000–45,000

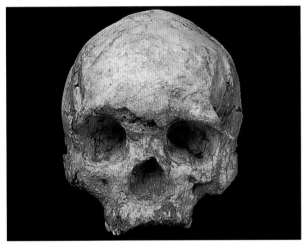

Left above **Homo erectus of Southeast Asia shows detailed similiarities to early Australians.** *Left below* **The skeleton from Wadjak comes from the boundary of the two great landmasses and near the origins of agriculture in the region. This individual is a link between Aboriginal people to the south and Asian people to the north.**

Right **Mungo 3, a man buried on the edge of Lake Mungo in southeastern Australia perhaps as much as 60,000 years ago, has been shown to carry a version of mitochondrial DNA (inherited through the female line) within the Australian family and distinct from African lineages.**

years ago, others claim that 60,000 years is a conservative estimate. Debates can become heated, as excavation strategies, sampling methods and dating techniques are queried. A further problem is that given the sea-level rise of the last 10,000 years, much of the evidence for great antiquity is buried under 100 m (300 ft) of water along the coast.

At any rate, we do know that people had spread throughout the continent by 40,000 years ago. There are now dates greater than 35,000 from Warreen in Tasmania, Allen's Cave on the Nullarbor plain, Upper Swan in southwestern Western Australia, Willandra Lakes near the Murray and Darling rivers, Ngarrabullgan in Cape York, the Huon peninsula in New Guinea and Matenkupkum in New Ireland. Aboriginal people had made the desert core their home by at least 22,000 years ago.

These first Australians would have encountered changing climates and different environments. During periods of low sea levels, when Tasmania and New Guinea were attached to Australia, small glacial caps topped the southern dividing range and the higher peaks of Tasmania. Spring melt waters fuelled rivers nine times the volume of present-day ones. These ancestral rivers, including Willandra Creek, flowed through a much drier, colder and windier land. During such times the man known as Mungo 3 was buried. Like many since, he was buried facing the water of Lake Mungo, with his feet to the east. He has recently been dated at about 60,000 years and while his exact date of burial is being debated, he is still the oldest known Australian.

Who were the first Australians?

Modern indigenous Australians vary physically from region to region, as do Europeans or any other continental group. There are two main explanations for this variation. Migration models assume multiple origins and different ancestral groups, while evolutionary models account for biological variation by examining processes of selection for different environments as well as marriage patterns across

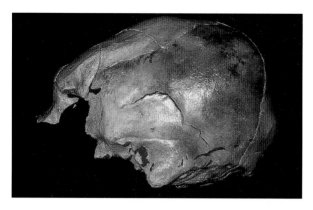

A skull from Nacurrie: with their high, sweeping foreheads and heavy build, the people of the Kow Swamp-Coobol region of the Murray River were the most robust Australians.

social and geographic boundaries. So did the observed range of biological variation develop as people adapted to the ecological variety of a new country, or was it created by the arrival and subsequent inter-marriage of different colonizing groups?

For much of the 20th century, migration models were used to explain the range of physical difference. In 1941, before radiocarbon dating was invented, Joseph Birdsell argued that three waves of migration by different colonizing groups accounted for the observed differences. By the early 1970s, Alan Thorne had proposed a dual migration model. His discoveries at Kow Swamp provided the evidence for heavily built, robust people living along the Murray River in southeastern Australia. The remains from Lake Mungo, which were much older than Kow Swamp, were more lightly built. Thorne explained this variation by relating them to ancient fossils from the north. The larger and more robust group traced their ancestry to *Homo erectus* in Java, while the more gracile were from further afield in China.

As dates for initial occupation have moved back, evolutionary explanations for the range of physical variation among indigenous populations have gained ground. People living in a desert environment over tens of thousands of years tend to develop a slender, slighter appearance, with relatively longer limbs. The people of the Willandra Lakes were desert dwellers during glacial times. Equally, adaptation can explain to a significant degree the sturdy build of those living in resource-rich areas such as the Murray River.

About 90 skeletons that are thought to be older than 10,000 years have been discovered in Australia. Most are fragmentary. They come mainly from Willandra Lakes, Coobol Creek and Kow Swamp. The latter two are separated by about 50 km (31 miles) across the Murray River and both lie within what was historically Baraparapa tribal territory.

Investigation has shown that, on average, most of these individuals from more than 10,000 years ago were larger and more heavily built. The best known – Cohuna, Nacurrie, Kow Swamp and Coobol Creek – are from a restricted area of the Murray River. They exhibit the largest teeth of any human group, a sweeping forehead and well-developed brow ridges. Others, such as Keilor and many of the Willandra Lakes skeletons, are less ruggedly built and are physically closer to modern Aboriginal people.

Who were the ancestors of the first Australians?

Recent research into the origins of anatomically modern humans and their spread throughout the world has polarized into two models: Regional Continuity and Out-of-Africa. In the first, *Homo erectus* spread through Eurasia from Africa and reached Java by 1.74 million years ago. Evolution from *Homo erectus* occurred across the Old World with all populations linked by inter-marriage. Modern *Homo sapiens* appears about 130,000 years ago. Under this model, the fossils of *Homo erectus* found at Solo and Ngandong are the ancestors of Aboriginal Australians. Many researchers have noted similarities between Australians of about 10,000 years ago and the Javan fossils that point to an unbroken lineage.

Under the Out-of-Africa model modern humans developed in Africa 130,000 years ago and in a geological instant moved across Asia, perhaps sailing the coasts of India and Southeast Asia, to settle Australia by 60,000 years. Along the way they killed all resident populations of *Homo erectus* and made the step to Australia that eluded the people that had lived so close for more than one and a half million years. This is the blitzkrieg model of evolution.

So according to the Out-of-Africa model, the fossils of *Homo erectus* from Java – Solo and Ngandong – are pruned from the Australian family tree and the first Australians are descended from ancestors who appeared in Africa 130,000 years ago. The Regional Continuity model still identifies *Homo erectus* as the ancestor of the first Australians. Perhaps the most surprising question then, is why *Homo erectus* did not make the last short crossing to Australia? Or did they? The Regional Continuity model leaves open the possibility that we will eventually see evidence of humans in Australia at more than 100,000 years ago. Although unlikely, it is not impossible.

The First Americans & Kennewick Man

Time: before 15,000 to 9,300 years ago
Location: North and South America

I believe the picture that emerges will show us one of the most intricate, thrilling, and inspiring episodes of the human adventure on earth.

TOM DILLEHAY, 2000

IN 1493, CHRISTOPHER COLUMBUS, Admiral of the Ocean Sea, paraded a small group of native Americans before the Spanish court. The intellectual debate began almost at once. Who were these strange people? How had they reached their homeland? Had they travelled by land or by sea from Asia? Or had some 'unknown pilot' crossed the Atlantic from the Mediterranean long before Columbus? Were the Indians survivors of either the lost continent of Atlantis or the Ten Lost Tribes of Israel? For over five centuries, mythmakers and scientists alike have speculated over the first Americans in one of the most enduring of all controversies about the human past.

As early as 1590, Jesuit missionary José de Acosta speculated that the first Americans had arrived in the Americas from Asia, with 'only short stretches of navigation', this was almost two centuries before the discovery of the Bering Strait in 1743. Except for a few, wild claims for Ice Age voyages across the Atlantic or long canoe journeys from Australia to South America, few scientists now challenge the Asian antecedents of native Americans: the main scholarly debates revolve instead around the manner of first settlement and the critical issue of exactly when initial colonization took place.

Folsom, Clovis and pre-Clovis

Until the 1920s, most experts assumed that the first Americans had arrived within the past 4000 years or so. Then the discovery of stone projectile points in direct association with the bones of extinct bison at Folsom, New Mexico, demonstrated once and for all that humans had lived in the New World for at least 10,000 years. The development of radiocarbon dating by Willard Libby in 1949 helped put the chronology of both Folsom and even earlier Clovis Paleo-Indian cultures on a firmer footing. Today, dozens of radiocarbon dates place the Clovis occupation of North America to between 13,500 and 13,350 years ago, which means that Stone Age peoples had settled in the New World within a few centuries of the end of the Ice Age, if not earlier. The question of questions is just how much earlier.

Everyone agrees that only modern humans, *Homo sapiens sapiens*, settled in the Americas. More than a century of diligent search has revealed no traces of archaic humans such as Neanderthals. Beyond this fact, there is little agreement. Scientists belong to

Excavations at Meadowcroft Rockshelter in Pennsylvania, a cave occupied from as early as perhaps 15,000 years ago.

Left **A Folsom point found with ribs of extinct subspecies of bison at Folsom, New Mexico. Finds of such direct associations between humanly made artifacts and bones of extinct animals in the 1920s proved that humans had settled in North America within a few centuries of the end of the Ice Age if not earlier.**

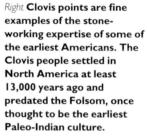

Right **Clovis points are fine examples of the stone-working expertise of some of the earliest Americans. The Clovis people settled in North America at least 13,000 years ago and predated the Folsom, once thought to be the earliest Paleo-Indian culture.**

two broad schools of thought. A minority faction believes that humans crossed from Asia into Alaska as early as 40,000 years ago, pointing to some highly controversial excavations in northeastern Brazil as evidence for such early settlement. Except for this questionable site – Boqueirão da Pedra Furada – there is no archaeological evidence for 40,000-year settlement. Most scholars favour a much later date, somewhat earlier than 13,500 years ago, with settlement taking place during the late Ice Age, when sea levels were up to 90 m (300 ft) lower than today and a land bridge linked Siberia and Alaska – the sunken continent of Beringia.

Few archaeological sites document pre-Clovis settlement in the Americas. The best known is Monte Verde far to the south in Chile, where some wooden huts and simple stone artifacts date to between 14,000 and 13,600 years ago, a little earlier than Clovis. A scatter of less well-known sites, including Cactus Hill in southeastern Virginia, may take the chronology back slightly further, but there the well-documented record stops. There is no reason why first settlement could not have taken place considerably earlier, but the numbers of people involved were small and the archaeological 'signature' they left behind them so inconspicuous that it is difficult now to find them.

Which route?

The routes by which humans entered the New World are also controversial. Until recently, everyone agreed that the first settlers crossed into Alaska dry-shod, across the windy and bitterly cold steppe-tundra of the Bering Land Bridge. From Alaska, they passed through a narrow, ice-free corridor between

Right **Foundations of wooden structures found at Monte Verde, southern Chile. This waterlogged site preserved the remains of small huts built alongside one another, as well as wood and stone artifacts, some of the earliest in the Americas.**

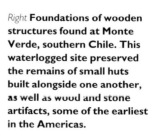

the two great ice sheets that covered Canada and the northern United States during, and immediately after, the late Ice Age, before settling in the heart of North America. Most Paleo-Indian sites were found in the North American Plains, so the first settlers were assumed to be big-game hunters, with a fondness for bison and mammoth or mastodon.

In recent years, this scenario has been challenged as a result of new excavations that reveal the Paleo-Indians as highly diverse hunter-gatherers, who exploited a very wide range of foods. At the same time, new geological researches have shown that the ice-free corridor from Alaska to the Plains was not vegetated and could not support animal or human life, so it would have been impossible for the first settlers to move south, unless they took a coastal route. Under this scenario, the first settlers would have coasted their way from Siberia along Beringian shores, then south and east along the continental shelf of Alaska. Unfortunately, the archaeological sites that would document such a route lie many metres under water, but there is no reason, at least in theory, why late Ice Age people equipped with skin boats could not have subsisted off fish and sea mammals and made their way southward at a time when sea levels were lower than today. The controversy over routes remains unresolved.

Enter Kennewick Man

The first Americans are one of those mysteries that generate remarkable passion among scientists and lay people alike. Nowhere did this passion become more apparent than in Benton County, Washington, with the discovery of Kennewick Man in 1996. A human skull and limb bones were washed out of a river bank, apparently belonging to a male Caucasoid with worn teeth, aged 40–45 years old at death and about 1.73 m (5 ft 8 in) tall. At first, archaeologist James Chatters assumed he was dealing with a modern European, until closer inspection revealed some form of projectile in a healed wound in his right hip. The bones were then radiocarbon-dated to between 9330 and 9380 years ago, making them some of the earliest human remains found in the Americas, while a CT (computerized tomography) scan identified the mysterious projectile as a leaf-shaped Cascade-type stone point.

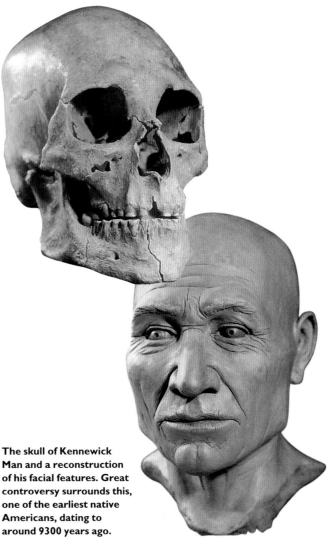

The skull of Kennewick Man and a reconstruction of his facial features. Great controversy surrounds this, one of the earliest native Americans, dating to around 9300 years ago.

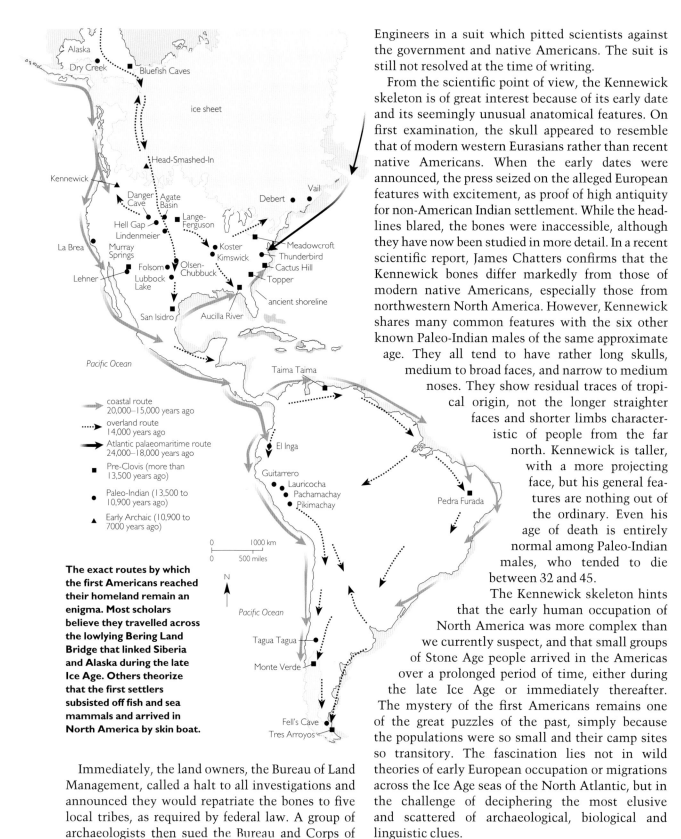

coastal route
20,000–15,000 years ago

overland route
14,000 years ago

Atlantic palaeomaritime route
24,000–18,000 years ago

■ Pre-Clovis (more than
13,500 years ago)

● Paleo-Indian (13,500 to
10,900 years ago)

▲ Early Archaic (10,900 to
7000 years ago)

0   1000 km
0   500 miles

N

**The exact routes by which
the first Americans reached
their homeland remain an
enigma. Most scholars
believe they travelled across
the lowlying Bering Land
Bridge that linked Siberia
and Alaska during the late
Ice Age. Others theorize
that the first settlers
subsisted off fish and sea
mammals and arrived in
North America by skin boat.**

Engineers in a suit which pitted scientists against the government and native Americans. The suit is still not resolved at the time of writing.

From the scientific point of view, the Kennewick skeleton is of great interest because of its early date and its seemingly unusual anatomical features. On first examination, the skull appeared to resemble that of modern western Eurasians rather than recent native Americans. When the early dates were announced, the press seized on the alleged European features with excitement, as proof of high antiquity for non-American Indian settlement. While the headlines blared, the bones were inaccessible, although they have now been studied in more detail. In a recent scientific report, James Chatters confirms that the Kennewick bones differ markedly from those of modern native Americans, especially those from northwestern North America. However, Kennewick shares many common features with the six other known Paleo-Indian males of the same approximate age. They all tend to have rather long skulls, medium to broad faces, and narrow to medium noses. They show residual traces of tropical origin, not the longer straighter faces and shorter limbs characteristic of people from the far north. Kennewick is taller, with a more projecting face, but his general features are nothing out of the ordinary. Even his age of death is entirely normal among Paleo-Indian males, who tended to die between 32 and 45.

The Kennewick skeleton hints that the early human occupation of North America was more complex than we currently suspect, and that small groups of Stone Age people arrived in the Americas over a prolonged period of time, either during the late Ice Age or immediately thereafter. The mystery of the first Americans remains one of the great puzzles of the past, simply because the populations were so small and their camp sites so transitory. The fascination lies not in wild theories of early European occupation or migrations across the Ice Age seas of the North Atlantic, but in the challenge of deciphering the most elusive and scattered of archaeological, biological and linguistic clues.

Immediately, the land owners, the Bureau of Land Management, called a halt to all investigations and announced they would repatriate the bones to five local tribes, as required by federal law. A group of archaeologists then sued the Bureau and Corps of

What Wiped Out the Big Game Animals?

Time: End of the Ice Age
Location: Americas, Eurasia, Australia

... the hunters swept down the Americas like a bloody wave that washed away much of the land's bounty.

PAUL MARTIN, 1999

W E LIVE IN AN appallingly impoverished world compared to that of our ancestors living as little as 13,000 years ago, at the end of the the last Ice Age. Whether those hunter-gatherer peoples lived in Africa, Europe, Asia or the Americas, they were able to watch megafauna – a range of wild animals of great size. Today it is virtually only in Africa that such animals survive: the elephant, giraffe, rhino and hippopotamus.

The Ice Age hunter-gatherers would have seen, and perhaps hunted, mammoths throughout Europe, northern Asia and North America. Giant deer, woolly rhinos and cave bears were also part of the European fauna, while the Americas supported a

Below **Palaeolithic paintings and engravings of woolly mammoths dominate the animal imagery from Pech-Merle cave, south-central France.**

remarkable array of creatures that had taken natural selection millions of years to produce and which disappeared effectively overnight in the timescale of evolution. In North America, for instance, there were not only two types of mammoth, but also an array of giant ground sloths – slow lumbering, plant-eating creatures that reached up to 6 m (20 ft) in length and 3 tonnes in weight. These shared the landscape with creatures such as castorides (a giant beaver the size of a bear), glyptodon (a giant armour-plated armadillo), camelops (appropriately known as 'yesterday's camel') and an assortment of carnivores which included smilodon, a sabre-toothed cat with 20-cm (8-in) serrated canines. A similar story is found in Australia where there was once a remarkable variety of giant kangaroos and wombats, together with marsupials that resembled rhinos, and giant cats.

The sudden disappearance of these large animals from all continents at the end of the last Ice Age is one of the great mysteries faced by those who study the past. Only Africa remained largely unscathed by this wave of extinctions, and why this should have been so compounds the problem yet further. There are two principal theories – that the animals were wiped out either by the dramatic changes in climate that accompanied the end of the Ice Age, or by the one lethal predator that was found in each continent, *Homo sapiens*.

The demise of the mammoth

Much of the debate has centred around just one of the extinct animals: the mammoth. Actually two species of mammoth became extinct: the woolly mammoth (*Mammuthus primigenius*) that had lived throughout northern Eurasia and North America; and the Columbian mammoth (*M. columbi*) that had been exclusive to North America, living as far south as Mexico. As with other types of megafauna the mammoths went extinct between 13,000 and 11,500 years ago – except for a relict population of woolly mammoths that survived on Wrangel Island in the Arctic Ocean for another 6000 years. Quite why these survived adds to the mystery of mammoth extinction; though to do this they became dwarfs, no more than 1.8 m (6 ft) high, compared with the normal 3–3.6 m (10–12 ft) of a full-size mammoth.

The climate hypothesis

The mammoths on Wrangel Island may have survived because the vegetation of that island

Columbian mammoths feeding on the Colorado Plateau, southwestern United States, about 15,000 years ago.

remained much the same as it had been during the Ice Age – a particularly diverse mix of grasses and herbs which provided perfect forage for mammoths. This type of vegetation, which has been termed the 'mammoth steppe', was once pervasive across northern Eurasia and North America but was replaced with new types of vegetation as the climate grew so much warmer and wetter after 20,000 years ago. In the most northern areas the steppe was replaced by a boggy tundra, one that is slow growing and poor in nutrients. This was only suitable for highly specialized feeders, such as the lichen-eating reindeer. Further south, the rich mix of grasses, herbs and shrubs that the mammoths had depended on was lost to thick forest, prairies and semi-desert. These changes in vegetation patterns, ultimately caused by the increased warmth and wetness, resulted in severe habitat loss for the mammoths, whose numbers dwindled and then disappeared completely.

This climate/vegetation change hypothesis for mammoth extinction initially sounds very compelling, but has run into some difficulties. The most significant is the fact that mammoths had survived many previous periods of climate change, very similar to that which occurred between 20,000 and 11,600 years ago. The last Ice Age was just one of many that had occurred during the last million years. These had been interspersed with periods of warm and wet climate very similar to the climate today, when forests, grasslands and tundra became prevalent. Yet mammoths had survived all of these, presumably by retreating into refuges where some semblance of mammoth steppe survived, to then spread out again once climate and vegetation conditions returned to their liking. There seems no reason why they could not have done this at the end of the last Ice Age. Another problem with the climatic theory of extinction is that the mammoths were not the only animals to go extinct – many of the others lived in quite different habitats and may even have seen their preferred foodstuffs expand with the increasing warmth and wetness.

Human overkill

These problems have led some scientists to favour the idea that mammoths and the other megafauna were hunted to extinction. This theory was championed by Paul Martin of Arizona University more than 30 years ago, and it remains a compelling idea. He was most concerned with North America and stressed the coincidence between the arrival of humans in that continent and the extinction of the megafauna. His idea was that as the new arrivals swept southwards across the continent, having originally arrived in Alaska after crossing through the now-flooded landscape of Beringia (around the Bering Strait), they wiped out the megafauna.

These people are known as the Clovis culture – after the site of that name where they were first identified – and are distinguished by their large

Above **The carcass of a 40,000-year-old baby mammoth – nicknamed Dima – was found in 1977 in Siberia.**

An excavation at Dent, Colorado, in 1932 produced the first clear evidence for the association of projectile points with mammoth remains in North America.

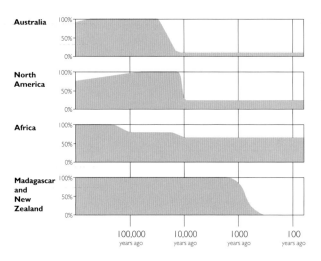

Percentage of surviving large animal species.

stone spear points, part of a lethal hunting technology. This culture is found throughout the North American continent and flourished between 13,500 and 13,350 years ago. 'Yesterday's camel', the ground sloths and the mammoths had never been faced with such a predator – one that combined deadly weapons with the abilities to hunt in large co-operative groups and to set traps and ambushes. The situation in North America would have been quite unlike that in Africa where the large mammals had effectively co-evolved with humans as predators, and may have developed patterns of social behaviour that formed a protection against human hunting. This would explain why there were few extinctions within that continent.

There is direct evidence that mammoths were hunted by the Clovis people. At several archaeological sites the bones of mammoths are found together with spear points, an association first discovered at the excavations at Dent, Colorado, in 1932. At Lehner Ranch in the San Pedro Valley of Arizona, for instance, the remains of 13 mammoths were found with spear points and fire-places. This seems to have been a family herd, slaughtered in its entirety as it gathered at a watercourse.

The overkill theory, however, also runs into serious problems. Although we have some mammoth kill sites, there is no direct evidence that the other megafauna were being hunted, with a few rare exceptions such as mastodon (a relative of the elephant and mammoth) bones at Kimmswick, Missouri. The ground sloths, for instance, appear to have once been abundant on the evidence of their dung found in caves, and are likely to have been easy prey. As we learn more about the Clovis people, it seems in fact that they were more concerned with hunting smaller animals and gathering plants.

It is also now becoming clear that the Clovis people were not the first to live in the Americas. Evidence dating from around 14,000 years ago at a settlement at Monte Verde in southern Chile shows that people had been in North and South America for a few thousand years before the extinctions occurred. Likewise in Australia, where a similar argument can be made about the arrival of humans as a new predator, hardly any bones of the extinct fauna have been found associated with human activity.

Climate change or human hunting? Scientists remain divided as to which of these was the cause of megafaunal extinction. Some even suggest a quite different explanation – a lethal plague carried around

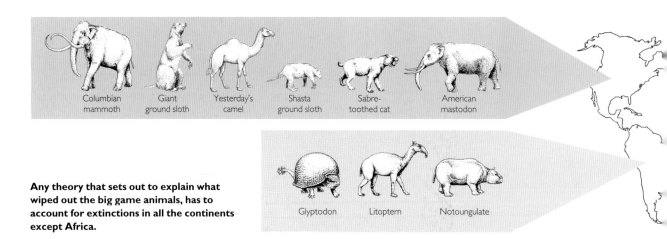

Any theory that sets out to explain what wiped out the big game animals, has to account for extinctions in all the continents except Africa.

112

the world by humans but which attacked the megafauna. It may be that there is no single explanation: some species were killed by hunting, some lost their habitats and could not cope with the new climate. We must remember that in any one region all species were members of dynamic ecological communities. Once one species was lost, the balance between predators and prey would change and may have led to a cascade of population explosions and crashes. Indeed mammoths have been described as keystone species. But as neither climate change nor overkill appears sufficient in themselves, it seems most likely that it was the combination of these that had such a devastating impact on the animal communities.

When the Ice Age came to its end mammoths would certainly have suffered, especially during the droughts that occurred in the American southwest during the Clovis period and immediately afterwards in the very cold and dry phase of the Younger Dryas (12,600–11,500 years ago) that came immediately before the global warming. During those periods, relatively weak animals may have congregated at waterholes, much like African elephants during drought conditions today – and provided easy pickings for the Clovis hunters. Even the killing of a few animals may have made all the difference between a species whose numbers would bounce back once more conducive climatic conditions returned, and one that had become condemned to extinction.

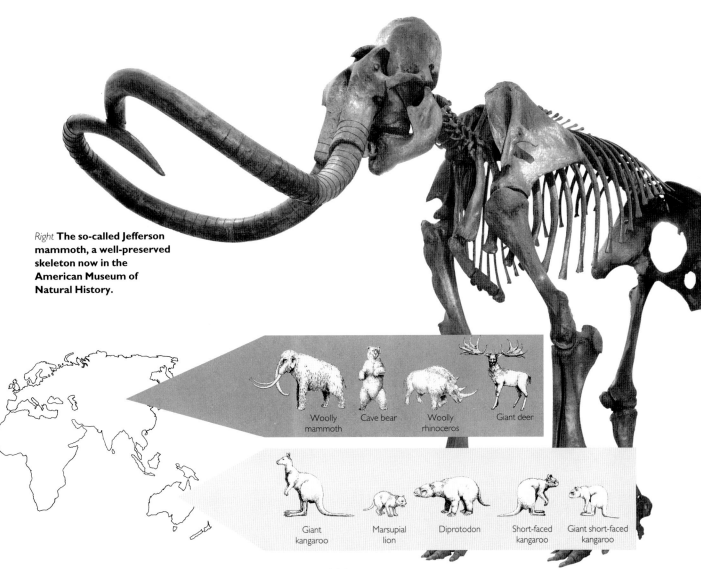

Right **The so-called Jefferson mammoth, a well-preserved skeleton now in the American Museum of Natural History.**

Woolly mammoth Cave bear Woolly rhinoceros Giant deer

Giant kangaroo Marsupial lion Diprotodon Short-faced kangaroo Giant short-faced kangaroo

How Did Farming Begin?

24

Time: after 12,000–4500 years ago
Location: Near East, Mexico, China, Andes,
Eastern United States, Sub-Saharan Africa

It was a Neolithic Revolution.

V. GORDON CHILDE, 1936

FOR THE VAST MAJORITY of the human past people have lived by hunting and gathering for their food. We evolved as a species long before our ancestors began to live in settled communities with domesticated plants and animals – farming is a novel event and archaeologists are still far from understanding why such a radical change in human lifestyles took place. It occurred for the first time a little under 12,000 years ago in the fertile crescent of the Near East. Farming was also independently invented in six other regions of the world soon after that date: in central Mexico at around 9000 years ago; a little later in both southern and northern China; then in the central Andes at around 7000 years ago; and finally in the eastern United States and Sub-Saharan Africa at about 4500 years ago.

A common factor in all these separate developments is that farming began after the end of the last

goats in the Near East, maize in Mexico, rice in China, and millet, sorghum and cattle in Sub-Saharan Africa. In addition, each area appears to have had its own unique set of specific events and causes that led people to give up the ancestral hunting-and-gathering lifestyle.

The Near East: a case study

The study of the origins of farming in the Near East has a very long history, with pioneering work undertaken by Robert Braidwood during the 1940s in the

Ice Age and was probably closely related to the environmental changes associated with global warming and a marked increase in human population. But the type of farming invented in each region was quite different, being largely determined by the indigenous plants and animals – barley, wheat, sheep and

Left **At the base of the settlement mound at Jericho are the remains of an early farming village in which people lived in small circular dwellings, but also built this large tower.** *Above* **Neolithic plaster head from Jericho.**

Right & below **The hunter-gatherer settlement at Abu Hureyra, Syria, was found below the mud-brick houses of the farming town, drawn below; this had a mixed farming economy, with grains and animals.**

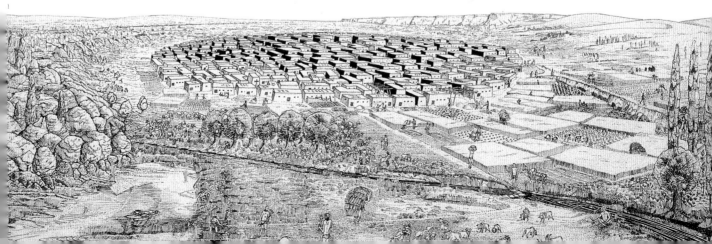

Chemchemal Valley of northeastern Iraq, followed in the 1950s by Kathleen Kenyon's excavations at Jericho in the Jordan Valley. This early work focused on the first Neolithic farming communities in the Near East, which still lacked pottery. More recently, archaeologists such as Ofer Bar-Yosef have shown that we need to look further back if we are to understand fully why farming began, while the archaeobotanist Gordon Hillman has provided great insights by studying the still-existing wild flora of the Near East and making microscopic studies of plant remains from excavations.

It is now evident that we must also pay attention to the many fluctuations in climate during the last millennia of the Ice Age, rather than just the dramatic global warming at 11,600 years ago. At about 14,500 years ago the coastal lands and river valleys of the Near East were covered with thick mixed oak woodland, while elsewhere there was a lush steppe with a vast array of edible plant foods. These included the wild ancestors of domesticated wheat and barley, the seeds of which were apparently gathered in large quantities by hunter-gatherers of the Natufian culture who began to live in permanent settlements, such as at Ain Mallaha in Israel and Abu Hureyra in Syria. This was an unprecedented step for our ancestors to take, one partly facilitated by the abundant herds of gazelle available for hunting.

For about 2000 years these communities flourished, developing many of the cultural attributes normally associated with farmers – stone architecture, rich burials, art and an elaborate plant-grinding technology. And then at about 12,600 years ago the climate took a marked turn for the worse. Instead of warm temperatures and plentiful rainfall, the hunter-gatherers were suddenly faced with ice age conditions for another 1000 years, with associated drought and a significant decline in the availability of both plants to gather and animals to hunt. This short climatic period of the Younger Dryas appears to have occurred just as the hunter-gatherer populations had reached unprecedented levels, and hence caused maximum distress.

A permanently settled way of life could no longer be sustained and once again highly mobile lifestyles were adopted, with people never staying more than a few months in any one place. Yet some links with the previous way of life were retained. Abandoned villages were maintained as cemeteries – groups appear to have periodically gathered at these ancient sites to bury their dead communally, in some cases bringing bags of bones, or just skulls, exhumed from temporary burials made on their searches for food. It is possible therefore that the period of sedentary lifestyles between 14,500 and 12,500 years ago had engrained cultural attitudes that remained with the people during the Younger

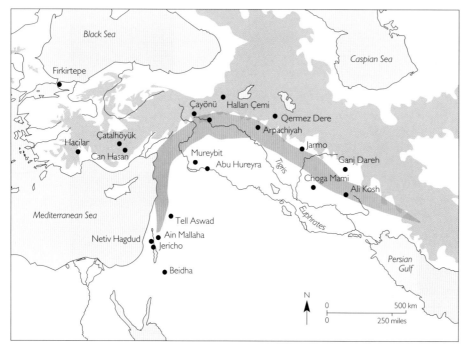

The fertile crescent. This arc of major river valleys was the scene for the first farming settlements and the first civilizations. One of its critical features was the presence of the wild ancestors of the domesticated species which had been exploited by hunter-gatherers for many thousands of years.

Dryas, and which were essential to the later development of farming villages.

In order to acquire sufficient food during the drought conditions of the Younger Dryas it seems likely that people began to manage plants by weeding, replanting and watering. Indeed they had probably begun such practices many years previously, when they had lived in sedentary villages, as these activities are well documented among many recent hunter-gatherer groups. Cultivation of wild plants provided increased yields and allowed people to plan their movements; unknown to them it was also an essential step towards the evolution of domesticated plants.

The key feature of domesticated cereals is that the grain remains on the stem as it ripens, rather than being automatically scattered for self-seeding. This means the farmer can retrieve the grain for use, and retain sufficient for re-planting. Similarly, domesticated peas remain within their pods – they 'wait for the harvester', in the phrase of Daniel Zohary the renowned specialist in plant domestication. Within the wild stands of wheat and barley there would have been a few mutant plants that retained their seed in this fashion; as the plant gatherers and cultivators of the Younger Dryas cut the cereals, and collected seed grain to save and to plant elsewhere, these few mutant plants gained a disproportionate presence within the cultivated stands.

It seems likely that these pre-farming plant cultivators soon discovered that the wild cereals grew particularly well on the alluvial soils of the Jordan Valley, especially in the vicinity of natural springs. And when the marked increase in rainfall and warmth arrived with the sudden global warming of 11,600 years ago, it was in this valley that people were able to return to a sedentary lifestyle. They also began to build mud-brick houses, most notably at Jericho, where a large stone tower and wall were constructed – the latter probably as a defence against flooding and mud flows rather than for warfare. A few kilometres to the north, the village of Netiv Hagdud was established, where there are traces of barley cultivation – although this may still have been of essentially wild plants. Both here and at Jericho there is a continuation and elaboration of the burial rituals of the mobile hunter-gatherers of the Younger Dryas – especially the practice of removal and re-burial of human skulls. Many of their tools also remain the same, suggesting that hunting and wild plant gathering continued. Similar develop-

A grinding stone at Abu Hureyra. The start of farming brought a good deal of hard work.

ments occurred throughout the fertile crescent. Some of the most elaborate early Neolithic villages were built in southern Turkey and northeast Iraq, where clay figurines suggest the emergence of a new ideology. The French archaeologist Jacques Cauvin believes that this was associated with new attitudes to the land, essential for the full development of farming.

Once these villages were established there was no turning back on the path to farming. We know that the villages were linked to each other by trade networks for materials such as obsidian (volcanic glass) and sea shells; it seems likely that seed grain of fully domesticated plants also travelled along those networks. And so these villages soon had fields of cereals, as well as peas and lentils, to support populations that began to grow at a rapid rate. Within 1000 years the first goats had been domesticated, followed by cattle. The villages turned into towns with large two-storey stone-built houses, streets, courtyards and storerooms. This was the culmination of the start of farming, a development which had its roots with the first sedentary hunter-gatherers of 14,500 years ago, was then ushered in by the climatic shock of the Younger Dryas and which set the scene for the emergence of the first civilizations.

The Mysteries of Rock Art

Time: late Ice Age onwards
Location: worldwide

Sculpture and drawing almost simultaneously make their appearance, and the best examples attain to so high a pitch of excellence that enthusiastic discoverers have spoken of them as superior in some respects to the work of the Greeks.

W.J. SOLLAS, 1911

MOST OF OUR ARCHAEOLOGICAL material consists not of shining gold but of detritus, things that were lost or abandoned when worn out, broken or useless. Scholars write entire books about collections of fragments of pottery without ever having seen a single complete example of the vessels they are describing, and then try to reconstruct the lives of the potters. By contrast, rock art is a direct record: these are pictures from the past which preserve for us an image of how ancient people experienced their own worlds. 'Experienced' is a more accurate term than 'saw', because experience shapes what the human eye sees and takes notice of, and what it overlooks.

Although it is the Ice Age art in French and Spanish caves that is most famous (pp. 96–100), the majority of rock art is later in date, more scattered across the world and found on open or slightly protected surfaces rather than deep in grottoes. Wherever there is rock, there may be rock art. Many of the great rock art regions of the world – Scandinavia, the far western United States, outback Australia, the mountain ranges of central Sahara – are, naturally enough, rugged regions with much exposed rock. At the same time rock art's distribution is capricious, in a way that hints at strong ancient patterns: of Alpine rock art, a million or two figures occur in just two north Italian valleys –

Left **The sandstone rocks of Australia carry one of the great treasuries of rock art. This is an archaic image of a kangaroo painted in red ochre, Kakadu National Park, north Australia.**

Right **South African rock art has famous elegance of line and colour. In the foreground is a line of eland antelopes; behind stand large human figures in cloaks and above run animated stick figures. Game Pass shelter, Drakensberg mountains, South Africa.**

Right **As well as paintings, rock art includes images made by the technique of chipping away the rock surface, as with this bear at Alta, north Norway.**

Valcamonica and Valtellina – and about 30,000 are on just one French mountain, Mount Bego, while the rest of the mountain chain has only a couple of thousand figures altogether.

Rock art of hunting peoples

So what is the world that is depicted? It is varied – pictures of kangaroos and echidnas in Australia, eland and springbok in southern Africa, bears and reindeer in Norway. But there is a strong consistency in the rock art of hunting peoples. Animals are nearly always predominant, and there is a deliberate choice at work: they are not usually the ones which would have been most common in the ancient landscape, or the ones whose bones we find in the contemporary archaeological sites. So there is some strong selection for animals which had meaning in some other way. By contrast, images of plants are rare (but plants are harder to recognize than the distinctive shapes of animals) – although we know that hunting-and-gathering peoples depend more on plants than animals for their nutrition. Images of landscapes are practically unknown. What is the reason for this?

Knowledge of hunter-gatherer peoples living today or who survived into historic times provides clues. Many hunter-gatherers hold certain animals special – bears in the northern lands of Eurasia, eland

Left **These images of bighorn sheep are pecked into a basalt rock-surface at Coso Range, near Death Valley, California, USA.**

among the San people of the Drakensberg in South Africa, bighorn sheep in the arid desert of south-eastern California – and these are the animals of the art. Some animals are connected to visionary experience, and occasionally we know their meaning: the bighorn sheep in California is related to rain-making and is found in the mountains close by Death Valley, the driest place in North America.

Visionary understanding, involving trance and the special knowledge and skills of 'shamans' or 'clever men', is commonplace in modern hunter-gatherer

Right **A human 'Dynamic Figure', holding two boomerangs in one hand and wearing a headdress and a great 'bustle' behind the waist, from Western Arnhem Land, north Australia.**

societies, so it is reasonable to expect it in hunter-gatherer societies of the past. A repeated emphasis on one animal species may indicate such beliefs, and so will other ways in which the feelings of trance – weightlessness, 'floating', flying, an otherness like death – are expressed in visual metaphors. Perhaps this is how the archaic 'Dynamic Figures' of north Australia should be interpreted. The placing of rock art in caves – in the Palaeolithic of Ice Age Europe, as well as in southeast America and in the Maya lands – makes sense in these terms also, for such underground places, dark and inaccessible, are often regarded as places to encounter another world.

In the West today, most of us have a reduced spiritual world – we do not believe in spirits or beings which are human-like, but other, living among us. But when we have first-hand access to knowledge about rock art, we often discover that pictures of animals and birds are not what they superficially seem to be. A figure may be of a deer, but it is a creature of a spirit world rather than a mundane and physical reality. Accordingly, when we look at prehistoric pictures we need to think of them in two ways. On one level, we can interpret them as surface pictures: images of bears and whales and halibut tell us that those creatures were found in the contemporary environment, and were known to its people. But the whale may have been more than a biological creature, and the image of the whale may have carried greater meaning.

The same goes for the figures we recognize as 'anthropomorphic' – in the form of humans. While they take human form, they may at the same time belong in the spirit world. Or they may not fall simply into one category: the Virgin Mary in Christian iconography is 'just' a picture of a young woman – but she carries many and sacred meanings beyond her physical self.

When the image takes a form which is only partly human, we can be sure it has meaning beyond simple depiction. Such is the 'Water Ghost Woman', who lives in the water and pulls mortals to their death, who is depicted in the rock art of the Bighorn Basin, Wyoming. A characteristic and unambiguous rock art motif connected with the spirit world is the 'therianthrope' – a single figure combining both human and animal elements – in South Africa a human figure with the head and the hooves of an eland, or in Australia a human figure with the head of a flying fox (fruit-bat). Often therianthropes are

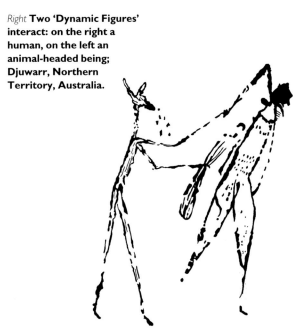

Right **Two 'Dynamic Figures' interact: on the right a human, on the left an animal-headed being; Djuwarr, Northern Territory, Australia.**

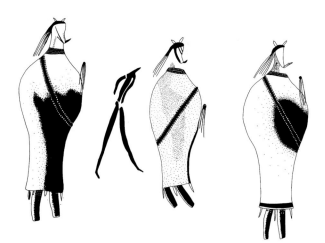

painted alongside or interacting with 'simple human' depictions. Perhaps such figures are humans involved with animal spirits, or they may themselves be spiritual beings – benign or malicious or indifferent or dangerous or sacred, or all at once – that chance to take human form.

Rock art of the first farmers

As we see it depicted in their rock art, the world – and world-experience – of farming people is decidedly different from that of hunter-gatherers. So in Europe the hunter-gatherer rock art of the later Ice Age gives way to very different imagery in the Neolithic and Bronze Ages, much of it pecked into

Above **Therianthropic figures combine human elements with those of animals – eland in this example from the Drakensberg mountains, South Africa.** *Right* **The rock art of the early farmers reflects their experiences of the world, and the innovations and artifacts of their new way of life. Here a four-wheeled wagon is drawn by two horses; Valcamonica, Brescia, north Italy.**

open-air and flat stone surfaces, rather than painted in shelters and caves. The innovations and artifacts of this new way of life are conspicuous: ploughs, and the oxen which pulled them, metal daggers and halberds, boats, timber-built houses. But again there is a deliberate selection. In the Alps, a characteristic motif in rock art is the halberd, a kind of axe which is rare in the archaeological record. So we know that the halberd was special as an object, without knowing what it meant. Both daggers and halberds are characteristically associated with human figures that are gendered male; so we think their meaning was in some way man's business.

The origins of rock art

The enduring mystery of rock art is in its origins. Unlike ancient technologies such as pottery or stone-working, which show a progressive improvement as craft skills develop, early rock art is already wonderfully accomplished. Two great new finds of painted caves in France, Cosquer and Chauvet, are as fine or finer than the celebrated cave of Lascaux and seem decidedly earlier in date. The mounting evidence for early art in continents other than Europe tells the same story, of an elegant skill from an early date, or even from the very beginning.

So how is it that superb painting 'flashed up' already developed – perfect even – rather than climbing gradually from clumsy first essays? But perhaps this is just how we see it now, rather than how it actually was: maybe there was a long evolution, but the early art was made on wood or other perishable materials or, when on rock, was exposed in the open and has not survived. The balance of evidence, however, still favours a sudden birth of accomplished images in art.

Left **Although in the world of farming people, the later rock art of prehistoric Europe is from an era when things were very different. The land below this Bronze Age rock engraving at Massleberg, Bohuslän, Sweden, now a ploughed field, would have been the beach of a shallow bay when the figures were cut into its surface.**

The Meaning of the Megaliths

Time: c. 5000 BC onwards
Location: Europe

I hardly know, sir, whether most to admire the grandeur and method of these vast remains; or the strangeness of their fate, in being found here, without a single chronicle or legend of their original structure or use.

REVD GROVER, 1847

THE REVEREND GROVER'S MUSINGS well express the attraction the megaliths have held for centuries: wonderful and striking places, yet mysterious and strange in the blankness of our knowledge about them. The word 'megalith', from the Greek words for 'big' and 'stone', means just that, a 'big stone', and a megalithic structure is one built of big stones, such as Stonehenge. So, potentially, megaliths can be used for building in any region and at any period. Of special interest are those regions, like the Khasia Hills in India, where megaliths were used until recent centuries or – in Ethiopia and in Madagascar – so recently there is still modern understanding of them. A Madagascan from an indigenous Malagasy people knowledgeable about megaliths who recently visited Stonehenge gave a fluent account of its purpose in which the key point is that the stones stand for the ancestors – a contemporary account which may capture or parallel its ancient meaning.

In building, megaliths are used like great planks or baulks of wood, rather than as stone is used in masonry. (There is also a giant kind of masonry, called 'cyclopean', using great blocks but otherwise following standard techniques of masonry-work.) We have indirect evidence also, and very occasionally surviving wood, to show that timber was used alongside stone in the same kind of engineering. At some English sites, a timber setting was replaced by a stone one; similarities in other forms make it clear that timber-and-earthen and megalithic arrangements could be equivalent, each in a variant suited to its building material.

At Carnac, southern Brittany, megaliths stand in great rows of alignments.

This monolith stands in the village churchyard at Rudston in Yorkshire, England. Now a sacred place in a Christian sense, we can conjecture that it was a special or sacred place in prehistoric times also.

The megaliths of ancient Europe

The best-known megaliths of prehistory are those of ancient Europe. There are single standing stones, some of immense height: the Rudston monolith, the largest in England, stands 7.8 m (25½ ft) high. Le Grand Menhir Brisé ('The great broken menhir'), the largest in France, weighs about 280 tonnes; now on the ground in four pieces, it would have stood 20 m (65½ ft) high – if it was ever successfully erected. There are also standing stones in twos and threes, or set in long parallel rows. At Ménec, on the south coast of Brittany, 11 rows stretch over 1100 m (3610 ft) and include 1099 granite megaliths.

Stone circles

Special in the British Isles are the stone circles, where the standing stones are placed to make neat circles, or oval or egg-shaped rings. Stonehenge is the most famous example (see pp. 136–40). Avebury, largest of the English stone circles, has more than 100 stones in a ring over 400 m (1300 ft) across; from it rambles a long Avenue of paired stones. Two isolated stones were proved, in 1999, to be fragments of another long Avenue. Examined with care, the circles show subtle geometries in their plans, and their dimensions seem often to be multiples of a unit of length, a 'megalithic fathom' or 'megalithic yard'; but we are not sure if either the geometry or the unit was intended by the builders. We may have invented it ourselves in our search for ancient precision. Some Scottish circles, with a mixture of tall and low stones, do seem to show a relation to the position of the moon on the horizon at the periods when it is exceptionally low in the sky. Alignments at varied sites can be found to relate megaliths to movements of the sun, the other great heavenly body.

Megalithic chambers

The other common kind of European megalith is more of a building: megalithic uprights supporting massive stones which make a roof. Together, these may make a long rectangular chamber, or a chamber with a narrow passage. Often this structure is under a stone cairn or earth mound, and many of those now freestanding were, we believe, once under a mound.

Right **An early modern idea of how megaliths were built – by giants. A 17th-century Dutch print of one of the Netherlands'** *hunebedden,* **the old Dutch word for these structures.**

The stones of some, the most famous being Newgrange and Knowth in eastern Ireland, bear the elaborate geometrical designs of 'megalithic art'. Newgrange is aligned so that its chamber is directly illuminated by the sunrise on midwinter's day, much as Stonehenge is aligned towards sunrise on midsummer's day. Knowth, grandest of the Irish megalithic sites, has two separate chambers with passages, back-to-back under a great round mound, with decorated stones inside each passage and on the kerb-stones which mark the edge of the mound. A whole series of smaller satellite mounds with megalithic chambers of more normal scale surround this monster.

In folk knowledge, these megalithic chambers were often connected with giants: there are both a 'Giant's Grave' and a 'Giant's Load' in Ireland, and the common type in Sardinia is the 'tomba di giganti', the 'giants' grave'; the old Dutch word for the Netherlandish type is 'hunebed', 'Hun's bed'. They often contain burials, so they are commonly called 'chambered tombs'. Yet sometimes they contain no bones, or the megalithic structure and mound is enormous in relation to the quantity of human remains inside. And odd things are done with the bones; skeletons may be sorted into the different types of bones – skulls together, long bones

Left **A singular element in the great megalithic structures of the Boyne Valley, in eastern Ireland, is the art: intricate images carved into the surfaces of the stones, such as this one from Knowth.**

Right **One type of European megalithic chamber takes the form of a long rectangle, the 'gallery grave'. This one, which would have originally been covered with a mound of earth, is at Mougou Vihan, Finistère, France.**

Left **Where rock is of a type that splits easily into long and narrow slabs, the standing megaliths may be singularly tall and thin, like those at Callanish on the isle of Lewis, Scotland.**

Right **Avebury, greatest of the English stone circles, has a complex structure that was much interfered with in medieval times. Many of the stones which now stand in the great circle round its edge, and in other groupings inside, were recovered from burial-pits by 20th-century archaeologists.**

together, or animal bones are also found. The grandest, at Bagneux in northwest France, now stands in the courtyard of the local café; 20 m (65½ ft) long by 7 m (23 ft) wide and a sufficient 3 m (10 ft) high, it would make a suitable hall for a party. Like many, it was explored long ago, and we do not know what was found inside.

In our own culture, a church usually contains burials – but its central purpose is not to be a grave. It marks the focal point of a community with a defined territory, the parish. In some regions where we think most or all of the megalithic 'tombs' survive, they are distinctly spaced as one would expect were each hamlet or farm community to mark its own land with a megalith.

Hidden meanings

The European megaliths mostly date to the Neolithic, the era of the first farmers, from 5000 BC or before onwards. The long forms of the chambers echo the long forms of timber houses built by the first-generation farmers of central Europe. Many of their 'ritual monuments', like the megaliths, are singular in form and enigmatic in purpose: circular enclosures with ditches that do not look to have a military or defensive point, pairs of ditches that wander across a landscape for kilometres, settings of split-oak posts. If we see them in terms of modern-day, Western attitudes, one could imagine farmers clearing the woodland to make fields, settling down to live in one place instead of constantly moving about like the hunter-gatherers had done. By degrees they would build up Neolithic 'savings', a bit of a surplus – time to be able to spend the effort and energy to build a megalith. But some megaliths date to *early* in the Neolithic: these are not optional luxuries, added to after the hard early years when they can be afforded. A functional purpose of burial is not the whole story.

The megalithic 'tombs' also provide signs that bodies were not 'disposed of' – put away once and for all at the funeral. There is clear evidence of a two-stage ritual: first the body was exposed, perhaps on a wooden platform, as in Australia in recent times; then the remaining and larger bones – for the smaller ones from the fingers and toes were likely lost with the flesh – would be put inside the megalithic chamber. The remains were actively used; at the least the bones from older 'burials' were pushed to one side while those of a newer body took their place. We now conceive of Neolithic communities as much concerned with their own pasts – societies in which the dead had an active life, in which the ancestors were central to social identity. If the megalithic chambers are tombs, they are in a sense 'tombs for the living'.

Among the most conspicuous and captivating of the ancient places, the megaliths are enjoying much contemporary interest. At sites like West Kennet, a 'chambered tomb' near the great rings and avenues of Avebury, one today finds burning incense sticks and offerings of flowers and bread. That is their modern-day meaning – they are seen as sacred sites where the natural forces of the earth and of appropriate human reverence are rightly expressed. To archaeologists, these new ideas do not seem to capture or express the specifics of ancient meanings as we can infer them; but it is right and fitting that these old sites are active places once more finding a social expression.

Was There a Mother Goddess Cult?

27

Time: 7000–2000 BC
Location: Anatolia, Europe and the Mediterranean

The goddess is nature and earth itself, pulsating with the seasons, bringing life in spring and death in winter.

MARIJA GIMBUTAS, 1999

IN THESE GENDER-AWARE DAYS, when male representations of the Christian god are increasingly called into question, the argument for a prehistoric mother goddess cult has gained many adherents. The idea itself goes back at least to the 19th century, with theories that the original human society was matriarchal and that the patriarchy which has been dominant in recent times developed

at a later stage. Adherents of this hypothesis claimed support from the analysis of myths of the ancient Near East and Aegean. Anthropologists sought to distinguish an early universal religion in which the dominant figure, a 'Great Goddess', was attended by a 'dying god' whose birth and demise symbolized the annual seasonal cycle. The most compelling statement of this belief was found in Sir James Frazer's

By the late 1960s, however, archaeologists were increasingly challenging this interpretation. Sweeping generalizations about prehistoric religion, it was held, should be based on something more substantial than representations of females. It was pointed out that figurines placed in graves, for example, may not necessarily represent divinities; and in any event, female gender was not always indicated. Some of these genderless figures might well be male; in other cases, the gender may not have been important. The corpulent 'lady' from Tarxien temple on Malta, of which only the base survives, could as easily have been male as female. The few clearly female forms found among the megalithic carvings in western Europe were likewise dismissed as inadequate grounds for identifying 'mother goddesses' in the much more numerous abstract images from these tombs.

Above **'Mother goddess' figurine from Çatalhöyük, Turkey, 7th millennium BC. Recent research shows that figurines at Çatalhöyük were not placed in 'shrines' within the settlement, as previously thought, but were deposited in courtyards and open areas. There is nothing to suggest that these figurines represent deities, though some may be connected with death.**

Left **This sculpture of a sleeping female figure from Tarxien, Malta, 3rd millennium BC, helped give rise to the theory of a prehistoric 'goddess' religion.**

The Golden Bough, a massive and wide-ranging comparative study of myth and religion throughout the world that was published in 12 volumes between 1911 and 1915.

Such was the general background that led the English archaeologist Sir Arthur Evans so readily to subscribe to the theory that the Minoan religion of Crete was centred on the cult of a 'great goddess', a female figure depicted in frescoes and figurines at Knossos. So too on Malta, Themistocles Zammit saw in the imagery from Tarxien and Hal Saflieni the evidence of a prehistoric 'goddess' religion, and the concept was soon extended to the sketchy or enigmatic representations in the Neolithic tombs of northwest Europe.

Faience figurine from the Minoan palace at Knossos, Crete, 2nd millennium BC, depicting a bare-breasted female grasping a small snake in each hand. Snakes are associated with the divine in early Aegean mythology, but whether this figure represents a goddess or an attendant engaged in some ritual practice remains in doubt.

Base of a colossal limestone statue from the prehistoric temple of Tarxien on Malta, 3rd millennium BC. Lacking its upper part, this statue may as well have represented a leading male member of Maltese society as a corpulent mother goddess.

The theories of Gimbutas

This sceptical trend was directly challenged by archaeologist Marija Gimbutas in a whole series of books, beginning with *The Gods and Goddesses of Old Europe* in 1974 and ending with *The Living Goddesses*, published posthumously in 1999.

Gimbutas used the Neolithic figurines of southeast Europe to develop a model of peaceful early farming societies that venerated goddesses and were organized matriarchally. This social order extended from the Near East (frescoes and figurines from Çatalhöyük in southern Turkey) to western Europe, where it was revealed not through figurines but in the spiral motifs of megalithic art, in the 'womb-like' character of Neolithic passage graves and in the circular plan of major ritual monuments. Gimbutas argued that these goddess-worshipping matriarchies were eventually supplanted by warlike patriarchies in a series of invasions by horse-riding peoples from the Eurasian steppes in the 4th and 3rd millennia BC.

Archaeologists readily accept the notion that prehistoric societies were probably very different from those of the recent past. The main objection to Gimbutas' theory, however, is that her analysis ignores the diversity and context of the evidence. Anthropomorphic representations of female gender are found widely in prehistoric and early historic sites. The figure with collar and breasts carved in outline on the wall of the Coizard hypogeum in northwest France, and the 'Snake Goddess' from the palace of Knossos on Crete are just two of the many examples. However, male images and male symbols (such as phalluses) are also common in prehistoric European contexts, often in those same societies where female figurines are found.

Furthermore, there is no reason to assume that all such representations are divine. This applies as much to male representations as to female. They may as easily have represented ancestors or the recently deceased: images of the dead kept in the household, perhaps, until the period of mourning was completed.

The 'womb-like' character of the passage-graves of western Europe – like this example from Ile Longue in Brittany, France – was held by Marija Gimbutas as further support for her matriarchal interpretation of early European society.

Plan.

The spirals in the chambered tomb of Newgrange in Ireland, c. 3100 BC, were another indicator for Marija Gimbutas of a matriarchal society.

The likelihood that there were a number of different explanations for these figurines makes any single overarching explanation, whether in terms of religious belief or social organization, very doubtful. One striking fact about the evidence mustered by Gimbutas is its very diversity, and this is also one of its greatest weaknesses: figurines in houses, in graves and in 'temples', as well as spiral carvings on megalithic tombs. Careful study of each of these cases suggests not a single universal religion, but a wide variety of diverse beliefs and practices.

Finally, the hypothesis that early prehistoric Europe was a peaceful matriarchal society until violence, warfare and a destructive ethos of competition was introduced by invasions of patriarchal horse-riders from the steppes can be challenged at almost every point. Gimbutas' 'Old Europe' was not peaceful: the butchered individuals – men, women and children – despatched by an axe-blow to the head at Talheim in Germany would certainly not have thought so. Nor are invasions from the steppes supported by the archaeological evidence. There is nothing to show new peoples sweeping across Europe in the 4th and 3rd millennia BC; quite the contrary, everything points to the steady, in situ development of indigenous societies.

The 'mother goddess' hypothesis in the terms envisaged by Marija Gimbutas and others must accordingly be rejected in the light of current archaeological understanding. Indeed, it provides an object lesson in the imposition of wishful thinking on the archaeological record. That, however, is not to reject the belief that women, and female deities, may have played very different roles in human societies of the past. To reject the idea of a widespread prehistoric matriarchy is not to suggest that patriarchy is the natural or necessarily the desirable condition for human society.

The Iceman: Shepherd or Shaman?

28

Time: 3300–3200 BC
Location: Italian Alps

Alpine incident: body discovered at Hauslabjoch – The dead man's identity has not as yet been established. On the strength of the articles found near the body it may be assumed that the accident happened as long ago as the nineteenth century.

POLICE REPORT, IN KONRAD SPINDLER, 1994

ON 19 SEPTEMBER 1991, two German mountaineers discovered the oldest preserved human body ever recorded in modern times. The site of the discovery was the Italian South Tyrol, close to the main ridge of the Alps and only a little more than 90 m (300 ft) from the international frontier with Austria. This section of the Alps is known as the Ötztaler Alps, taking its name from the long narrow Ötztal Valley. The body is commonly known today by the nickname 'Ötzi', coined by an Austrian journalist through conflation of 'Ötztal' and 'yeti'. Many, however, simply refer to the body as the 'Iceman'.

The desolate and remote setting of the discovery has led to numerous hypotheses as to how the Iceman met his end. Scientific analysis has yielded a considerable amount of detail about his state of health, and about the equipment which he carried and which was found around the body in the narrow gully. It is the equipment which provides evidence of the identity of the Iceman, and enables archaeologists to speculate as to what he was doing here in the high Alps.

Body, clothing and equipment

The body proved to be that of a man aged somewhere between 25 and 45 years old; its excellent state of preservation meant that even the molecular structure of the tissues had survived. The reason for this unusual degree of preservation lay in the sequence of events which had led to and followed the Iceman's death. It is thought that the man died after being overcome by an early autumn blizzard. The thin covering of snow prevented attack from insect larvae

as the corpse was gradually desiccated by autumn winds. In essence, what occurred was a natural freeze-drying. The condition of the corpse was already largely stabilized when the heavy winter snows came to cover it. Radiocarbon dating of tissues from the body – undertaken separately in four different laboratories for greater reliability – indicated that these events took place between 3300 and 3200 BC. The corpse must thus have lain buried for over 5000 years before the melting of the ice –

Opposite **The Iceman in September 1991, still partly encased in ice, though first attempts have freed the body as far as the hips. Only when the corpse had been removed to the Institute of Forensic Medicine in Innsbruck did its true age and significance become clear.**

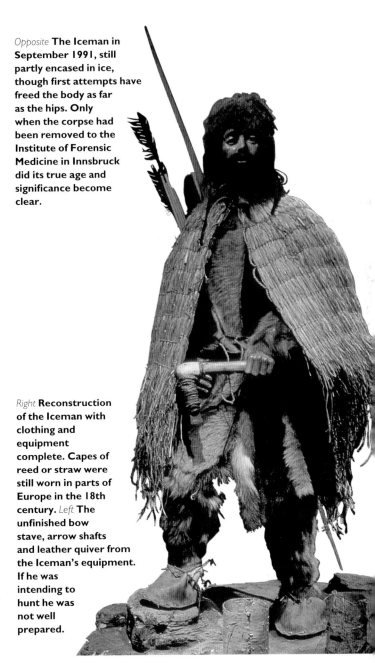

Right **Reconstruction of the Iceman with clothing and equipment complete. Capes of reed or straw were still worn in parts of Europe in the 18th century.** *Left* **The unfinished bow stave, arrow shafts and leather quiver from the Iceman's equipment. If he was intending to hunt he was not well prepared.**

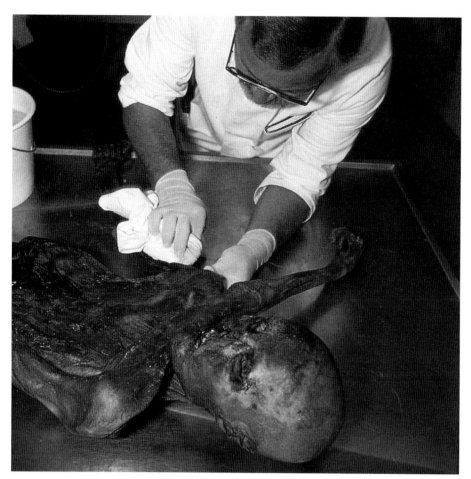

Above **The polished white marble bead and the attached leather tassels have been claimed to indicate that the Iceman was a shaman.** *Right* **The Ötztal body laid out with some of its equipment. The copper axe, lashed to its wooden haft, was found close to the body and gave one of the first indications of its date.**

Left **An international team of specialists undertook detailed examination of the Iceman to determine his age, state of health and any evidence for cause of death.**

accelerated by wind-borne Saharan dust in July 1991 – exposed it to view once again.

The preservation of the Iceman is thus more remarkable than mysterious, but the circumstances of his death, and the significance of the objects that he was carrying, do indeed pose many questions. Lying around the body in the ice hollow were a copper axe hafted in a yew handle, an unfinished bow, also of yew, a backpack made of larch planks and animal hide, a flint knife and scabbard, a deer-skin quiver with 2 flint-tipped arrows and 12 unfinished arrow shafts, and a calfskin pouch which hung from a belt. In addition to this equipment the remains of his clothing also survived: fur leggings and cap, fur outer garment of poncho type, leather shoes stuffed with grass for warmth, and a grass cape which could have doubled as a ground-sheet or blanket. Despite the absence of warm, modern waterproof materials, this was a set of clothing well able to cope with the harsh Alpine climate, at least outside the winter months.

The same cannot be said of his equipment, and the unfinished nature of his bow and the majority of his arrows suggest that he was not well prepared for his journey. Furthermore, he was not in the peak of health. Analysis of one of his fingernails revealed that he had suffered from serious illnesses (resulting in interruptions to their growth) at least three times during the six months before he died. He also bore tattoos on his lower back, left leg, and right ankle and knee. These may have been decorative, but more probably had a therapeutic function, since the Iceman suffered from arthritis. Analysis of his colon contents has indicated that he was also afflicted by an intestinal infestation which could have caused chronic diarrhoea. Most serious of all, however, was direct evidence that eight of his ribs had been frac-tured not long previously. They had begun to mend, but this evidence for trauma has led some to specu-late that the Iceman had been involved in violence which had driven him from his village, and that it was while he was fleeing across the Alps with

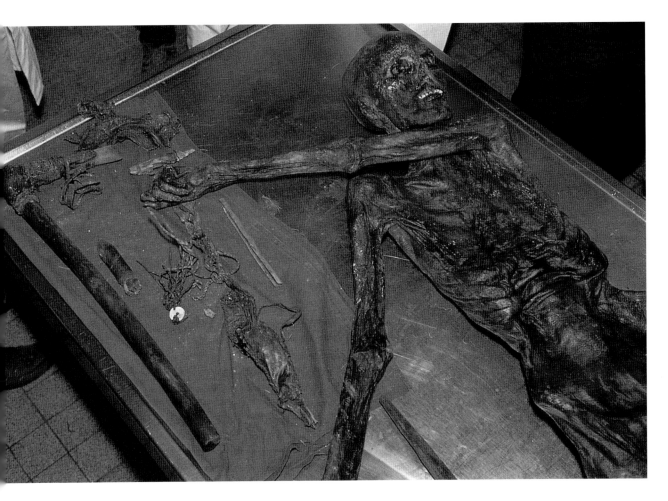

unfinished equipment that an early winter storm overcame him.

Shepherd or shaman?

Other interpretations are equally possible. One such is that he was simply a shepherd. Analysis of moss from the body showed that it had come from the south side of the Alps, and it is quite possible that the Iceman's home was in the Vinschgau, only some 20 km (12.5 miles) due south of the place where he met his end. Pollen suggests that his death occurred in the early autumn, thus making him perhaps a victim of misadventure – shepherding his flock in upland pastures, and in none-too-good a state of health, when an unseasonable wintry storm overwhelmed him. He may have sought shelter in the shallow hollow where he was found, only to freeze to death.

Not all have been content with such prosaic explanations, however, and some have argued that the Iceman was in fact a shaman or ritual specialist. The unfinished hunting equipment, the body tattoos and the perforated bead of white marble, with twisted leather tassels, have all been adduced in support. Shamans commune with the spirit world, often in remote locations, and this might explain his journey to the high mountains. Ethnographic examples indicate that bright or polished stones are often held to have special significance or power, though quartz rather than marble is the more usual material. The evidence that the Iceman was a shaman cannot be said to be overwhelming, though it is a possibility that is difficult to discount. The unique nature of the discovery, and the exceptional conditions of preservation, give us little with which to compare him. Were fuller evidence available, we might be less inclined to attribute to the Iceman some ritual or religious status, and more willing – notwithstanding curious features of his equipment – to regard him as a typical member of a high Alpine community of the late 4th millennium BC, distinguished more by the fate that befell him and his body than by his status in life.

How Did They Build Stonehenge?

29

Time: c. 2950–1600 BC
Location: southern England

A voiceless vision of a vanished age,
These solemn triliths of a temple stand
On the unquestioning plain – a hoary band
And mystery of ev'ry modern sage.

EDWARD G. ALDRIDGE, MID-19TH CENTURY

SO HOW *DID* THEY BUILD STONEHENGE? The pat answer must be 'with difficulty', and the true answer is 'with less difficulty than we think'. Stonehenge is unique, as well as specially famous, and it is that uniqueness which gives a clue. The other stone circles in Britain – there are several hundred, some of them of much larger diameter – are of stones left in their natural state. Only at Stonehenge are the great stones neatly trimmed into squared-off shapes. The horizontal stones that span

Left **Stonehenge today – ruined, missing some stones, and perhaps never completed to the full, intended plan.** *Above* **Most of the wooden monuments from the age of Stonehenge have rotted away completely, leaving only their traces as dark marks in the soil. This is a rare exception – the strange monument on the Norfolk coast christened 'Seahenge'.**

the gaps between the uprights, like the lintel across a doorway, are held in place by mortise-and-tenon joints – as if they were beams of timber. And adjacent horizontal stones are held tight against each other by tongue-and-groove joints, again a timber-worker's technique. We have known these facts from the beginning: our earliest record of Stonehenge, as early as the 11th century, talks of the place as being built 'like doorways'.

Woodhenge and Seahenge

So Stonehenge, although built of stone, is constructed as if it were made of wood. Early in the 20th century, within a few kilometres of Stonehenge, pioneering air photographers spotted from the air a set of marks in the grass, altogether much the same size as Stonehenge and organized the same way into concentric settings. This site was evidently something like Stonehenge, but made of timber, so it was named 'Woodhenge'. It even has an axis orientated towards the midsummer sunrise, like Stonehenge.

In 1998–99, for the first time one of these timber monuments was recovered intact, rather than as marks in the earth where its elements had rotted away. Preserved in the coastal mud just off the Norfolk coast of east England, and dated by dendrochronology (tree-ring dating) to precisely 2050 BC, it was immediately named 'Seahenge'. In the centre of a ring of wooden posts was a single great oak tree set vertically into the ground, and what had at first looked like the branches were in fact roots: the tree had been put in upside down.

So the builders of Stonehenge had a traditional craft knowledge not just of transporting great stones and setting them upright, but also of moving great tree-stumps and – as we see in the other traces of timber-work – of splitting massive oak logs into slabs. It was these skills which made Stonehenge possible. We do not know what these wooden structures were like above ground. They may have been buildings with roofs, or simple standing timbers, or carved like Native American totem poles. Seahenge, our first material sight of the above-ground component, has surprised us in being different again, rather than resembling a part of Stonehenge. As Stonehenge is our only close analogy, it is reasonable to think the timber structures looked like Stonehenge. Instructively, other stones at Stonehenge, originally eight in number, which are more overlooked than the famous settings at the heart of monument and dated rather earlier, were not trimmed on the model of woodworking.

Moving the stones

The first requirement in building Stonehenge was obtaining the right kind of stones. Of the several types used, the most numerous are 'bluestones' brought from west Wales, some 240 km (150 miles) away. Typically about the dimensions of a coffin, they weigh up to about 4 tonnes; it would not have been so hard to drag them overland or to float them on skin coracles along the coast and up one of the English rivers close to Stonehenge. But not so easy either: in 2000 a team attempting to transport a bluestone of the correct size to Stonehenge struggled to find enough volunteers to pull it. And once on the boats, the stone slipped into the water and was lost; it had to be fished up off the bottom of the sea so that the trial could continue.

The larger 'sarsen' stones at Stonehenge are much heavier, but they come from closer to hand, some 30 km (18 miles) away. The main difficulty for the builders would have been in finding enough sarsens of sufficient size – a Stonehenge built to its full design needed 79 of them. The older megalithic

Opposite **The classic view from Stonehenge, looking northeast past the distant 'Heel Stone' over which the sun rises on midsummer day.** *Above* **In a modern re-enactment, a Welsh bluestone was dragged towards Stonehenge mounted on a sled.**

circles and avenues at Avebury would have already used up several hundred. Many of the sarsens at Stonehenge have very little of their length underground for foundation support, and Stonehenge does not seem to have been completed to its intended design. Did they run out of stones?

Moving the sarsens, which weigh up to 40 tonnes and more, was the first task. Experiments with a replica stone in 1994 by archaeologist Julian Richards and engineer Mark Whitby give us confidence as to how this may have been done. The stone would have been levered on to a timber cradle, and the cradle pulled by teams with ropes. It has usually been thought that the cradle would have run over rollers, but the engineer in the 1994 tests found a better way – sliding the cradle on timber rails plentifully greased. Their stone 'stuck' until rocked free, and then went well, with a team of 130 volunteers pulling. Modern ropes were used for safety's sake, but it is known that good ropes of sufficient strength could have been made in prehistoric times from the inner bark of trees. It was estimated the stone could have been pulled a full kilometre in a day on a

modest uphill slope, and a full 10 km (6¼ miles) on the level or downhill! And we know that Neolithic people were skilled in splitting oak trees to make the rails. Between the Marlborough Downs, where the sarsens are found, and Stonehenge is the Vale of Pewsey – the stones would have had to be taken down the steep scarp of the valley's north wall, across the damp valley, and up the slope on to the high downland where Stonehenge was built.

Shaping and raising the stones

The sarsens can be shaped by hammering with the same stone – a slow business since the sarsen is so very hard and does not break off in large pieces, but is worn away grain by grain. Many mauls and hammerstones of varied size have been found at Stonehenge, where they were later used to hold uprights steady in their foundations. Some of the stones show parallel dips, where the gangs of stone-shapers had worked.

Raising the upright stones was also tested by experiment in 1994. The stone was tipped into a prepared hole, and ingeniously made to topple well by sliding a smaller stone across it, abruptly changing its balance. Neolithic technology could have done that, but would Neolithic minds have had the same idea? Then the stone was pulled upright by ropes running over a timber 'A-frame' by a team of about 130 labourers (men and women of varying ages and strength). The final task, once the uprights were wedged securely in their holes with small sarsen stones, was to raise the lintel stones on to the top. This could have been done either by pulling the stone up a sloping ramp, or levering it up first on one side, then on the other, on a rising scaffold of stacked logs. Whichever method was used, once raised to the required height the lintels had to be trimmed into shape and moved into their final position. Since no trace of any ramps has been found, it seems the method using stacked logs is the more likely one.

So, given a labour force of 130 or more, and with the skills in moving stones and shaping timbers that we know Neolithic people possessed, perhaps building Stonehenge was not so hard as it seems to us today. At least in the West, we are so accustomed to machinery that we forget what can be done by skill and human muscle-power alone. So part of the mystery is in ourselves, not 'how did they build Stonehenge?' but 'why are we so puzzled as to how they built Stonehenge?'

There is a curious footnote to the fragment of Stonehenge built in the experimental test. Not intended to be left, it looked superb in its north Wiltshire field, and the notion took hold to let it remain as a modern curiosity. Then it was taken down when rumour had it that an unofficial 'rave' or festival would take place there. Rumour now has it that the component stones are in store, available to anyone who also wants to have a go at building their own Stonehenge the ancient or the modern way.

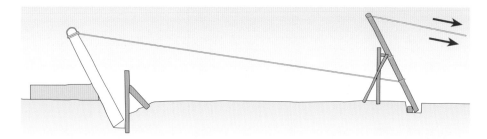

Right **In this reconstruction, an A-frame is used to increase the leverage when pulling a great Stonehenge upright. Were Neolithic engineers so accomplished?** *Below* **In this raising of a Stonehenge lintel, modern engineers used manpower, but also scaffold and safety helmets.**

Where Did the Indo-Europeans Come From?

Time: c. 7000–3000 BC
Location: Eurasia

30

My leisure hours, for some time past, have been employed in considering the striking affinity of the languages of Europe; and finding, every day, new and most engaging entertainment in this pursuit, I was insensibly led on to attempt following them to their source.

JAMES PARSONS, 1767

ALTHOUGH EUROPE and western Asia have seen many cultures and peoples, most Europeans and a significant part of western and southern Asians have spoken related languages belonging to a single language family which began to expand across Eurasia some time during the Neolithic or Early Bronze Age. We can gain an impression of this linguistic continuum if we take several words, cognate in most Indo-European languages, and follow them from Ireland in the west to the Tocharians of the oasis towns of the Silk Road in western China.

The similarities between these words is explained by deriving them all from a common ancestral language (much as we derive French, Spanish or Italian from Late Latin) known as Proto-Indo-European. Precisely when and where this Proto-Indo-European was spoken has exercised the ingenuity of scholars for two centuries. The correspondences between the items of vocabulary in the different Indo-European languages assists linguists in reconstructing the general shape and at least some of the content of Proto-Indo-European. It reveals the names of trees (birch, oak, willow, ash, etc), wild animals (bear, fox, elk, lynx, deer, etc), and, more importantly, a series of domestic animals (cattle, sheep, goats, pig) and technology (pot, sickle, plough) associated with farming (grain, grinding stone) and wagons (wheel, wagon, yoke). All of this suggests that the proto-language did not dissolve until its speakers at least

shared a common Neolithic vocabulary, the period when these innovations appeared.

Many have attempted to use the evidence of the proto-language, particularly reconstructed words for environmental terms, to locate where it was spoken.

Above **A silver-gilt Thracian plaque, from Letnitsa, showing a 'sacred marriage', dating to 400–350 BC.**

Right **Table tracing three words across Europe, from Ireland in the west to the Tocharians of western China. The similarities can be explained by a common ancestral language.**

	Celtic Old Irish	Germanic Old English	Italic Latin	Baltic Lithuanian	Slavic Russian	Greek Greek	Indic Sanskrit	Tocharian Tocharian B
three	tri	thrie	tres	trys	trije	treis	trí	trai
mother	máthair	modor	mater	móte	mat'	meter	matár	macer
door	dorus	dor	foris	durys	dver	thúra	dváras-	twere

141

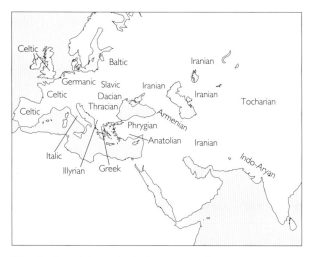

Distribution of the major Indo-European language groups.

Unfortunately, there seems to be a general rule that the more diagnostic or distinctive the meaning of the reconstructed word, the less secure is its reconstruction and so the use of the vocabulary alone to locate the earliest Indo-Europeans has never led to convincing results.

Why do we need to look for the Proto-Indo-Europeans in a confined location? The problem here is both empirical and theoretical. To begin with, we know that there were non-Indo-European languages spoken in some of the margins of Europe, e.g., Iberian in Spain, Etruscan in Italy, Hattic in Anatolia. We also know that some Indo-Europeans spread over earlier non-Indo-European-speaking populations, e.g., the Iranians assimilated the Elamites of

southern Iran, the Indo-Aryans had to spread their language over earlier Dravidian and Munda speakers. Furthermore, one non-Indo-European language has survived in Europe – Basque, which is spoken in northern Spain and southern France.

The theoretical problem concerns the entire nature of language change. To position the Indo-Europeans from the Atlantic to western China since deepest antiquity greatly exceeds the size of area which any single language could have maintained in the prehistoric period. Languages are constantly evolving (although not at a constant rate) and it would be impossible to imagine how the speakers of a single language, spread across several thousand kilometres, could maintain the same language changes for thousands of years.

The homeland models

Proposed locations of the Indo-European homeland (or Urheimat as a German might put it) have ranged from the North to the South Pole, from the Atlantic to the Pacific. Basically, there are three types of models of Indo-European origins currently under discussion. The first suggests that the Proto-Indo-Europeans may be found before the Neolithic, during either the Palaeolithic or Mesolithic, in some broad expanse across Eurasia. By pushing their origins back so far and over such a broad area – most of Europe – this reduces the demand on the archaeologist to demonstrate later, long-distance migrations to account for the dispersal of the Indo-European languages. This is the least acceptable model because it does not account for the shared Neolithic, indeed late Neolithic vocabulary, that we find in the reconstructed proto-language.

The second model initiates Indo-European expansions with the spread of agriculture, a model which has also been extended to other language families. This means that the Indo-European language(s)

1. Some propose an Indo-European homeland in the Paleolithic or Mesolithic that embraced a large region of Europe. 2. The Anatolian model associates the expansion of Indo-Europeans with the spread of agriculture from the Near East to Europe. 3. The Kurgan model sees the expansion of Indo-Europeans from the European steppelands at the end of the Neolithic.

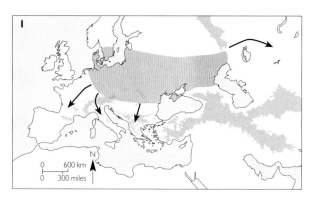

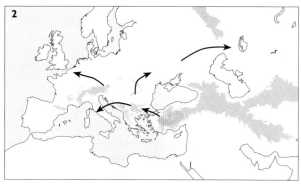

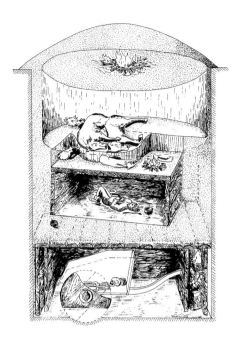

Bronze Age chariot burials at Sintashta, southern Urals, are often seen as evidence of early Indo-Iranian expansions.

spread with a new, far more productive economy and that the new Indo-European speaking farmers gradually filled up Europe to replace earlier hunting-gathering populations. Some have argued that the expansion was entirely demic, that is it involved largely a population replacement, while others have suggested that the periphery of Europe did not see an influx of new farmers but rather underwent language shift. All these models would set the earliest Indo-Europeans in Anatolia (ancient Turkey) in about the 7th millennium BC, and argue for their expansion into Greece and the Balkans and then progressively westwards to the Atlantic.

As for the major Indo-European languages of Asia, they generally follow the third hypothesis. This third model requires major language shift among most of the Neolithic–Bronze Age populations of Europe and western Asia. The theory generally situates the earliest Indo-Europeans in the steppe and forest-steppe north of the Black and Caspian seas and argues that the earliest Indo-European expansions were accomplished by semi-nomadic or at least highly mobile populations who possessed the domestic horse and wheeled vehicles. As they typically buried their dead under a mound, Russian *kurgan*, this is often termed the Kurgan theory. It argues that from the 5th to the 3rd millennia BC, mobile populations began moving off the steppe into southeastern and central Europe and progressively assimilated the native populations to their own Indo-European language.

This model does not depend so much on population movement as a social shift – the Indo-European languages spread because of the nature of early Indo-European social institutions which were more aggressive and attractive than those previously found in Europe. As for the Indo-Europeans of Asia, the Kurgan model suggests that by *c*. 2000 BC, chariot-driving aristocracies had developed in the Volga-Ural region and had then crossed eastwards and south through Central Asia to form Bronze Age élites in greater Iran and India.

Although there is not a wholly acceptable model to explain Indo-European origins and expansions, the problem itself continually stimulates scholars to consider how language, one of the most intrinsic elements of human culture, can be tracked in the archaeological record.

Below **The most detailed version of the Kurgan model envisages three waves of Indo-European expansions across Europe.**

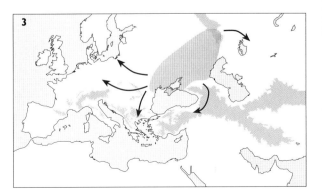

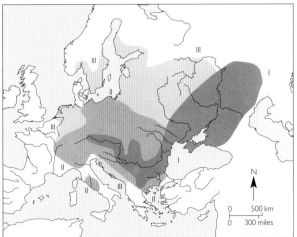

Ancient Civilizations

THE WORLD'S FIRST CIVILIZATIONS cast an irresistible spell over us – among them the ancient Egyptians, Greeks and Romans, as well as the Maya, the enigmatic Olmecs and the imperial Incas of the Andes. For all their many differences, all pre-industrial civilizations share important features. Each was a society driven by a distinctive ideology, where a handful of powerful people and a supreme ruler managed to acquire and retain the loyalty of thousands of subjects who laboured to maintain the apparatus of state. We marvel at this ability to achieve conformity, at the religious and social controls which permitted Egyptian pharaohs to govern millions for 3000 years and Maya lords to exercise mastery over complex city-states.

For all our familiarity with the names of the pharaoh Ramesses II or the Maya lord Pakal, many mysteries and controversies remain, some of them simple technological questions, others matters of cultural identity with powerful implications in today's world. Generations of archaeologists have argued about how the Egyptians built their obelisks and pyramids – both the methods used to fashion and raise them, and also the miracles of bureaucratic organization involved in their construction. Equally remarkable perhaps is the feat of the ancestors of the Polynesians, who navigated over vast distances of open ocean using their knowledge of the stars and natural phenomena to settle on remote islands.

Such debates pale into emotional insignificance, however, beside the passionate arguments over the cultural identity of the ancient Egyptians, whom

The Temple of Apollo at Delphi was the focus for the most famous oracle in the ancient world. Just what kind of help visitors to such oracles could expect remains a mystery.

some insist were of black African origin. Afrocentrist scholars make the blackness of ancient Egyptian culture a cornerstone of their theory that blacks were responsible for Western civilization; the debate is fraught with racist arguments and deep-felt conviction. So also is the question of the cultural identity of the Olmecs of Mexico, a founder society of ancient Mesoamerican civilization, whose monumental statuary, some claim, displays black African features. In Europe, too, the question of who were the Celts? is now, perhaps surprisingly, being asked.

Less controversial but just as enduring are issues such as the manner of the pharaoh Tutankhamun's death (was he murdered?), and the contentious 'riddle of the Sphinx', which continues to excite those who believe it is as much as 10,000 years old. We are also fascinated by aspects of the past that are now lost – whether it is the location of the Land of Punt, or of Site Q, swallowed up by the forests of the Maya; or the fate of the IXth Roman legion, who, some believe, marched into the mists of Scotland and into legend.

The ancient dead, especially if well preserved, have intrigued people for centuries. The most spectacular mummies of recent times come from the Tarim Basin in Central Asia, where they were preserved naturally in the dry desert. Waterlogging preserved the bodies yielded up by peat bogs of northern Europe. Both men and women have been found, all met violent deaths – were they victims of murder or human sacrifice? In the high peaks of the Andes, the deep-frozen corpses of children sacrificed by the Incas have been discovered above the snow-line. On the other side of the world, we examine the

evidence that Carthaginians also sacrificed children. Why was human life, especially of the young, considered to be such a powerful offering to the gods?

The monuments of the early civilizations present us with profound enigmas, such as the courts and platforms of Tiwanaku near the shores of Bolivia's Lake Titicaca, and the mysterious Nazca Lines of southern Peru's coastal desert. Tiwanaku's builders used their complex religious beliefs to fashion a blueprint for the city. A visitor in AD 650 would have marvelled at palaces, plazas and brightly coloured temples shimmering with gold-covered reliefs – hard to imagine from the remains of masonry gateways and buildings that survive today. The Nazca Lines with their vast animal figures and long, straight lines are also religious architecture on an enormous scale. Attempts have been made to attribute them to ancient astronauts from space or to explain them as maps of the heavens. Current scholarly opinion connects them to the religious beliefs of the indigenous people, who created a huge symbolic landscape on the surface of the desert which they themselves would not have been able to view overall.

The religious and cultural beliefs of ancient societies perhaps present us with the most profound mysteries, such as the place of oracles in ancient Greek society, the secrets of the cult of Mithraism in the Roman world, and the remote statues of Easter Island, unique ancestor figures quite unlike any others on earth. All these mysteries form part of the palimpsest of ancient societies, whose spiritual life and relationships with their environment were as complex as, and sometimes one suspects more satisfying than, our own.

The pyramids at Giza, Egypt, have aroused considerable debate about how, and why, they were built, and how the ancient Egyptians aligned these colossal monuments so accurately.

Were the Ancient Egyptians Black Africans?

Time: c. 3100–332 BC
Location: Egypt

From various Egyptian legends I have been able to conclude that the populations settled in the Nile Valley were negroes, since the goddess Isis was said to have been a reddish-black woman.

ÉMILE AMÉLINEAU, 1899

SINCE EGYPT IS undoubtedly part of Africa, its inhabitants – both ancient and modern – are, in a strict geographical sense, certainly 'African'. The question of whether the ancient Egyptians were 'black', however, is a much more complicated issue. To many modern writers – particularly those 'Afrocentrists' who want to define Egypt as a purely 'black African' civilization – the geographical location of Egypt is sufficient proof that its people were fundamentally 'black'. But if we are to attempt to answer the question properly, we need to define not only what the word 'black' means now but also what it may have meant in ancient times.

What do we mean by black?

Unfortunately, even a cursory examination of modern writing on the subject reveals that the use of the term 'black' as a means of categorizing groups or individuals differs largely according to the views of the individual writer. Sometimes the word is used to refer specifically to the classic Negroid physical type, but very often it has a much vaguer sense, roughly equivalent to 'African', 'non-European' or even 'oppressed ethnic group'. In contrast – perhaps surprisingly – there appears to be far more consensus and clarity in the ancient sources. Three main types of evidence from the ancient world tend to be used: the skeletal remains from Egypt and adjoining regions; the texts and depictions of the ancient Egyptians; and the texts written by Classical authors.

Over the years, increasing numbers of Egyptian skeletons of many different periods have been

Below **Two 4th-Dynasty 'reserve' heads from private tombs at Giza. One shows the more typical Egyptian physical features, while the other, female, head has more negroid features.**

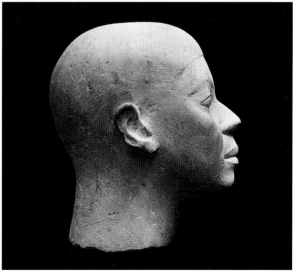

Two troops of model soldiers from the tomb of Mesehti – one *(opposite)* shows Egyptian soldiers, with reddish-brown skin, the other Nubian mercenaries with much darker skin.

studied, and the conclusions reached have often had significant effects on Egyptologists' ideas concerning population movements in and out of Egypt and Nubia. For instance, the British Egyptologist Brian Emery claimed, on the basis of skull measurements, that the late Predynastic Egyptians were conquered

The handle of a ceremonial cane of Tutankhamun, with figures of an Asiatic and an African.

by a New Race from the east, while Flinders Petrie at one stage suggested, on similar grounds, that the pyramid builders of the Old Kingdom were a group of non-Negroid invaders from Asia. However, as the methodology of biological anthropologists has improved, such simplistic assertions have become less common, and it is now widely recognized that the slippery idea of racial types cannot readily be assessed purely on the basis of skeletal remains.

The anthropology of Egyptians

Although the history of anthropological influences on Egyptological historians has periodically focused on possible confrontations between Negroid and Caucasoid groups, there has been a certain amount of continuity in the study of Egyptian human remains. At the end of the 18th century, the pioneering anthropologist Johann Friedrich Blumenbach reached the conclusion that there were three basic physical types among the Egyptians: (1) 'Ethiopian'; (2) 'approaching to the Hindoo'; and (3) a mixture of 'Ethiopian' and 'Hindoo'. It was partly through the influence of Blumenbach's work that many anthropologists in the 19th century continued to stress potential racial connections between Egypt and

southern Asia, and in the early 20th century several anthropologists used a so-called 'coefficient of racial likeness' (based on cranial measurements) claiming to provide hard scientific evidence for such a link between the Egyptian and south Asian physical types. Although the statistical validity of this coefficient has since been discredited, analyses of Egyptian skeletal material undertaken during the 1990s suggest that the people of ancient Egypt had stronger links with the peoples of Europe and south Asia than with the occupants of Sub-Saharan Africa.

In addition, the most recent anthropological work suggests that the gradual north–south change in the Egyptian physical type is not even an indication of the mixing of two distinct races (i.e. Negroid and Caucasoid) but a kind of spectrum or 'cline', whereby the physical type gradually adapts to environmental changes according to latitude and local conditions. The American anthropologist C. Loring Brace therefore concludes that, 'attempts to force the Egyptians into either a "black" or "white" category have no biological justification.... The old-fashioned chimerical concept of "race" is hopelessly inadequate to deal with the human biological reality of Egypt, ancient or modern.'

The Egyptian world view

How, then, did the Egyptians view themselves? We can answer this question first by looking at the way in which they portrayed themselves in painting and sculpture, and secondly by analysing their depictions of 'foreigners'. As in many other cultures, the Egyptians seem to have gained a sense of their own identity primarily by contrasting themselves with the peoples of the world outside Egypt. The iconography of the Egyptians' depictions of themselves and foreigners suggests that for most of their history they saw themselves as midway between the black, woolly-haired Africans and the pale, bearded Asiatics. The tombs of the New Kingdom pharaohs Seti I and Ramesses III in the Valley of the Kings include scenes specifically depicting figures representing the various human types in the universe over which the sun-god Re presided. These types included reddish-brown Egyptians whose skin colour contrasts equally starkly both with the black-skinned Kushites (Nubians) and with the paler-skinned Libyans and Asiatics. Although partly based on skin colour and other physical characteristics, these ancient ethnic types were also based on varieties in hairstyles and costume, and their function was clearly to allow the

Painted relief scenes from the tomb of the 19th-Dynasty pharaoh Seti I in the Valley of the Kings, showing stereotypical figures of Egyptians and Asiatics.

Egyptians to define themselves as a national group, relative to the rest of the world. Such depictions, however, would have been recognized by the Egyptians themselves as simplified stereotypes, given that the thousands of portrayals of individual Egyptians on the walls of tombs and temples show that the population as a whole ranged across a wide spectrum of complexions, from light to dark brown.

There is therefore also a sense in which the 'Egyptians' regarded themselves as a distinct population in purely cultural, non-racial terms. Thus there are many examples of individuals who are clearly considered to be Egyptian in social and political terms, despite the fact that they were obviously 'foreign' in their physical appearance.

Black people in the Classical world

As far as Greek and Roman writers were concerned, the most common yardstick of 'blackness' was Ethiopia. The Ethiopians (literally 'those with burnt faces') are constantly described as the blackest of all Africans known to the Classical world, and it is significant that they are rarely confused with the Egyptians in the writings of authors such as Aristotle, Xenophanes and Ptolemy. Indeed, Manilius, in his *Astronomica*, specifically lists a number of people in order of decreasing blackness: Ethiopians, Indians, Egyptians and Moors, while Strabo suggests that Ethiopians were like southern Indians and Egyptians were like northern Indians. It is also evident that Greeks and Romans did not tend to describe skin colour or other racial characteristics in pejorative ways. Instead, geography and ethnicity were much more important methods of categorizing peoples in the Classical world. However, carefully selected quotations from Classical authors, often cited totally out of context, have repeatedly been used by modern authors with axes to grind on the subject.

Conclusion

So who were the ancient Egyptians? A number of facts can be determined with some confidence on the basis of the evidence currently available to us. First, as stated at the outset, Egypt was undoubtedly part of the African continent, although it is worth pointing out that it was also the African country best positioned to establish close contacts with the Near East and the Mediterranean. Secondly, the language spoken by the Egyptians seems to have been primarily African in origin, but increasingly influenced by Semitic tongues (especially from the New Kingdom onwards). Thirdly, as far as their physical appearance was concerned, the overwhelming weight of evidence of ancient Egyptian and Classical art and literature indicates that the population of the lower Nile valley was racially and ethnically mixed, ranging from fully Negroid individuals in the south to paler-skinned, straight-haired Caucasian types in the north. Fourthly, the traditional Egyptian iconography of the pharaonic period used a form of racial stereotyping (primarily based on skin colour and hair-types) to distinguish between themselves and the peoples of Africa, Asia and the north Mediterranean.

Finally, and perhaps most importantly, the concept of 'black' people is a modern construct which only confuses the situation when attempts are made to apply it to ancient contexts. Just as there has never been any serious 'white Anglo-Saxon Protestant' plot to define Egypt as a 'white' civilization, so there are no scientific grounds for describing it as a 'black' civilization. The ancient Egyptians themselves would not have understood the modern racial concept of 'blackness' and they clearly never defined their 'Egyptian-ness' in purely racial terms. The culture and the archaeological record of ancient Egypt were the product of the interaction of many racial groups. In other words, the Egyptians were not quintessentially black, brown or white – they were simply Egyptian.

How Did They Erect Pyramids & Obelisks?

Time: c. 2551 BC–AD 100
Location: Egypt

The pyramid was built in tiers, battlementwise, as it is called, or, according to others, stepwise. When the pyramid was completed in this form, they raised the remaining stones to their places by means of machines formed of short beams of wood.

HERODOTUS, C. 430 BC

SINCE AT LEAST the time of Herodotus there has been considerable debate concerning the means used by the Egyptians to construct the pyramids and raise obelisks. Unfortunately very few Egyptian textual records referring to such matters have survived, leaving experimental archaeology as the principal means of testing the various theories. There are many unanswered questions concerning the quarrying, dressing and transportation of stone blocks and obelisks, but perhaps the greatest mystery of all surrounds the techniques by which both pyramids and obelisks were actually erected.

How did they align the pyramids so accurately?

In 1880–2, Flinders Petrie, the unquestioned father of modern archaeology in Egypt, undertook meticulous survey work on the Giza plateau, site of the pyramid complexes of the 4th-Dynasty rulers Khufu, Khafre and Menkaure of the mid-3rd millennium BC. His findings suggested the area was carefully levelled, probably by cutting a series of trenches as a grid and flooding them with water, then reducing the surrounding stone 'islands' to the desired level. A century later, the American Egyptologist Mark Lehner carefully mapped and studied the various holes and trenches cut into the bedrock around the Giza pyramids, and this led him to suggest that the process of fine levelling took place not over the whole area but simply along the narrow perimeter strips around the edges of the pyramid on which the lowest course of casing would be placed. The Giza pyramids each contained a core massif of bedrock (visible at a number of points inside the pyramids). These cores of natural rock would also have prevented the pyramid-builders from measuring diagonals to achieve a perfect square.

Judging from surviving tools, Egyptian architects, surveyors and builders used two particular implements, the *merkhet* and the *bay*, which allowed them to lay out straight lines and right-angles as well as orientating the sides and corners of structures in accordance with astronomical alignments.

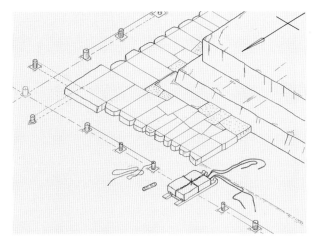

Left **Diagram of an early stage of pyramid construction, with stakes forming a line parallel to the base of each of its sides which may have formed a reference for orientation and levelling.** *Below* **Model of a wooden cradle or rocker – it is possible that such rockers were used to help move the pyramid blocks, though no full-scale examples have survived.**

British Egyptologist I. E. S. Edwards argued that true north was probably found by measuring the place where a particular star rose and fell in the west and east, then bisecting the angle between these two points. More recently, Kate Spence has put forward a convincing theory that the architects of the Great Pyramid sighted on two stars rotating around the position of the north pole (b-Ursae Minoris and z-Ursae Majoris), which would have been in perfect alignment around 2467 BC, when Khufu's pyramid is thought to have been constructed. This hypothesis is bolstered by the fact that inaccuracies in the orientations of earlier and later pyramids can be closely correlated with the degree to which the alignment deviates from true north.

How were the pyramids built?

The surviving evidence (particularly from unfinished pyramids) at such sites as Saqqara and Giza suggests that at least five different systems of ramps might have been used to convey the blocks up to their final positions in the pyramids. The easiest and most obvious method would have been the so-called linear ramp (probably used in the 3rd-Dynasty pyramid of Sekhemkhet at Saqqara), but in general the necessary width of such ramps would have meant that they were rarely used. The staircase ramp, a narrow set of steps leading up one face of the pyramid, would have been set at a steeper angle than others; traces of this type have been found at Sinki, Meidum, Giza, Abu Ghurob and Lisht. The principal objection to the spiral ramp (perhaps described in the 19th-Dynasty Papyrus Anastasi I), is the question of what it would have rested on and how corrective calculations and checks could have been made from the corners if most of the pyramid was covered up. The reversing ramp, a zigzag course up one face of a pyramid, would probably have been most effective for the construction of step pyramids, although, frustratingly, there are no signs of its use on the step pyramids at Saqqara, Sinki and Meidum.

Traces of interior ramps have survived inside the remains of the pyramids of Sahure, Niuserre and Neferirkare at Abusir and of Pepi II at Saqqara, but some kind of exterior ramp would still have been needed after the interior was filled in. It has been

Left **The 5th-Dynasty pyramids at Abusir, with their 4th-Dynasty predecessors at Giza visible in the background. Although the outer casing of fine limestone was removed in ancient times, the core blocks of these pyramids have survived.**

Right **Two of the three 18th-Dynasty obelisks still standing in their original locations in the Temple of Amun at Karnak.**

suggested that the terraced nature of the pyramid core would often have made it more convenient to use a series of much smaller ramps built along the sides of the pyramid from step to step. The remains of these would no doubt have been lost when the outer casing was applied. It is also possible that the causeways stretching from pyramid to valley temple might originally have served as builders ramps from quay to construction site (the quay being connected with the Nile by canal).

Apart from the question of the types of ramps employed, debate has also tended to centre on the methods by which individual stone blocks were raised into position. Since the Egyptians made no use of block-and-tackle methods or cranes, it is usually assumed that wooden and copper levers were used to manoeuvre the blocks into position.

What were the secrets of the obelisks?

One of the most distinctive icons of ancient Egyptian civilization was the obelisk, a tapering, needle-like stone monument, the tip of which was carved in the form of a miniature pyramid (also

known as a pyramidion or *benben*-stone). The first obelisks seem to have been erected in the temple of the sun god at Heliopolis during the Old Kingdom (*c.* 2575–2134 BC); by the New Kingdom (*c.* 1550–1070 BC), large monolithic examples, usually of granite or quartzite, were often erected in pairs in front of temples, such as those at Karnak and Luxor.

An unfinished granite obelisk, probably dating to the New Kingdom, still lies in the northern quarries at Aswan. With a length of 41.75 m (137 ft) and a planned weight of around 1150 tonnes, it would have been the largest monolithic obelisk ever cut if it had not been abandoned at a fairly late stage in the quarrying process, when a disastrous flaw appeared. Experiments by Reginald Engelbach, the British Egyptologist who first studied the Aswan obelisk, showed that it would have taken one person an hour to remove 5 mm (0.2 in) of stone from a strip 0.5 m (1 ft 8 in) wide across the obelisk, using a basalt pounder.

The very large size and weight of most obelisks means that the final stage – the raising of the obelisk into a stable, vertical position – was one of the most ambitious and dangerous of the technological achievements mastered by the Egyptians. Opinions of Egyptologists and engineers vary considerably as to how this was achieved. In the absence of any precise Egyptian information, one suggestion is that levers

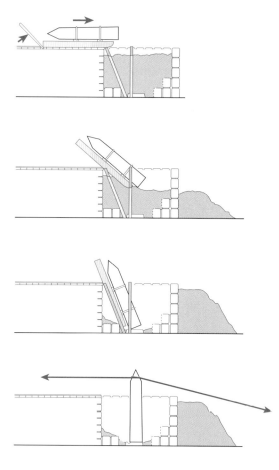

were used in combination with stones packed under the base and gradually removed, as well as the use of ropes in order to pull the obelisk the last few degrees into a vertical position, but this method would only really be feasible with relatively small examples. As far as larger obelisks were concerned, one suggestion was that the monument was slid gradually over a very steep artificial embankment, although this method would have required an almost impossible control over the huge mass of stone as it made its descent towards the pedestal. Each pedestal had a turning groove cut into it so that the obelisk could be correctly aligned before being raised into position.

Engelbach suggested that the obelisk could have been slid down into a funnel-shaped pit full of sand. The idea was that the sand was allowed to drain away out of the pit in such a careful way that the obelisk would gradually have settled into the correct vertical position. The inspiration for this theory was provided by the above-mentioned 19th-Dynasty Papyrus Anastasi I, which takes the form of a problem to be solved by a scribal pupil. This document includes the command: 'Empty the magazine that has been loaded with sand under the monument of your lord which has been brought from the Red Mountain ... with 100 chambers filled with sand from the river bank'.

Experiments with obelisks

Two different methods were attempted by a team of archaeologists and engineers in 1999, using a 25-ton, freshly quarried obelisk. The first attempt, conducted at Aswan, was the so-called swigging method, whereby complex sets of ropes and timber beams (an A-frame) were used to lower the obelisk gradually over the edge of an embankment, using a large log as a pivot and a granite block a counterweight. This eventually failed, primarily because the rocking action of the obelisk slowly moved the pivot dangerously close to the edge of the embankment.

An experimental version of Engelbach's sandpit theory, conducted near Boston, Massachusetts, was entirely successful, however. In this method, a concrete enclosure filled with sand was built in front of an embankment. An obelisk was tipped over the edge of the embankment and the sand was then gradually removed, causing the monument to descend gradually into a vertical position.

The moving and raising of obelisks was a major feat of organization, a task that has presented difficulties even to those who have attempted it in the 19th and 20th centuries AD, when obelisks were successfully re-erected in London, Paris and New York.

Opposite **Diagram of the sandpit method of erecting an obelisk, as hypothesized by the English archaeologist Reginald Engelbach. The obelisk is pushed on a sledge over the prepared pit filled with sand. The sand is gradually removed and the obelisk is lowered on to its base. The final steadying and positioning is done with ropes attached to the top of the stone, pulling in opposite directions.**

Right **Reconstruction of the swigging method of erecting an obelisk, attempted by a multi-national team of archaeologists and engineers near the granite quarries at Aswan, Egypt.**

The Riddle of the Sphinx

33

Time: c. 2500 BC
Location: Giza, Egypt

A thing with one voice, but four, then two, then three feet; nothing more changeable than this thing to be found in earth or sky or sea. When this thing goes on most feet, then its strength is at its weakest and its pace most slow.

RIDDLE POSED BY THE SPHINX TO OEDIPUS

The riddle most commonly associated with the sphinx is the one solved by Oedipus in Greek legend. More than one riddle, however, surrounds the Great Sphinx next to the pyramids at Giza, which was the distant ancestor of the malevolent Greek sphinx. When was it made? Who made it, and for whom? Are there any secret chambers inside it

or below it? The possible answers to these questions lie in a mixture of archaeology, ancient history and geology.

What is a sphinx?

The ancient Greeks thought that the word sphinx came from a Greek word meaning 'to strangle' (*sphingein*), but it seems likely that its real origin is the Egyptian phrase *shesep ankh* ('living image'), which was an epithet applied to sculpture and occasionally to the Great Sphinx itself. In Egypt sphinxes were usually portrayed with the body of a lion (identified with the sun god) and the head of a man, often wearing royal headgear such as the nemes-cloth. It is assumed that the combination of lion and man was intended to symbolize the union of the king with the sun god Re. One major difference between the Egyptian sphinxes and their Greek counterparts was that the earliest Egyptian versions were always male, until the Middle Kingdom (when the first winged sphinxes also began to be depicted).

The history of the Great Sphinx

The Great Sphinx, located beside the causeway of the pyramid of Khafre (*c.* 2500 BC), measures nearly 73 m (238 ft) long and a maximum of 20 m (66 ft) in height. Carved from a knoll of rock left behind after quarrying, over the centuries it was often almost completely buried by sand, though it has been repeatedly recleared.

An incomplete temple, apparently made from the same stone as the Sphinx itself, was built immedi-

Statue of Khafre, from his Valley Temple at Giza. It is likely that this pharaoh was responsible for creating the Sphinx, the head of which was probably carved in his image.

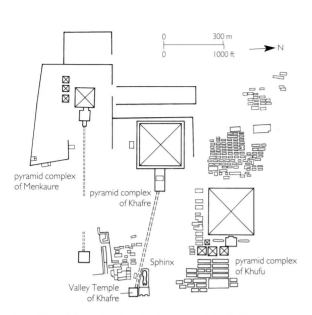

Above **Plan of Giza showing the location of the Sphinx, next to the Valley Temple of Khafre's pyramid.** Right **The Dream Stela between the paws of the Sphinx.** Below **The variation in erosion of different parts of the Sphinx has been shown to be due to the various geological layers that it was carved from.**

pyramid complex
of Menkaure

pyramid complex
of Khafre

Sphinx

Valley Temple
of Khafre

pyramid complex
of Khufu

0   300 m
0   1000 ft

N

ately in front of the monument in the 4th Dynasty (c. 2575–2465 BC). It was probably intended for the worship of the three forms of the sun: Khepri in the morning, Re at midday and Atum in the evening (a scenario which intriguingly parallels the three ages of humans in the Greek riddle of the sphinx quoted above). In the New Kingdom, the Sphinx was identified with Horemakhet ('Horus in the horizon'), perhaps inspired by the fact that the buried sphinx simply appeared to be the head of a colossal ruler emerging from the horizon. The most famous instance of reclearance was recorded on the 'Dream Stela' erected directly in front of the Sphinx by Thutmose IV (c. 1400 BC). The inscription describes the promise made to the young prince in a dream that if he rescued the Sphinx from the sand covering it he would become the next king.

As early as the 18th Dynasty (c. 1550–1307 BC), the Sphinx was already being reconstructed using limestone cladding, and at this date a standing royal statue was added between its paws. In recent years, there has been growing concern about the gradual deterioration of the monument, which lost its nose centuries ago. Fragments of its missing beard and uraeus were excavated by Giovanni Battista Caviglia

and later excavators and these are now in the British Museum and the Egyptian Museum, Cairo. More recently, erosion and rising ground water have become a problem, and the site has increasingly been subject to close environmental monitoring intended to identify the main causes for the monument's decay.

How old is the Sphinx?

Since the Sphinx is surrounded by 4th-Dynasty royal pyramid complexes and the mastaba-tombs of royal officials, it has usually been assumed that it was built at roughly the same date. In 1853, Auguste Mariette's excavation of the nearby Valley Temple of the 4th-Dynasty ruler Khafre suggested that this pharaoh was the likely creator of the monument, and that the Sphinx's head was probably carved in his image. The inscription on the 18th-Dynasty Dream Stela even includes a possible fragmentary reference to Khafre. Certainly, the various features of the head of the Sphinx, its nemes headcloth, its uraeus and its general physiognomy are comparable with royal statues of the 4th Dynasty.

However, this apparently convincing archaeological and art historical dating evidence was

The Sphinx, still mostly buried in the sand, as depicted in a lithograph by the artists of Napoleon's expedition to Egypt in the late 18th century.

temporarily shaken in 1992, when an American geologist, Robert Schoch, claimed to have found evidence showing that the rock of the Sphinx and its surrounding enclosure had been severely eroded by rainwater run-off at least 2500 years earlier than the 4th Dynasty. He argued first that this distinctive erosion had taken place only after the Sphinx's body had been carved, secondly that the high levels of rainfall necessary to create such weathering could only have occurred in the Neolithic period, between 7000 and 5000 BC, and thirdly that the monument and its temple had been built in two stages, the first being the carving of the core and the second the provision of casing blocks on the exterior. He explained the much later art historical dating of the head by suggesting that it might have been carved or re-carved by a 4th-Dynasty ruler.

Support for the conventional Egyptological dating of the Sphinx came from another American geologist, James Harrell, who suggested that the erosion might instead have been caused by a covering of saturated sand or floodwaters from the Nile. Harrell also argued that the

Computer reconstruction of the Sphinx, with a New Kingdom royal statue standing between its paws.

nature of the topography of the plateau would have caused rainwater to drain down towards the Sphinx, so that the levels of rainfall in the Old Kingdom might in fact have been sufficient to produce the weathering observed by Schoch, particularly if the rainwater saturated the sand surrounding the monument.

The archaeologist Mark Lehner, who directed a painstaking photogrammetric survey of the Sphinx in the 1980s, has refuted a number of Schoch's arguments, including the suggestion of a two-stage process of construction for the Sphinx and temples, which he points out was totally contrary to the known building methods employed by ancient Egyptians. A typical 4th-Dynasty pottery jar was

The Sphinx in Classical style, as imagined by the 17th-century Jesuit Athanasius Kircher, who never actually visited Egypt.

found at the western end of the Sphinx enclosure along with stone hammers with traces of copper, suggesting that tools of this type (not available in Egypt before the 4th millennium BC) were used to carve out the enclosure and presumably also the monument itself. In addition, a large stone block destined for the unfinished Sphinx temple was found immediately above a stratigraphic layer containing 4th-Dynasty pottery. Finally, Lehner argued that the unusually high numbers of large-scale statues excavated from Khafre's pyramid complex make it even more likely that he was the creator of the Sphinx.

Are there any secret chambers?

From at least the Middle Ages onwards, tales began to be told about secret chambers under the Sphinx. Two Arab writers (al-Makrizi and al-Kodai) described a chamber beneath the Sphinx from which three passages extended, each leading to one of the three pyramids. Stories of this kind were taken up by early European travellers, such as Johannes Helferich (1579), who described a tunnel leading up into the head, as a result of which ancient priests were said to have convinced worshippers that the Sphinx could utter oracles. The reliability of Helferich's account, however, is put into perspective by his publication of a woodcut depicting the Sphinx with breasts, as if it were the Greek female version.

Although the archaeological investigations of Caviglia (1816), Gaston Maspero (1881–1914), Émile Baraize (1926–34) and Selim Hassan (1936–8) revealed no secret chambers under either the Sphinx

or its temples, the association between the monument and a buried repository of secret knowledge was revived in the 1930s by Edgar Cayce, an American psychic. Cayce claimed that the wisdom of Atlantis had been placed in a subterranean hall of records associated with the Sphinx, and that its rediscovery during the 20th century would result in some huge disaster. Resistivity surveys in 1977–8 and 1992–3 revealed anomalies (fluctuations in electrical resistance perhaps caused by cavities) in the vicinity of the Sphinx, but subsequent work, including the use of electromagnetic surveys, showed that these anomalies were natural fissures and cavities.

Mark Lehner's study of the Sphinx has resulted in a much improved understanding of the various phases of construction and ancient and modern restoration of the monument. He has determined that there are three passages associated with the Sphinx. One is a small shaft which is known to have been drilled into the top of the neck (immediately behind the head), by Colonel Richard Vyse in the mid-19th century. The two others are of unknown date and do not appear to have contained any artifacts or inscriptions.

Thus the current evidence suggests that the Sphinx was neither a precocious Neolithic monument nor an Atlantean filing cabinet, but until we know precisely why it was sculpted and why we can find no obvious mention of it in Old Kingdom records, there will continue to be an aura of mystery around this most colossal of Egyptian statues.

Below **Modern photogrammetric survey of the Sphinx has mapped out the monument in immense detail.**

Where Was the Land of Punt?

34

Time: c. 2450–1170 BC
Location: Somalia/Sudan/Ethiopia?

Turning my face to sunrise I created a wonder for you, I made the lands of Punt come here to you, with all the fragrant flowers of their lands, to beg your peace and breathe the air you give.

STELA IN THE MORTUARY TEMPLE OF AMENHOTEP III

FOR AT LEAST THIRTEEN HUNDRED YEARS – from the reign of King Sahure (*c.* 2450 BC) until the time of Ramesses III (*c.* 1170 BC) – the ancient Egyptians periodically sent trading expeditions to a region they knew as Punt. Although it is clear that Punt lay somewhere to the south of Egypt, modern scholars have long argued over its precise location and the particular land or sea routes taken by Egyptian trading missions.

Our evidence for the nature of the land of Punt and its inhabitants consists of a mixture of textual and pictorial information. The painted scenes and inscriptions indicate that traders were sent there to obtain such exotic products as gold, aromatic resins, fine woods, ivory and wild animals (such as giraffes, monkeys and cynocephalous baboons). Scenes in certain New Kingdom temples and tombs depict the inhabitants of Punt as a people with a dark reddish complexion and fine features; they were shown with

long hair in the earlier paintings, but from the late 18th Dynasty onwards they were portrayed with a more close-cropped hairstyle.

The location of Punt was once identified with the region of modern Somalia, but a strong argument has now been made for its location in either southern Sudan or the Eritrean region of Ethiopia, where the indigenous plants and animals equate most closely with those depicted in the reliefs and paintings or described in the texts.

The Punt scenes of Queen Hatshepsut

A particularly elaborate set of scenes in the cult temple of Queen Hatshepsut at Deir el-Bahri was perhaps painted to commemorate the resumption

Relief scenes from Hatshepsut's temple at Deir el-Bahri showing Parahu, ruler of Punt, and Ati his wife *(left)***, and the saddled donkey that carried her** *(right)***. It was still relatively unusual for Egyptians to ride donkeys or horses at this time.**

Left **A modern-day Dinka village in Sudan, with houses raised on stilts, very similar to the houses of the Puntites as depicted on reliefs at Queen Hatshepsut's temple at Deir el-Bahri (below).**

Right **Map showing three suggested locations of Punt. The southernmost (Somalia) is now regarded as unlikely, and the consensus is that the country lay somewhere between Eritrea and Sudan.**

of trading contact with Punt after a long period of inactivity. The scenes include depictions of very distinctive Puntite settlements, with conical reed-built huts built on poles above the ground, entered via ladders. Among the surrounding vegetation depicted at Deir el-Bahri are palms and myrrh trees, some of the latter already being hacked apart to extract the myrrh.

The ruler of Punt (distinguished from the Egyptians primarily by his long beard and unusual costume) is seen emerging from the settlement to greet the Egyptian trading party. The ruler's name is given as Parahu, and it is implied that he is the sole leader of the Puntites. However, many of the other inscriptions suggest that the Egyptians encountered several different groups in Punt, each with their own leader, in the same way that the peoples of Lower and Upper Nubia were divided into various named tribes. It is possible that Parahu was the ruler of a loose confederation of chiefdoms or the representative of a coastal group acting as middle-men between the Egyptians and the more inland regions of Punt.

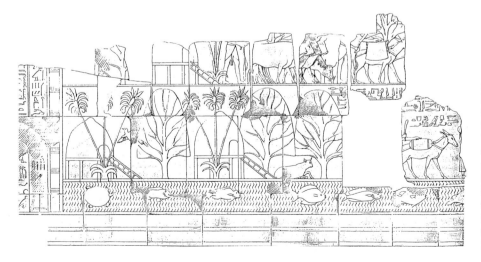

A scene from the reliefs on Hatshepsut's temple at Deir el-Bahri showing a Puntite village, with houses on stilts. The fish depicted are characteristic of the Red Sea and Indian Ocean. Queen Hatshepsut's soldiers brought back myrrh trees from Punt, and these may have been planted at Deir el-Bahri, as tree-pits have been found there.

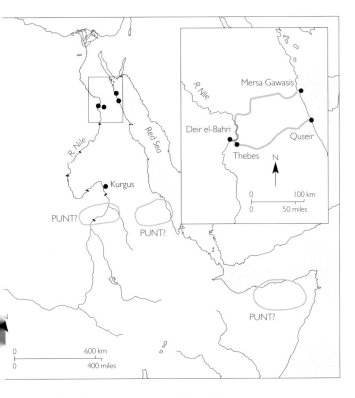

made by sailing south up the Nile to the 4th cataract, then either trading with Puntites in the vicinity of the fortress at Kurgus or taking an overland route direct to Punt itself (or perhaps to one of the regions between Punt and Nubia).

The argument for the combined Nile and overland route, as opposed to the Red Sea voyage, has been suggested by an American Egyptologist, Louise Bradbury. She points out that scenes in the 18th-Dynasty tomb of Min, Chief Treasurer in the reigns of Thutmose III and Amenhotep II, show him overseeing a trading encounter with Puntites, who are apparently arriving in flat rafts more suited to river transport than the rigours of the Red Sea. She also argues that the lack of New Kingdom inscriptions in the eastern part of the Wadi Hammamat makes it less likely that this overland/Red Sea route was frequently used at this date, whereas the large numbers of 18th-Dynasty graffiti at Kurgus suggest that this site was operating as a busy emporium for Puntite and Egyptian traders.

Even after Punt had become firmly established as a trading partner, it continued to be regarded as a kind of distant Shangri-La. In the Middle Kingdom story of The Shipwrecked Sailor the eponymous hero encounters a magic serpent supplying myrrh and describing himself as the King of Punt. After the end of the New Kingdom (c. 1070 BC), however, Punt is rarely mentioned in Egyptian records. The last surviving reference to the region occurs on a fragmentary 26th-Dynasty stela (c. 600 BC), and even here the emphasis has shifted from trade to climate, with an intriguing description of Punt as a mountainous area where high rainfall could affect the height of the Nile flood down in Egypt.

A land or sea route to Punt?

It has usually been assumed that trading parties travelled from Thebes to Punt in two stages: first on foot across the Eastern Desert and then by boat down the Red Sea coast (probably embarking from the ports of Quseir or Mersa Gawasis). Although the Deir el-Bahri images confirm the arrival and departure of at least one major Punt expedition by boat via the Red Sea (the fish in the waters around Hatshepsut's fleet are marine species rather than riverine), it seems possible that some contacts might also have been

Right **Part of a relief scene from the mortuary temple of Sahure at Abusir, showing Egyptian ships on an expedition to Punt in about 2450 BC.**

Was Tutankhamun Murdered?

35

Time: *c.* 1323 BC
Location: Thebes, Egypt

My husband is dead and I have no son ... I am afraid.

ANKHESENAMUN, QUEEN OF EGYPT, WIDOW OF TUTANKHAMUN, *C.* 1323 BC

THE DISCOVERY OF the tomb of the Egyptian pharaoh Tutankhamun (*c.* 1333–1323 BC) by Howard Carter in 1922 dazzled the world. Its four chambers contained well over 2000 objects, which revealed the incredible wealth of a pharaoh at the zenith of Egypt's ancient power. Among the most awe-inspiring was the king's innermost coffin, made of over 10 kg (22 lb) of solid gold, and within it was the kernel of the tomb, the mummy of the king himself. Although in very poor condition, the body provided one of the key facts about the king: that he had died at a tender age of no more than 20 years.

The first autopsy was carried out by Dr Douglas Derry in 1925, shortly after the coffins were opened. He noted noted a lesion '[o]n the left cheek ... a

Left **One of the greatest treasures from Tutankhamun's tomb is the boy-king's second, gilded-wood coffin. It was originally made for another king but, like a large number of other objects found in Tutankhamun's tomb, had been appropriated for his burial equipment.**

Right **The mummy of Tutankhamun. The body has a number of unusual features, including a missing front part of the rib-cage. This may be linked with the position of the arms, laid over the stomach area. In other royal mummies of the period, they are crossed over the chest.**

rounded depression, the skin filling it resembling a scab. Round the circumference of the depression, which had slightly raised edges, the skin was discoloured'; he was unable to express any opinion as to the cause of death.

X-rays taken in 1968 by Professor R.G. Harrison allowed tuberculosis to be ruled out. A shot of the skull showed a stray fragment of bone within, and a defect which might indicate a haemorrhage, conceivably caused by a blow to the head. The X-rays also revealed that the front of the rib-cage was missing, presumably removed during the embalming process. It has been suggested that the king might have suffered a catastrophic chest injury that could only be 'cleaned up' for burial by radical post-mortem surgery. However, there are no signs of other injuries, and it may be simply another of the unexplained variations on the standard embalming process that turn up every so often in the archaeological record.

Thus, there is no unequivocal physical evidence of the cause of Tutankhamun's death. However, many have suspected that foul play might have been involved, particularly in view of the circumstantial

Queen Ankhesenamun, third daughter of Akhenaten and wife of Tutankhamun. After her husband's death, having borne only two still-born daughters, she wrote to the King of the Hittites offering to marry one of his sons and make him pharaoh.

Below left **Ay performs the funeral rites of Tutankhamun, as shown on the wall of the latter's burial chamber. Under Egyptian law, carrying out a person's burial confirmed one's status as heir. Although common in private tombs, such a scene is not otherwise found in a royal sepulchre, and may indicate Ay's need to emphasize his legitimacy in the wake of the events surrounding Tutankhamun's death.**

evidence provided by events both before and after the young king's death.

The boy king

Tutankhamun was the successor, and probably the son, of the 'heretic' pharaoh, Akhenaten, who had abolished the traditional polytheistic religion of Egypt in favour of a single sun god, the Aten. Even while Akhenaten was still alive there had apparently been moves back towards the ancient cults, and with that pharaoh's death, the forces of counter-reformation gained in power.

As a child of no more than 10, Tutankhamun was under the protection of high officials, notably a group of army generals headed by Ay and Horemheb, the latter holding the title of King's Deputy. Ay was possibly the father of Nefertiti, who was the wife of Akhenaten and the mother of Tutankhamun's wife, Ankhesenamun. Under the generals' direction, the king had officially returned to the traditional religion and undertaken a major temple restoration programme. However, by the time he had reached his late 'teens, Tutankhamun would have been in a position to make his own decisions, which may – or may not – have coincided with the views of his advisors.

The fact that the king was dead within a short time of attaining adulthood has been regarded as suspicious. And the fact that his successor was none other than the general Ay, his erstwhile advisor, has also been entered into the equation. There was also a remarkable correspondence between Queen Ankhesenamun and the King of the Hittites (an empire roughly corresponding to modern Turkey). The queen states that her husband is dead, that she is unwilling to marry one of her subjects and make him king, that she wishes to marry a Hittite prince instead – and that she is 'afraid'. Many have assumed that the 'subject' in mind is Ay.

A Hittite prince was sent, but was killed *en route* to Egypt. Ay duly became king, seemingly having married Ankhesenamun, who disappeared shortly afterwards. While this could be interpreted as more skulduggery by Ay, it should be noted that Ankhesenamun's offer of the Egyptian throne to a foreigner would have been tantamount to treason. Indeed, *if*

Tutankhamun was murdered, Ankhesenamun could be suggested as the culprit, plotting to rule thereafter through a foreign husband, backed by Hittite military power. Such an alternative scenario, far from casting Ay as a villain would make him the defender of Egypt's liberty against a criminal, scheming queen!

However, it must be emphasized that no examination of the body has revealed conclusive evidence as to the cause of death, and that all such scenarios are merely potential interpretations of extremely sketchy evidence. All that can be said with certainty is that Tutankhamun died young; while murder is certainly a possibility, so are a whole range of alternatives. As far as violent death is concerned, blocks from a now-demolished temple strongly suggest that Tutankhamun may have taken part in military campaigns, despite his tender years: could he have died in battle? And the possibility that his death was merely accidental or natural cannot, on the available evidence, be ruled out; it is quite probable that we will never know.

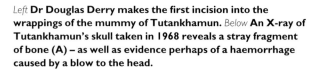

Left **Dr Douglas Derry makes the first incision into the wrappings of the mummy of Tutankhamun.** *Below* **An X-ray of Tutankhamun's skull taken in 1968 reveals a stray fragment of bone (A) – as well as evidence perhaps of a haemorrhage caused by a blow to the head.**

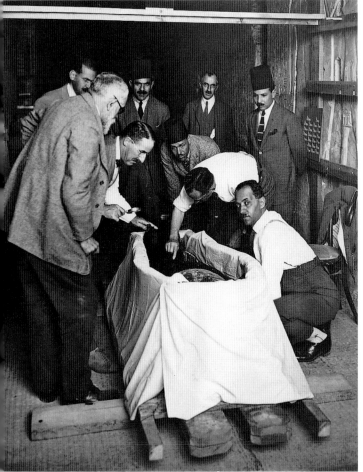

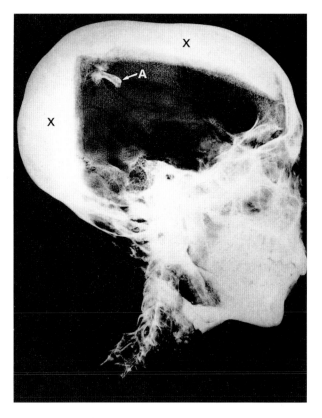

The Tarim Mummies: Who Were They?

36

Time: 1800 BC–AD 400
Location: western China

It was not without a strange emotion that I looked down on a figure which, but for the parched skin and the deep-sunk eye cavities, seemed like that of a man asleep, and found myself thus suddenly brought face to face with a representative of the indigenous people who had inhabited, and no doubt had liked, this dreary Lop region in the early centuries of our era.

AUREL STEIN, 1928

THE BEST-PRESERVED MUMMIES in the world do not come from Egypt or Peru – they are found in the sands of the Täklimakan, the vast desert of western China that forms much of the Tarim Basin. Unlike the mummies of the ancient Egyptians, the Incas and their predecessors, whose civilizations sought to preserve the human form artificially after death, the mummies of the Tarim were preserved naturally in the arid and salt-laden sands of Eurasia's second greatest desert.

The Tarim mummies were first discovered at the turn of the 20th century, when Western expeditions by Sven Hedin of Sweden, Albert Von La Coq of Germany and Aurel Stein of Britain sought to uncover the antiquities of the oasis towns that formed the northern and southern spines of the Silk Road linking China to the West. These early expeditions excavated mummies, photographed and described them, but no facilities existed to preserve or transport them to Western museums.

Mummified man from Zaghunluq (c. 1000–600 BC), with ochre spirals about his temples and a strap to bind his mouth closed in death.

It is only recently that Chinese and Uyghur archaeologists have been able to make more scientific investigations of the region, and it is their truly spectacular discoveries of mummified remains that has awakened international attention. There are at least 300 mummies now known from western China which date from *c.* 1800 BC until the historic period when the Han dynasty attempted to extend its power westwards in the first centuries BC. Even more mummies are known from the historic period.

Tombs and textiles

There is in fact no mummy people: the mummies derive from different sites and cultures, primarily along the southwestern and northwestern sections of the ancient Silk Road. Archaeologists have uncovered their remains in shallow pit graves, deep pits covered with layers of reeds, brushwood, timber logs and animal hides, and brick-built chambers. The earliest mummified remains, uncovered at the cemetery of Qäwrighul and other sites in the vicinity of the desiccated salt-lake of Lopnur, are clothed in the simplest of wrappings, effectively woollen blankets, but after 1000 BC we find individuals fully dressed and boasting feathered caps (one man was buried with no fewer than ten caps), shirts, cloaks, trousers and colourful woollen stockings; and, even more striking, plaid tartans! At Subeshi on the northern route of the Silk Road three women were found with enormously tall hats resembling the oversized head-gear of witches.

The mummies provide an enormous quantity of prehistoric clothing for the textile experts, who are only now beginning to analyse the remains in detail. But the greatest mystery concerning these mummies derives from their faces. These are not those of the Mongoloid physical type who dominate East Asia today: the light hair and beards clearly indicate that these early settlers of the Tarim region were Caucasoids or Europoids. Identifying these strangers from the west is one of the major mysteries of recent archaeological discovery.

Who were they?

Before the Bronze Age, that is *c.* 1800 BC, the archaeology of Xinjiang is very poorly known, and the first settlement of the region remains so obscure that we can only speculate as to who was first to settle in the uninviting world of the Tarim Basin. But for the Bronze and Iron ages, the overwhelming body of evidence suggests that it was primarily people of

Below **One of three women from Subeshi (c. 500–400 BC) with long tall 'witches' hats. She wears a woollen skirt and blouse, leather shoes and a sheepskin cloak. Her left hand is still covered with a leather mitten, while her right hand is bare.**

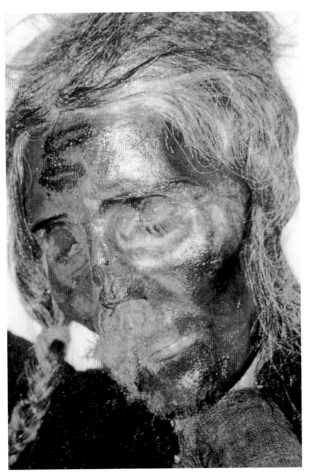

Woman from Zaghunluq (c. 1000–600 BC) with tattoos on her forehead and eyelids. Her eyebrows had recently been painted in black and her hair is braided.

Caucasoid stock who migrated either from the western mountain ranges or northern steppes. Besides the mummies we have skeletal remains, and of these only 11 per cent of the over 300 prehistoric human skulls examined so far belong to people of the Mongoloid physical type, and these are found primarily to the east of Xinjiang. It seems apparent that the early Chinese farmers of Gansu Province, immediately to the west of Xinjiang, found little to attract them into the desert oases.

So who were these people that fortune has preserved so well? If they belonged to a totally anonymous group who did not survive to be recorded in written history, we might remain eternally in the dark and could at best assign them the names of the various archaeological cultures that have been identified for the Bronze and Iron ages of Xinjiang. However, there is some reason to hope that

their descendants did survive into the written record; indeed, many believe that their descendants left their own accounts of their existence.

The Tarim Basin has preserved not only a large quantity of human and other organic remains, but also a vast library of early manuscripts – this was one of the first regions of China to adopt Buddhism, a religion that placed great emphasis on the written word. Many of the manuscripts are in the more recently imported languages of India, such as Sanskrit, and confined to the Buddhist monasteries. Others, however, contain the languages of the native populations and these may be divided into two major groups. The first is Khotanese or Khotanese Saka, spoken in and around the ancient town of Khotan in the south Tarim and in some of the oases of the northwest of the Tarim Basin. The language belongs to the Iranian group which includes Persian and many of the languages of west Central Asia; the closest language to Saka was probably that of the steppe nomads whom history records in Europe as the Scythians. Although the language is well represented in the south and western parts of the Tarim Basin, the mummies are primarily concentrated in the southeast and northeast where we have no evidence of Khotanese. Iranian languages are attested in these areas but these are generally trade languages and not the common language of the people.

Tocharians

The northeast of the Tarim and Turpan basins as well as the region around Lopnur, all areas from which we recover most remains of mummies, coincide better with the later distribution of the Tocharian languages. Tocharian is a group of the Indo-European languages, that is it derives from the same prehistoric ancestor to which most of the languages of Europe are assigned, as well as the Iranian and Indian languages of Asia (p. 141–3). In the best-attested Tocharian language we may read *pācer, mācer, procer, ser, keu, okso, $\bar{a}_u$, twere, ñuwe* which are cognate, i.e., share the same Indo-European ancestor, with English *father, mother, brother, sister, cow, ox, ewe, door* and *new* respectively. Although we have no pure Tocharian texts from the southern region of the Silk Road, Indic documents there are filled with native loanwords and personal names which linguists suggest represent the Tocharian substrate.

Tocharians are portrayed in paintings on the walls of Buddhist caves dating from the early Middle Ages,

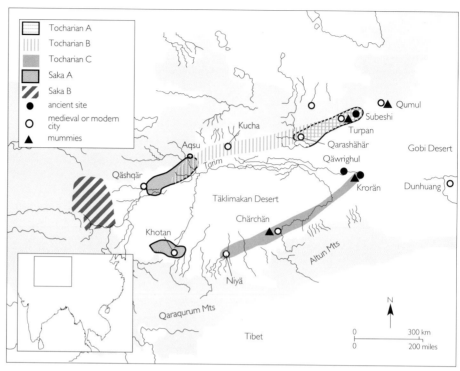

and here we find a population – much like that of the mummies – depicted with Caucasoid features and light hair, eyes and beards. DNA analysis of one of the prehistoric mummies has indicated that it shares the same genetic inheritance as is typical among some 40 per cent of modern Europeans. The tartans found with the mummies after 1000 BC are remarkably similar to the earliest tartans in Europe, from the site of Hallstatt in the Austrian Alps. Elizabeth Barber has proposed that the European and Tarim tartans share a distant common origin north of the Caucasus, for this is where the earliest evidence for such fabrics is known.

The Tocharian languages appear to have separated from the other Indo-European languages at a very early date and developed in isolation from their immediate neighbours, those who spoke Indic and Iranian languages. It has been suggested that the ancestors of these Tocharians may have been part of a substantial movement of a Caucasoid population eastwards from the Volga-Ural region some time in the mid-4th millennium BC. These people, known as the Afanasevans, settled in the Minusinsk Basin and the Altai mountains to the north of Xinjiang. There is some evidence that the Afanasevans may have moved southwards by c. 2000 BC to settle in the Tarim Basin.

Although far from substantiated, this model does provide an attractive explanation for how an isolated Indo-European language, spoken by a population originally deriving from Europe, found its way into the west of the Tarim Basin. Such a movement would also provide a linguistic identity for the earliest mummies.

Above left **Depiction of a Tocharian monk (on the left) from Bezäklik (9th–10th centuries AD).** *Above right* **The location of the mummies (triangles) correlates better with the Tocharians than the Iranian Saka.** *Below* **The earliest Bronze Age settlers of the Tarim Basin, the Qäwrighul culture, may have come from the south Siberian Afanasevo culture.**

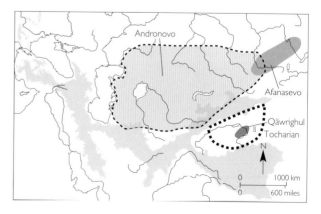

Were the Olmecs African?

37

Time: 1200–900 BC
Location: southeast Mexico

I was struck with surprise: as a work of art, it [Tres Zapotes Colossal Head 1] is without exaggeration a magnificent sculpture ... but what astonished me was the Ethiopian type represented. I reflected that there had undoubtedly been Negroes in this country, and that this had been in the first epoch of the world.

MELGAR Y SERRANO, 1869

WERE THE OLMECS, creators of ancient Mesoamerica's oldest civilization, migrants from Africa? All the evidence indicates that they were Native Americans descended from Paleo-Indians who entered the Americas from northeast Asia. Furthermore, there is absolutely no evidence to support the suggestion that Africans reached the Americas prior to the voyages of Columbus. Archaeologists have not identified a single African artifact, plant or animal remain, human skeleton, linguistic element, or any other concrete evidence of African presence in Olmec country or elsewhere in the Americas. How then, a reasonable person might ask, did this question ever arise, and why?

Background

While visiting a sugar *hacienda* in southern Mexico's Tuxtla mountains in 1862, José Melgar y Serrano was shown a giant human head carved from basalt uncovered by a worker there several years before. Melgar, an educated man interested in ancient Old World civilizations as well as those of his native land, realized that the sculpture – now known as Tres Zapotes Colossal Head 1 – was a highly unusual find. In later years he speculated on the meaning of the head, and the ethnic identity of the person depicted, in two published articles. The diffusionist ideas that dominated the intellectual climate of the time held that, like their oppressed 19th-century descendants, pre-Columbian Native Americans must have lacked sufficient intelligence or capacity for culture to create large or beautiful works of art. Thus, Melgar assumed that migrants from the Old World must have carved the head and identified the personage as an African, specifically an 'Ethiopian'.

Melgar's head lay almost completely forgotten until 1939 when archaeologist Matthew W. Stirling cleared it once again in the course of his pioneering investigations of Olmec culture. Stirling's investigations at Tres Zapotes, La Venta, Cerro de las Mesas and San Lorenzo brought Olmec culture to the attention of the scholarly world, while his widely read articles in *National Geographic* magazine made the Olmecs a household name.

Subsequent investigations into Olmec culture have recovered hundreds of stone sculptures, including 17 other Colossal Heads. Most modern scholars believe

Matthew W. Stirling making the first scientific observations on the Tres Zapotes colossal head in 1939.

these unusual monuments are portraits of living or recently deceased Olmec rulers. Interestingly, none of the other 17 look particularly 'African' and in fact no professional archaeologist since Melgar's time has ever accepted his ethnic identification of the Tres Zapotes head. How then did the question of African Olmecs emerge as a serious concern in recent times?

The modern myth

In a recent comprehensive examination of the issue, Gabriel Haslip-Viera and his associates trace the history of the idea to the writings of Ivan Van Sertima, particularly his book *They Came Before Columbus* (1976). Van Sertima, who is not an archaeologist, argues that 'Negroid' Africans made numerous voyages to the Americas long before Columbus' voyages and created or at least strongly influenced the earliest civilizations of Mesoamerica and South America. Although no serious scholar accepts these claims, they have become a central foundation myth for the contemporary Afrocentric movement in North America. According to Haslip-Viera, Afrocentric revisionist history argues that 'all the world's early civilizations, including those of ancient Egypt, ancient Mesopotamia, India, China, Europe, and the Americas, were created or inspired by racially "black" peoples'.

Van Sertima and other writers cite five basic lines of evidence to support their claims: written documents from various times and places in the Old World; the 'Negroid' features depicted on Olmec Colossal Heads; architectural correspondences between Olmec earth mounds and the stone pyramids of Egypt and Nubia; plants native to one hemisphere found in the other; and the practice of mummification in the Americas. Haslip-Viera and his colleagues examine the evidence for each claim in detail and refute every one of them.

Given the prominent role the Olmecs played in the origins of Mesoamerican civilization, it is not surprising that Afrocentrists have revived the fanciful ideas of a 19th-century savant to bolster their claims. Ironically, they also perpetuate the equally mistaken racist ideas of the same period, ideas that relegated Native Americans to an inferior status incapable of major cultural developments on a par with peoples of the ancient Old World.

Tres Zapotes Colossal Head 1: the features may represent a compromise between the minimal removal of stone from the basalt boulder and the need to portray an actual living or recently deceased ruler.

Why Did the Carthaginians Sacrifice Children?

38

Time: 8th–2nd century BC
Location: Carthage, Tunisia

Out of reverence for Kronos (Ba'al Hammon), the Phoenicians, and especially the Carthaginians, whenever they seek to obtain some great favour, vow one of their children, burning it as a sacrifice to the deity, if they are especially eager to gain success.

CLEITARCHUS, LATE 4TH CENTURY BC

CARTHAGE was settled in what is now north-eastern Tunisia by Phoenicians from the eastern Mediterranean as their 'New City' (Kart Hadasht). Tradition ascribes the foundation to Queen Dido, and the year to 814 BC, although nothing in the archaeological record has been found so far which predates the mid-8th century BC. Carthage's position at the very centre of the Mediterranean and its control of a fertile hinterland enabled it to expand and flourish, and in the 4th and 3rd centuries BC it ruled a considerable empire. Its sway extended over much of present-day Tunisia as well as over many settlements on the North African coast from Morocco to western Libya; in addition there were overseas possessions in Sicily, Sardinia and Spain. Carthage's territorial ambitions, however, brought it into conflict with that other contemporary Mediterranean

View of Carthage from the Byra hill: the *tophet* lay to the right (west) of the Punic harbour, just visible in the middle distance.

superpower, Rome. The resulting power struggle was fought out in three Punic Wars, culminating in the utter destruction and humiliation of Carthage at the hands of Rome in 146 BC.

Baal and Tanit

The deities of the Carthaginian pantheon were dominated by the sky-god Baal and his companion Tanit, often enigmatically described in inscriptions as 'face of Baal', i.e. the female counterpart or 'reflection' of Baal. Whereas Baal was a familiar deity in the Phoenician homelands, Tanit was not, and in Carthage she took over from Astarte as the principal female divinity after her introduction in the 5th century BC. Baal was a somewhat remote and frightening deity: god of the remote hill regions, especially of mountain tops, but also of the fertile plains, he was also lord of the sky – a god, in other words, of the entire universe. Tanit, TNT in Carthaginian (neo-Punic) script, 'Thanneth' or 'Thinith' in Greek, was above all a goddess of the sky, and therefore provider of the rain which was such a vital contributor to agricultural prosperity; she was also the principal guardian deity of the city of Carthage.

Places of sacrifice

Both Baal and Tanit demanded and received heavy sacrifices, which took place in the sacred open-air precincts, known as *tophet*. In Carthage it is clear from the many thousands of *tophet* inscriptions that it was principally Tanit who was the focus of cult and sacrifice; the 800 dedications from the *tophet* at Constantine in eastern Algeria, on the other hand, are mainly in honour of Baal. Other *tophet* have been excavated at Sousse in Tunisia, at Sulcis (Sant'Antioco), Tharros and Monte Sirai in Sardinia, and at Motya in Sicily. The term *tophet* does not occur on inscriptions but is used in the Bible to refer to places in the Phoenician homelands where child sacrifice took place (Jeremiah 7: 31–2; II Kings 23: 10).

The *tophet* at Carthage was discovered in 1921, some 50 m (165 ft) west of the site of the Punic artificial harbours on the southern edge of the ancient city. It consisted of a vast open-air walled precinct covering at least 6000 sq. m (64,500 sq. ft). Excavations over many years have revealed thousands of urns containing partially cremated bones, each pot buried in a pebble-lined pit. Most were marked at the surface, at first by a small carved throne or a stone block (*cippus*) carved with a betyl (an oval or bottle-shaped stone, a representation of the deity). From the 4th century BC

onwards, however, it was customary to place a tall stone slab (stela) bearing simple relief or incised carving, and sometimes also an inscription in honour of Baal and Tanit, together with the name of the dedicator. Fashions in the form and decoration of these stelae inevitably varied over time; especially common was the depiction at the apex of the 'sign of Tanit' – a triangle surmounted by a horizontal bar and circle. One stela, now in the Bardo Museum in Tunis,

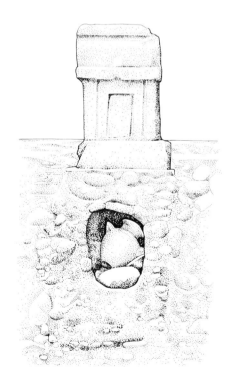

Left **These stelae came from excavations of the Carthage *tophet* and have been arranged in a garden and so are not in their original positions.** *Right* **A stela with the sign of Tanit, dedicated by Hanno, son of Mathan-Baal, 2nd–1st century BC.**

appears to show a Priest with a baby (presumed to be a sacrificial victim) in the crook of his arm.

Although there were clearly fluctuations in frequency, dedications at the Carthage *tophet* are continuous between the mid-8th century BC and the destruction of the city in 146 BC, and it has been estimated that an average of approximately 100 urns were deposited each year, making a total of some 60,000 sacrifices in all.

Left **Diagram to illustrate the position of the sacrifice (the incinerated bones were placed in the urn and buried below ground), and the stela on the surface above, marking its position.** *Right* **Stela in the Bardo Museum, Tunis, 3rd century BC, showing a man (a priest?) with a flat cap and hand raised in an act of reverence, carrying a child in the crook of his left arm (for sacrifice?).**

Modern excavations

The excavations in the Carthage *tophet* in the late 1970s have provided the first detailed statistical figures for these depositions. The cremated bones consisted of both human and animal remains, but contrary to what was expected, there was not a gradual substitution of human sacrifice by animal offerings. Animal sacrifice constitutes as much as a third of the total in the earliest depositions, whereas in the 4th century BC this figure had dropped to as little as one urn in ten: 90 per cent of the remains of sacrifices at that period were human. A further distinction is that whereas in earliest times (8th–6th centuries BC) the bones were those of still-born or neonatal babies, the majority of the sacrifices in the 4th century BC are of children between the ages of 1 and 3; in fact as many as a third of the urns at this time contain the remains of two and sometimes even three children.

Why sacrifice children?

The reason for these changes, and indeed why human sacrifice was thought necessary at all, is hard to explain in the absence of explicit written testimony. It would be tempting to think that the switch from sacrificing new-born infants to that of killing toddlers was prompted by military or economic crisis, but such a neat link is unprovable and probably unlikely. In particular, the evidence for *tophet* ritual in the final period leading up to the biggest crisis of all, the destruction of Carthage in 146 BC, was largely erased by later Roman activity and cannot therefore be accurately assessed.

Various hypotheses have been advanced. The votive inscriptions show a clear predominance of wealthy dedicants, and it is possible that it became the practice of the Carthaginian élite to sacrifice their first-born, recalling the biblical command that 'the first-born of thy sons shalt thou likewise give to me' (Exodus 22: 28). Unfortunately, the condition of the bones does not allow their sex to be determined, though early DNA tests have been able to establish sex in a few cases. DNA may also be able to show whether the multiple infants in some urns came from the same family or not. Some have seen infant sacrifice as a form of birth control, akin to the Spartan practice of exposing unwanted children on a hillside to die. The sacrifice of older children, however, is harder to explain. It has been suggested that a baby was promised to Tanit while still in the womb, and if it proved to be still-born an older child in the same family was sacrificed in its place; but such a practice presupposes a very high incidence of infant mortality.

Sabatino Moscati has suggested that the Greek and Roman authors (and the biblical writers) were peddling vicious anti-Semitic propaganda, and that both babies and young children had already died from natural causes before they were incinerated. Such a view, however, contradicts everything that we know about the act of 'sacrifice' in the ancient world, which must involve hardship (in this case to the parents) for it to stand any chance of being successful with the deity – rather than counting merely as an alternative method of disposal of the dead. Forensic archaeologist Charlotte Roberts has also studied the bones of 20 infants from the Motya *tophet* and found no signs of disease or ill-health.

After the Roman take-over in North Africa, the cult of Baal and Tanit continued under a thin Romanizing veneer: the deities were renamed Saturn and Caelestis, and their worship endured strongly until the advent of Christianity. Even the site of the *tophet* at Carthage was not forgotten: there is some evidence that both Saturn and Caelestis were honoured there under the Romans. But the practice of human sacrifice, the one aspect of foreign religions everywhere that Rome did not tolerate, appears to have stopped in 146 BC, in Carthage and elsewhere. Nevertheless the notion that the animal now offered was only a 'substitute' (*vicarius*) for a human being was not forgotten, as some stelae inscriptions make clear, and the 3rd-century AD Christian apologist, Tertullian, even darkly muttered that human sacrifice continued in some parts of Africa in his own day. Re-excavation under modern conditions of those *tophet* which continued after 146 BC, like Sousse and Constantine, together with detailed examination of the burnt bones, may one day be able to test whether Tertullian was right; but even if he was not, his testimony is a vivid reminder that the practice of Carthaginian child sacrifice was still remembered nearly four centuries after the fall of Carthage.

Stelae still in position in the *tophet* at Carthage, with a later (Roman) vaulted structure above.

Ancient Oracles: Prophets or Profiteers?

Time: c. 6th century BC–4th century AD
Location: Greece

The lord whose Oracle is in Delphi neither speaks out nor conceals, but gives a sign.

HERACLITUS, 6TH CENTURY BC

THE ANCIENT GREEKS believed gods spoke to mortals and might offer guidance about the future. Divine communication was part of daily life. Seers travelled from city to city selling prophecies or offering to interpret omens. The pattern of a bird's flight, remains of a sacrifice, images in a dream, even the timing of a sneeze – any of these signs might, if construed correctly, reveal the gods' will.

The divine messages considered most significant by the Greeks were delivered by Oracles. These were fixed sites, usually sanctuaries, where gods or heroes could be directly consulted. (The same word is used for both the sites and the messages they produced: here Oracles will be used for the former and oracles for the latter.) The most famous Oracle is, and was, that of Apollo at Delphi, but numerous others are mentioned throughout ancient literature.

The popularity of individual Oracles rose and fell over the centuries – new sites sprang up, others fell into disuse. Nevertheless, for over 1000 years individuals and city states visited these institutions for guidance on crucial decisions and in return presented them with elaborate gifts, often extraordinary treasures of great value.

But what kind of help visitors to Oracles received has long posed a puzzle. Many of the well-known stories in ancient Greek literature portray their messages (especially those from Delphi) as tricky and misleading – often with catastrophic results for their recipients. It is unclear why the Greeks wanted to trust Oracles with important decisions. Nor are we certain about the methods of prophecy used at these sites. The mystery of the Oracles continues to seduce – and stump – scholars today.

Raving women and turbulent priests?

The Oracle of Apollo at Delphi has received the most attention in both ancient literature and modern scholarship. Here the prophetess (called the 'Pythia') was believed to enjoy divine inspiration, considered the most prestigious method of prophecy among the ancients. How this worked is controversial. Tradition asserted that she entered a state of divine ecstasy brought on by chewing laurel leaves and inhaling intoxicating vapours from a mysterious chasm over which she sat on Apollo's tripod. Her

On a cup dated from the late 5th century BC, Aegeus, a king of Athens, consults the goddess Themis, a mythical predecessor of Pythia. Aegeus consulted the oracle about his lack of children; he later fathered the hero Theseus.

Above **View of the sanctuary of Delphi, with the remains of the treasuries, the temple of Apollo and the theatre.** *Left* **The Treasury of the Siphnians (525 BC) was probably one of the most richly decorated buildings in the sanctuary.** *Opposite below* **Detail of the north frieze of the Treasury, depicting the battle between the gods and the Giants.**

Opposite above **This head of ivory and gold is part of a life-size statue thought to represent Apollo, Delphi's patron god. It was found among the remains of a shrine dating to around the middle of the 6th century BC which had been destroyed by fire and then buried beneath the Sacred Way at Delphi.**

incoherent ravings were translated into verses by sanctuary priests called *prophetai*.

Initially, scholars accepted this portrayal while trying to rationalize it. Some theorized that the *prophetai* were merely passing on information gained from one visitor to another. Others suggested more venal motivations were at work, describing the priests as wily psychologists who found out people's secrets and told them what they wanted to hear, or even as political schemers who used their unique position to support favoured causes.

Profits or prophets?

The success of such scams seems unlikely, however. The Greeks were perfectly aware of the dangers of fraud in this area: in the popular comedies of Aristophanes, characters frequently criticize crooked and greedy seers. No such accusations were made against the Oracles even though we know their visitors were charged some kind of fee (the details are obscure). A very few stories do describe attempts to bribe the Delphic Oracle, but these are rare, and are clearly meant to emphasize the execrable nature of the corruptor rather than any inherent dishonesty of the Oracle.

Indeed, it is difficult to work out how anyone could be described as

making a profit from Oracles and their treasures since the Greeks were careful to ensure that no individual, group or state could claim their ownership. The riches belonged to the god alone and were left on display in each sanctuary for his glory. Only very rarely, and in the direst straits, did anyone dare to borrow them – and there was a heavy penalty.

Delphi and other Oracles were perceived as, and so far as we can tell, intended to be, sincere agents of prophecy. Even the early Christian writers in their anxiety to discredit the Oracles do not accuse them of corruption, preferring to denounce their oracles as the creations of evil demons.

This still leaves us wondering how Oracles functioned in Greek society. Recently, two areas of research have raised interesting, though controversial, insights into this question. Anthropological studies of Oracles in contemporary cultures have introduced comparative material which widens our understanding, while close analysis of the phrasing and content of surviving ancient oracular consultations has prompted a reconsideration of traditional accounts.

Questions and responses

It appears that the Greeks, like peoples in many cultures which use Oracles, did not turn to them out of general curiosity about the future. Instead they consulted them about particular courses of action and seem usually to have been seeking confirmation of decisions already made. Questions were most often phrased so that they suggest a 'yes' or 'no' response.

The Oracle in the sanctuary of Zeus at Dodona provides most of the evidence for individuals'

enquiries, though we are told Delphi heard similar questions. These covered many aspects of daily life, including marriage, children, work and travel. State enquiries included consultations about political issues and the founding of settlements. Oracles also appear to have functioned as arbiters of religious matters – crucial in a society which otherwise had no religious experts. Individuals frequently asked Oracles to identify which god they should address to ensure the success of a project, while state enquiries

Below **The sanctuary at Dodona has yielded thousands of inscribed strips of lead bearing questions put by inquirers at the oracle (and, very occasionally, answers from the god). On this one Hermon is asking to what god he should pray in order to get children from his wife Kretaia.**

Left **The east frieze of the Siphnian Treasury, showing the combat of Achilles and Memnon in the Trojan War.** *Below* **The Delphic Charioteer is one of the few and earliest of the original life-size bronzes to have survived from the early Classical period. He was part of a larger group (including a chariot, horses and perhaps a groom) dedicated at Delphi to Apollo by Polyzelus, tyrant of Gela, Sicily, in the 470s BC.**

often concerned adjustments and innovations in religious practice.

An analysis of historical responses indicates that visitors at Oracles did not normally suffer the ambiguous riddles of traditional stories. Instead they could expect straightforward pronouncements in prose. Some think the Pythia at Delphi spoke these directly to her clients herself. The nature of her divine ecstasy is debated. Comparisons with similar institutions in other cultures suggest that it may have functioned as a form of 'resistance' – that is a mechanism which reinforces an appearance of objectivity in the speaker. The vaporous chasm and the effects of chewing laurel were almost certainly figments of later writers' imaginations.

Prosaic affirmation

These analyses may make it easier to understand how and why the Greeks consulted Oracles, but it leaves us wondering about the ambiguous messages of traditional stories. Did the Oracles ever really make such prophecies? The ancient Greeks believed they did, attributing them to an earlier practice which died out – and this is still a popular explanation. Other scholars suggest these stories are simply mixtures of proverbs, folktales and the kinds of general prophecies which were in widespread circulation at the time.

Whatever explanation we accept, however, these stories clearly explain how the Greeks viewed the difference between mortal and divine knowledge – and that in turn helps us to understand why they turned to Oracles for what they saw as guidance about the future.

Who Were the Celts?

40

Time: c. 600 BC–c. AD 100
Location: Europe

To many, perhaps to most people outside the small company of the great scholars, past and present, 'Celtic' of any sort is ... a magic bag, into which anything may be put, and out of which anything may come.... Anything is possible in the fabulous Celtic twilight, which is not so much a twilight of the gods as of the reason.

J.R.R. TOLKIEN, 1963

TODAY, WE ARE used to thinking of the Celts as a people of Europe's Atlantic fringe, but they were once one of the continent's most widespread peoples. The first Celts known to history appear in the writings of Greek historians of the 5th and 6th centuries BC. The term 'Celt' (Greek *Keltoi*) was initially used to describe the peoples who lived inland from the Greek colony of Massalia (modern Marseille). Later, the term was used virtually synonymously with the Roman word *Galli* (Gauls) and a related Greek word *Galatoi* (Galatians) to describe a powerful group of peoples who in the 3rd century BC dominated a vast swathe of Europe from the Atlantic Ocean to the Black Sea, with offshoots in Spain, Italy and Anatolia. Classical writers also recognized close similarities between these continental peoples and the inhabitants of Britain and Ireland, though they never described them as either Celts or Gauls.

The Celtic identity

What united these peoples in Classical eyes was shared customs and beliefs and, above all, a shared language – all these peoples spoke what are now called Celtic languages, part of the great Indo-European family of languages (pp. 141–3). The modern representatives of these languages are Welsh, Breton and Irish and Scottish Gaelic, but several more Celtic languages are known to have been spoken in ancient and even recent historic times. The word Celt was one which some, but certainly not all, continental Celtic-speaking peoples used to describe themselves, as it features as an element in both tribal and personal names; however, there is no evidence that any of the peoples of Britain and Ireland ever did so. This has helped make the

Celtic identity one of the most controversial issues in modern British archaeology: can the prehistoric inhabitants of Britain and Ireland really be described as Celts if neither they nor their contemporaries described them as such? The question is only partly the result of political correctness.

The Celtic languages probably began to develop about 5000 years ago. Until recently it was believed that they had developed in a small area of central Europe and then been spread by waves of migrations. This view is no longer universally accepted because archaeological and genetic evidence for major prehistoric migrations in western Europe, Britain and Ireland has not been found. Instead a picture of long-term ethnic and cultural continuity has emerged

Left **Detail from a statue of an armoured Celtic warrior, found in a tomb at Glauberg in Germany, dating from the 5th century BC. Carved from red sandstone, the complete figure is 1.86 m (6ft) high.**
Opposite **Impressively defended hillforts such as Hambledon Hill in Dorset, England, served as the residences of pre-eminent chieftains and tribal refuges in time of war.**

which has forced a reconsideration of long-held assumptions about British and Irish prehistory. It seems that no ancient people calling themselves Celts lived in Britain and Ireland and, though there was certainly some exchange of population, there were no major migrations of continental Celts to the islands either. One response to this has been simply to write the Celts out of British and Irish prehistory but, not surprisingly, modern-day Celts have reacted angrily to this. What does it mean to be Celtic if the historic communities you claim descent from were not Celtic? Accusations of ethnic cleansing have been made.

How must we define the Celts, then, if we are not to write them out of British and Irish prehistory? We cannot define the ancient Celts as a genetic community (a 'race') since ethnic identity is essentially cultural. Genetic studies demonstrate considerable continuity in European populations over thousands of years; identities have changed but to a great extent the people have stayed the same. A better approach is to define the ancient Celts in linguistic terms as the group of peoples speaking Celtic languages. Whatever they called themselves, there is no doubt about the linguistic affiliation of the peoples of Britain and Ireland in late prehistory – most, if not all, of them spoke Celtic languages – while the discrediting of the migration-based interpretations of British and Irish prehistory makes it most likely that the islands formed part of the area where the Celtic languages first developed: there is little evidence to suggest they were introduced by trade or a conquering aristocratic élite.

The making of a myth

If the ancient Celts rank among the mysteries of the ancient world it is largely because modern romantics have placed them there. Until the birth of modern archaeology, historical knowledge of the ancient Celts was necessarily based on the works of Classical Greek and Roman writers whose attitudes to them were coloured by varying degrees of fear, loathing and condescension. These writers paint a fairly consistent picture of the ancient Celts as a proud warrior race with a powerful priesthood. Celtic warriors were fierce, undisciplined and boastful, addicted to feasting and drunkenness, and jealous of their status and honour. Poetry and cleverness with words were admired and the priestly class of the Druids enjoyed respect, influence and power, not only as intermediaries with the gods but as custodians of tribal traditions and laws which they committed to

memory in a 20-year apprenticeship. The Druids conducted their rituals in sacred oak groves and carried out gruesome human sacrifices. This picture was by no means dispassionate reporting: it was intended to contrast the Celts unfavourably with the well-ordered world of Greek and Roman civilization. But times change, and values with them.

The late 18th century saw one of the most influential cultural developments of European history, the beginning of the Romantic movement, an intellectual rebellion against the inexorable rise of scientific rationalism. For the Romantics, what the Greeks and Romans had presented as vices were virtues. The Celts' violence and lack of discipline became a passionate independence and individualism, their superstition became spirituality and a love of nature. A new knowledge of Celtic myths and legends, recorded mainly by medieval Irish monks, added to the Classical stereotype an otherworldly aura, eventually to be characterized as the 'Celtic twilight'. Two hundred years on, this highly attractive view of the Celts as heroic, poetic and spiritual – the antithesis of modern industrial society – is still accepted uncritically by people as diverse as Celtic nationalists and 'New Age'

Rather than face capture and enslavement, a defeated Celtic warrior commits suicide after killing his wife. The Celts probably believed that such actions guaranteed them an honourable position in the afterlife. Roman copy of a 3rd-century BC Hellenistic original from Pergamon, Turkey.

travellers. But this actually has more to say about the values and concerns of modern society than it has about the ancient Celts. What kind of people were they really?

The reality of the Celts

If we look at the developed Celtic world in its heyday of the 3rd to the 1st centuries BC we can quickly see that the Celts were actually very like their contemporaries, the Romans, the ancient Greeks and the early Germans. By this time the Celts had developed political institutions such as monarchies, elected magistracies and assemblies ('senates') which paralleled those of the Classical world. Increasingly, the Celts lived in large well-planned settlements called *oppida*, many of which were fully developed towns. Like the Greeks and Romans, the Celts used coinage on an everyday basis as exchange-based trade was gradually replaced by a cash economy. Writing too was coming into use. The Celts were technologically so up to date that the Romans adopted many of their innovations, such as barrels, shipbuilding techniques, chain mail and the design of their legionaries' helmets. The Celts were certainly warlike and some of their customs, particularly head-hunting, are distinctive to them. Celtic society was highly competitive and war was an important arena for the élite to win prestige and wealth. In this they were no different from their contemporaries – the expansion of the Roman empire itself was the result of aristocrats pursuing identical ends.

In their religious beliefs the Celts possessed no unique sense of spiritu-ality. Their reverence for natural places, such as groves, springs and rivers was shared with the Germans, Greeks and Romans. This reverence did not make them any more likely to live in harmony with the environment than anyone else in human history – they cleared most of Europe's forests for agriculture. Like their contemporaries, the Celts wanted to maximize the return for their labour on the land because this was the primary source of wealth in pre-industrial societies. Druidic worship might seem a world away from the formality of Classical religion, but shrines and temples had become a common feature of the Celtic world by the 1st century BC, indicating a shift to more formalized patterns of worship among the Celts too. Nor does their practice of human sacrifice set them completely apart, as this was common among the early Germans, while even the deadly gladiatorial combats which the Romans enjoyed originated as part of a funeral rite.

The ancient Celts were, then, by the standards of the day, a sophisticated, rational and thoroughly modern people, neither the barbarians prejudiced Classical writers made them out to be nor the twi-light fairy folk of modern romantics. It was their very sophistication that made their conquest by Rome (3rd century BC–1st century AD) both attractive and practical because it meant that the Celts could easily be assimilated within the Roman system. It is telling in this respect that the only parts of the Celtic world that escaped Roman rule – northern Britain and Ireland – were also the least socially and economically developed parts.

Barrels, seen here being used to carry wine for the Roman army, were invented by the Celts.

Bog Bodies: Murder Victims or Sacrifices?

41

Time: 1st century BC–4th century AD
Location: northern Europe

In the spring of 1640 the dead body of a human being was dug up on Schalkholzer Moor; the individual had probably been murdered and buried on the spot.

BAUERNCHRONIK DES HARTICH SIERK AUS WROHM, 1615–64

THE AMAZINGLY PRESERVED bog bodies of northern Europe have long stirred both the popular imagination and scientific speculation. What were these people doing in these desolate and dangerous wetlands? How came they to be so astonishingly well preserved? And how and why did they meet their deaths here, a question given added significance by the evidence of violence discovered on a large number of the bodies? Were they sacrificed as offerings to the gods or spirits of these watery places? Or is the prosaic verdict of mishap and casual murder a more plausible explanation?

The first mystery of the bog bodies, that of their preservation, is easily dispelled. The crucial requirement is Sphagnum moss forming peat in a marshy hollow. The particular conditions resulting from this mean that bacteria are unable to flourish, and hence organic materials (including bog bodies) that are deposited in Sphagnum moss are free from bacterial attack. The moss also contains a natural tanning agent, preserving the skin of the bog bodies while at the same time turning it dark brown in colour in a process known as a Maillard reaction. As the Sphagnum moss dies it turns to peat, leaving the bog body trapped deeper and deeper within its accumulating layers. Only with the great upsurge in peat-cutting for fuel in recent centuries, and more recently still its use in gardens, have these bog bodies seen the light of day once again.

Discovery and dating

The earliest surviving accounts of the rediscovery of ancient bog bodies date to the 17th century, and become more numerous as the 18th and 19th centuries progressed. Most of these bodies disappeared without trace; some were reburied in consecrated ground, but quickly decayed outside the protective environment of the peat bog. At

Tollund Man, found in Denmark in 1950, still had the noose around his neck with which he had been hung.

least one bog body became a source of 'mummy powder', sold as an expensive medicine. Only in the 1870s did proper scientific study begin in earnest, but it was during the 20th century that the most famous discoveries were made. At the same time, advances in technology meant that detailed forensic analysis of bog bodies, such as those from Tollund in Denmark (1950) and Lindow Moss in Britain (1984), could be undertaken.

The excellent preservation of the bog bodies masks their true antiquity, and much effort has been devoted to ascertaining how old these bodies really are. The peat-cutters who discovered Tollund Man in Denmark in 1950 thought they had come upon a recent murder victim and accordingly notified the police. In 1983, a skull from Lindow Moss in Cheshire with hair, eyeball and part of the brain preserved was assumed by police to be the remains of a known murder victim; and when confronted with the evidence, the suspect confessed to the crime. Radiocarbon dating, however, has shown that Tollund Man and Lindow Woman are both around 2000 years old.

The oldest bog body – that of the Koelbjerg Woman from the Danish island of Fyn – has been dated to the early Mesolithic period, some 10,000 years ago. In this case, however, as well as in subsequent Neolithic examples, no soft tissue is preserved. Bog bodies proper begin in the Iron Age. They come from Britain and Ireland, the Netherlands, Denmark and Germany. A small number date to the medieval or post-medieval period, but the vast majority of bog bodies belong to the period between the 1st century BC and the 4th century AD. This concentration in itself suggests that they did not die through random accident, but represent particular practices of sacrifice or execution which were common to several areas of northern Europe at that particular period.

Murder or sacrifice?

It is clear that many of these individuals had met an untimely and violent end. Lindow Man, found close to Lindow Woman in 1984, had been knocked unconscious by two blows to the head, then killed by having his throat slit and his neck broken by a garrotte. Grauballe Man, along with other Danish bog bodies, had apparently had his throat cut, but also had a forehead wound and a broken leg which were not accidental. Tollund Man had met his death by hanging. Borremose Woman may have been

scalped. The Yde Girl was stabbed and strangled. It is indeed remarkable how many of these bodies had been killed in a number of different ways. There are other peculiarities which suggest that these were not casual murder victims but the result of planned executions or sacrifices. A large number of bodies were buried naked, and where clothing was

Above **The Windeby Girl had had one side of her head shaved and a blindfold tied over her eyes, evidence that death was not accidental.**

Right **Some bog bodies had been stripped naked before death, but the Huldremose Woman was found fully clothed, with lambskin cape and check skirt and headscarf.**

preserved it was not always on the body; as if the individual had been stripped before execution. The young girls from Windeby and Yde had each had one side of their head shaved.

Archaeologists have looked to Tacitus, a Roman writer of the early 2nd century AD, for an explanation of these bodies. In his *Germania*, a treatise on the Germanic peoples, he describes the punishment meted out among the native societies of northern Europe for certain offences: 'Traitors and deserters are hanged on trees; cowards, shirkers and those guilty of unnatural vice are pressed down under a wicker hurdle into the bog.' The 'unnatural vice' referred to here may include both homosexuality and promiscuity.

The punishment of adulterous wives is described separately: 'A guilty wife is summarily punished by her husband. He shaves off her hair, strips her naked, and in the presence of kinsmen turns her out of his house and flogs her all through the village.' The nakedness of many of the bodies may be interpreted in these terms as a mark of disgrace. A Burgundian law of the early medieval period prescribes death in a swamp for a woman who repudiates her husband.

Whether the bog bodies were criminals or sacrifices still remains uncertain. There is a long tradition of ritual offerings being deposited in the lakes and peat bogs of northern Europe, including spectacular finds of metalwork such as the Trundholm sun chariot. The bog bodies – human lives representing the ultimate offering – could be viewed as part of this tradition. At the same time, we cannot discount the evidence that bog burial was employed as a form of punishment by Germanic societies in the early centuries AD.

Tantalizing further clues to the mystery are provided by analyses of stomach contents that allow us to reconstruct the victim's last meal: a thin gruel in the case of both Tollund and Grauballe Man. Yet Grauballe Man's finger ends showed no sign of manual labour and he had presumably been a high-status individual; while the gruel that he consumed was infected with ergot, and he may mercifully have gone to his death in a coma. There may, in the last analysis, be no single explanation for all the bog bodies of northern Europe, but it is clear that relatively few met their end by simple misadventure in the mist.

The North European practice of ritual deposition in peat bogs and watery places is documented not only by finds of human remains but also of sophisticated metal objects such as the Trundholm sun chariot, dated to c. 1650 BC.

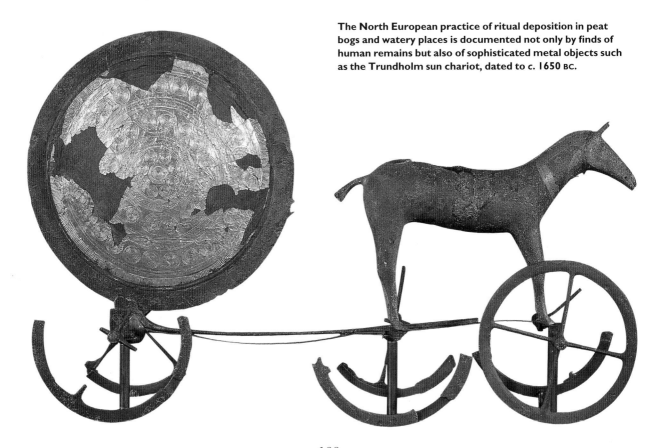

The Lost Legions
of Rome

42

Time: 1st/2nd centuries AD
Location: Roman empire

Oh when I joined the Eagles
(As it might be yesterday)
I kissed a girl at Clusium
Before I marched away

ROSEMARY SUTCLIFF, 1954

THE LEGIONS WERE the troops with which Rome conquered first Italy, then a vast empire stretching, at its fullest extent, from Scotland to the Sahara, and from Spain to the Persian Gulf. Each legion consisted of some 5000 men, drawn initially from Rome and Italy, but increasingly from the conquered provinces and from areas ever closer to the permanent bases the legions soon began to occupy along or near the frontiers. Under the Roman emper-

ors, all soldiers were professionals, serving for 25 years. From historical sources, and more importantly from epigraphy and archaeology, we can establish where they were stationed, who served in them, their transfer from one province or frontier to another, their participation in various wars and their internal organization. Many of their fortresses are known, and have been excavated, so that we can build up a picture of the lifestyle of the soldiers, their diet, and the equipment and weaponry in use.

Fortunes of war

Some legions remained in existence for 400 years or more, changing titles and the sources of their personnel, and adapting to changing conditions, pressures and threats as the decades and centuries passed. Others had a shorter lifespan, and were lost in battle or were disbanded after disgrace or disobedience, or after unluckily finding themselves on the losing side in a civil war. For example, three legions (XVII, XVIII and XIX) were lost in the forests of Germany in AD 9, under the governor Quinctilius

Left **Monument found at Xanten, Germany, to Marcus Caelius, centurion of the 18th legion, who 'fell in the Varian War' AD 9.** *Below* **Coin issued by Caligula, commemorating the successes of his father Germanicus, in particular his recovery of two of the eagles of Varus' legions, in AD 15–16.**

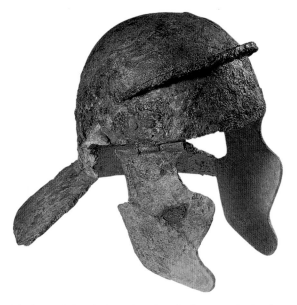

A legionary's iron helmet found at the fortress of Brigetio (Hungary). Dating to the early 2nd century AD, it has the characteristic broad neckguard and cheekpieces.

Varus (the so-called Varian disaster); the numerals were never re-used. The event is securely recorded in the historical writers, particularly for its psychological impact on the ageing emperor Augustus, and the site of at least part of the defeat was found in 1987 in fields at Kalkriese north of Osnabrück, by a British army officer metaldetecting. Legions I *Germanica* ('Victor over the Germans'), IV *Macedonica* ('Victor over the Macedonians'), XV *Primigenia* ('First Born'), XVI *Gallica* ('Victor over the Gauls') and V *Alaudae* ('The Larks'), all found themselves on the losing side in a civil war of AD 69 (the Year of the Four Emperors). They were disbanded (I, V and XV), or reconstituted (IV and XVI) with a fresh title (*Flavia*), reflecting loyalty to the winning side, the Flavian dynasty.

Missing in action?

A few legions disappear from the historical record without modern scholars being able to identify the precise historical context: XXI *Rapax* ('Grasping', as of a bird of prey descending on its victim) is lost to view sometime towards the end of the 1st century AD. Stationed on the Danube frontier, it may have been destroyed in wars against the Dacians of modern Romania in about AD 86–92. Legion XXII *Deiotariana*, which had its origin in forces raised and equipped as legionaries by Deiotarus, King of Galatia (central Turkey) in the mid 1st century BC, is

last heard of in Egypt in AD 119; very probably it succumbed during fighting in Judea against rebels under Bar Kokhba in AD 132–5.

The Ninth Legion

The disappearance of another legion, the IX *Hispana*, has exercised scholars for many decades now, and has remained in the public imagination as the supreme example of a 'lost' legion. The Ninth, which had its origins in a legion which campaigned under Julius Caesar in Gaul from 58 to 49 BC, served for a time in Spain, hence its title *Hispana*, 'Spanish'. By 13 BC it had been transferred to the Balkans, where it stayed for a time in modern Croatia, then in AD 43 it was chosen to become part of the force earmarked for the landings in Britain; thereafter it became a permanent part of the garrison of the new province of *Britannia*.

Its activities in Britain can be partially reconstructed: by about AD 60 it was based at Lincoln, where some tombstones of serving soldiers have survived, and from *c.* AD 70 it was at York, where again tombstones and an altar testify to its presence. The legion undoubtedly took part in the successful campaigns by the governor Julius Agricola into northern

Fragment of a building inscription at York, dated to AD 108, recording the construction of a gateway by the Ninth Legion, the last datable evidence of its presence in Britain.

Left **Tombstone commemorating L. Duccius Rufinus, a standard-bearer of the Ninth Legion, who came from Vienne in southern France. He died at York.**

Below **The Ermine Street Guard, in wedge formation, charging towards the enemy led by their centurion bedecked with military decorations. Members of this re-enactment group are equipped with armour, helmets and shields of the Roman army of the later 1st century AD.**

Britain, and its soldiers must have been present at the climactic victory at *Mons Graupius*, somewhere in northeast Scotland, in AD 83. Thereafter it returned to York, where it is attested building one of the gateways of the new stone fortress above the River Ouse (on the site now occupied by York Minster) in AD 107–8. After that, silence.

'The Eagle of the Ninth'

Various theories have been advanced to chart the final years of the Ninth Legion and explain its demise. Until fairly recently it was generally accepted that the legion must have been destroyed in Britain, perhaps in known troubles on the northern frontier of the province in AD 115–17; we also know that the new emperor Hadrian ordered another legion, VI *Victrix* ('Victorious'), to Britain in AD 122, most probably as a replacement for the Ninth. One theory has the legion marching northwards into the Scotch mists of northern Britain, and simply failing to return. This version of events has entered the public consciousness, and served as the central theme in

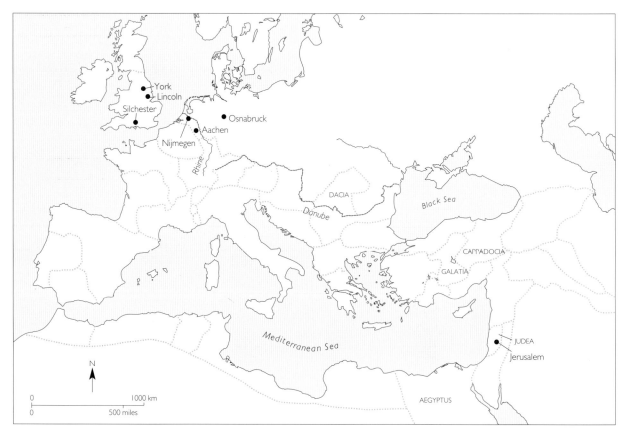

the novel, *The Eagle of the Ninth*, by Rosemary Sutcliff (1954). The novel's title drew inspiration from
the discovery long ago at Silchester in Hampshire of
a small bronze eagle, which the author chose to identify as the eagle-standard of the Ninth Legion. More
probably the Silchester find belonged to a cult statue
of the god Jupiter or that of an emperor. The shape
does not really match the eagle-standard of a legion
as depicted on coins and relief sculpture.

Increasingly detailed examination of the careers of
officers and soldiers of the Ninth, as evidenced on
inscriptions, casts doubt on the view that it could
have been lost as early as AD 115–17. More recently,
evidence has accumulated that the legion, or part of
it, spent time in garrison at Nijmegen in the Roman
province of Lower Germany; but the date of its
sojourn there remains imprecise. Some have argued
that it then moved much further east, to the
Euphrates frontier in Cappadocia (Turkey), or even to
Judea, and met its end there. We simply have insufficient information to know what happened. If there is
no good evidence that it was lost or disbanded in
Britain, then there is equally no solid evidence that it
was not. The matter remains unresolved.

Above **The Roman empire at
its greatest extent, during
the reign of the emperor
Trajan (died AD 117), with
sites which have links with
the possible movements of
the Ninth Legion.**

**A bronze statuette of
an eagle, found at Silchester,
England – the inspiration for
the 'Eagle of the Ninth',
though it was probably part
of a cult statue of Jupiter.**

The Mysteries of Mithraism

Time: 1st–4th centuries AD
Location: Roman empire

'Mithras god of the morning,
Here where the great bull dies,
Look on thy children in darkness
O hear our sacrifice!

Many roads thou hast fashioned:
All of them lead to the light.
Mithras, also a soldier,
Teach us to die aright!'

RUDYARD KIPLING, 1906

ITHRAISM AS WE know it appeared in Rome towards the end of the 1st century AD. The central mystery of the cult focused on the killing of a white bull by the god Mithras in a cave, an act which was believed to have brought salvation to mankind. The bull-slaying scene (the 'tauroctony') was depicted with minor variations in every temple to the god (*mithraeum*) the length and breadth of the empire. Within it lies the key to unlocking the secrets of the Mithraic mysteries as there are no liturgical texts to guide us, apart from a few painted verses in some *mithraea*, and a recently discovered papyrus fragment in Berlin. Unravelling these mysteries is no easy task.

Origins and spread

Mithraism is often described as an 'oriental' religion, and it was the central tenet of the founding father of mithraic studies, the Belgian scholar Franz Cumont, that the cult originated in the East, probably in Iran, and then migrated westwards to Rome. Mithra(s) was indeed in origin an eastern deity, and the clothes he is shown wearing are almost invariably eastern (close-fitting leggings and tunic). The conical hat ending in a peak, the so-called 'Phrygian' cap, emphasized the eastern connections, and already in the 1st century BC we see him so dressed greeting King Antiochus (*c.* 80–32 BC) on the reliefs from Nemrud Dagh in Commagene (southern Turkey). Certain words in the liturgy, such as 'nama' ('hail'), as well the names of other figures in the Mithraic entourage, such as the torchbearers Cautes and Cautopates and the enigmatic figure of Ahriman, are Iranian or Mesopotamian in origin.

But how deep do these 'oriental' features go? A key element in Cumont's thesis in support of an eastern

origin for Mithraism lay in a passage of Plutarch describing an episode when Pompey the Great was flushing out pirates from around the Mediterranean in 67 BC. The pirates of Cilicia in southern Asia Minor (Turkey) are reported to have 'brought strange offerings and performed some secret mysteries, which still exist in the cult of Mithras'. This passage has been taken as firm evidence for the existence of the Mithraic mysteries in the eastern Mediterranean in the mid-1st century BC, and the Cilician pirates have been claimed as the agents by which Mithraism reached the west. But if so, why are no

A relief from Nemrud Dagh, Turkey, showing Antiochus I (left) greeting Mithras, with Phrygian cap; 1st century BC.

examples of temples of Mithras, or of the bull-slaying scene, known in the Mediterranean world (or indeed beyond) throughout the entire Hellenistic period, and why, if the origin of Mithraism is really to be sought in the east, are *mithraea* so rare there in imperial times? And why, if Mithraism did indeed reach the west in the middle of the 1st century BC, does a century and a half elapse before we find any evidence for it there? Plutarch was writing in the first half of the 2nd century AD, when the cult of Mithras was just becoming widespread, and the reference to 'mysteries' may therefore be anachronistic: the Cilician pirates may have acknowledged Mithras as one of their gods (just as Antiochus did in neighbouring Commagene at the same time), but the iconography of the bull slaying and the full panoply of Mithraic ritual and mystery had probably not been invented at that time. An alternative view, which places the origins of Mithraism in philosophical and scientific circles at Tarsus in eastern Turkey in the 2nd century BC, is open to the same criticisms.

The earliest reference to what sounds like the bull-slaying scene is by Domitian's court poet, Statius, who in a poem published in AD 92 refers to 'he who beneath the rocks of a Persian cave twists the horns of the stubborn bull'. The first datable representation of the tauroctony is one now in the British Museum dedicated by Alcimus, slave of the praetorian prefect of the emperor Trajan (AD 98–117). The cult may therefore have emerged from intellectual groups in Rome, who in effect 'created' a new religion at a time when cults which promised salvation and an after-life seemed more promising than the emptiness of traditional state religion.

From *c.* AD 125 onwards the religion spread rapidly, particularly along the northern frontiers and in cosmopolitan urban centres such as Ostia, the port of Rome, where 16 *mithraea* have been discovered. It seems to have been especially popular with the army and the mercantile class; but its appeal was not (like Christianity) universal, above all since it was restricted to men.

The bull-slaying scene

The tauroctony was very quickly standardized, and although there are a few regional variations the iconography is more or less identical in all parts of the empire. Mithras is shown kneeling on the back of the bull, plunging his dagger into the animal's neck. The inspiration for this pose almost certainly derives from the scenes of Victory subduing a bull by kneeling on its back – seen in reliefs from Trajan's Forum in Rome and elsewhere. The god looks back over his shoulder at the figure of the sun god, Sol; often a sun ray between the two served to emphasize the close relationship between them in the Mithraic liturgy, and Sol's bird, the raven, often also appears. A bust of Luna, the moon-goddess, balances that of Sol. Cautes with torch upright, symbolizing light, and Cautopates, with torch reversed representing darkness, flank the bull-slaying. This dichotomy between light and darkness is a central feature of Mithraism. Below the bull are a scorpion, a snake (a symbol of the earth and of regeneration, since it

sheds its skin), and a dog, often leaping up to lick the blood spurting from the bull's wound. Ears of corn sprout from the bull's tail, symbolizing the new life that sprang from Mithras' heroic act.

Representations on the Rhine and Danube frontiers often add also a lion and a crater (a mixing bowl for wine) below the bull, probably symbolizing fire and water (making a trinity with earth, represented by the snake). Tauroctonies from this area also frequently show other deeds of Mithras – the birth of Mithras from the rock, the pact with Sol, the miracle of the water (shooting an arrow at the sky), the capture of the bull, the meal in the cave with Sol on the bull's flesh, and so on.

Many of the elements in the bull-slaying scene are closely linked with astrological symbolism (e.g. Taurus [bull], Leo [lion], Scorpio [scorpion]), and the Mithraic tauroctony has been seen as a 'star map': one particularly elaborate theory sees it as a symbolic representation of certain constellations which lay on the celestial equator when the spring equinox was in Taurus. Certainly Mithras and his mastery over the cosmos is central to the cult: the stars of the firmament are shown on the back of his cloak, as well as on the vaulted roofs of *mithraea* where these survive.

Above **Reconstruction of a *mithraeum* at Heidelberg.** *Below* **Cast of the Heddernheim (Roman Nida) bull-slaying relief. This and the reconstruction, both from Germany, incorporate scenes from the life of Mithras around the central panel.**

Left **A *mithraeum* beneath the church of San Clemente, Rome, with the customary side benches and low vaulted ceiling.** Right **A floor mosaic from the *mithraeum* of Felicissimus, Ostia, with the seven grades of Mithraism (in the foreground is the Raven, with cup and Mercury's caduceus).**

Below **Temple of Mithras at Carrawburgh, northern England, outside the Roman fort of Brocolitia, excavated in 1949.**

Temples and rituals

Mithraic temples are rectangular and usually small: the largest known, at Sarmizegethusa in Romania, is 26 m (85 ft) long. They generally consist of a narthex or vestibule, and a main chamber in which a central 'nave' leads to the tauroctony at the far end; the worshippers reclined on mattresses on raised platforms on either side. The *mithraeum* was therefore a meeting room for cult members at which (secret) rituals were enacted – much like the Christian church but quite unlike the standard pagan temple, which simply housed the image of the deity, and where ritual sacrifice occurred at an altar in the open air outside.

What exactly went on inside a Mithraic temple, however, remains a mystery. We know that there were seven grades of initiation, from the Raven at the bottom to Pater (Father) at the top, who was leader of the local Mithraic community. The fourth grade, the Lion, seems to have been particularly important, and some texts appear to refer to the temple as a whole as the *leonteum*. Initiation between one grade and another seems to have involved a kind of 'hardship' ritual with the initiate blindfolded (branding with torches and pain inflicted by the sword are represented in some frescoes); one temple (Carrawburgh on Hadrian's Wall) is even alleged to have had a torture pit, in which the initiate suffered symbolic burning. We also know that Sol and Mithras' meal of the bull's flesh and blood was ritually re-enacted, usually with some lesser meat (like sheep and chicken, to judge from the bones found in certain *mithraea*) rather than with expensive beef. Sometimes the flesh and blood of a bull were substituted by bread and wine, bringing Mithraism into clear conflict with Christianity. The official acceptance of Christianity in the early 4th century led directly to the decline of Mithraism, and many temples suffered destruction, most probably at the hands of Christians.

Lost City of the Maya: The Hunt for Site Q

Time: AD 250–909
Location: Central America

… we considered that in its medallion tablets the people who reared it had published a record of themselves, through which we might one day hold conference with a perished race, and unveil the mystery that hangs over the city.

JOHN LLOYD STEPHENS, 1841

TO OVERFLY THE EXPANSE of lowlands straddling Guatemala, Mexico and Belize, is to see the last great wilderness of Central America. Though suffering ever-increasing pressure from logging and land clearance, this verdant forest remains both a haven for wildlife and one of the most important archaeological landscapes in the world. Thirteen hundred years ago it was the densely settled heartland of Maya civilization: with numerous great cities dominated by lofty pyramids and sprawling palaces, their wide plazas the setting for intricately carved monuments glorifying god-like rulers. Long abandoned, these cities are today little more than clusters of mounds bound together by tree roots.

Maya ruins, even some of the most impressive, rarely escape the pages of dusty academic journals, but there are some that achieve a certain notoriety, even mystique. In the 1970s a series of plundered

sculptures, all with fine hieroglyphic inscriptions, appeared on the art market at much the same time. Were they the product of some hugely important capital still to be discovered in the jungle? Many began to think so and took up the evocative label 'Site Q' (based on the Latin American Spanish *¿que?*, meaning 'which?').

The only clues to Site Q's whereabouts lay in its inscriptions. Several stones feature the same 'emblem glyph' – a royal title that identifies the 'divine lord' of a particular kingdom. The political landscape of the Classic period (AD 250–909) was divided into 50 or more such kingdoms, most of them city-states of very limited extent. This particular emblem glyph was one of the most famous, representing the kingdom of *kaan* or 'snake', a tremendously important but elusive entity whose home capital was still in doubt.

Throughout a 20-year debate, in which the fortunes of favoured options variously waxed and waned, there were always those who held fast to the idea that the massive ruins of Calakmul would prove to be the Snake capital. The great quantity of monuments there, at least 117, would normally make this an easy question to resolve. But its soft local limestone has weathered badly and a thousand years of tropical rain have scoured most clean of their inscriptions. It is only in recent years that close

Left **Map with locations linked to Site Q.** *Right* **Site Q monuments make references to the 'emblem glyph' reading *k'uhul kaan ajaw*, or 'Divine Lord of the Snake [Kingdom]'. This belonged to Calakmul, one of the great powers of the Maya world.**

Map labels: Gulf of Campeche · Yucatán Peninsula · Calakmul · La Corona · El Perú · Caribbean Sea · N · 0 150 km · 0 100 miles

analysis of eroded texts and newly excavated finds are yielding firm answers. The most important contribution has come from the recognition of two place-names linked to the Snake capital: *oxte'tuun* ('Three Stones') and *chiik naab'* (meaning still unclear). Both make frequent appearances in the texts of Calakmul, where they clearly name the city and its surrounding environs.

So, if Calakmul is the city of the Snake, is that where the Site Q sculptures come from? The latest readings suggest not. Calakmul was one of the great *hegemons* or superpowers of the Classic Maya world and for about 130 years its rulers acted as 'overkings', dominating the affairs of lesser contemporaries. There are clear signs that the Site Q stones celebrate the rule of lords subject to the Calakmul dynasty, and come, in fact, from more than one locale. Some of the larger pieces are now known to originate at the city of El Perú. What hope is there of identifying the others?

A jungle discovery
In 1996 a NASA satellite scanning the Maya forest in search of ancient roadways detected some kind of feature near Lo Veremos, Guatemala, a lakeside camp built by *chicleros* (chewing-gum tappers). An initial expedition found a possible canoe port, while some nearby mounds produced a broken hieroglyphic monument. A full exploration by Ian Graham and David Stuart of the Peabody Museum,

Above **Panel from Site Q with a ballgame at Calakmul, featuring Chak Ak'ach Yuk ('Great Turkey'), whose name appears at the top right-hand corner. The appearance of this lord's name on a monument at La Corona** *(right)* **gives good reason to think that it originally came from there.**

Harvard University, the following year mapped these ruins, naming them La Corona ('The Crown'), and uncovered several longer inscriptions.

These reveal La Corona's close ties to Calakmul. Crucially, Stuart identified the name of Chak Ak'ach Yuk ('Great Turkey'), seemingly the local ruler, who attends an important ritual performed by the great Calakmul king Yich'aak K'ak' ('Claw of Fire'). Chak Ak'ach Yuk appears on one of the finest Site Q monuments, where he is shown playing the Maya ballgame at Calakmul itself. This connection strongly implies that this panel, at least, came from La Corona or somewhere close by.

Even if La Corona solves part of the Site Q puzzle, we know that the forest continues to conceal the remaining pieces. Further work, and a degree of good fortune, may yet expose the others. The hunt for Site Q is a true jungle adventure, but it also illustrates how the decipherment of Maya hieroglyphs – the most complete writing system of Precolumbian America – has become an effective tool in unfathoming Maya history and political geography.

The Mystery of the Nazca Lines

Time: c. 100 BC–AD 700
Location: southern Peru

To put it simply: whatever it is, the message on the pampa *may not be intended for us! The zoomorphic figures give me the gut feeling that the secret that lies within them is closer to* Alice in Wonderland *than Darwin's* Origin of Species.

ANTHONY AVENI, 2000

THE NAZCA PEOPLE of southern coastal Peru were a confederation of minor kingdoms – farmers, fisherfolk and expert weavers, whose pots and textiles reveal a complex iconography. They lived on the fringes of the Pampa de Ingenio, a desert with all the potential of a fine sketch-pad. Here they swept away the topsoil of fine sand and small stones to form an intricate web of lines and figures in the white alluvium so large that they cannot be fully viewed from the ground. High above the desert, from an aeroplane, the lines, some as wide as an airport runway, are visible extending for kilometres across valleys and low hills. Others radiate from hubs. Some lines coalesce into giant birds, monkeys, a whale, spiders, even plants, but those who created them never saw them in their entirety. Why, then, did people without aeroplanes draw such lines and figures?

Aerial view of a bird drawn on the desert at Nazca. Why did the Nazca people sweep away the thin topsoil to create figures which were invisible in their entirety on the surface?

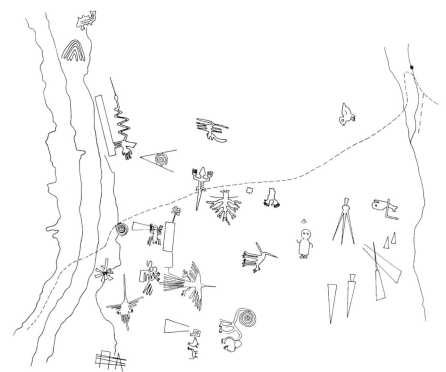

Above **Map of South America with the location of Nazca (the shaded area is the later Inca empire).** *Right* **Diagram of the various geoglyphs on the desert surface of the Pampa de Ingenio.**

Research into the lines

German-born mathematician Maria Reiche fled Germany for Peru in 1939 and became a teacher in Nazca. Soon she became obsessed with recording and preserving the lines, surveying them over many years with a tape measure. She became convinced that the lines pointed to celestial activity on the distant horizon, while the animals represented constellations in the heavens. Until 1963, Reiche worked almost alone. Then the tide of popular culture, with its preoccupations with mysteries and occult phenomena, flooded over the pampa. Pseudo-archaeologist Erich von Däniken even claimed that the lines were runways created by ancient astronauts for their spacecraft!

In the late 1970s, scientists realized that the Nazca Lines were similar to ground drawings, often called 'geoglyphs', found along much of the Peruvian coast. Anthony Aveni and Gary Urton have mapped over 62 raylike centres and measured the orientation of 762 straight lines near Nazca, some up to 13 km (8 miles) long. Aveni plotted the orientations on a computer and found that many of them lined up with the point on the horizon where the sun appeared during critical days in early November when the annual rainwater runoff began to flow into coastal rivers from the Andes.

Archaeologist Persis Clarkson has surveyed over 1600 km (1000 miles) of lines for cultural remains. She recovered thousands of Nazca potsherds, traces of crude shelters and a system of cairns, which may have been markers for people walking the lines. Aveni and his colleagues believe the Nazca Lines were pathways, maintained, swept and ritually cleansed by local kin groups as an important part of ritual activity surrounding the arrival of water on the pampa. The ray centres are concentrated close to places where water comes into the river valleys adjacent to the pampa. Trapezoid glyphs lie on splits of elevated land between ancient streambeds. Perhaps they pointed to the direction of water flow.

The meaning of the lines

Everyone agrees that the lines played an important symbolic role in ancient Nazca life, but the precise significance of the animal and plant geoglyphs eludes us because we have no knowledge of Nazca beliefs. Throughout the Andes, mountain gods are believed to protect humans and control the weather. They are associated with lakes, rivers and the ocean – the ultimate source of both fertility and water. Local mountains have always figured prominently in Nazca rainmaking rituals, for they are the source of water for the irrigation canals. Archaeologist

Johan Reinhard records how some rural churches and crosses in modern Bolivia lie at the end of long ground lines. For instance, a sacred line leads from the Bolivian village of Sabya, where the headman makes offerings for rain each January.

Another archaeologist, Helaine Silverman, has excavated a ceremonial centre named Cahuachi, a complex of mounds, cemeteries and shrines which faces outwards, towards the pampa with its geoglyphs. The river adjacent to the site is almost never dry, a sacred place where water bubbles to the surface year-round. Nazca art from Cahuachi and other locations emphasizes masked performances by priests and mythical beings.

Perhaps the lines were political, social and religious phenomena deeply entrenched in the local world. Those who traversed them became transformed into ritual beings as they arrived at the sacred place, a transformation brought about by dance, elaborate costumes and masks, and by shamanistic trance.

The mysterious Nazca Lines will always generate controversy. But the latest researches point to a close connection between the lines in the desert and the life-giving water that nourished crops and people along the Pacific.

Above **A Nazca polychrome vessel. Nazca pots depict mythic themes, as well as animals, people and plants, often painted against red or white backgrounds. The rich iconography behind the decorated pottery is lost to us.**

Below **The Nazca capital at Cahuachi was a ceremonial centre adorned with mounds, plazas and platforms. Cahuachi's Great Temple was a stepped platform capping a natural rise. Rooms, courts and a plaza lay at the base.**

Who Built Tiwanaku?

46

Time: 6th–12th centuries AD
Location: Bolivia

[Tiwanaku] is not a large town, but it is mentioned for the large buildings found there that are certainly notable things to see. Near one of the principal lodges is an artificial hill built over large stone foundations. Further on from this hill are two stone idols in human form ... that are so large that they appear to be small giants.... Near these stone statues is another building whose antiquity and lack of inscriptions is cause for not knowing who made such great foundations nor how much time has passed since they were made ...

CIEZA DE LEÓN, 1553

THE ARCHAEOLOGICAL SITE of Tiwanaku, located in the high plains or 'altiplano' of Bolivia, near Lake Titicaca, was one of the earliest ancient monuments in the Americas to capture the attention of the early European chroniclers. By some accounts, even the great Inca emperor Pachacuti was impressed by the stoneworking of the ruins when he made a triumphal march around the region in the late 15th century. Legend has it that the emperor ordered stonemasons from the Tiwanaku area to Cuzco, where they were to direct the construction in the Inca capital.

Tiwanaku was the capital city of one of the great civilizations of the ancient Americas. This vast, planned urban centre sprawled over the grasslands of the southern Titicaca Basin in the majestic Tiwanaku

Valley. At its height in the 9th century AD, Tiwanaku was a huge concentration of people surrounding an impressive architectural core of pyramids, palaces, streets and state buildings. The city is dominated by a large, terraced, artificial stone-faced pyramid. Known as the Akapana, this pyramid measures 197 × 257 m (646 × 843 ft) at its base and is 16.5 m (54 ft) high. Adjacent to the north face of the Akapana is a large, walled enclosure

Right **A gold diadem mask with turquoise inlays, from the Kalasasaya complex.**
Far right **A reconstruction of the Akapana temple, a stepped pyramid with a courtyard on the uppermost level.**

known as the Kalasasaya measuring approximately 120 × 130 m (394 × 426 ft). Other buildings at the site include palaces, residential compounds for craft specialists, temples and lower-class housing. Surrounding the architectural core of the capital was a hinterland of labourers and farmers who lived in adobe structures in dozens of villages up and down the valley.

The total urban settlement is estimated to have covered 4–6 sq. km (1.5–2 sq. miles), with a population ranging from 30,000 to 60,000. The valley between Tiwanaku and the lake was also heavily settled. The combined population of these settlements and the capital itself would have made Tiwanaku one of the largest cities in the ancient world by the end of the 1st millennium AD.

Origins and growth of Tiwanaku

Archaeological research in the Tiwanaku Valley and around the central Andes has provided a solid picture of the origins of Tiwanaku. The first period of human occupation recorded for the site is around 1500 BC, when Tiwanaku was one of hundreds of small villages that flourished throughout the

Right **One of the large monolithic statues standing in Tiwanaku.** *Below* **Detail of the Gate of the Sun: the central relief depicts one of the principal Tiwanaku deities, sometimes known as the Gateway God.**

The monumental stairway into the Kalasasaya was the principal entrance into the great enclosure that dominated the centre of Tiwanaku.

Titicaca Basin. For almost a millennium, the site continued to grow in influence. By the first centuries of the 1st millennium AD, Tiwanaku became one of two major political centres in the region. To the north, the site of Pucara also grew into a small city of around 100–150 ha (247–370 acres) by AD 200–300. Tiwanaku was most likely similar to Pucara in scale and complexity at this time.

Then around AD 350 Pucara collapsed as a political centre; Tiwanaku continued to grow. By AD 500 it was the primary political power in the southern Titicaca Basin. By AD 650 the Tiwanaku peoples began to expand out of their home territory. They conquered the Island of the Sun in the southern part of the lake and built the first regional pilgrimage centre there, while continuing to expand throughout the area. By AD 800, Tiwanaku had established colonies up and down the entire Lake Titicaca area.

We now understand how the Tiwanaku peoples were able to build one of the first states in the Americas in this harsh environment. They settled colonies in distant regions, up to several hundred kilometres away, to obtain obsidian, maize and other products not available in the altiplano. Within the Lake Titicaca region, huge areas of lake-edge swamp land were converted to highly productive agricultural land through an ancient technique, known as *waru waru*. *Waru waru* are areas of fields raised above the swamps that provide rich planting surfaces. These fields are found throughout the Tiwanaku territory and beyond, and provided the agricultural base for the Tiwanaku state.

Who built Tiwanaku?

Tiwanaku has been a mystery for generations. It is one of a handful of ancient sites around the world that have spawned fantastic origin theories. Early scholars asked how could a great urban centre flourish on the high, cold and windswept altiplano where maize, cotton, fruits and other important crops cannot be grown? Who were the people that built this great centre? Were they immigrants from the south as some histories suggest? Or did the original inhabitants who lived there for millennia build Tiwanaku?

The first European writers, seeing the statues found on the ruined site, talked about a race of antediluvian giants. The late 19th-century scholar Arturo Posnansky suggested that Tiwanaku was originally built on the Pacific coast 10,000 years ago, and had since been geologically uplifted. By the beginning of the 20th century, some writers suggested that Tiwanaku was the birthplace of humanity, the original Garden of Eden or that it was Atlantis. Theories that Tiwanaku was built by Chinese immigrants, Vikings and others abound in the non-academic literature.

Linguists generally believe that the ancestors of modern Aymara-speaking peoples immigrated into the Tiwanaku area in the 12th century. According to these theories, the people who built Tiwanaku spoke a now-extinct language known as Pukina. Archaeological and place-name evidence suggests otherwise, and indicates that the Tiwanaku peoples were early Aymara-speakers who had been in the area for hundreds of years before Tiwanaku was founded. Like the great civilizations of the ancient Mediterranean and Near East, Tiwanaku was built by the ancestors of the modern inhabitants of the Lake Titicaca region.

Why Did the Incas Sacrifice Children?

Time: 14th–15th centuries AD
Location: Ecuador, Peru, Chile, Argentina and Bolivia

Once a fourteen-year-old girl was brought to this island to be sacrificed, but the chief attendant exempted her. In carefully examining her body, he had found a small mole under one of her breasts. For this reason she was not considered to be a worthy victim for their god.

FATHER BERNABE COBO, 1653

FATHER BERNABE COBO, an early Spanish chronicler of the Inca empire, tells us this story of a young girl brought to the Island of the Sun in Lake Titicaca, in what is now the Republic of Bolivia. The girl was to be sacrificed at the temple of one of the great pilgrimage centres and religious shrines of the ancient Andes. But she lived to tell her story to some Spaniards who arrived on the island a few years after the conquest of the Inca empire in 1532.

Our information about the Incas comes from the early chroniclers such as Cobo, and from modern archaeological research. We know that the Inca empire was a huge, multi-ethnic, multi-lingual state that stretched over 4000 km (2500 miles). The peoples who founded the ruling dynasties sometime in the 13th or 14th century AD lived in Cuzco, high in the Andes, the physical and spiritual centre of their world. In a period of a few generations,

Left **The mummy of an Inca maiden, freed by an avalanche in 1995 from the ice at the summit of Ampato, highland Peru.**
Below **A modern-day *maestra*, or shaman, officiates at the burning of coca leaves and incense during a sacrifice ritual.**

Above **Detail of the silver female figurine found with the male mummy shown opposite. It is dressed in fine textiles fastened with a *tupu* pin.** *Left* **Archaeologists survey the excavation on the summit of Llullaillaco, where a female Inca sacrifice was found at an altitude of over 6700 m (22,000 ft).**

Quechua-speaking ancestors of the Inca empire conquered scores of different ethnic groups, peoples and territories over this vast area of western South America. Rebellions were endemic and controlling the large expanse of territory and people was difficult. As with other ancient empires throughout the world, a state religion became a principal means of incorporating the disparate groups under their control and projecting the power of the ruling dynasties.

Andean sacred places
During the Inca empire, and for centuries before, Andean peoples built shrines at sacred places called 'huacas'. Huacas were any natural or humanly modified feature in the landscape that was endowed with spiritual power; they were built in caves, at springs, on large rocks, on hilltops, near fountains and bridges, and on mountain peaks. Sacrifices were common at these huacas. The most popular offerings were baskets of coca leaf, colourful marine shells, llamas, alpacas, maize beer, cloth, metal

figurines, and occasionally children. Throughout the Cuzco area, the early Incas built hundreds of shrines, each maintained by kin groups from the nascent empire.

As the empire grew, the state built larger shrines, such as that on the Island of the Sun. Temple complexes were dedicated at major huacas the length of the Andes to the Sun, Moon, Thunder and other gods. Substantial amounts of energy and resources were invested in developing a religion around the worship of these huacas, the magnificent temples emphasizing the political as well as ideological power that the Cuzco nobility held over the lives of their subjects.

Human sacrifice
Human sacrifice was not an invention of the Incas. Prehispanic Andean iconography is replete with images of sacrificed individuals, usually war captives – in fact, some of the first carved stelae in Peru depict decapitated war captives. Other cultures took human heads as trophies as well. The Incas merely elaborated such practices as part of the state religion and imperial ideology that welded the empire together.

It is in this context that child sacrifice must be understood. Children were sacrificed in a politically significant ritual called *capac hucha*. This term, according to Colin McEwan and Maarten van de Guchte, translates as 'royal obligation'; these scholars describe how children, aged six to ten years, were sent from villages and towns from throughout the empire to the capital in Cuzco. For some, it was a journey of hundreds or even thousands of kilometres. Throughout the journey, the children and their attendants passed through villages singing as they walked in procession. Once in Cuzco, the children assembled in the middle of the city and were symbolically married by Inca priests. After great sacrifices of animals and other offerings, the children were paraded around Cuzco's great plaza. They were then sent back to their home villages and towns, where new celebrations were held. At the culmination of the ceremony, the children were drugged with alcohol and other substances, and killed at a huaca associated with their homeland.

Archaeologists have found a number of child sacrifices throughout the Andes. Remains of these *capac hucha* ceremonies are reported from islands, caves and mountaintops. In particular, the archaeologist Johan Reinhard has discovered sacrifices on snow-capped mountain peaks – often volcanic – throughout the Andes. The recovery of these sacrifices constitutes some of the most difficult archaeological work in the world: Reinhard and his colleagues must climb peaks over 6000 m (20,000 ft) high, battle altitude fatigue, ice, ash and snow. The determination of the ancient peoples to climb those same mountains without modern equipment is astonishing.

Discovering these mummies involves a combination of luck and skill. The skill comes from knowing where to look from surface traces, and the luck lies in the right environmental conditions coming together to expose the bodies. To recover the mummies before looters steal them or the weather destroys the exposed bodies, Reinhard and his team have to cut through ice and rock-hard soil, scientifically record their finds, and transport the mummy back to their base camps safely.

The chronicles contain descriptions of great ceremonies associated with the sacrifice of children. Now, archaeological evidence from Ampato near Arequipa, Peru, indicates that the documents were correct. The Ampato maiden was a young girl buried with a magnificent feather headdress, pottery, spoons, wooden cups, fully dressed metal figurines, food and

beautiful textiles. Red soil, a sacred colour, had been carried to the mountaintop to place in the base of her tomb. Platforms and possibly other buildings were constructed around the sacrifice area, where several other young children were most likely sacrificed as well.

Compared with other empires in both the Old World and New, human sacrifice was relatively rare in the Inca state. However, child sacrifice did exist, and it served profoundly important religious and political purposes. For a local lord to offer his child was both a statement of loyalty to the Inca state and to the creator gods that they worshipped. The sight of dozens of children in a ritual procession to Cuzco to be prepared for sacrifice served as an annual reminder of the power of the Inca state. Only by understanding the political logic and religious principles of the Inca empire in its historical context can we fully appreciate this tragic, but powerful, state institution.

The southernmost Inca mummy, found at Cerro el Plomo, at an altitude of 6000 m (20,000 ft); this child sacrifice was accompanied by numerous figurines and a bag of coca leaves.

How Did the Polynesians Find Their Homeland?

Time: 30,000 years ago – AD 1200
Location: The Pacific

In these Proes or Pahee's as they call them from all accounts we can learn, these people sail in these seas from Island to Island for several hundred leagues, the Sun serving them for a compass by day and the Moon and Stars by night.

CAPTAIN JAMES COOK, 1769

IN 1766, CAPTAIN SAMUEL WALLIS in *HMS Dolphin* approached the island of Tahiti in a dense morning mist. When the mists cleared, he was astonished to find his ship surrounded by dozens of canoes manned by tall, 'well-shaped' warriors. Tahiti soon became known in Europe as a distant tropical paradise, where the women were beautiful and poverty unknown, the home of human beings who were the epitome of the noble savage. But when a more sober observer, Captain James Cook, visited Tahiti in 1769, he puzzled over a question which has fascinated scholars ever since: how had the

Tahitians colonized their remote homeland? How had humans with only simple canoes and no metals sailed across vast tracts of open ocean and settled on the remotest islands of the Pacific?

Cook himself was in no doubt that the Polynesians had come from further west. He wrote prophetically: 'We may trace them from Island to Island quite to the East Indies.' The great British navigator talked to a local canoe pilot named Tupaia and asked him how their skippers made their way to remote islands far out of sight of land. Tupaia explained how they used the sun and the heavenly

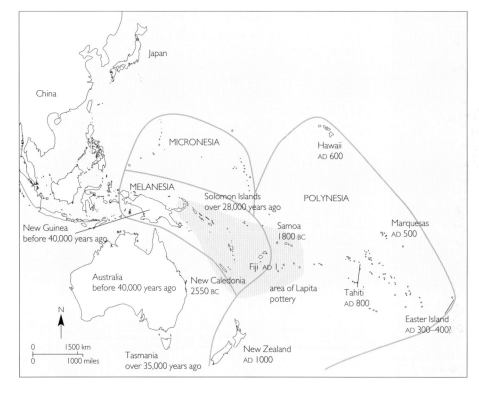

Left **The first human settlement of the Pacific depended on the invention of seaworthy open-water canoes and the availability of easily stored foods. Seafarers were navigating some of the Melanesian islands as early as 30,000 years ago, but the offshore islands were colonized much later, within the past 3000 years.**

Opposite above **Pacific navigators learned their craft from their elders at sea, both memorizing the movements of heavenly bodies and by using simple lattice charts showing islands and constellations.** *Opposite below* **A modern replica of a Hawaiian twin-hulled canoe, the *Hokule'a*. Interest in traditional navigation has taken *Hokule'a* and other replicas on voyages along ancient canoe routes.**

bodies as a compass. When Cook marvelled at the Polynesians' ability to sail against the prevailing trade winds for hundreds of miles, Tupaia pointed out that westerlies blew from November to January, and that these were months when canoes could make good progress to windward. Tupaia carried a mental image of Polynesia around with him. He listed islands, the number of days required to sail to them, and their direction, which Cook made up into a rough sketch map. Modern scholars believe Tupaia could define an area bounded by the Marquesas in the northeast, the Tuamotus to the east, the Australs (Tubai) to the south, and the Cook Islands to the southwest. Even Fiji and Samoa to the west lay within his consciousness – a mental map of an area as large as Australia or the United States. Cook persuaded Tupaia to accompany him to the southwest when he voyaged to New Zealand, so he could observe his methods. Unfortunately, Tupaia died of fever while *Endeavour* was in southeast Asia.

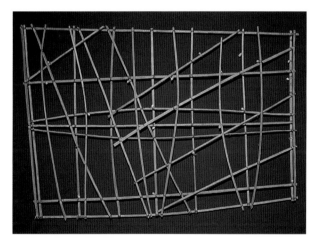

From speculation to experiment

No later explorers interviewed Tahitian navigators. Many armchair scholars assumed the Pacific Islands had been colonized by canoes blown accidentally far offshore. But in 1965 English cruising sailor David Lewis encountered aged canoe navigators in the Caroline Islands of Micronesia. He learned how the pilots used the zenith passages of key stars to navigate far from the land, as well as swell direction, waves reflected off distant land, and even the flights of sea and land birds, to make landfall on island archipelagos far from their departure point. These navigators were able to return to their homes safely, using the same signs of sea and sky. Determined to preserve a rapidly vanishing art, Lewis sailed his European-designed ocean-going yacht from Rarotonga in the Cook Islands to New Zealand, using only a star map and a Polynesian navigator to help him. In the 1970s, Lewis apprenticed himself to the pilots of the Caroline Islands.

Thus speculation gave way to experimentation. In the late 1960s, anthropologist Ben Finney began long-term experiments with replicas of ancient Polynesian canoes. Finney's first replica was *Nalehia*, a 12-m (40-ft) copy of a Hawaiian royal canoe. Tests in Hawaii's windy waters showed the vessel could sail across the wind, so Finney planned a voyage from Hawaii to Tahiti and back, using a replica built from a composite of known canoe designs from throughout the Pacific Islands. *Hokule'a*, designed by Hawaiian Herb Kawainui Kane, is 19 m (62 ft) long, with double hulls and two crab-claw-shaped sails. Finney, Micronesian navigator Mau Piailug and a mainly Hawaiian crew successfully sailed *Hokule'a* from Hawaii to Tahiti

A restored ancient *marae* (shrine) at Tuputaputia on Raiatea Island in Polynesia, where long-distance voyages began.

and back in 1976. This journey was followed by a two-year voyage around the Pacific using only indigenous pilotage. Thanks to the successful *Hokule'a* experiments, ancient Polynesian navigational skills have been preserved for posterity.

Ancient migrations

At the same time, archaeologists and linguists have traced the ancient migrations across the Pacific. A recent analysis of 77 Austronesian languages has placed the ultimate origins of the Pacific Islanders in Taiwan, from where they island-hopped through the Philippines and New Guinea, passed east through Fiji and from there to Tahiti, Hawaii, New Zealand and Easter Island. This complex journey is estimated to have taken little more than 2000 years, a mere blink of an eye in prehistoric terms. Humans had settled in the Solomon Islands of the southwestern Pacific by at least 28,000 years ago.

By 5000 years ago far-flung exchange networks transported sea shells, obsidian (volcanic glass) and other commodities over enormous distances from the Asian mainland deep into the central Pacific. We can trace these people from their characteristic 'Lapita' pottery, which may have developed in the Bismarck Archipelago off New Guinea and is found as far east as Fiji dating to the 1st millennium BC. The ocean-going double-hulled canoe and easily storable root crops like taro were the catalyst for bolder offshore voyaging, to islands far over the horizon, hundreds of miles apart. New Zealand archaeologist Geoffrey Irwin, himself a sailor, has used computer modelling and his own voyages to show that the offshore passages were systematic, deliberate and based on an intimate knowledge of the ocean environment and the heavens.

The achievements of the navigators were remarkable, but not mysterious, given their pilotage system, passed from generation to generation. Micronesia and eastern Polynesia were colonized within the last 2000 years, originating in Fiji by AD 1. Tahiti was settled by AD 800, Hawaii by 600, Easter Island possibly between 300 and 400, New Zealand by AD 1000. With these voyages the last chapter of the 150,000-year spread of modern humans across the world ended.

Statues & Survival on Easter Island

Time: AD 1000–1700
Location: Easter Island, southeast Pacific

If people ask you if we have 'solved the riddle', you can say that we do not claim to have done that, but we have found much that is new and interesting.

KATHERINE ROUTLEDGE, 1915

THE GEOGRAPHY, GEOLOGY and ecology of Easter Island (Rapa Nui or Rapanui) shaped the destiny of Polynesians who settled there at an uncertain date in the 1st millennium AD. The island's watery isolation, combined with the impoverished landscape seen by European voyagers in 1722, seemed an impossibly barren stage on which to raise the majestic *moai* (stone statues). This gap between nature and culture baffled Western science for generations. Recent international scholarship, however, has enriched the Rapa Nui archaeological database and revealed more of the ecological context. At the same time linguists and physical anthropologists have contributed new models of Polynesian origins and dispersal. In the words of Katherine Routledge, co-leader of the Mana Expedition to Easter Island in 1913–15, 'much that is new and interesting' is emerging.

The island

Rapa Nui lies in the southern hemisphere on the Nazca Plate in the southeast Pacific Ocean, a dynamic focal point of geological tension and seismic instability. It is a roughly triangular, basaltic high island formed by the coalescing flows of three undersea volcanoes. At 63 sq. miles (163 sq. km) Rapa Nui is small, but not the smallest of habitable Pacific islands. Geographically isolated but culturally linked to the rest of Polynesia, Rapa Nui is a sub-tropical 'outlier' in rainfall and temperature. This produces a marginal local ecosystem, limited natural resources and patterns of slow plant growth or recovery, although there was once lush palm cover. Rano Raraku, a volcanic cone of consolidated *lapilli* tuff, assumed an important role in pre-contact Rapa Nui culture. Over the course of at least 500 years, this near-perfect sculptural material was quarried to produce 95 per cent of 883 known statues. It was a major impetus to the development of monumental public works and innovative ceremonial architecture.

Engraving of a drawing by Duché de Vancy, the artist accompanying a French expedition to Easter Island in 1786. One of the expedition members is measuring a statue which still stands on its platform.

All Rano Raraku statues fall into one of four body shapes or types, and the proportionate relationships of design attributes are unvarying. This demonstrates proof of aesthetic continuity, uninterrupted social patterns, significant food management strategies and political stability for multiple generations. By the end of the 16th century AD about one-third of known *moai* had been successfully transported to and erected upon ceremonial platforms (called image *ahu*). Major *ahu* sites along the Rapa Nui shoreline evolved into elaborate, multi-phase struc-

A total of 883 statues have been inventoried on Easter Island and they all fall into one of four body types. The tallest statue is an important variant of Type 4.

| 3.56 m | 4.05 m | 5.88 m | 9.94 m | 20.65 m |

Left **The stone *moai* of Rapa Nui were erected in honour of venerable and, perhaps, deified ancestors. Their sacred *mana* was contained within and transmitted to the natural world through their eyes.**

Below **Ahu Nannau at Anakena is associated in Rapa Nui legend with Hotu Matu'a, the founding ancestor of island society.**

tures with massive dressed stone walls capable of supporting multiple numbers of statues. Most of these coastal *ahu* and some *moai* were embellished with distinctive red scoria features quarried from a single volcanic source called Puna Pau.

Origins and isolation

The Polynesians built massive sailing rafts and double-hulled canoes capable of long-distance voyaging. Their vessels were characterized by robust construction, flexible but tough lashed joinery and durable, seaworthy design. Heavy timbers, some more than three times the length of the largest *moai* successfully raised, were moved over rough terrain.

Trained navigators set courses according to wind direction, adjusted to wind shifts and attended to the natural movement patterns of birds and fish.

Early Polynesian movements in the East Pacific were underway by the 1st millennium AD. Discovery of Rapa Nui may have taken place between AD 300 and 400, but certainly by AD 800. Mangareva, Pitcairn (Rapa Nui's nearest neighbour) and Henderson were in sporadic but repeated trade contact from AD 800 to 1600. While the specific island of embarkation for Rapa Nui settlement is not known, there are suggested archaeological affinities to Mangareva and to Mangaia in the Cook Islands. Monumental stone carvings in red scoria link Rapa Nui to Pitcairn and, perhaps, to Raivavae in the Austral Islands.

Archaeological, linguistic and ethnographic evidence of Polynesian strategic voyaging in the east Pacific has, in the words of P.V. Kirch, 'turned the tables on Thor Heyerdahl's theory of an American origin for the Polynesians'. The increasingly convincing hypothesis is that Polynesian voyagers reached the vicinity of the South American coast, where they acquired, perhaps in trade, the domesticated sweet potato (*Ipomoea batatus*) and the *Lagenaria* gourd. Subsequently introduced into pre-contact Polynesia, the sweet potato evolved into

Statues carved from red scoriaceous material are found on Easter Island and elsewhere in East Polynesia, such as this one on Raivavae, Austral Islands.

an invaluable food staple throughout the Pacific. On Rapa Nui it was intensively cultivated in large plantations and household plots. It fuelled massive megalithic building projects and surpassed other staples in religious importance.

Megaliths and mariners: a transport project

How did the Easter Islanders move and erect the giant statues? There are three stages of *moai* production: quarrying, transporting and erecting. Each required specialized expertise, tools and co-ordinated work parties. Repeated experience with similar statues was essential and invaluable. Estimates of the time and labour required to carve a statue vary, but the first informed calculations were made by William Scoresby Routledge, co-leader of the Mana Expedition to Easter Island, 1913–15. He estimated that a master carver and crew of 54 men using stone tools could carve a 10-m (30-ft) tall statue in 15.5 days, but more recent studies suggest that double that time may have been required.

Routledge accurately described how a statue 'blank' was quarried as a rectangular block balanced on a stone spine or 'keel' and then undercut. While gigantic statues embedded in the slopes of Rano Raraku are awesome, over 95 per cent of the *moai* transported to *ahu* are less than 6 m (18 ft) tall. Only one 10-m (30-ft) tall statue fitting Routledge's calculations was successfully erected on an *ahu*. The statistical average for the island is, in fact, just 4 m (12 ft) tall and between 8 and 10 metric tonnes. The megalithic tasks achieved by Rapa Nui people are impressive, but the majority of them are well within Polynesian canoe building capability.

Several methods of transport have been suggested. One, involving a complex tripod, was proposed but not demonstrated, and has since been found impractical. Two versions of upright methods were actually tried on flat ground. Both were found possible but dangerous, and unlikely on rolling terrain. The logical method of transport for the average statue is in a prone or supine position, perhaps with bracing of posts and ropes when moving up or down slopes. The prone position is required for raising on most coastal *ahu* sites.

The Polynesians were adept at moving heavy canoes out of the water and over land in several ways. Some were carried, others rolled over rollers or moved along on a 'canoe ladder' composed of lateral 'rungs' spaced a metre apart and providing a surface over which a canoe could slide. Over steep terrain, rungs may be kept in place by lashing – becoming a 'rope ladder'. Rungs also may be fixed to longitudinal rails to provide support and a uniform surface.

A transport hypothesis, based upon canoe technology, was recently tested on Rapa Nui. A perfectly proportioned concrete replica of a statistically average *moai* was laid on an A-frame sledge lashed in the form of a Polynesian outrigger canoe hull. Three documented and replicable tests using rollers,

Left **This supine statue in Rano Raraku exterior quarry is the largest on the island.** *Right* **Replica statue within inches of being set upright successfully. The transport frame was indispensable in protecting and lifting the statue.**

A real example *(right)* of a statistically average *moai* was located and documented at Ahu Akivi, and photogrammetric analysis and laser scan produced an accurate 3-D model *(left)* for experimental use.

levers and a 'canoe ladder' configuration were conducted. Rollers were not viable but, using the 'canoe ladder', the replica *moai* was pulled with ease 100 m (300 ft) over level terrain and then up a ramp to a replica *ahu*. The sledge doubled successfully as a gantry to protect the statue and raise it with its accompanying headdress.

Putting people into the transport equation

Forty people are required to pull the average *moai* on an A-frame sledge over level terrain. Twenty expert

individuals can raise the same statue in three days. The average Rapa Nui chiefdom required to carve, transport and erect an average *moai*, and to feed everyone involved, is estimated to have consisted of 8.7 extended families, or about 395–435 people. The resources resulting from approximately 20 ha (50 acres) of sweet potatoes and other crops supported workers, but Rapa Nui traditions say that master carvers required prestige foods such as tuna and lobsters. As long as the environment co-operated, the Rapa Nui social system and political structure thrived. When larger than average *moai* needed proportionately greater resource investment, economic decline based on resource depletion and slow resource regeneration resulted. If drought or cold descended for long periods intense stress may have erupted into aggression.

The role of the *moai* in Rapa Nui society was both sacred and secular. They contained *mana*, the ancient Polynesian spiritual force, but were also powerful tokens of successful, co-operative food production, display and redistribution. Today, many *moai* once thrown down have been resurrected. They stand on restored *ahu* to represent the 'living faces' of Rapa Nui ancestors, facing the future and reminding us all of the past.

Tombs & Lost Treasures

THE MAGIC MOMENT in 1922 when Howard Carter and Lord Carnarvon opened the tomb of the Egyptian pharaoh Tutankhamun is etched in every archaeologist's consciousness. To many people archaeology still is buried treasure and untold wealth lurking underground, a science that offers limitless adventure, fame and fortune – if you are lucky enough to find another Tutankhamun. There are other archaeological treasures, too, not precious metals or lavish burial equipment, but priceless documents that illuminate religious beliefs, even the purported tomb of Christ himself. The search for elusive graves and hidden riches continues unabated, over three-quarters of a century after Howard Carter marvelled over the 'wonderful things' in the boy-king's burial place. The mysteries, and potential for spectacular discovery, remain as challenging as ever.

Egypt's Valley of the Kings contains one of the most closely scrutinized clusters of archaeological sites on earth – the rock-cut tombs of some of Egypt's most famous pharaohs. Tutankhamun was the last ruler to be found here, but the search goes on for undisturbed sepulchres to this day. Modern research in the Valley is a complex jigsaw puzzle, not only of ancient Egyptian tombs themselves, but of the work of previous archaeologists who excavated here. Howard Carter alone moved tons of granite rubble from one side of the valley to the other, complicating the careful survey and conservation work of today. Tomb 55 is a case in point: found by American Theodore Davis in 1907 it contained a badly damaged woman's coffin and a male mummy. At first, experts thought this was the body of the

A cavalryman, part of the terracotta army that guarded the still-unopened tomb of China's first emperor.

heretic pharaoh Akhenaten, or, perhaps, that of his co-regent and successor Smenkhkare – the debate still rages today and here we look at the evidence.

Alexander the Great died in Babylon in 323 BC, and was buried in Alexandria, Egypt, after a frenzied power struggle over his body by his successors. At first the body was displayed in a golden coffin, near an imposing mausoleum close to the palace complex next to the eastern harbour, but both body and memorial vanished during Roman times. The search for Alexander's tomb has continued ever since. It is probably now deep under the modern metropolis, or even, perhaps, under the Mediterranean. Despite numerous claims, no one has ever found any trace of Alexander's resting place, either in the city named after him, or in the Siwa Oasis in Egypt's western desert, where the great king is said to have wished to be buried.

Everyone knows the location of the great sepulchre of Emperor Qin Shihuangdi, the first ruler of a unified China, who died in 210 BC. Chinese legend and contemporary writings tell of a vast burial chamber containing a three-dimensional map of China with the rivers delineated in mercury. So far, Chinese archaeologists have declined to excavate the mausoleum, on the grounds that they lack the technology, resources and know-how to undertake what would be the archaeological excavation of a millennium. But they have investigated burial pits around the mound, where they have unearthed the famous terracotta army – consisting of over 7000 men and horses and chariots – which guarded the tomb. The investigation of the royal burial complex has hardly begun.

What does this stupendous find tell us about the life and times of the emperor? And what spectacular discoveries await future generations of archaeologists when they finally excavate the royal tomb?

The discovery of the Dead Sea Scrolls by a Bedouin youth searching for a goat near Qumran in 1947 caused an archaeological and political sensation. Important religious texts probably belonging to a nearby and long-forgotten Jewish community, the Scrolls soon became political symbols, religious tourist attractions and the intellectual preserve of a narrow coterie of learned men. It is only in recent years that their control has been challenged and the texts made widely available. The Scrolls are a different form of archaeological treasure, which bears witness to the historical milieu in which Christianity was to emerge. The contents of some of the Scrolls are very enigmatic, and none more so than the Copper Scroll, which seems to record almost unbelievable quantities of treasure hidden in various places around the Dead Sea.

The search for tangible relics of Christ continues unabated, including a long and controversial debate over the site of his tomb. The location of the burial place was lost for two centuries, before the Roman emperor Constantine ordered the building of a huge church at the site. A tomb was located under the foundations of a Roman temple and was immediately declared to be Christ's resting place. Did oral traditions lead Archbishop Makarios to the sepulchre, or was a convenient empty tomb just co-opted for the shrine? Herein lies an enduring mystery of archaeology and Christianity.

The Church of the Holy Sepulchre, Jerusalem, said to stand on the site of Christ's tomb. Within the church, the Aedicule, or 'little house', most recently rebuilt in 1808, encloses the tomb itself.

The Puzzle of Tomb 55

50

Time: c. 1335–1322 BC
Location: Amarna & Thebes, Egypt

I believe in the end the identity of the owner of the coffin may prove a surprise.

GASTON MASPERO, 1907

IN JANUARY 1907, the expedition of American Theodore M. Davis to the Valley of the Kings at Thebes found a tomb. Like most tombs in Egypt, its damaged contents were in chaos, but in this case the disturbance was not the result of tomb robbery, but apparently the outcome of official activity in ancient times. Resolving the mystery of what had occurred has exercised the minds of Egyptologists for nearly a century, and even today there almost as many 'solutions' as researchers.

The tomb, with the official number KV (Kings' Valley) 55, comprises a stairway, a corridor and a single chamber. Many objects lay scattered around the tomb; the largest was a dismantled shrine, originally made to surround the sarcophagus of Queen Tiye, a wife of Amenophis III, by her son, Akhenaten (c. 1353–1335). Akhenaten is often known as the 'heretic pharaoh', having abolished the traditional religion of Egypt in favour of the worship of a single sun god, known as the Aten. Four protective charms ('magic bricks') were placed around the chamber, one of which bore this pharaoh's name. In a niche in the north wall of the chamber were four canopic jars, originally made to contain the internal organs of a junior wife of Akhenaten, Kiya, but with their inscriptions erased. Clay seal-impressions found on the floor of the tomb bore the name of Akhenaten's successor Tutankhamun (c. 1333–1323 BC).

Below **A reconstructed view of KV55, showing how material was strewn through the tomb, much of it on top of chippings that had once largely blocked the descending corridor.**

Left **View across the chamber of KV55 as discovered. On the left are some panels of the shrine, leaning against the wall, and beyond them is the coffin. The niche in the wall holds the canopic jars.**

Left **The canopic jars from KV55 were made for Kiya; they had had their texts removed in two stages. First Kiya's name and titles were erased, and later those of Akhenaten and the Aten, which occupied a panel to the left.**

Below **The burial chamber of KV55. The coffin, with the lid jolted off the trough, lies at the far end of the room, while panels from the shrine lean against the left-hand wall and lie on the floor.**

The mystery of the mummy

The key item in the tomb, however, was a coffin, also made for Kiya, but extensively modified for a king. Unfortunately, the identity of that king had been hidden by the deliberate erasure of his name wherever it occurred, and the removal of the coffin's gold face-mask. The shrine had suffered similar damage, with the images and names of Akhenaten all destroyed. A mummy, badly damaged by damp, lay within the coffin. An initial examiner was misled by the collapsed pelvis into declaring the corpse to be that of a woman. Davis thus christened the sepulchre 'the Tomb of Queen Tiye'; but by the time his book of this title had come out, a proper examination had shown the body to be that of a man. The almost-universal opinion was that it belonged to Akhenaten himself. His memory had been condemned after his death, thus explaining the erasures on the coffin and shrine.

However, others suggested that the body might be that of Smenkhkare, who seems to have ruled as Akhenaten's co-regent during his last few years, and suffered from the same posthumous opprobrium as the 'heretic pharaoh' himself. There has been much debate over the identity of this individual, and another named Neferneferuaten who appears around the same time. The evidence seems best interpreted as identifying them both as the same person, who underwent a name change during the three years as co-ruler.

Important additional evidence was supplied by the discovery of the tomb of Tutankhamun, in 1922. First, Tutankhamun's mummy showed that he and the KV55 individual were closely related – being either siblings or parent and child; secondly, the tomb contained numerous items that had originally been made for Smenkhkare's burial, but never used. In particular, there were four miniature coffins intended for Smenkhkare's internal organs, as well as one of his full-size coffins. All had been re-inscribed for use by Tutankhamun, but showed traces of their original owner, both in the areas occupied by the royal names, and in the fact that the faces of the coffins were clearly not that of Tutankhamun. That all these items are the very ones in KV55 represented ate to Akhenaten). Many scenarios have been produced to explain history of the tomb, most of them mutually exclusive. The only broadly common thread is that the mummy, whoever it was, had originally been buried at Tell el-Amarna, the new capital city built by Akhenaten some 300 km (180 miles) north of Thebes, and had been moved to KV55 following the abandonment of the new city.

Two solutions

Amarna ceased to be the capital around the middle of the reign of Tutankhamun, and was definitively abandoned after his death. The establishment of KV55 will thus have taken place at some point between the middle of Tutankhamun's reign and his burial, when his seal will have gone out of use.

One view is that Smenkhkare and/or Akhenaten, together with the latter's mother, Tiye, who had been buried with him at Amarna, had all been transferred to KV55 as soon as the government abandoned the city. The mutilation of the tomb's contents is attributed to either the violently anti-Atenist kings of the early 19th Dynasty, or the officials of Ramesses IX. It was perhaps during the construction of that pharaoh's adjacent tomb that KV55 may have been rediscovered. Under this scenario, Tiye's body will have been removed and reburied elsewhere, her shrine left behind when a section of it became jammed in the only partly unblocked entrance corridor. One other body may also have been removed, and the remaining one was deprived of its identity. The images of Akhenaten on the shrine were destroyed before the tomb was closed and its last remaining occupant abandoned to eternal obscurity.

Another option, however, is that the move occurred after Tutankhamun's death, but before his burial. As is now becoming clear, the demolition of Akhenaten's monuments had begun even during Tutankhamun's lifetime. The presence on the throne of Akhenaten's son must have acted as some restraint on the forces of reaction, but with Tutankhamun's death, that tether will have disappeared. According to this scenario, the KV55 body will have been installed alone, and nameless, in its new tomb from the outset. The ultimate disorder will then have been the result of the rediscovery of the tomb during the reign of the economically troubled Ramesses IX. Gold-hungry officials would have been keen to remove the gilded contents for salvage – frustrated by a section of shrine jamming in the entrance passage.

The coffin had been purposely mutilated – as well as losing its face, all cartouches had been cut out.

by material that once belonged to Kiya has been regarded as significant by some researchers favouring Smenkhkare as the occupant of that tomb.

Others have continued to argue that the body is that of Akhenaten. Estimates of the age of death of the mummy have been little help, different anatomists producing figures ranging from around 20 (favouring Smenkhkare) to 30–40 (more appropri-

Left **A reconstruction of the face of the KV55 skull** *(right)*, **showing it wearing the nemes headdress. The face corresponds closely with that depicted on the second coffin of Tutankhamun's coffins** *(far left)*. **This is known to have been made for a king other than Tutankhamun, the cartouches having been removed and new ones inserted.**

A solution?

Both basic scenarios could be appropriate to the corpse being that of either Akhenaten or Smenkhkare, but there remain two fundamental questions: why was a king placed in an elaborately altered woman's coffin; and what had happened to his own? The alterations did not affect the pure Atenist nature of the coffin's texts, and this suggests it had been prepared for use in the *primary* burial of a pharaoh during the reign of Akhenaten since, after his death, apostasy was rapid and dramatic. Akhenaten must have had a full set of coffins completed long before his death, which were almost certainly used for his interment. However, as we have already noted, it is certain that while Smenkhkare had completed at least one coffin, together with his canopics, he was not buried using his own equipment, which instead was put into service for the young king Tutankhamun.

Smenkhkare was by no means a devoted Atenist, in spite of later adopting the name Neferneferu*aten*. His funerary equipment was completely traditional, and the head of the conventional pantheon, Amun, was worshipped in his temple. However, he seems to have died while his father Akhenaten, the author of the Atenist revolution, yet lived. Given Akhenaten's complete lack of toleration of anything connected with deities other than Aten – visible in his widespread mutilation of polytheistic monuments – it is quite likely that Akhenaten denied Smenkhkare burial with the traditionalist equipment which the latter had prepared for himself.

If so, alternative containers for the mummy and viscera would have been required. Accordingly, the appropriate 'religiously-correct' equipment that had once belonged to Kiya was altered for the young king, and was used in his funeral, almost certainly in a tomb in the Royal Wadi at Amarna, where he was sheltered by Queen Tiye's shrine. It was from here that the body was ultimately moved to the Valley of the Kings.

Only the lid of the KV55 coffin is currently in the Cairo Museum; the gold from the rotted remains of the trough seems to have been stolen from the museum during the First World War, and has recently turned up in Germany. Unconfirmed reports indicate the presence of one intact cartouche of Smenkhkare, corroborating the indications of a fragment of gold from the coffin in Cairo and the solution noted just above. It is to be hoped that this side of the question may finally be put to rest when the restored coffin-trough is returned to its rightful owner, the Cairo Museum.

The Lost Tomb of

Alexander the Great 51

[Julius] Caesar ... paid a hurried visit to the rock-hewn tomb which housed the body of that mad if glorious adventurer Alexander the Great, whom Death had cut off in his prime, thus avenging a defeated world.

LUCAN, 1ST CENTURY AD

WHEN ALEXANDER DIED in Babylon in 323 BC, it was no doubt envisaged that his mortal remains were destined for the ancestral royal burial ground of the Macedonian kings at Aegai (modern Vergina in northern Greece). In Babylon his body was (highly unusually) embalmed rather than cremated; it then became the focus of a power struggle as various claimants to Alexander's empire competed for the succession – burying one's predecessor was the legitimate right of the new monarch. Alexander himself is reported to have expressed the wish to be buried at Siwa, the oracular shrine of Zeus Ammon in the western Egyptian desert. Here Alexander had been flattered by being told that he was 'son of Ra', meaning in this context son of Zeus Ammon. It was after this that the attribute of this god, ram's horns, were sometimes added to Alexander's image. Whether burial at Siwa was really his expressed wish, however, or was merely a story invented as part of the propaganda war in the aftermath of Alexander's death, we are unlikely ever to know for certain.

The journey to Egypt

In the event it was Ptolemy Soter, the ruler of Egypt (304–284 BC), who managed to win possession of Alexander's corpse: he went to Damascus in Syria and intervened with Arrhidaeus, the satrap responsible for conveying the body from Babylon. Probably following the offer of a massive bribe, the funeral cortège was diverted, and wended its way

Left **Marble head of Alexander the Great, with characteristic hairstyle and distant gaze. Istanbul Museum.** *Right* **Posthumous coin portrait of Alexander as Zeus Ammon (with ram's horns), issued by Lysimachus (late 4th/early 3rd century BC).**

not back to Macedonia but to Egypt. It is ironic that we know more about the elaborately decorated hearse (which had taken two years to build) that bore Alexander's body on this journey than we do about the details of his final resting place: Diodorus, the Sicilian historian, writing in the 1st century BC but drawing on eye-witness accounts, has left us a meticulous description.

What happened next is uncertain. One historical tradition reports that Alexander's body was first taken to Memphis before being transferred to Alexandria. It seems likely that he was in fact interred at Memphis, at least for a brief time. Whether, however, it was for the 'few years' that one source, Curtius Rufus, reports, is open to question, especially since our main authorities for what happened to Alexander's corpse, Diodorus and Strabo, make no mention of Memphis. At any rate, probably well before the end of Ptolemy Soter's reign, Alexander's body was transferred to Alexandria, where it was kept on permanent display in a gold coffin. This was not to be Alexander's last resting

place, however. A later successor of Ptolemy Soter, Ptolemy Philopater (221–205 BC), was responsible for building a mausoleum for the Ptolemaic dynasty, known as the Sema or Soma (our sources vary), which contained the body of Alexander and also Ptolemy's immediate predecessors as rulers of Egypt. This monument may have been erected around Alexander's original resting place in Alexandria, but it is more likely to have been built on a fresh site nearby, in which case the location of the original burial place was presumably soon forgotten. Even then Alexander was not allowed to rest in peace: Ptolemy X (107–88 BC) stole the gold coffin, after which one of alabaster was substituted instead. The last recorded visitor to the tomb was the Roman emperor Caracalla, in AD 215. The monument was probably destroyed in the riots which engulfed Alexandria around AD 273, and it is astonishing that bishop John Chrysostom, visiting Alexandria a little more than a century after this, reports that even its location had already been forgotten.

Suggested reconstruction of Alexander's elaborate funeral hearse, which reputedly took two years to build, based on a description by Diodorus.

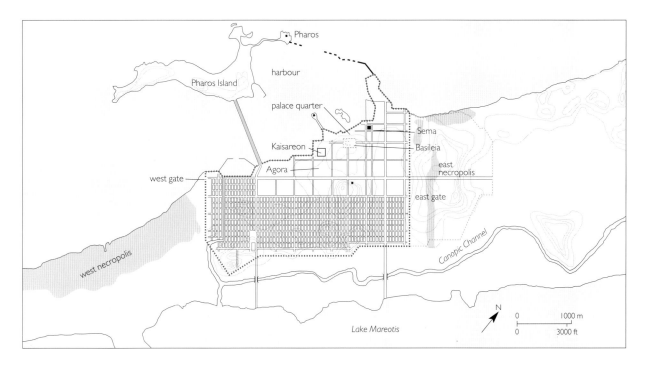

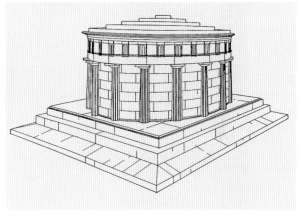

Top **Plan of Alexandria in Ptolemaic times, showing the probable position of Alexander's tomb, in the Sema of the Ptolemaic dynasty.** *Above* **A reconstruction drawing of a Greek circular mausoleum at Ptolemais, Libya, dating to c. 200/150 BC.**

The lost tomb: Classical sources

No trace of the tomb of Alexander has ever been found, and what remains of it is likely to be buried deep below modern Alexandria. We know roughly where it was: Strabo says specifically that it lay in the area known as 'The Palaces', a vast complex of royal residences, shrines and pleasure parks next to the eastern harbour. Alexander's tomb therefore lay probably on or close to the sea in this northeastern quarter of the city. But of its appearance and size no clear clues are provided by the extant written sources, and attempts to locate it on small-scale representations of the city, such as on decorated clay lamps, are unconvincing. A passage of the 1st-century AD Latin poet Lucan indicates that the body lay (not surprisingly) in an underground chamber, and he implies that the roof was pyramidal in form; but that is hardly enough to attempt a convincing reconstruction of its appearance.

We do not even know if it was square or rectangular in shape, as had been the norm for monumental mausolea up to this time (most notably at Halicarnassus in Turkey, where Mausolus' famous tomb gave us the word 'mausoleum'), or whether it broke with tradition by being circular. The fact that Lucan employs the word *tumulus*, used in archaeological parlance to describe a circular tomb (usually capped by an earth mound, or in prehistoric times entirely of earth), cannot be taken as evidence that Alexander's tomb was circular, since poetic licence and metrical demands rather than descriptive accuracy may explain the choice of the word. The truth is that we are entirely in the dark about the form and decoration of this tomb, and it is unfortunate that written accounts (which must have existed in antiquity) by those who had seen and been impressed by this monument have simply not come down to us.

A circular mausoleum at Le Medracen, near Batna in Algeria, c. 200/150 BC. The roof is in the form of a stepped pyramid, and the vertical face is ornamented with Doric half-columns.

Numidian parallels

In the absence of hard evidence we are left to speculate. The most impressive surviving monuments of pre-Roman North Africa outside Egypt are undoubtedly the mausolea of the Numidian kings and princes: examples are known near Siga, Tipasa, Constantine and Batna in Algeria, and at Dougga in Tunisia. All show close links with the Greek Hellenistic world, and the tall false-door divided into four unequal compartments, a feature found in nearly all of them, is a commonplace in Macedonian tomb architecture.

Of these Numidian tombs the largest and most impressive are the massive, circular mausolea of Le Medracen near Batna (59 m or 194 ft in diameter) and that near Tipasa known as 'The Tomb of the Christian Woman' (wrongly so-called from the cross-like shape of the division lines on the false-door), which is even larger (65 m or 213 ft in diameter). The former is certainly earlier, having probably been built between about 200 BC and 150 BC; the Tipasa tomb is a century or so later. Le Medracen is especially dramatic – standing alone in a wild and desolate landscape, it is a mysteriously isolated mausoleum, as the settlement

Detail of the false door of the 'Tomb of the Christian Woman', Tipasa, Algeria, c. 100/50 BC.

to which it must have belonged is so far unlocated. At present these circular Numidian tombs are without forerunners in the Mediterranean world. Both share the two known features of Alexander's tomb, an underground burial chamber (reached by a passageway which starts outside the monument) and a pyramidal roof.

Is it possible that both used Alexander's tomb at Alexandria as their model? Is it coincidence that in Cyrenaica (eastern Libya), the part of the Greek world closest to Egypt, circular mausolea appeared in the late Hellenistic period? And is it coincidental, too, that when Augustus wished to express his dynastic ambitions early in the period of his consolidation of power over the Roman empire, he chose to erect for himself on the Campus Martius at Rome, in 28 BC, a massive *circular* mausoleum? This in turn became a model for the showy tombs of the aristocratic élite throughout the Roman period. The circular form is reflected in such monuments as Hadrian's mausoleum (Castel Sant'Angelo) in Rome and Theoderic's tomb at Ravenna – and much later, in the 18th century, it was rediscovered as a suitable means of expression for impressive family mausolea in other parts of Europe, such as splendid examples at Castle Howard (Yorkshire) and Brocklesby (Lincolnshire).

It is tempting to speculate, therefore, that Alexander's tomb in Alexandria was circular, and that first the Numidian kings and later Augustus were taking a lead from the mausoleum of their illustrious predecessor. We can further guess that Alexander's tomb was decorated by either freestanding or more probably engaged columns round the exterior (as at Le Medracen and Tipasa), and was no doubt richly embellished with sculpture. But all this is incapable of strict proof. A recent attempt by the late Achille Adriani to identify Alexander's tomb with a simple tomb made of alabaster slabs in the eastern cemetery at Alexandria is unconvincing. But until what remains of the actual tomb is (by chance) unearthed by archaeologists under modern Alexandria, we are unlikely ever to know what the final resting place of this remarkable man really looked like.

The Tomb of China's First Emperor

52

Time: 210 BC
Location: Xian, China

*As soon as the first emperor became king of Qin, excavations and building were started at Mount Li....
The tomb was filled with models of palaces, pavilions and offices, as well as fine vessels, precious stones
and rarities. Artisans were ordered to fix up crossbows so that any thief breaking in would be shot.*

SIMA QIAN, 145–86 BC

IF YOU TRAVEL EAST from Xian, past intensively farmed fields framed by rolling hills, you may notice a low mound known as Mount Li. Local people for centuries assumed it to be simply a natural part of the landscape, but even 60 years ago, intriguing large terracotta human figures had been turned up in the vicinity. The chance digging of a well in 1974 increased speculation that this was a very special place in the history of China: peasants encountered a jumbled mass of life-sized clay soldiers, still bearing their original paint and holding bronze weaponry. The locals had stumbled upon the silent army that, for two millennia, had protected the tomb of Qin Shihuangdi, the first emperor of China.

In the year 221 BC, a vital phase of China's history, known as the Warring States period, drew to a close. Since 453 BC, the major states had been embroiled in a virtually continuous conflict for supremacy. It was a time when armies measured in tens and possibly hundreds of thousands were locked in combat, when the art of war and weaponry advanced in great leaps. By 311, the state of Qin conquered the rich basin of Sichuan. In 277, Chin fell, followed by Han and Wei.

Mount Li covers the subterranean palace and tomb of China's first emperor. Now 47 m (155 ft) high, it must once have been much higher, but erosion has taken its toll.

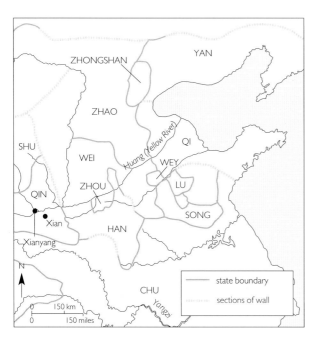

Map showing China during the Warring States period, and the location of Xianyang and Xian.

And so the victorious King Zheng proclaimed himself Qin Shihuangdi. The tomb of Master Xi, one of his high officials who died in 217 BC, contains the oldest surviving legal documents in China, 500 precious bamboo slips which record a new legal regime based on the strict application of universal laws under the unified state. The emperor divided his domain into 36 commanderies, and from his capital at Xianyang he ordered the construction of the Great Wall to the north, and a splendid new palace. Obsessed with notions of immortality, already in 246 BC he also ordered 700,000 conscripts to build a tomb hardly rivalled in the history of humankind.

The emperor's army

Set within a vast rectangular walled precinct, the tomb complex is known to us from two sources. The first is archaeology, and the second contemporary historic records. Within the enclosure, before the tomb itself, are the pits containing the terracotta army. There are few sites in world archaeology that can prepare visitors for the spectacle that confronts them as they descend into the viewing area of pit 1, now partially revealed by Chinese archaeologists. Serried rows of silent terracotta warriors within long, parallel chambers disappear into the distance. A chariot and four horses are positioned towards the front. The infantry soldiers stand ready, proudly

erect, arms holding long-handled bronze spears, or a quiver of arrows, the edges still sharp to the touch. Closer inspection reveals the intricacy of the body armour, and the scarves to keep out the blast of Siberian air for those sent to the northern frontier.

Earlier historians had long appreciated the advances in military organization which propelled the Qin to supremacy on the battlefield, but who could have imagined that an entire division of over 7000 soldiers, within a subterranean pit covering 12,600 sq. m (135,630 sq. ft), would one day emerge from oblivion? Who would have thought it possible to inspect every member of the army, from the tall general down to the meanest foot soldier?

This army, frozen in time, is but the tip of the iceberg. A second pit nearby contains the cavalry division of over 100 chariots and 100 war horses. A third pit houses the army headquarters staff.

The contents of the tomb

No one can guess at what other treasures may await discovery: already a superb bronze chariot and its horses have been unearthed, surely representing the emperor's own vehicle, which would have taken him on his many tours of the empire before his death aged 50 in 210 BC. There are chambers containing the skeletons of horses, each looking towards the central

Above **Each clay warrior in the huge terracotta army was rendered as an individual, using various clay moulds and applied details. The figures were then painted – traces of pigment survive.**

Left **An archer kneels and prepares a bow that was probably taken by robbers soon after the death of the First Emperor.** *Right* **Recently discovered chariots complete with horses and all their equipment: only a fraction of the army has so far been uncovered.**

Chinese archaeologists are still in the painstaking process of uncovering the army in the pits located outside the tomb mound, but have not yet ventured to explore the tomb itself – its contents remain a mystery.

mausoleum, some incorporating the skeletons of animals which probably belonged to the emperor's menagerie. Yet no visitor can for long ignore the lowering summit of Mount Li itself in the distance. Still rising around 47 m (154 ft) above the plain, and measuring 350 by 340 m (1148 by 1115 ft) at the base, its contents remain a mystery, for no archaeologist has ever ventured within.

Yet the historian Sima Qian has provided us with tantalizing clues. Underneath, he says, lies a veritable palace of treasures. The rivers of the empire, the mighty Yangzi and Yellow, are represented in mercury, which by mechanical means is made to flow into an inland sea. Huge torches of whale oil were once lit, to illuminate the interior if not for eternity, then for a very long time. The tomb was encased in cast bronze, and the emperor's finest furniture and fittings were set in place for his future needs. His successor decreed that all the emperor's wives who had not borne him sons should accompany him in death. Crossbows were set in place to eliminate unwelcome plunderers and tomb robbers. And, in a final autocratic decree, all those involved in the interior construction and fitting out of the tomb chambers were executed. Pits containing the skeletons of many men, some bearing the scars of butchery, have been found nearby.

Yet perhaps there is little left to find. Only recently, a superb Qin Dynasty bronze bell embellished with gold and silver was found in the shadow of the tomb. The historic accounts of the period recount that, only a few years after his death, the emperor's tomb was entered and sacked. Rebels under their leader, General Xiang Yu, plundered the riches within the actual burial palace and entered the underground chambers which contained the terracotta armies and took their weapons. But some of the clay soldiers and their weapons survived unscathed. If, as the records suggest, 300,000 people in 30 days could not empty the entire contents of the tomb, then some chambers may survive untouched to this day. Perhaps the quicksilver still flows to the sea within – a mystery that only excavation can solve.

But we can be sure of one historic fact. Even if his dynasty barely outlived his own death, and the emperor's palace-tomb has been destroyed, his administrative reforms lived on through the succeeding centuries down to modern times.

The Hidden Treasure of the Dead Sea

Time: mid-1st century BC – mid-1st century AD
Location: Qumran, Jordan Valley

... the Copper Scroll treasure, whether real or imaginary, is probably the Jerusalem Temple treasure.

KYLE McCARTER, 1992

I N THE LATE 1940s a hidden deposit of scrolls was found by chance in caves at Qumran, near the northwestern shore of the Dead Sea, then in the British Mandate of Palestine. On the withdrawal of the British the area became part of the Hashemite kingdom of Jordan. The cache of documents, which were mostly written on leather, then tightly rolled up and placed in pottery jars, was spread over several caves. The scrolls themselves were found to contain fragments and large portions of nearly all the books of the Hebrew Bible and also a considerable amount of literature that probably emanated from the sect that inhabited the site of Qumran itself. These documents have come to be known as the Dead Sea Scrolls – and of all of them the Copper Scroll, named after the metal it is made from, is certainly the strangest.

Discovery and restoration

Père Roland de Vaux, one of the chief excavators of Qumran, found the Copper Scroll in Cave 3, in two pieces, in 1952. It looked so different that he was not even sure if it belonged with the other Scrolls, and neither he nor any of the other archaeologists was able to open it because of its corroded condition. They could discern just enough of the contents to guess that it might contain a description of hidden silver and gold treasure. But, frustratingly, there was absolutely nothing they could do about it.

Eventually, three and a half years later, the Copper Scroll was taken to the then Manchester College of Science and Technology in northern England, where

Professor H. Wright Baker of the Engineering Department was able to open it with a specially designed miniaturized disc saw. The 12 columns of text, preserved in the 23 concave panels or segments that resulted from this delicate operation, were found to contain a tantalizing list of treasures and a description of their hiding places throughout ancient Palestine.

The cliffs east of Qumran are full of caves in which the Dead Sea Scrolls were hidden, probably around AD 66 at the outbreak of the First Jewish Revolt against Rome.

231

The Scroll must have been a very costly item to make and was clearly intended to be highly durable. It is composed of three extremely thin sheets of copper which is 99 per cent pure. The sheets were originally riveted together to make a scroll 2.4 m (8 ft) long by 23 cm (9 in) wide. It is also unique: first, it is made of copper not leather like the other Dead Sea Scrolls. Secondly, it is written in a Hebrew that is later than the Bible but earlier than the earliest Rabbinic texts. On palaeographic grounds it appears to date to the mid-1st century AD or slightly later. Its script is so clumsy that it could not have been set down by a professional scribe. Finally, unlike the other Dead Sea Scrolls it does not contain a biblical text nor sectarian literature that might have emanated from the monastic community at Qumran itself.

A few scholars used to think of it as a legendary list, a kind of secret treasure trail of the sort that occurs in folklore all over the world. Today most experts believe that it records the hiding places of treasure taken from Herod's Temple in Jerusalem just before the Romans attacked the city in AD 67.

Above **A section of one of the opened panels from the Copper Scroll. Some letters, such as the 'aleph' in the sixth line down and 'beth' in the last, are clearly visible, written in the square script that is still used to print modern Hebrew today.**

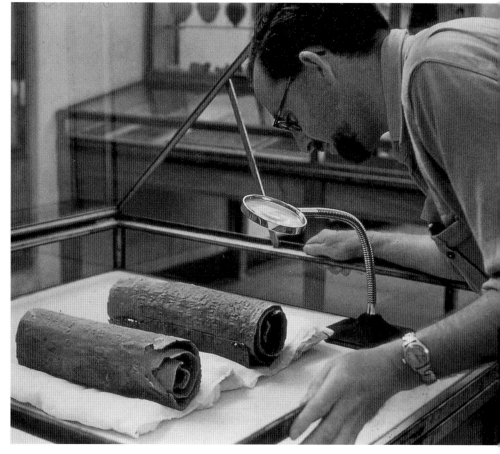

Right **John Allegro examining the two pieces of the Copper Scroll, lying in its display case in the Palestine Archaeological Museum (now the Rockefeller Museum) in Jerusalem. The photograph was taken soon after the discovery of the Scroll, and before it was taken to England to be opened and examined.**

What is the treasure?

Not one single item of this treasure has ever come to light, although many have travelled hopefully the length and breadth of Israel and Jordan in search of it. The first to do so was John Allegro, who had been instrumental in bringing the Copper Scroll to Manchester, and who published the first English translation of it. Like all those who followed him he was unsuccessful. Can the Scroll possibly be what it seems – a simple list of treasure hidden about the country? The nature of each cache is given, and its location is supplied with a note of the distance in cubits from some neighbouring landmark and even at what depth it has been hidden. Even more mysteriously a few entries include two or three Greek letters. No one has any idea what they signify.

In total there are 64 entries. Between them they set out details of an enormous amount of treasure, mostly in gold and silver bullion, but also in costly ritual vessels and containers of incense. Surely only the Temple – which was in effect the State Treasury – could possess such wealth or would have use for ceremonial objects and incense? Its dating fits in with the time of the First Jewish Revolt (AD 66–70). In AD 70 the Romans entered Jerusalem and the Temple was destroyed in a huge conflagration.

These days majority opinion believes that, while it does give details of real deposits, the Scroll is not entirely what it seems. The hiding places of the treasure appear to be mostly in the wadis that run down from Jerusalem to the Dead Sea, yet not a single piece has ever been found. In addition the total amount of the treasure recorded on the Scroll (itself so valuable) is so incredible that most scholars think that some sort of code is in operation in the text. It is one that we are never likely to unravel.

There is one final mystery: was the treasure originally stolen from the Temple by the Zealot guerrilla fighters who opposed the Romans so vigorously and who ultimately perished at Masada? Or was it removed from the Temple for safekeeping by the priests or other parties on the approach of the Roman army? It is one of the many questions still surrounding the Copper Scroll.

The 23 sections of the Copper Scroll displayed in the specially built case at the Jordan Archaeological Museum, Amman. Unfortunately, the edges of the sections have deteriorated over the years since it was opened and some of the text has been lost. Conservation work is now underway to ensure that no more of the unique text disappears.

The Tomb of Christ

Time: 1st century AD
Location: Jerusalem, Israel

And Joseph took the body, and wrapped it in a clean linen shroud, and laid it in his own new tomb, which he had hewn in the rock; and he rolled a great stone to the door of the tomb, and departed.

MATTHEW 27: 59–60

MANY PEOPLE BELIEVE with great confidence that at the heart of the Church of the Holy Sepulchre in Jerusalem lies the genuine tomb of Christ. Yet, considering that the site of Jesus' burial was lost for over two centuries when Jerusalem was a pagan city, how can there be such certainty? In the early 4th century AD, Constantine, the first Roman emperor to become a Christian, declared Christianity the state religion of his empire. In AD 325, after the Council of Nicaea, he asked Archbishop Makarios of Jerusalem to find the tomb of Christ and to erect a great church over it. The Archbishop seems to have known exactly where to look – without hesitation he set about the destruction of the massive Roman temple built by the emperor Hadrian some 200 years previously. Reaching the temple's foundations the excavators quickly came upon a tomb which was unanimously declared to be the place where Joseph of Arimathea had hurriedly laid the body of Jesus Christ before the onset of the Sabbath, some 300 years earlier. Was this truly a miracle directed by the hand of God, or was there perhaps already a tradition that led Makarios straight to the tomb? Or might there have been some other reason?

The Gospel tradition

The Gospels tell us that the Romans crucified Jesus in a place of execution near the walls of Jerusalem, so that the citizens would have a good view of the punishment meted out to criminals. Just beyond the northwest corner of the city there was a quarry for the hard *malaki* limestone which is still used to face the buildings of Jerusalem. The quarry has been found to date to the 8th and 7th centuries BC and by the time of Jesus it was an area of gardens and orchards. In one place in the quarry there was a seam of faulty rock that the masons had left standing because it was not suitable for building purposes. This is the rock that many people accept as Calvary or Golgotha (the Place of Skulls) where Jesus was crucified between the two thieves.

Nearby, some of the wealthy citizens of Jerusalem had had their tombs carved out of the solid rock of the quarry's walls. Joseph of Arimathea's tomb could well have been one of these – near a place of public execution just beyond the walls of the city, as recounted in the Gospel of Matthew (27: 57–60). The Gospel story also tells us that the entrance to the tomb was closed with a huge and heavy rock shaped like a millstone, and archaeologists have found a few tombs like this in the area of Jerusalem dating to the time of Jesus. They probably belonged to aristocratic families who buried several generations of their dead in them, sealing them with great round stones that

Left **This gold fingerring appears to show the original Aedicule built around the Tomb of Christ in the reign of the emperor Constantine (AD 306–37). The ring itself possibly dates to the 6th century AD, and was found in excavations near the Temple Mount in Jerusalem.**

Right **Aerial view of the Church of the Holy Sepulchre. The large dome covers the Rotunda, above the Tomb itself; the smaller one on the left is at the crossing of the short transept.**

rolled in a groove across the entry. These 'rolling stones' took an enormous amount of strength to move, just like the one in the account of the Gospel of Matthew.

Before interment, each body had to be bathed and anointed in accordance with the rituals of Jewish law of the time. Then it was shrouded in a winding sheet and placed on a rock-cut bench on one side of the tomb chamber. It was to wash and anoint the body of Christ that the women returned to the tomb in the early hours of the day after the Sabbath, only to find the stone miraculously rolled aside and the burial bench empty.

Jerusalem under Roman rule

For years the Christians of Jerusalem venerated the site, but it was lost in the early 2nd century AD when Hadrian destroyed the city and founded his pagan colony of Aelia Capitolina on its ruins. In around AD 135 he built a great temple complex on a high platform, dedicating it to Aphrodite, goddess of love. Perhaps there really was a persistent tradition that it was over the site of the tomb and the place of the crucifixion that the emperor built his temple. According to St Jerome, writing about AD 395, there may even have been a large statue of the goddess erected on the rock of Calvary nearby. In the later, Christian, view Hadrian built the temple on the site

of the holy tomb in order to deny Christians access to their holiest places; it is certainly true that he discouraged Christians and Jews alike from practising their faiths in his new city. However, a tiny Christian presence survived in Jerusalem throughout the Roman period.

By the time Constantine ordered the whereabouts of the crucifixion and burial of Christ to be located, the size of the city and even the extent of its walls had changed a great deal. Even if the general location of the tomb remained a traditional memory, how could the Christians have still been aware of the exact site of Christ's burial, especially when there had been so few of them in the city in its pagan Roman days? Yet without a glance beyond the city walls, Archbishop Makarios instantly went to the great Roman temple, on the north side of the forum at the heart of Hadrian's city. At the time of the crucifixion, this area had indeed been outside the city and had only been incorporated into it about 10 to 15 years after Christ's death.

Finding the tomb

We have one, possibly eye-witness, account of the finding of the tomb. About AD 337, quite late in his life, Eusebius, Bishop of Caesaria and church historian, wrote a biography of the emperor Constantine. According to Eusebius the excavators were amazed to find the tomb of Christ so easily. But did they really find the right tomb among the many that once stood in the area? Or did they simply find a tomb and assume it was the right one? Perhaps it was marked in some way, with the name of Jesus scratched on it, although this is not mentioned by Eusebius or any later sources. Martin Biddle of Hertford College, Oxford, has pointed out that this is how the tomb of St Peter was identified deep beneath the high altar of the basilica of St Peter's in Rome.

In any case the church that arose in Jerusalem, the Church of the Martyrion (or 'Witness'), was the greatest of its age, the ancestor of today's Church of the Holy Sepulchre. Beyond the great church, across the Holy Garden, lay the tomb itself, cut free from its surrounding rock and standing proud, the ground levelled all around it. Sometime after dedicating the church in AD 335, Constantine enclosed the rock

View from the interior of the so-called 'Tomb of Herod's Daughters' in western Jerusalem, beyond the ancient city walls – as were all tombs of the period. The great round stone running in its groove can clearly be seen, and the short flight of steps leading down into the rock-cut tomb.

tomb in a small shrine called the Aedicule ('little house') and created a great Rotunda (called the Anastasis or 'Resurrection') around it, roofing the whole with a huge dome.

Today, the third descendant of the original Aedicule enshrines the tomb; but even if we accept, as most people do, that it is indeed the tomb of Christ, one final mystery still attaches to it, for we have no idea if anything of the original tomb survives. Over the many centuries since the original Aedicule and the church that houses it were built, it has several times been totally or partly destroyed by fire, earthquake and human hand. The last time the Aedicule was rebuilt was after a disastrous fire in 1808. Most recently the structure became unstable during the British Mandate, after an earthquake in 1927, when it was shored up by steel scaffolding. This scaffolding is still in place and it has become clear that substantial building work on the Aedicule must be undertaken in the near future. When this happens, with the permission of the Christian religious communities who are responsible for the Church of the Holy Sepulchre, it should be possible to detect whether anything remains of the actual tomb in which Christ's body was originally laid to rest.

Left **The Aedicule as it appears today, shored up by British scaffolding of the Mandate period in the first half of the 20th century. Beyond can be seen some of the arches of the Rotunda that encircle the Aedicule.**

Below **A section east–west through the current Church of the Holy Sepulchre. At the lowest (eastern) end is the Chapel of the True Cross, supposedly where Helena, Constantine's mother, located the Cross on which Jesus was crucified. Steps lead up from it to the ambulatory; the small dome is above the transept crossing, the area of the original Holy Garden with the Rock of Calvary in its southeastern corner. At the extreme right is the Rotunda, with the Aedicule in its centre.**

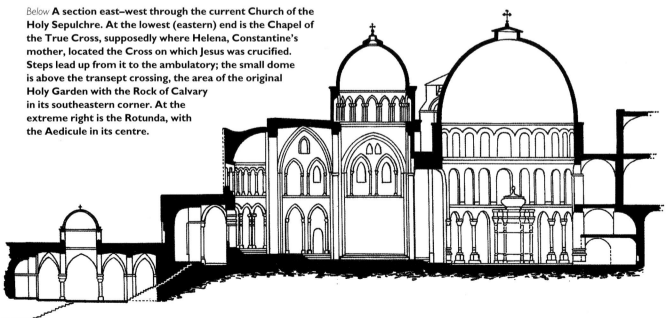

Ancient & Undeciphered Scripts

WRITING IS ONE of humanity's great inventions. Today, we mostly take it for granted, learn how to write in school, and put pen to paper, or fingers to computer keyboard, without thinking about it. We rarely pause to consider the complex mental and physical processes that enable us to put thoughts into symbols and words, so the invention of writing at least 5000 years ago seems almost miraculous. Small wonder that the decipherment of ancient scripts has fascinated layperson and scholar alike for centuries. Andrew Robinson takes us on an engaging journey through the arcane world of epigraphy and decipherment.

How did writing begin? Robinson believes it began in southwestern Asia with accountancy and the need to keep track of increasingly intricate commercial transactions. Perhaps the first scribes lived in Uruk in Mesopotamia. Or conceivably writing developed from humble clay tokens, long used to keep an inventory of caravan loads. We will probably never be certain. But we know that writing was a highly successful innovation, widely used in Mesopotamia and Egypt by 3100 BC. The new scripts opened fresh vistas for humanity. Writing gave people the ability to record details easily lost in human memory, a way of reminding people of tasks to be completed, of recording inventories and ration allocations. Writing also became the currency of international diplomacy, a vehicle for religious devotion, for education, self-expression, and, above all, of political power. To be literate was to have access to information, a power over people. The office of scribe was highly prized in ancient Egypt, and rightly so. Literacy passed from

Detail of the Franks Casket, c. AD 700, depicting the story of Romulus and Remus, with runic inscriptions above and below.

father to son, starting with hesitant glyphs brushed on potsherds and small stones, then on papyrus reed, the paper of ancient Egypt. A school book adjures reluctant pupils: 'Be a scribe, your body will be sleek, your hand will be soft.... You will go forth in white clothes, honoured, with courtiers saluting you.'

The first writing was in the form of pictograms – symbols wholly insufficient to express all kinds of words or parts of words. As Robinson points out, the first true writing came with the discovery or invention of the rebus principle, which gave phonetic values to pictographic symbols. While the idea of writing spread widely, it seems that different scripts developed in separate places, and evolved quite independently in the Americas.

The decipherment of ancient scripts requires infinite patience, a passion for detail, considerable mathematical ability, and great linguistic ability. Few decipherments have come from individual scholarship, or simply from spectacular discoveries like the Rosetta Stone or the Great Rock of Behistun. Some were achieved by collaboration, though often the race to decipherment was driven by fierce rivalry and the desire to be first, as much as by a spirit of co-operation. The Frenchman Jean-François Champollion deciphered Egyptian hieroglyphs in 1823 on the shoulders of earlier workers. Edward Hincks, Jules Oppert and Henry Rawlinson worked on Mesopotamian cuneiform in tandem and with frequent consultation, each contributing to the complex puzzle. Teamwork has continued into modern times: the decipherment of Maya glyphs ranks as one of the great scientific achievements of the 20th century and was the result of inspired collaboration between scholars living in several countries working on royal genealogies and religious almanacs.

Years of arduous research go into successful decipherments: a combination of brilliant insights, inspired guesswork and sheer hard work. The triumphant stories of Champollion, Rawlinson, Michael Ventris and the Maya researchers are well known. But many ancient scripts still defy epigraphers. Robinson describes the mysteries surrounding several important, but lesser-known, scripts. Ventris and others deciphered Linear B in the 1950s, but the more primitive Linear A remains a mystery, partly because the language in which it was written is unknown. The Indus script of the Harappan civilization is still an enigma, but may be written in a proto-Dravidian language. Final decipherment may come from current researches into early Dravidian languages. The Etruscan script was written in an extinct language, of which we know only some 250 words. Much of the corpus comes from brief entries on gravestones, hardly the best archives for researching a language. The cursive and hieroglyphic script of Meroe owes much to ancient Egyptian writing, but is set down in an unknown language, undecipherable until more bilingual inscriptions come to light.

Right **The majority of surviving Etruscan inscriptions are epitaphs on tombs and grave monuments, which has hampered the decipherment of the underlying language even though the inscriptions can be 'read'.**

The Zapotec and Isthmian scripts of Mesoamerica still elude decipherment, despite some resemblance to the Maya script and the fact that we have a fair idea of the language they are written in; the problem in this case is that there is so little text available. Some other scripts, like Pictish symbol stones and (probably) proto-Elamite from ancient Iran, were not full writing systems, while the celebrated *rongorongo* wooden tablets of Easter Island will probably never be deciphered because the exquisite script is complex and again so few inscriptions have survived. That, however, will not prevent scholars and amateurs from continuing to try.

The Origins of Writing

Time: 3300 BC?
Location: Mesopotamia

You, who are the father of letters, have been led by your affection to ascribe to them a power the opposite of that which they really possess.... You have invented an elixir not of memory, but of reminding; and you offer your pupils the appearance of wisdom, for they will read many things without instruction and will therefore seem to know many things, when they are for the most part ignorant.

WORDS OF THE EGYPTIAN KING TO THOTH, DIVINE INVENTOR OF WRITING, AS SPOKEN BY SOCRATES

HOW DID WRITING BEGIN? The favoured explanation, until the Enlightenment in the 18th century, was divine origin. Today many, probably most, scholars accept that the earliest writing evolved from accountancy, though it is puzzling that accountancy is little in evidence in the surviving writing of ancient Egypt, India, China and Central America (which is no guarantee that once upon a time there was not such bureaucratic record keeping on perishable materials in these civilizations). In other words, some time in the late 4th millennium BC, the complexity of trade and administration in the early cities of Sumer in Mesopotamia, the 'cradle of civilization', reached a point where it outstripped the power of memory of the governing élite. To record transactions in an indisputable, permanent form became essential. Administrators and merchants could then say the Sumerian equivalent of 'I shall put it in writing' and 'May I have this in writing?'

Some scholars believe that a conscious search for a solution to this problem by an unknown Sumerian individual in the city of Uruk (biblical Erech) in about 3300 BC, produced writing. Others believe writing was the work of a group, presumably of clever administrators and merchants. Still others think it was not an invention at all, but an accidental discovery. Many regard it as the result of evolution over a long period, rather than a flash of inspiration. One particularly well-aired theory holds

Clay 'envelope', and clay 'tokens', from Mesopotamia. Marks on the 'envelope', apparently made by the 'tokens' to indicate its contents, may be a stage in the development of writing.

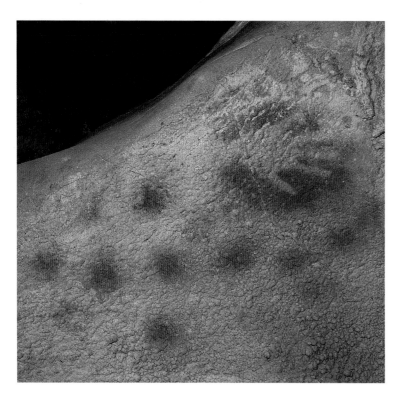

Left **'Proto-writing'? These marks in a cave at Pech-Merle in France are probably 20,000 years old. Their meaning is unknown.**

Right **Modern 'hieroglyphs', a contemporary form of 'proto-writing'. Their meaning is known but they are of limited use – unlike alphabetic letters.**

that writing grew out of a long-standing counting system of clay 'tokens' (such 'tokens' – varying from simple, plain discs to more complex, incised shapes whose exact purpose is unknown – have been found in many Middle Eastern archaeological sites): the substitution of two-dimensional symbols in clay for these three-dimensional tokens, with the symbols resembling the appearance of the token, was a first step towards writing, according to this theory. One major difficulty is that the 'tokens' continued to exist long after the emergence of Sumerian cuneiform writing; another is that a two-dimensional symbol on a clay tablet might be thought to be a less, not a more, advanced concept than a three-dimensional 'token'. It seems more likely that 'tokens' accompanied the emergence of writing, rather than gave rise to it.

'Proto-writing'

Apart from the 'tokens', numerous examples exist of what one might call 'proto-writing'. For example, there are the Ice Age symbols found in caves in southern France, which are probably 20,000 years old. A cave at Pech-Merle, in Lot, contains a lively Ice Age graffito showing a stencilled hand and a pattern of red dots. What does this mean? 'I was here, with my animals'? – or is the symbolism deeper?

Other images show animals, such as horses, a stag's head and bison, overlaid with signs; and notched bones have been found that apparently served as lunar calendars.

'Proto-writing' is not writing, in the sense of the word as we use it today. A distinguished scholar of writing, John DeFrancis, has defined 'full' writing as a 'system of graphic symbols that can be used to convey any and all thought'. By this definition, 'proto-writing' includes, as well as Ice Age cave symbols, Middle Eastern archaeological 'tokens', Pictish symbol stones (pp. 264–5) and tallies such as the fascinating knotted Inca *quipus*, such contemporary sign systems as international transportation symbols, highway code signs, computer 'icons', and mathematical and musical notation. None of these systems is capable of expressing 'any and all thought', but they are each good at specialized communication.

To express the full range of human thought, we need a system intimately linked with spoken language. For as Ferdinand de Saussure, the founder of modern linguistics, wrote, language may be compared to a sheet of paper. 'Thought is on one side of the sheet and sound the reverse side. Just as it is impossible to take a pair of scissors and cut one side of the paper without at the same time cutting the

Above **When is a pictogram not a pictogram?** *Metamorphosis III* (detail), **1967–68, by M.C. Escher.**

Right **Two gold pectorals from the tomb of Tutankhamun. The scarab beetle in the top one, pronounced** *kheper,* **is a rebus forming part of Tutankhamun's prenomen, Nebkheprure. The 'ankh' sign (with cross) in the talons of the falcon is, however a pictogram: it stands for 'life'.**

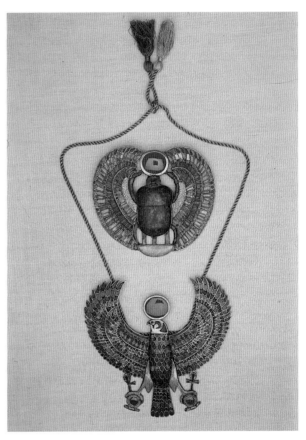

other, so it is impossible in a language to isolate sound from thought, or thought from sound.'

The development of full writing

The symbols of what may have been the first 'full' writing system are generally thought to have been pictograms: iconic drawings of, say, a pot, or a fish, or a head with an open jaw (representing the concept of eating). These have been found in Mesopotamia and Egypt dating to the mid-4th millennium BC, shortly after that in the Indus Valley, and even earlier in China, according to the (doubtful) claims of some Chinese archaeologists. In many cases, their iconicity soon became so abstract that it is barely perceptible to us. Here is how the Sumerian pictograms developed into cuneiform signs:

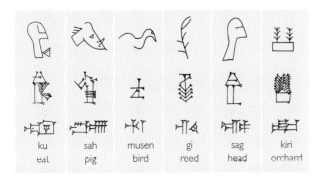

ku eal	sah pig	musen bird	gi reed	sag head	kiri orchard

But pictograms were insufficient to express the kinds of words, and their constituent parts, that cannot be picturized. Essential to the development of 'full' writing, as opposed to limited, purely pictographic 'proto-writing', was the discovery of the *rebus* principle. This radical idea, from the Latin meaning 'by things', enables phonetic values to be represented by pictographic symbols. Thus in English, a picture of a bee with a picture of a figure 4 might (if one were so minded) represent 'before' and a bee with a picture of a tray might stand for 'betray', while a picture of an ant next to a buzzing bee hive, might (less obviously) represent 'Anthony'. Egyptian hieroglyphs are full of rebuses, for instance the 'sun' sign, ☉, pronounced *R(a)* or *R(e)*, is the first symbol in the hieroglyphic spelling of the pharaoh Ramesses. In an early Sumerian tablet we find the abstract word 'reimburse' represented by a picture of a reed, because 'reimburse' and 'reed' shared the same phonetic value *gi* in the Sumerian language.

Once writing of this 'full' kind, capable of expressing the full range of speech and thought, was invented, accidentally discovered or evolved – take your pick – did it then diffuse throughout the globe from Mesopotamia? The earliest Egyptian writing dates from 3100 BC, that of the Indus Valley (the undeciphered seal stones, pp. 247–9) from 2500 BC, that of Crete (the undeciphered Linear A script, pp. 250–2) from 1750 BC, that of China

(the 'oracle bones') from 1200 BC, that of Central America (the undeciphered Zapotec script, pp. 261–2) from 500 BC – all dates are approximate. On this basis, it seems reasonable that the *idea* of writing, but not the symbols of a particular script, could have spread gradually from culture to distant culture. It took 600 or 700 years for the idea of printing to reach Europe from China (if we discount the unique and enigmatic Phaistos disc of *c.* 1700 BC, found in Crete, which appears to be 'printed'; pp. 252–3), and even longer for the idea of paper to spread to Europe: why should writing not have reached China from Mesopotamia over an even longer period?

Nevertheless, in the absence of solid evidence for transmission of the idea (even in the case of the physically much nearer civilizations of Mesopotamia and Egypt), a majority of scholars prefers to think that writing developed independently in the major civilizations of the ancient world. The optimist, or at any rate the anti-imperialist, will prefer to emphasize the intelligence and inventiveness of human societies; the pessimist, who takes a more conservative view of history, will tend to assume that humans prefer to copy what already exists, as faithfully as they can, restricting their innovations to cases of absolute necessity. After all, the latter is the preferred explanation for how the Greeks (at the beginning of the 1st millennium BC) borrowed the alphabet from the Phoenicians, adding in the process signs for the vowels not written in the Phoenician script; and there are many other examples of script borrowings, such as the Japanese taking the Chinese characters in the 1st millennium AD. If ever the *rongorongo* script (pp. 266–7) of Easter Island – the most isolated inhabited spot on earth – is deciphered, it may shed light on the fascinating question of whether the Easter Islanders invented *rongorongo* unaided, brought the idea of their writing from Polynesia in their canoes, or borrowed it from Europeans who first visited Easter Island in the 18th century. If we could prove that *rongorongo* was invented unaided on Easter Island, we would at last be sure that writing must have had origins, rather than one origin.

Left above **A Sumerian rebus, c. 3000 BC. The 'reed' in the top left-hand corner is a rebus for 'reimburse'.** *Left below* **Chinese 'oracle bones' c. 1200 BC. Some of the signs resemble modern Chinese characters.**

The Proto-Elamite Script

Time: 3050–2900 BC
Location: Iran

56

For most students of antiquity Elam appears aloof, somewhat exotic – a place of hard-to-pronounce names, unfamiliar sites, a poorly understood language and a somewhat barbaric population to the east of Mesopotamia.

DANIEL T. POTTS, 1999

PROTO-ELAMITE is the world's oldest undeciphered script – assuming that it is a fully developed writing system. It was used for a brief period 5000 years ago, *c.* 3050–2900 BC, in Elam, the biblical name for the province of Persia and the area known to the Classical geographers as Susiana, from the name of its ancient capital Susa; today it corresponds very roughly to the region of the oil fields in western Iran. However, the proto-Elamite script seems to have been used over a much wider area than just Elam; it has been found as far east as the Iranian border with Afghanistan.

The prefix 'proto-' is used because the script preceded a much later, partially deciphered script known as Linear (Old) Elamite, also found at Susa, which was employed by the ruler Puzur-Insusinak, again for a brief period, *c.* 2150 BC. (A third, largely deciphered script, Elamite cuneiform, was used from the 13th century BC for many centuries, including by the Persian king Darius at his capital Persepolis.) The relationship between proto-Elamite and Linear Elamite is controversial. Scholars were formerly convinced that the two scripts wrote the same language and that Linear Elamite had developed from

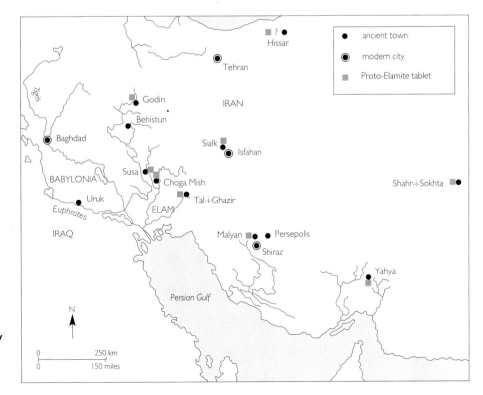

Proto-Elamite settlements on the Iranian plateau, with tablet finds marked. The proto-Elamite script slightly postdates the proto-cuneiform script used at Uruk in Mesopotamia.

A proto-Elamite account text from Susa. Only the numerals are properly understood.

proto-Elamite. But today they are increasingly persuaded that there is no evidence for a shared language and culture.

The proto-Elamite corpus is a substantial one: almost 1500 texts (clay tablets), containing some 100,000 characters, though many of them are so badly damaged they are known only from reconstructions; whereas Linear Elamite, by contrast, can boast only 22 texts. It is therefore ironic that Linear Elamite is somewhat better understood than proto-Elamite, because some of its few inscriptions are bilinguals (the second, known, script/language being Akkadian cuneiform), while the proto-Elamite script lacks bilinguals and its language is totally unknown.

We do nevertheless know quite a lot about the script. The most productive method of decipherment has focused on the numerals, since all tablets contain them; in fact the tablets clearly record lists of people and objects with calculations, like the much better-understood Sumerian tablets from Mesopotamia. Here is an example concerning herdsmen and sheep:

Careful study of the numerals in many tablets shows that the proto-Elamite scribes employed a variety of counting systems, not just the simple decimal system illustrated here. For example, a sexagesimal system was used to count inanimate objects, as in Babylonia. But while we can understand many proto-Elamite calculations, we do not yet know if the non-numeral signs are phonetic or logographic, so we cannot translate the many signs that apparently name individuals and institutions. Only knowledge of the language could prove that the script is a full writing system, rather than a complex system of noting economic records.

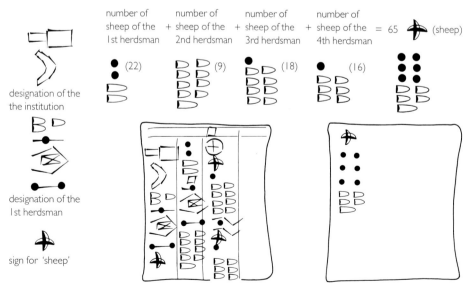

designation of the the institution

designation of the 1st herdsman

sign for 'sheep'

number of sheep of the 1st herdsman + number of sheep of the 2nd herdsman + number of sheep of the 3rd herdsman + number of sheep of the 4th herdsman = 65 (sheep)

(22)   (9)   (18)   (16)

A proto-Elamite administrative document concerning four flocks of sheep. It uses a decimal system.

The Indus Script

Time: 2500–1900 BC
Location: Pakistan/India

At their best, it would be no exaggeration to describe [the Indus Valley seals] as little masterpieces of controlled realism, with a monumental strength in one sense out of all proportion to their size and in another entirely related to it.

SIR MORTIMER WHEELER, 1953

THE INDUS VALLEY civilization was lost even at the time of Alexander the Great. When his emissary Aristoboulos visited the area in 326 BC, he found 'an abandoned country, with more than a thousand towns and villages deserted after the Indus had changed its course'. It was not mentioned again in historical records for over 2000 years. In the early 1920s, an Indian archaeologist out searching for non-existent victory pillars put up by Alexander on his retreat from India, stumbled across the true significance of the ruin mound at Mohenjo-daro (now in Sind province of Pakistan). His discovery, and a similar discovery 560 km (350 miles) away at Harappa, also in what is now Pakistan, would double the recorded age of civilization in India at one stroke – shifting it from the imperial inscriptions of Ashoka in 250 BC back to about 2500 BC. Immediately, a team under Sir John Marshall, Director-General of the Archaeological Survey of India, began excavating at both sites.

Over the past eight decades, they and their successors have revealed some 1500 sites belonging to the Indus Valley civilization in Pakistan and northwest India, covering an area approximately a quarter the size of Europe, larger than either the ancient Egyptian or the Mesopotamian empires of the 3rd millennium BC. Most sites were villages, but five were major cities. At the Indus civilization's peak, between 2500 and about 1900 BC, Mohenjo-daro and Harappa were comparable with cities like Memphis in Egypt and Ur in Mesopotamia. They could not boast great pyramids, palaces, statues, graves and hoards of gold, but their well-planned streets and advanced drainage put to shame all but the town planning of the 20th century AD, and some of their ornaments – such as the long, drilled carnelian beads found as far afield as the royal cemetery of Ur – rival the treasures of the pharaohs for loveliness and technical sophistication.

But this advance in understanding how the Indus Valley dwellers lived has served to highlight the embarrassing fact that we can only speculate about how they thought – because their writing remains undeciphered. Unlike Egyptian hieroglyphs and Mesopotamian cuneiform, the Indus script appears not on walls, tombs, statues, stelae, clay tablets, papyri and codices, but on seal stones, pottery, copper tablets, bronze implements and ivory and bone rods, found scattered in the buildings and streets of Mohenjo-daro, Harappa and other urban settlements. (No doubt it was written too on perishable materials, such as the palm fronds traditionally used for writing in India.) The seal stones are the most numerous of the inscriptions and are justly celebrated for their exquisiteness and unique style of carving. Once seen, they are never forgotten.

The Great Bath at Mohenjo-daro, one of the two major cities of the Indus Valley civilization.

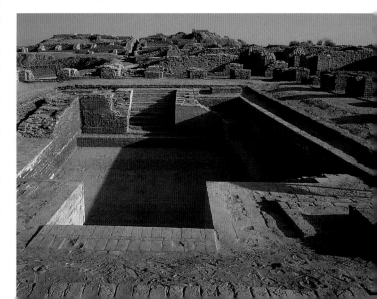

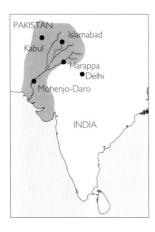

Left **The sites of the Indus Valley civilization cover an area about one quarter the size of Europe.**

Right **'Proto-Shiva': this Indus seal impression may show a precursor of the much later Hindu deity Shiva.**

About 3700 inscribed objects are known, 60 per cent of them seals, but some 40 per cent of these are duplicate inscriptions, so the useful total for the decipherer is not as large as it seems. More have been found in the 1990s, but it is not an abundant corpus, especially as the inscriptions are tantalizingly brief: the average has fewer than four characters in a line and five in a text, the longest is only 26 characters, divided between three sides of a triangular terracotta prism. In addition to the characters, many seal stones are engraved with a detailed intaglio of animals. These are generally recognizable – rhinoceroses, elephants, tigers, buffaloes, zebus, for instance (though curiously no monkeys, peacocks or cobras) – but some are fantastic or chimerical, including a one-horned animal which the early excavators promptly dubbed a 'unicorn' (a creature legendarily originating in India). Unidentified anthropomorphic figures, sometimes seated in yogic postures, also feature and may be gods and goddesses. Various scholars, beginning with Marshall, have therefore suggested that some of these figures are precursors of the Hindu deities first mentioned two millennia later in Sanskrit texts; one in particular Marshall dubbed 'proto-Shiva'.

The evidence of the signs

There have been more than a hundred serious attempts to decipher the Indus script, but although important work has been done in collecting, cataloguing and publishing all the inscriptions, notably by Asko Parpola, the leading Indus script scholar, there is little general agreement about a decipherment. Most of the attempts differ so radically – one compared the Indus signs with Egyptian hieroglyphs, another with the Easter Island *rongorongo* script – that there is hardly any common ground.

All that is certain, or at least highly probable, is the direction of writing and reading; the approximate number of signs in the writing system; the identification of some numerals; and the fact that certain texts are segmentable into words.

An important initial deduction is that the seal *impression* was what was intended to be read, not the seal intaglio (in which the characters are naturally reversed). There is room for some doubt here, as seals far outnumber seal impressions, and many of the seals show hardly any wear, suggesting that they were not used but carried, perhaps as identity 'cards' or even charms. We know it was the seal impression that was read, however, because we can compare the sign sequences and sign orientations of seal impressions with the same sequences in inscriptions that were definitely meant to be read directly, for example those written in pottery graffiti and on metal implements. Generally, they match. The seal images shown here are all seal impressions.

As for the direction of writing, the most dependable evidence comes from the spacing of the inscriptions. If a short text starts from the right-hand edge and leaves a space on the left, it may be assumed to run from right to left. And if it shows cramping of symbols on the left-hand edge, the same conclusion may be drawn. In the case of one seal, the reader plainly started at the top right-hand corner, turned the seal impression clockwise through 90 degrees twice, and part of the third edge and all of the fourth edge was blank. The direction of Indus writing is normally from right to left in the seal impression. (See photographs on the opposite page.)

The widely accepted figure for the number of signs is 425 ±25 signs. This is a significant figure, being too high for a syllabary in which the basic signs are phonetic, representing syllables, as in Linear B, and too

Right **Evidence for the direction of writing of the Indus script. These two seal impressions are read from right to left (see text).**

Below **The two chief language families of the Indian subcontinent: Indo-Aryan (the white areas) and Dravidian (which includes Brahui).**

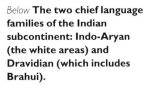

low for a highly logographic script such as Chinese, in which several thousand signs each represent a word or concept in the Chinese language. The nearest comparisons are probably Hittite hieroglyphs, with about 500 signs, and Sumerian cuneiform, with perhaps 600+ signs. Most scholars therefore agree that the Indus script is a logosyllabic script like its west Asian contemporaries, though there has been little progress in identifying the signs for phonetic syllables.

Which language?

To determine these would require knowledge of the likely language spoken in the Indus Valley civilization – and presumably written in the inscriptions. If we discard the possibility that this language is not related to any other language (a reasonable assumption in the Indian subcontinent where cultural continuities are especially strong), there are two strong candidates for related languages: proto-Indo-Aryan (Sanskrit) and proto-Dravidian, i.e. the ancestors of the two great language families of north India and south India. (Sanskrit, the chief Indo-Aryan language, is the root language of most of the modern languages of north India.)

Geographically, proto-Indo-Aryan has the edge over Dravidian, since today's Dravidian speakers belong almost exclusively to south India, far from the Indus Valley region. But proto-Dravidian is favoured on historical grounds, because the Indo-Aryan 'invasions' of north India are thought to date to the 2nd millennium BC – *after* the disappearance of the Indus Valley civilization. In support of this, there exist pockets of Dravidian languages in north India, one of which, Brahui, spoken by around 300,000 nomadic people in Baluchistan (west Pakistan), is significantly close to the Indus Valley. These Dravidian speakers are probably remnants of a

Dravidian culture once widespread in north India which was submerged by encroaching Indo-Aryans. The proto-Dravidian hypothesis is therefore the one favoured by a majority of scholars. They are searching for sensible links between the meanings of words in early Dravidian languages such as Old Tamil, Telugu, Malayalam and Kannada, and the iconic and iconographic signs and images of the Indus seals and other inscribed objects, with support from archaeological evidence about the Indus Valley civilization and cultural evidence about Dravidian civilization and religious beliefs. The method is inherently speculative, but some intriguing 'decipherments' of individual signs have been suggested, which may one day be testable if enough new inscriptions come to light.

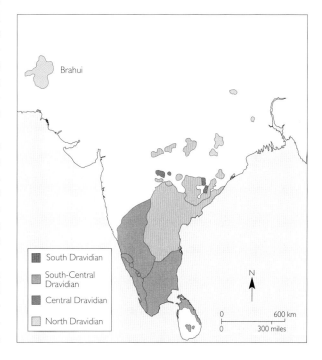

Brahui

South Dravidian

South-Central Dravidian

Central Dravidian

North Dravidian

N

0   600 km
0   300 miles

Linear A & the Phaistos Disc

58

Time: 1750–?1450 BC
Location: Crete

Suggested decipherments of the Phaistos disc are legion, and the propositions go in all possible and imaginary directions: Basque, Chinese, Dravidian, Greek, Hittite, Luwian, 'Pelasgian', Semitic, Slavic, Sumerian, to name a few.... Anyway, if one of the decipherments is correct, all the others are wrong.

YVES DUHOUX, 2000

WHEN SIR ARTHUR EVANS began excavating what he called 'Linear Script B' a century ago at the 'Palace of Minos' at Knossos, Crete, he discovered a second script also written mainly on clay tablets which strongly resembled it and which he named 'Linear Script A'. He also found a third type of writing, at Knossos and elsewhere on Crete, principally on seal stones, which he termed 'hieroglyphic'. According to the archaeological record, the 'hieroglyphic' was the oldest of the three scripts, dating chiefly to 2100–1700 BC; Linear A belonged to the period 1750–1450 BC; while Linear B post-dated Linear A. Evans therefore came to the conclusion that all three scripts wrote the same 'Minoan' language, and that Linear B had developed from Linear A, which had probably developed from the 'hieroglyphic' script – on the basis that the later Egyptian scripts such as demotic were derived from

Left **Sir Arthur Evans at Knossos, as painted in 1907. Evans holds a tablet written in Linear B, one of the three scripts he discovered in Crete.**

Right **A major findspot of Linear A: the Minoan palace at Haghia Triada in southern Crete. The clay tablet with Linear A inscription** *(opposite)* **was found there.**

Egyptian hieroglyphs and all of them wrote one Egyptian language. Lastly (and not discovered by Evans), there was the unique Phaistos disc, which he could not relate to any of the other three scripts.

Today, Evans's simple picture has been abandoned, apart from the isolation of the Phaistos disc. Linear B has been deciphered as Greek (by Michael Ventris in 1952); Linear A has been to some degree deciphered but appears to write an unknown language, probably but not definitely Cretan, so that we cannot really read it; while the meaning of the 'hieroglyphs' remains almost wholly mysterious. Furthermore, all three scripts have been found outside Crete, and the spans of their dates are now seen to overlap; we can no longer postulate a straightforward line of descent purely within Crete: Linear A and Linear B may be cousin scripts, rather than one being the parent of the other.

Linear A

The bulk of the early discoveries of Linear A were made at the site of a Minoan palace in the south of the island at Haghia Triada. But much has been discovered since then, including on Greek islands all over the Aegean, at one place on the Greek mainland, on the Turkish mainland (at ancient Miletus), and even at two sites in distant Palestine. Nevertheless, there is far less of Linear A than of Linear B: only about 1500 texts, many of them minimal or damaged, containing around 7500 characters. (This compares with tens of thousands of Linear B characters, and less than 2000 'hieroglyphic' characters.)

Two principal clues have been fruitful in deciphering Linear A: the numeral system, and the similarity of many Linear A signs to those of Linear B. It was not difficult to identify which signs were numerals: they stood out from the other signs just as they did in Linear B. The Linear A numerals are clearly the same as those of Linear B, except for the fractional signs plus an alternative sign for 10 – a heavy dot:

	= I unit		• or —	= I ten
O	= I hundred		-◇-	= I thousand

Thus we can count the numbers in a tablet and see that they add up to the correct total, given at the bottom of the tablet:

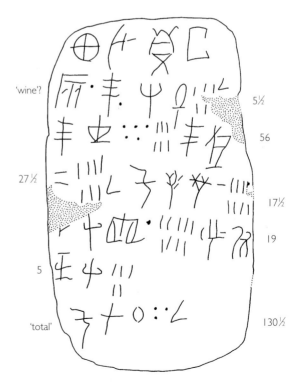

Working from the top down, we can pick out a series of numbers: 5½, 56, 27½, 17½ [unclear], 19, 5, and, at the bottom, 130½ – which is the correct total of the preceding six numbers. The two signs that appear to the left of the total probably signify 'total', as in Linear B. We can also identify a logogram ('word' sign), which means 'wine' in Linear B. (It may picture a vine growing on a trellis.) By general analogy with the Linear B tablets, this Linear A tablet is likely to concern amounts of wine given to various named individuals at a certain place, which is thought to be named in the first line of the tablet.

Comparison of Linear A signs with the sign list of Linear B yields an important conclusion: the vast majority of the Linear A signs resemble those of Linear B. Thus the two Linear A signs ⊢ ⊕ closely resemble the Linear B signs, ⊢ for *a* and ⊕ for *ru*, and the three signs ⊓ ⊤ ⊬ resemble the Linear B signs for ⊓ *di*, ⊤ *na*, and ⊬ *u*. In this way – equating unknown Linear A values with known Linear B values purely on the basis of the resemblance in shape of A and B signs – we can 'translate' Linear A tablets phonetically.

But even assuming that this comparison is valid, and that Linear A signs did originally have the same phonetic values as their Linear B equivalents, what do the Linear A words mean? For this we need to know the 'Minoan' language of Linear A. Well over a dozen candidate languages have been pressed into service by would-be decipherers; and of course the very notion that 'Minoan' is related to another language excludes the possibility that, like the unknown Etruscan language, it may have been an isolated language. The most seriously pursued comparisons have been with these three languages or language groups: Semitic, Greek (the language of Linear B) and Anatolian (Indo-European). They are all possible to the extent that these languages, or their archaic dialects, were spoken around the eastern Mediterranean in the 2nd millennium BC. The trouble is, there is not enough Linear A text to rule any of them in or out conclusively. The current favourite is the Anatolian hypothesis, which is reasonable on historical and archaeological grounds. Herodotus, in the 5th century BC, noted that 'The Lycians [of southwest Anatolia] are in good truth anciently from Crete'; and Linear A was recently found in Anatolia, at the site of ancient Miletus.

The decipherment of Linear A is therefore a partial one. The numerals can be read with confidence; the phonetic values may well be those of Linear B; but we do not have enough inscriptions to work out which of the likely candidates is the language of Linear A. So we can transliterate much of Linear A, but we cannot translate it.

The Phaistos disc

The Phaistos disc is undoubtedly the greatest puzzle of all among the scripts of ancient Crete. It was dis-

covered in 1908 by an Italian excavator in the ruins of a palace at Phaistos in southern Crete, in an archaeological context suggesting that the date of the disc was not later than about 1700 BC – in other words it was contemporary with Linear A. It is made of baked clay and on either side is an inscription, which consists of characters impressed on the wet clay with a punch or stamp. The disc is therefore, so to speak, the world's first typewritten document, created 2500 years before printing began in China, and more than 3000 years before Gutenberg's Bible.

But why should anyone have bothered to produce a punch/stamp, rather than inscribing each character afresh as in Linear A and B? If it was to 'print' many copies of documents, then why have no other documents in this script been found in over 90 years of intensive excavations? And why do the signs on the Phaistos disc fail to resemble any of the signs of the Cretan 'hieroglyphic' script, Linear A or Linear B? Could the disc have been imported into Crete, as a minority of scholars believes? Could it even be a fake – perhaps a hoax on the original excavators – as has occasionally been suggested? There are very few clues as to the meaning of the script, and no reliable answers. The signs themselves are of little help since they resemble no other 'Minoan' signs, are few in number (only 242 characters in all) and enigmatic in appearance;

and the language behind the signs is a total unknown. The context of discovery is of no real help either, other than to establish the disc's date, since there are no samples from other archaeological contexts with which to compare the disc. The only serious hope for a decipherment is that a cache of similar inscriptions will one day be found.

This has not stopped several scholars, and a great many amateurs, from proposing full decipherments, which vary wildly (itself proof of the hopelessness of the task). During 1999 alone, two books appeared in French and English, one proposing a total translation into proto-Ionian Greek, the other an interpretation of the disc as a calculating device, a 'Bronze Age computer disc'. Even Chinese has been put forward as the true language of the disc. For most professional scholars, anyone claiming to have deciphered the Phaistos disc must, *ipso facto*, be 'cracked' in the head. John Chadwick, collaborator of Ventris in the decipherment of Linear B, used to receive new disc decipherments at the rate of almost one a month for many years, and continued to analyse some of the better ones for the elements in them that were logical. He wrote: 'We must curb our impatience, and admit that if King Minos himself were to reveal to someone in a dream the true interpretation, it would be quite impossible for him to convince anyone else that his was the one and only possible solution.'

Left **The mysterious Phaistos disc. Its punched signs do not resemble any other script and its language is totally unknown. It was found in 1908 in the ruins of a palace at Phaistos, southern Crete** *(right)* **and was dated to not later than 1700 BC. So far, all attempts at its decipherment have proved fruitless.**

The Origins of the Alphabet

Time: early 2nd millennium BC
Location: Egypt or Palestine

Man has always been curious to know how alphabetic script began. Herodotus, the 'father of history', mentions that the Phoenicians came to Greece with a man named Kadmos. There they introduced writing and other arts.

JOSEPH NAVEH, 1975

IF THE ORIGINS OF WRITING (pp. 241–4) are full of riddles, even more perplexing is the enigma of the first alphabet. That it reached the modern world via the ancient Greeks is well known – the word alphabet is of course derived from the first two Greek letters, alpha and beta – but we have no clear idea of how and when it appeared in Greece, how the Greeks thought of adding letters standing for the vowels as well as the consonants, and how, even more fundamentally, the idea of an alphabet first occurred to the pre-Greek societies at the eastern end of the Mediterranean during the 2nd millennium BC.

Scholars have devoted their lives to these questions, but the evidence is too scanty for firm conclusions. Did the alphabet evolve from the scripts of Mesopotamia (cuneiform), Egypt (hieroglyphs) and Crete (Linear A and B) – or did it strike a single unknown individual in a 'flash'? And why was an alphabet thought necessary? Was it the result of commercial imperatives, as seems most likely? In other words, did business require a simpler and quicker means of recording transactions than, say, Babylonian cuneiform or Egyptian hieroglyphs, and also a convenient way to write the babel of languages of the various empires and groups trading with each other around the Mediterranean? If so, then it is surprising that there is zero evidence of trade and commerce in the early alphabetic inscriptions of Greece. This, and other considerations, have led some scholars to postulate, controversially, that the Greek alphabet was invented to record the oral epics of Homer in the 8th century BC.

From myth to speculation

In the absence of proof, anecdote and myth have filled the vacuum. Children are often evoked as inventors of the alphabet, because they would not have had the preconceptions and investment in existing scripts of adults. One possibility is that a bright Canaanite child in northern Syria, fed up with having to learn cuneiform, took the familiar idea of a small number of symbols standing for single consonants found in Egyptian hieroglyphs and invented some new signs for the basic consonantal sounds of his own Semitic language. Perhaps he doodled them

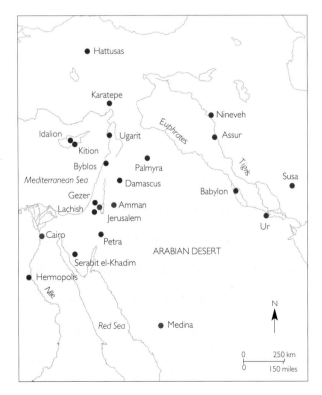

Land of many languages: the Middle East when the alphabet was born, c. 1500 BC.

first in the dust of some ancient street: a simple outline of a house, Semitic 'beth' (the 'bet' in 'alphabet'), became the sign for 'b'. In our own time, Rudyard Kipling's child protagonist in *How The Alphabet Was Made*, Taffimai, designs what she calls 'noise-pictures'. The letter A is a picture of a carp with its mouth wide open; this, Taffimai tells her father, looks like his open mouth when he utters the sound *ah*. The letter O matches the egg-or-stone shape and resembles her father's mouth saying *oh*. The letter S represents a snake, and stands for the

Above **Modern souk, Aleppo, Syria. Did the alphabet grow out of the need for more efficient interstate trade, polyglot haggling and record keeping in the bazaars of ancient Palestine, Lebanon and Syria?**

Left **The birth of the alphabet, according to Rudyard Kipling (see text).**

The riddle of the early alphabet. This sphinx, found in Sinai in 1905, carries proto-Sinaitic signs related to Egyptian hieroglyphs that appear to be an early alphabet. The signs were scratched by Semitic miners from Canaan. Was the alphabet conceived in Egypt or Palestine?

hissing sound of the snake. In this somewhat far-fetched way, a whole alphabet is created by Taffimai.

To quote a better poet, William Blake wrote in *Jerusalem*: 'God ... in mysterious Sinai's awful cave/To Man the wond'rous art of writing gave'. A small sphinx in the British Museum once seemed to show that Blake was right, at least about the origin of the alphabet. The sphinx was found in 1905 at Serabit el-Khadim in Sinai, a desolate place remote from civilization, by the Egyptologist Sir Flinders Petrie. He was excavating some old turquoise mines that were active in ancient Egyptian times. Petrie dated the sphinx to the middle of the 18th Dynasty; nowadays its date is thought to be about 1500 BC. On one side of it is a strange inscription. On the other, and between the paws, there are further inscriptions of the same kind, plus some Egyptian hieroglyphs which read: 'beloved of Hathor, mistress of turquoise'. There were still other inscriptions written on the rocks of this remote area, such as these:

Petrie guessed that the script was probably an alphabet, because it consisted of less than 30 signs (as distinct from text characters); and he thought that its language was probably Semitic, since he knew that Semites from Canaan – modern Israel and Lebanon – had worked these mines, in many cases as slaves. Ten years later, another Egyptologist Sir Alan Gardiner studied the 'proto-Sinaitic' signs and noted resemblances between some of them and certain pictographic Egyptian hieroglyphs. Gardiner now named each sign with the Semitic word equivalent to the sign's meaning in Egyptian (the Semitic words were known from biblical scholarship):

Proto-sinaitic signs	Egyptian sign	Semitic name
ᐁ ᐀	ᐁ	'aleph (ox)
☐ ☐	☐	beth (house)
＼	＼	gimel (throwstick)
☰ ☐	☐	daleth (door)

These Semitic names are the same as the names of the letters of the Hebrew alphabet – a fact that did not surprise Gardiner, since he knew that the Hebrews had lived in Canaan in the late 2nd millennium BC. But while the names are the same, the *shapes* of the Hebrew letters are different from the proto-Sinaitic signs, suggesting that any link between them cannot be a straightforward one.

Gardiner's hypothesis enabled him to translate one of the inscriptions that occurred on the sphinx from Serabit el-Khadim:

In English transcription, this would be 'Baalat', with the vowels spelt out. Hebrew and other Semitic scripts do not indicate vowels; readers guess the vowels from their knowledge of the language. Gardiner's reading made sense: Baalat means 'the Lady' and is a recognized Semitic name for the goddess Hathor in the Sinai region. So the inscription on the sphinx seemed to be a bilingual. Unfortunately no further decipherment proved tenable, mainly because of lack of material and the fact that many of the proto-Sinaitic signs had no hieroglyphic equivalents. Scholarly hopes of finding the story of the Exodus in these scratchings were scotched. Nevertheless, it is quite possible that a script similar to the proto-Sinaitic script was used by Moses to write down the Ten Commandments on tablets of stone.

We still do not know whether Gardiner's 1916 guess was correct, plausible though it is. For some decades after Petrie's discoveries in Sinai, the inscriptions were taken to be the 'missing link' between the Egyptian hieroglyphs and the first well-attested alphabets. (These belong to Ugarit, today's Ras Shamra on the coast of Syria, where a 30-sign cuneiform alphabet was used in the 14th century BC; and to the Phoenicians in Canaan in the late 2nd millennium, who used 22 consonantal letters.) But why should lowly – and presumably illiterate – miners in out-of-the-way Sinai have created an alphabet? *Prima facie*, they seem to be unlikely inventors. Subsequent discoveries in Lebanon and Israel have shown the Sinaitic theory of the alphabet to be a romantic fiction. These inscriptions, dated to the 17th and 16th centuries BC, suggest that the people then living in the land of Canaan were the inventors of the alphabet, which would be reasonable. They were cosmopolitan traders at the crossroads of the Egyptian, Hittite, Babylonian and Cretan empires; they were not wedded to an existing writing system; they needed a script that was easy to learn, quick to write and unambiguous. Although unproven, it is probable that the (proto-) Canaanites were the first to use an alphabet.

The world's first alphabetic writing? An inscription from Wadi el-Hol in Egypt, c. 1900–1800 BC.

New evidence from Egypt

Very recently, however, the picture has become complicated by new discoveries in ancient Egypt itself, and a revised version of the Gardiner theory now seems plausible. In 1999, an archaeologist from Yale University, John Coleman Darnell, and his wife Deborah, announced that they had found examples of what appeared to be alphabetic writing at Wadi el-Hol, west of Thebes, while they were surveying ancient travel routes in the southern Egyptian desert. The date of the inscriptions is *c.* 1900–1800 BC, which places them considerably earlier than the inscriptions from Lebanon and Israel, and would make them the earliest-known alphabetic writings.

The two short inscriptions are written in a Semitic script and, according to the experts, the letters were most probably developed in a fashion similar to a semi-cursive form of the Egyptian script. The writer is thought to have been a scribe travelling with a group of mercenaries (there were many such mercenaries working for the pharaohs). If this theory turns out to be correct, then it looks as if the alphabetic idea was, after all, inspired by the Egyptian hieroglyphs and invented in Egypt, rather than Palestine. But the new evidence is by no means conclusive, and the search for more inscriptions continues. The riddle of the alphabet's origin(s) has not yet been solved.

The Etruscan Alphabet

60

Time: 8th–1st century BC
Location: Italy

Even today, ninety per cent of the educated public firmly believes that Etruscan is totally indecipherable. This belief is echoed in the press and repeated in the majority of textbooks, even though it is over two hundred years out of date.

MASSIMO PALLOTTINO, 1975

THE ETRUSCANS, and their homeland Etruria (modern Tuscany), have exerted a special hold on the imagination of Europeans ever since Roman times. During the Renaissance, Cosimo de' Medici, grand duke of Tuscany, was poetically cast (by his biographer Vasari) as the Etruscan king Lars Porsenna, after the supposed discovery of the ancient ruler's tomb at Chiusi. And in the 20th century, D.H. Lawrence imbued much of his final poetry with imagery taken from his descents into Etruscan tombs. 'Reach me a gentian, give me a torch!/let me guide myself with the blue, forked torch of this flower/down the darker and darker stairs ... even where Persephone goes.'

In the history of language, the Etruscans are undoubtedly of great interest and importance. They adopted the alphabet from the Greeks, which they modified and passed to the Romans, from whom it reached the rest of Europe. But their spoken language became extinct, and so far as we can tell from reconstructions of it based on their inscriptions, it bore no resemblance to any European language. Simply by comparing the Etruscan words for numerals with their equivalents in Latin, Greek and Sanskrit, we can see that Etruscan was not an Indo-European language:

The Etruscans learnt the alphabet from Greek colonists who settled in Italy in about 775 BC at Pithekoussai (modern Ischia). They wrote the letters in the form of 'model' alphabets; these obviously enjoyed prestige, because they have been found on many objects at many sites. In practice, not all the letters were used since the Etruscan language had no need of signs for the voiced stops *b*, *d*, *g*, and the vowel *o*, so Etruscan writers did not use these Greek signs $, (, O – and they gave the Greek gamma (Γ, ⟨, or ⟨), the phonetic value *k* (instead of Greek *g*). This means that three Etruscan signs were used to write *k* (as in English 'think'): Κ before *a* (*ka*); ⟨ before *e* and *i* (*ce*, *ci*); and Q before *u* (*qu*). (Latin spelling initially adopted the same system, but since the Latin language, unlike Etruscan, did have the sound *g*, the early Latin letter 'C' could be pronounced either as *k* – as in Caesar pronounced *Kaiser* – or as *g* – as in Caius pronounced *Gaius*; later, the Romans introduced a new letter G, to make this phonetic distinction unambiguous.)

Right **An Etruscan vase or ink well in the shape of a rooster, c. 600 BC. It is incised with the letters of a 'model' alphabet borrowed from the Greek alphabet.**

English		Etruscan	Latin	Greek	Sanskrit
I	one	thu	oinos, unus	oine	e(kah)
2	two	zal	duo	dyo	dva
3	three	ci	tres	treis	trayah
4	four	sa	quattuor	tettares	catvarah
5	five	mach	quinque	pente	panca
6	six	huth	sex	hex	sat (sas)
10	ten	sar	decem	deka	dasa

Left **Gold plaques from Pyrgi, c. 500 BC. The plaque on the left is written in Phoenician, the one on the right is in Etruscan/ Greek script. The Greeks borrowed the alphabetic principle from the Phoenicians and then gave it to the Etruscans, who modified the letters** *(below).*

Model alphabet	Archaic inscriptions (7th-1st centuries BC)	Later inscriptions (4th-1st centuries BC)	Phonetic values
A	A	A	a
			(b)
↑	)	⊃	c (=k)
◁			(d)
∃	∃	∃	e
⫣	⫣	⫣	v
I	I	ⲧⳠ	z (=ts)
⊟	⊟	⊟⊘	h
⊗	⊗○	⊙○	θ (=k)
I	I	I	i
λ	λ		k
↓	↓	↓	l
ⱬ	ⱬ	ⱬ	m
Ⰰ	Ⰰ	Ⰸ	n
⊞			(s)
○			(o)
⌐	⌐	⌐	p
M	M	M	s
♀	♀		q
◁	◁	⬤	r
⟩	⟩	⟩	s
T	T	ⲦⲄ	t
Y	Y	V	u
X	X		s
Φ	Φ	⬤	ø (=ph)
Ψ	Ψ	V	x (=kh)
	(⟡8)	8	f

Although there are about 13,000 known Etruscan inscriptions, some 4000 of these are fragments or graffiti, and the vast majority of the other 9000 inscriptions are short, mainly epitaphs containing only names – the father's name, sometimes the mother's name, the surname of the deceased and, if she was a woman, perhaps the name of her husband and the number of children – maybe an age and a public office held, and formulaic phrases. There is not much problem in reading these, simply by substituting the phonetic values of the letters, as has been understood since the 18th century or before – but it is rather like trying to learn a language by reading only gravestones.

What is lacking is a substantial bilingual text, containing other subject matter. In 1964, three gold tablets were discovered at Pyrgi, the harbour of Caere (now Cerveteri), and they are the most important bilingual inscription in the Etruscan corpus. One of the plaques is written in Phoenician, the other two are in Etruscan, of which the longer one contains 36 or 37 words; but the Phoenician and Etruscan inscriptions are not word-for-word translations: the Pyrgi tablets are more of a 'quasi-bilingual' inscription than a true one. Both record the same event – the dedication by the ruler Thefarie Velianas in the third year of his reign of a cult place and perhaps a statue to the Phoenician goddess Astarte, or Ishtar, identified here with the Etruscan goddess Uni – but they do so in significantly different ways. In the end, 'ci', meaning 'three', was the only new Etruscan word to emerge from the Pyrgi plaques. And the same proved to be true of the latest inscription to be discovered, in the 1990s, the Tabula Cortonensis, containing 200 words which are mostly names (like Laris Celatina Lausa): the only new word appears to be that for 'lake'.

The Etruscan script is therefore no mystery, while the Etruscan language certainly is. Despite many other aids to decipherment, such as Etruscan art and Latin inscriptions, our total vocabulary for Etruscan is still only about 250 words, not all of which are of secure meaning; our knowledge of the grammar is extremely patchy, because of the limited nature of the inscriptions; and we know very little about Etruscan syntax, because no literature has survived. Nevertheless, our knowledge of each element has increased steadily decade by decade.

The Meroitic Script

Time: 3rd century BC – 4th century AD
Location: Sudan

To learn that ... nomads from the eastern desert once founded an empire in the valley of the Nile [at Meroe] ... would perhaps not be more surprising than the fact that a nation which ... pioneered the world in material and intellectual culture were the ancestors of the Egyptian fellahin.

FRANCIS LLEWELLYN GRIFFITH, 1909

LOOK AT A MAP of the course of the Nile, and you will see that the river flows in two great bends through six cataracts from Khartoum near the centre of Sudan to Lake Nasser and Aswan on the modern border between Sudan and Egypt. This vast area, rivalling that of ancient Egypt, is known to archaeologists as Nubia. In ancient times, it was the kingdom of Kush, a word of unknown origin, and its principal city was Meroe, between the 5th and 6th cataracts on the Nile .

The Meroitic civilization was one of the most important early states of sub-Saharan Africa, not a mere appendage of ancient Egypt. Its archaeological origins go back to the 3rd millennium BC, but it enters history – through references to it in Egyptian hieroglyphic inscriptions – only in the 8th century BC. From 712–656 BC, Kushite kings conquered and ruled Egypt and were accepted as its 25th dynasty, governing an empire that extended from the central Sudan to the borders of Palestine. Egyptian hieroglyphs were used in Kush until as late as the 1st century AD. But they increasingly co-existed with the Meroitic script, which was both hieroglyphic and cursive in form like the Egyptian script. Brief Egyptian/Meroitic bilingual inscriptions found at Meroe and elsewhere have allowed scholars, chiefly Francis Llewellyn Griffith, to decipher the phonetic values of the Meroitic script. There are only 23 hieroglyphic signs (and the same number of cursive ones), most of which were borrowed from the Egyptian script. In other words, the Meroitic hieroglyphs visually resemble Egyptian hieroglyphs, but they are actually an alphabet.

We can therefore translate many Meroitic names, and can also guess the meanings of a handful of Meroitic words that are not names, by comparing them with parallel Egyptian words. But the Meroitic language as a whole is a virtual mystery. The words we have seem to bear no relation to the Old Nubian language or to any other African language of the area from either the Nilo-Saharan or Afro-Asiatic families. Thus there is no simple linguistic solution: no Sub-Saharan equivalent of Coptic, the key to the decipherment of Egyptian hieroglyphs. The best immediate hope for advancing the decipherment would appear to be the discovery of a larger bilingual text, probably in Meroitic and Egyptian. Perhaps we shall eventually learn, as Griffith hazarded, that the people who created the kingdom of Kush spoke an early form of Beja, the language of today's nomads of the eastern desert near the Red Sea, whose name has given us the English 'Bedouin'.

Meroitic hieroglyphic and cursive letters and their phonetic values. Although the forms resemble Egyptian hieroglyphs, the system is alphabetic.

The Zapotec & Isthmian Scripts

Time: 500 BC?–2nd century AD
Location: Mexico

The La Mojarra stela is ... the oldest example of an extended written text, and perhaps the most important inscription ever discovered, in Mesoamerica.

MARTHA J. MACRI, 1993

OF THE SEVERAL PRE-MAYAN scripts in Central America, the Zapotec script (of Oaxaca state in Mexico) and the Isthmian script (named after the Isthmus of Tehuantepec), both of which are undeciphered, are the most significant. The former script is the earliest-known writing system in the Americas, dating from perhaps 500 BC, while the latter has a somewhat later date, the 2nd century AD. Geographically, the Zapotec script was a close neighbour of the Isthmian, which was itself contiguous with the area of the Mayan script (first recorded in the 3rd century AD). It is therefore quite likely that the Zapotec script influenced the Isthmian script, which in turn influenced the Mayan script.

The majority of Zapotec inscriptions – and the most significant ones – come from the Zapotec capital city built on the tremendous hill-top site of Monte Albán outside the modern city of Oaxaca. The glyphs do not resemble Mixtec, Aztec or Mayan writing visually, except for the fact that they use the same bar-and-dot numerals and a very similar calendrical system (as do the Isthmian glyphs), which were presumably invented by the Zapotecs.

Luckily for decipherers, a Spanish priest published a Spanish-Zapotec dictionary in 1578, which included the names of the 20 days in the Zapotec language of the time, though it does not match each name to a Zapotec glyph since the writing system had been extinct for many centuries. Modern scholars have been able to do this, however, by guessing the meaning of many of the glyphs from

	Zapotec	Spanish	English	Zapotec glyph(s)
1	Chilla	Lagarto	Crocodile	
2	Laa	Relámpago	Lightning	
3	Laala	?	?	
4	Lachi	Juego de pelota?	Ballgame?	
5	Zee	Miseria	Misfortune	
6	Lana	Flecha, Tizne	Arrow, Soot	
7	China	Venado	Deer	
8	Lapa	?	?	
9	Nica	Aqua	Water	
10	Tella	Nudo	Knot	
11	Loo	Mona, Mono	Monkey	
12	Pija	Planta jabonera	Soap plant	
13	Laa	?	?	
14	Lache	Corazón	Heart	
15	Naa	Milpa	Corn field	
16	Loo	Ojo	Eye	
17	Xoo	Temblor	Earthquake	
18	Lopa	?	?	
19	Lape	Gota	Drop	
20	Loo	Principal	Ruler, Lord	

Left **The Zapotec day names/glyphs.** *Right* **The Tuxtla statuette (see over), with Isthmian signs.**

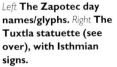

what they appear to depict, and then matching this meaning to the Spanish meanings of the day names.

The decipherment of the non-calendrical glyphs has proved to be much trickier. It depends on identifying the language of the glyphs. This may be related to the modern Zapotec language, but the link is likely to be a tangled one. Not only is there the issue of language change over some 2000 years to consider, the Zapotecan language group itself is highly diversified, with three major branches and several mutually unintelligible dialects. In addition, we know the names of only a very few ancient locations – which might be expected to appear in the inscriptions – in Zapotec, because many locations in Oaxaca have long been known by their names in Nahuatl, the language of the Aztecs, which intruded into the area well before the Spanish conquest.

Nevertheless, scholars have established that there are at least 100 basic Zapotec signs in the writing system, which is too high a figure for the script to be purely syllabic and too low for it to be logosyllabic like the Mayan script. Until more inscriptions are discovered, the exact nature of the Zapotec system must remain unclear.

The same is true of the Isthmian script but, curiously, given that there is much less of it available, we understand it better than the Zapotec script. This is because, first, most of the Isthmian script is concentrated in one long, dated inscription accompanied by the figure of a ruler, and, second, the linguistic situation is somewhat clearer in the Isthmus of Tehuantepec than in Oaxaca state.

The Isthmian story dates from 1902, when a strange little statuette made of jade was ploughed up in a field apparently in the Tuxtla Mountains near San Andrés Tuxtla in southern Veracruz. It depicted a man dressed as duck, and was inscribed with about 70 characters of unknown writing. Deposited in the Smithsonian Institution in Washington DC, it acquired a kind of cult status over the decades – like the Phaistos disc found a few years later – because no other examples of the script turned up. Then, in 1986, bare-footed fishermen at La Mojarra, a small ranching and fishing settlement on a river near the Gulf Coast not far from Tuxtla, stumbled upon a 4-tonne engraved stone underwater. The La Mojarra stela contains 400–500 text characters (including the dates AD 143 and 156) and is clearly written in the same script as the Tuxtla statuette.

There is general agreement that the most likely candidate for the Isthmian language is an early form of Zoquean, a branch of the Mixe-Zoquean language family spoken in the isthmus and adjacent areas today. Indeed, some scholars believe that the Olmecs, who created the earliest civilization in Mesoamerica (though one without writing) which flourished in the same area as La Mojarra, were Mixe-Zoquean speakers. They therefore call Isthmian, controversially, an 'epi-Olmec' script.

The Mixe-Zoquean hypothesis is, however, speculative (not unlike the Dravidian hypothesis for the Indus script, p. 249). When applied to the Isthmian inscriptions, by attempting to match apparent patterns and imagery in the signs with known words, grammar and syntax in the reconstructed Zoquean language, it produces a possible 'decipherment'. The difficulty is, there is no way of knowing if the proposed solution is correct because there are no further Isthmian inscriptions against which the 'decipherment' can be tested. Despite strong claims to the contrary, the Isthmian script therefore remains undeciphered.

A drawing of the La Mojarra stela. The inscription contains 400 to 500 text characters, including dates.

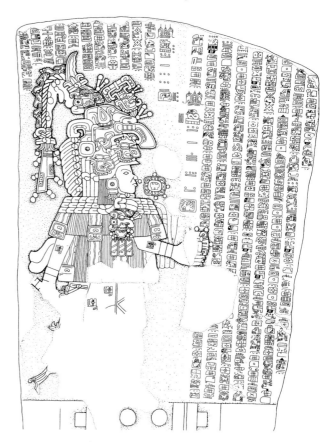

Runes & Pictish Symbol Stones

Time: 2nd?–9th centuries AD
Location: northern Europe, Greenland

For every runic inscription there shall be as many interpretations as there are scholars working on it.

'THE FIRST LAW OF RUNO-DYNAMICS'

THE VAST MAJORITY of European scripts derive from the Roman letters – which has tended to obscure the existence of one significant European script, runic, whose links with the Roman script are less certain. From as far back as the 2nd century AD, runes have been found that were used to record the early stages of Gothic, Danish, Swedish, Norwegian, English, Frisian, Frankish and various tribal tongues of central Germania.

The range of runic scripts reflects the range of languages involved. The total number of known runic inscriptions is probably in the region of 5000, almost all of which are located in Nordic countries. The great majority are in Sweden, where discoveries of rune stones are still frequently made. Norway has over 1000 inscriptions, and Denmark some 700; Iceland has about 60, all from comparatively late times, and there are also runic texts from Greenland

Rök stone, Östergötland, Sweden. The longest-known runic inscription, it was written by Varin, in memory of Vaenod, his dead son, in the Early Viking Age.

and the Faroes. Some of those in the British Isles – found in the Isle of Man, the Orkney islands, the Shetland islands, Ireland and the Western Isles – are the work of travelling Norsemen.

We do not know where and when runes were invented. Finds of early rune-inscribed objects in Romania, central Germany and Russia indicate that runes may have been invented in that general area, perhaps by Goths on the Danube frontier or beside the Vistula. Another hypothesis notes the resemblance between the runes and characters used in the inscriptions of the Alpine valleys of southern Switzerland and northern Italy and goes on to ascribe the invention to romanized Germani from that area; there may even be a link with the Etruscan alphabet. A third hypothesis prefers one of the Germanic tribes of Denmark, perhaps southern Jutland, as the progenitors of runes; many of the earliest inscriptions come from this general area, and early runic texts continue to be found in various regions of Denmark. But on one point all scholars of runes agree: the Roman alphabet exercised influence of some kind on the runic script.

The runic alphabet

The runic alphabet has 24 letters, arranged in a peculiar order known as the 'futhark' after its first six letters:

ᚠᚾᚦᚨᚱᚲᚷᚹᚺᚾᛁᛃᛇᛈᛉᛋ

f u þ a/œ r k g w h n i j i p z s
   (th)   (R)

ᛏᛒᛖᛗᛚᛜᛟᛞ

t b e m l n o d
              (ng)

Here it is written from left to right, but it could be written from right to left equally well in early times, or even boustrophedon (from right to left and from left to right in alternate lines). An individual letter could also be reversed on occasions, apparently at whim, and might even be inverted. No distinction was made between capital and lower-case letters.

Some of the letters are obviously related to letters of the Roman alphabet, such as the runes standing for *r*, *i* and *b*. Others could well be adaptations of Roman letters, such as those for *f*, *u* (Roman V inverted), *k* (Roman C), *h*, *s*, *t* and *l* (Roman L inverted). But other letters, such as those representing *g*, *w*, *j* and *p*, scarcely resemble Roman forms with the same sound value.

The sound values given above are approximate: the sounds of early Germanic languages are not exactly paralleled in modern English. There is a rune, for example, for the spirant sound *th*, as in 'thin' (it was used in early English spelling, and called 'thorn'). There is a vowel ᛁ, represented here as *i*, the pronunciation of which is disputed. Runic script could also distinguish between *ng* in 'ungrateful' (ᚾ + ᛉ) and *ng* as in 'sing', ◇.

But even though runic inscriptions can usually be 'read' – in the same sense as Etruscan inscriptions – their meaning is frequently cryptic, because of our lack of knowledge of the early Germanic languages. Hence the origin of today's expression 'to read the runes' – meaning to make an educated guess on the basis of scanty and ambiguous evidence.

Pictish symbol stones

The Pictish symbol stones are, if anything, even more tantalizing. They number about 630, including those recorded as lost, and are found only in Scotland, which was ruled by the Picts between the 4th and 9th centuries AD. There are about 425 legible symbols, which can be grouped into some 50 different signs, the most common of

Right **The Hunterston brooch, found at Strathclyde in Scotland. The runes to the left of the pin give the owner's name, Melbrigda, those to the right are pretend runes.**

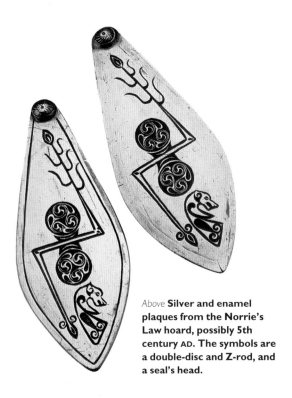

Above **Silver and enamel plaques from the Norrie's Law hoard, possibly 5th century AD. The symbols are a double-disc and Z-rod, and a seal's head.**

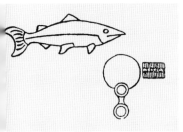

Left **The most common Pictish symbols.** *Above* **Golspie No. 2, from Scotland, a Class II symbol stone, shows, among other things, a Pictish beast, Pict man with double-headed axe and dirk facing a lion and fish, and two twined adders biting their own fish tails.**

which are the crescent and V-rod, the double disc and Z-rod, the 'dolphin', the fish and the mirror and comb. There is clearly no resemblance to the Roman alphabet and indeed Pictish symbols usually occur in pairs, only rarely in groups of more than four – so they are very unlikely to be alphabetic.

Two major classes of inscription exist. Class I consists only of symbols incised on undressed boulders and Neolithic and Bronze Age monoliths. Class II, with obviously Christian symbolism, consists of a cross and often-striking decoration carved on one side of a slab of local stone, and the same symbols as in Class I, also with decoration and sometimes a second cross, carved on the back or the side.

Since the Pictish language, a form of Gaelic, is lost to us, interpretation of the inscriptions rests entirely on the symbols themselves. (A few stones also carry letters of the Ogham alphabet, but since this is virtually incomprehensible, these stones are not useful 'bilinguals'.) Most likely the Pictish symbols represent chiefly personal names in the manner of later heraldic devices, or commemorate important events; some are almost certainly gravestones. Unlike the runic script, the Pictish symbols were not a full writing system.

Rongorongo

64

Time: ??–19th century AD
Location: Easter Island

Our ko hau rongorongo *are lost! Future events will destroy these sacred tablets which we bring with us and those which we will make in our new land. Men of other races will guard a few that remain as priceless objects, and their* maori *will study them in vain without being able to read them. Our* ko hau motu mo rongorongo *will be lost forever.* Aue! Aue!

HOTU MATU'A (LEGENDARY FIRST SETTLER OF EASTER ISLAND)

EASTER ISLAND (or Rapa Nui as it is known to its inhabitants) is the most isolated inhabited spot on earth: its nearest inhabited neighbour, some 2250 km (1400 miles) east-southeast, is Pitcairn Island. It is also small, as islands go, with a maximum length of 24 km (15 miles). One of its many mysteries, which include its unique and imposing stone statues (*moai*) (pp. 211–15), is the fact that the island possesses its own script, known as *rongorongo* – a word meaning 'chants' or 'recitations'. So exotic and enigmatic is it, that *rongorongo* has proved to be a permanent magnet for would-be decipherers ever since it was discovered by Europeans in the 1860s.

There are 25 *rongorongo* inscriptions, carved on wood probably with a shark's tooth, bird bone or flake of obsidian, scattered from Honolulu and Santiago to European capitals; not a single one remains on Easter Island itself. Most are named after their current locations, such as the Large St Petersburg tablet, but a few have names in the Rapa Nui language, such as Mamari ('egg'), from the object's egg-like shape, or in one case a French name Echancrée ('notched'), again because of the tablet's appearance. Many of the inscriptions are very short, but the largest and longest, the Santiago staff, has some 2300 characters on a wooden staff that measures 126 × 6.5 cm (50 × 2½ in), and a second inscription, Tahua, a wooden tablet made out of a European or an American oar, contains about 1825 characters; it is the longest tablet inscription.

How old is *rongorongo*?

Hardly anyone doubts that the *rongorongo* inscriptions are written in a Polynesian language related to today's Rapa Nui language. The problem is to deter-

mine how the language has changed since the time when the inscriptions were written and, of course, to relate it to the inscriptions. But no one can be sure how old *rongorongo* is as a system of writing. None of the inscriptions is dated. Was *rongorongo* brought to the island from Polynesia perhaps a millennium and a half ago, or invented on the island unaided by outside influences, or was it a product of contacts with the first European visitors in the 18th century? There is some evidence for all three possibilities. If independent invention on the island, were to be proved, it would constitute exceptionally strong evidence for the idea that there were origins, as opposed to one origin, of writing – a highly controversial issue (as mentioned on p. 244).

Oral tradition on Easter Island itself, recorded in the 19th century, has it that the first settler, the legendary Hotu Matu'a, brought 67 tablets with him from his homeland in Polynesia. But we know of no writing systems in the rest of Oceania which predate the colonial period. If writing was invented on the island, we might expect it to be found carved in

Left **'Signatures' by Easter islanders on a Spanish treaty, 1770.** *Opposite above* **The Mamari tablet, written in reverse boustrophedon, i.e. the reader reads line 1 from left to right, then turns the tablet through 180 degrees and reads line 2 in the same direction, and so on.**

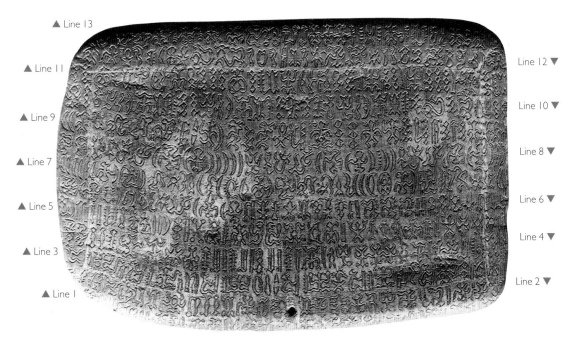

▲ Line 13
▲ Line 11   Line 12 ▼
▲ Line 9   Line 10 ▼
▲ Line 7   Line 8 ▼
▲ Line 5   Line 6 ▼
▲ Line 3   Line 4 ▼
▲ Line 1   Line 2 ▼

Right **A 'lunar calendar' in the Mamari tablet. It is not strictly speaking a calendar but rather a list of instructions about where to insert two intercalary nights in the 29.52 day lunar month, so as to maintain the traditional lunar calendar of 29- and 30-day months.**

Line 6
Line 7
Line 8
Line 9

stone on, for example, the *moai* statues and on the walls of caves. There is no evidence of this, but there are petroglyphs with a distinct resemblance to *rongorongo* signs – though not as a rule on the *moai*. Yet it is perfectly possible that the petroglyphs existed before European contact, but no one on the island had figured out how to use them to represent phonetic speech. The first European visitors, in 1722, saw no evidence of *rongorongo*, but in 1770, when two Spanish ships called in and claimed the island for the king of Spain with a military ceremony, they compelled the islanders to 'sign' a treaty. At least two of the signs used – the 'vulva' and the 'bird' – resemble common petroglyphs, but they do not resemble *rongorongo*. Perhaps, say some scholars, it was invented some time after 1770, as a result of seeing the Spanish writing?

Attempts at decipherment

Modern attempts to decipher *rongorongo* rely on a combination of internal analysis of the signs and the 'readings' of *rongorongo* collected from native informants in the 19th century before the tradition died out, supplemented by knowledge of Polynesian languages. Scholars from many countries have contributed, but progress has been slow. There is much disagreement about the validity of the 19th-century oral evidence, and about the number of signs in the writing system. Estimates of the latter vary from 55 or 60 basic signs to many hundreds of signs. One of the few generally accepted 'decipherments' is that the Mamari tablet contains a kind of lunar calendar. A proposed decipherment of the Santiago staff by Steven Roger Fischer in the 1990s claimed to show that it recorded a creation chant. Although the translation was greeted with enthusiasm by some, and widely published, no other *rongorongo* scholar accepts its validity. Unless more tablets are discovered, which is unlikely since wood rots quickly, we shall probably never know exactly what the *rongorongo* boards originally said.

The Fall
of
Civilizations

MANY SCHOLARS HAVE written about history in terms of cycles: the rise of complex societies, their brilliant apogees, and their sudden declines. Some of the world's first civilizations rose rapidly from a handful of villages to become powerful states and then apparently suddenly collapsed. The possible causes are much discussed, disputed and numerous: did outsiders overthrow the ruling dynasty and sack their temples and palaces? Or did an environmental catastrophe such as severe drought cause society to implode? Many of archaeology's most engrossing mysteries surround sudden social collapse of otherwise seemingly invincible and mighty empires.

Often, as with the Roman empire, the causes are complex and interrelated, but there is always a strong temptation to reach for simple, single explanations. Natural disasters are one such possibility. Around the middle of the 2nd millennium BC (the exact date is disputed) the island of Thera in the southern Aegean exploded in a violent eruption that ranks among the greatest cataclysms ever experienced by humanity. The Minoan civilization on Crete was nearing the height of its prosperity, trading timber and olive oil to Egypt, controlling routes of exchange throughout the Aegean. Did the explosion bring about the total destruction of Minoan society? Although falling ash and tidal waves may have done serious damage to the Minoan economy, Knossos and other Minoan palaces certainly survived the disaster. A straightforward connection between collapse and natural disaster does not seem the full answer. One benefit of the eruption for archaeology was that it preserved a Minoan town, and in particular its

The spectacular ancestral Pueblo Cliff Palace, Mesa Verde, Colorado. Along with other large pueblos near Mesa Verde, it was abandoned in the 12th century AD.

wonderful wall-paintings, which otherwise probably would not have survived the centuries.

All pre-industrial civilizations were vulnerable to short-term climatic change. A revolution in the study of climatology is producing startling evidence for abrupt short-term climatic changes over the past 5000 years: droughts weakened Mesopotamian cities and nearly toppled ancient Egyptian civilization, and strong El Niño climatic events helped overturn powerful states in Mexico and Peru. The Moche civilization of Peru's North Coast flourished off valley irrigation agriculture supported by mountain runoff and coastal fisheries in one of the driest environments on earth. Highly centralized and ruled by warrior-priests through rigid ideologies, the Moche were extremely vulnerable to strong El Niño events which brought disastrous flooding, such as those that struck at the height of a major drought identified from ice cores high in the Andes in the 7th century AD. The Moche rulers moved their capitals upstream, only to have them overwhelmed by further floods a century later. In this case, El Niños were knockout blows for a society which had nowhere to move and too rigid a political and economic system to adapt to disaster.

Collapse resulted not just from climate change, but many factors. The immediate fall of the western Roman empire resulted from Germanic invasions, but long-term military and political reverses and changes had long ushered in the decline. Eventually the empire split into two halves. Classic Maya city-states developed sophisticated agricultural systems which involved swamp agriculture, terracing and slash-and-burn methods. But drought, environmental degradation, and social unrest, possibly combined with the demands of Maya lords for labour and tribute, led to the precipitous collapse of civilization in the southern lowlands around AD 900. The cities imploded and the population dispersed into smaller communities.

The great Anasazi pueblos of the American Southwest are some of the most spectacular archaeological sites in North America. The 'great houses' of Chaco Canyon reached their apogee in the 10th century AD. Then, suddenly, they were abandoned. The centre of Anasazi culture moved northwards to the Four Corners region, to the Moctezuma Valley and the Mesa Verde area, where dense populations flourished until the 12th century. Then, again, the Anasazi mysteriously dispersed over a large area. Long called a catastrophe, the dispersal was in part a response to severe drought chronicled by tree-rings. Pueblo Indian culture has an ancient tradition of movement in response to drought, a logical strategy for combating arid conditions.

Then there are catastrophic events of an extra-terrestrial dimension, such as cometary impacts. Palaeoecologist Michael Baillie believes scientists have overlooked one of the major causes for the collapse of civilizations: comet swarms. We know about the huge impact that caused the extinction of the dinosaurs, but Baillie warns that we should also look for smaller, but possibly frighteningly frequent events. His tree-ring studies point to a series of global environmental traumas over the past 2500 years, which may mark such events as the biblical Exodus, the disasters which befell Egypt, a major famine in China and the onset of the European dark ages. Baillie believes that massive, long-forgotten cometary events devastated or seriously weakened civilizations whose collapse we are still at a loss to explain.

Comets have always aroused awe and fear, as here recorded in 1682; but could they have had more impact on human history than we have hitherto imagined?

The Thera Eruption & the Fall of the Minoans

Time: 17th or 16th century BC
Location: Thera (Santorini)

The thundering roar must have deafened and terrified the Cretans, who had, of course, no means of knowing what was its cause. Then must have come the rain of mud and ashes, some cold, some ablaze and burning. Worst of all, however, were the waves which broke over the island, much higher and more rapid than Krakatau.

SPYRIDON MARINATOS, 1972

THE EARTH TREMORS had rumbled on for weeks as the crater in the centre of the island spewed ash and lava. As volcanic debris rained down on their homes, Thera's farmers abandoned fields and villages, took to their boats and fled. Then, on a summer's day sometime in the 17th or 16th century BC, the volcano exploded with massive force. The volcanic cone collapsed in stages after the eruption. Dense ash blanketed much of Crete. But did the Thera eruption actually destroy Minoan civilization? Like so many archaeological mysteries, the answer to this puzzle is proving elusive.

The great cataclysm
Thera, also called Santorini, is an island in the southern Cyclades group of the Aegean Sea and was once about 16 km (10 miles) in diameter. The ancients called it *Kallistê*, 'the beautiful', a precipitous yet fertile island with a volcanic cone rising about 1600 m (5250 ft) above sea level. The 7500-megaton explosion, greater than the atomic blast at Hiroshima, created three islands from one. They surround a 80 sq.-km (31-sq.-mile) caldera, with steep cliffs of ash and pumice. Millions of tonnes of tephra – volcanic ash – rained down on the island, covering every community under layers of fine dust. The prevailing northwesterly winds carried the same volcanic ash far over eastern Crete and into the eastern Mediterranean. Several metres of ash fell on Minoan field systems on Crete, causing havoc with the harvest. Deep-sea cores have recovered samples of Santorini ash over an area of more than 300,000 sq. km (115,800 sq. miles) and up to 700 km (430 miles) downwind. The grain size in the samples is consistent with ash that could be carried by summer northwesterly winds.

Tsunamis (huge waves caused by seismic activity) may have flowed out from the centre of the eruption. Lesser Santorini eruptions in AD 365 and 1650 created tidal waves that caused severe damage on the north coast of Crete and as far afield as Alexandria, Egypt. An earthquake near Amorgos in 1956 generated 40-m (130-ft) tidal waves. Those from the much larger Thera cataclysm must have been commensurately greater, due to the force of the eruption and the depth of the ocean. The steeply sloping north Cretan coast only 100 km (62 miles) away, home to many Minoan communities, would have been vulnerable to tsunamis.

A casualty of nature: Akrotiri
The explosion of Thera ranks among the greatest natural disasters since the Ice Age. The stupendous Mount Tambora eruption of 1815 in southeast Asia exceeded it in intensity, but Thera dwarfs the cele-

Map showing the thickness of the fallout of tephra from Thera, from deep sea cores. Figures in brackets are an estimate of the corresponding tephra depth on land.

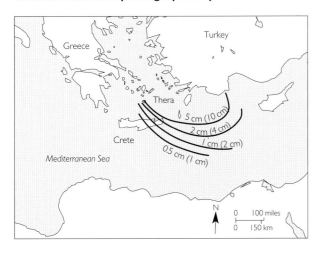

Right **The Thera eruption was preceded by violent earth tremors and showers of volcanic ash, which soon mantled fields and villages on the island. The inhabitants fled by boat, leaving settlements like Akrotiri deserted. Within a short time, the abandoned Minoan village lay under many metres of ash, until unearthed by archaeologists.**

Below **Akrotiri's houses still stand two storeys high, their owners' possessions lying where they were abandoned. The closely huddled dwellings offer a vivid picture of Minoan life at the time of the disaster.**

THE THERA ERUPTION & THE FALL OF THE MINOANS

The plastered walls of the Akrotiri houses are covered with superbly painted friezes providing a colourful portrait of village life over 3500 years ago. Two young boxing boys exchange fisticuffs on one wall, while elegant antelopes prance to the right.

Below **A detail from one of the miniature frescoes: a scene depicting armed warriors with hide-covered shields and possibly a shipwreck, with men falling into the sea.**

brated Krakatoa explosion of 1883, which killed tens of thousands and destroyed dozens of communities. In 1939, Greek archaeologist Spyridon Marinatos theorized that the Thera disaster had contributed to the decline of the Minoan civilization after 1500 BC. Most archaeologists greeted his theory with caution, until Marinatos discovered Akrotiri, a hurriedly abandoned Minoan settlement buried under volcanic ash at the southeastern corner of Thera. His excavations brought home the dramatic intensity of the eruption.

Akrotiri has been called the 'Pompeii of the Aegean', a complete settlement smothered in ash which preserved it for posterity, though here its terrified inhabitants had time to flee. Marinatos unearthed a town that covered more than 13 ha (32 acres), its substantial houses separated by narrow alleyways, just like numerous Greek rural communities to this day. Many houses still stand two or three storeys high. Marinatos excavated room after room with great care and unearthed a community frozen at a moment in time. Beds, storage jars and other artifacts lay where they had been abandoned by the fleeing inhabitants. Some of the walls were painted with brilliantly coloured friezes of warriors and towns, ships, animals and plants, even two boys engaged in a boxing match. Akrotiri was a humble community by Minoan standards, but tells us more of day-to-day life than any Cretan palace.

The Thera explosion blew up the centre of the island completely, leaving an active volcanic cone in the centre of the huge crater, overlooked by the modern village of Santorini.

The date of the eruption

When Marinatos tried to date Akrotiri and therefore the eruption, he based his chronology on ceramic vessels from the houses, which he compared with examples known from the famous 'Palace of Minos' at Knossos in northern Crete. Similar vessels appear in Egyptian sites along the Nile dated by historical records to about 1500 BC. Marinatos accordingly dated the cataclysm to around 1450 BC, just the time when Minoan civilization went into decline and signs of destruction appear at Knossos. He argued, with seemingly good reason, that the Thera eruption contributed to the fall of Knossos – and Minoan civilization as a whole – to the Mycenaeans of the Greek mainland.

Recent years have witnessed a revolution in our knowledge of ancient climatic fluctuations, due to the study of tree-ring sequences and deep ice cores, both of which chronicle year-by-year, decade-by-decade changes in temperature and rainfall. Some experts claim that tree-rings and ice-core data from northern Europe and Greenland reveal cooler temperatures and stunted tree growth over a wide area in 1628 BC, a phenomenon known to be linked to the effects of volcanic ash blocking out sunlight (p. 290). The same experts believe that this anomaly can be attributed to Thera and that the explosion therefore took place in the 17th century BC, a full century and a half before the final decline of Minoan civilization. However, those who support the Marinatos chronology point out that the climatic anomaly in ice cores and tree-ring sequences is from northern Europe and may reflect

not the Thera eruption, but an otherwise unknown volcanic event 150 years earlier.

Another recent discovery compounds the dating mystery. Across the Mediterranean in Egypt's Nile Delta, Austrian scholar Manfred Bietak has discovered pumice in layers dating to about 1550 BC at Tell el-Dab'a (Avaris). This pumice may also be evidence for a major volcanic eruption in the eastern Mediterranean. We still do not know within a century and a half when Thera blew apart.

What happened to the Minoans?

There can be no question that the Thera disaster had a serious impact on Minoan life, especially on palaces and farming communities living close to the north coast or in the path of the volcanic ash cloud in eastern Crete. The falling ash would have covered fields of growing crops, killing them and preventing subsequent ploughing. Hundreds, if not thousands, must have perished from famine, and from the infectious diseases that are the inevitable consequence of hunger. Knossos itself lies on higher ground some distance from the sea, so the tidal waves would not have flooded the palace, as they must have communities large and small on the shore. Hundreds of merchant ships, fishing boats and smaller craft must have been smashed by the tsunamis, with serious effects on the long-distance trade in wine and olive oil that nourished Minoan civilization. But the cataclysm itself probably did not destroy the Minoans, who seem to have survived and even prospered for, at minimum, a few generations after the disaster, and perhaps for much longer.

The Fall of Rome

Time: 5th century AD
Location: western Mediterranean

While these things were taking place in Jerusalem, a dreadful rumour reached us from the west. We heard that Rome was besieged, that the citizens were buying their safety with gold, and that when they had been thus despoiled they were again beleaguered, so as to lose not only their substance but also their lives. The messenger's voice failed and sobs interrupted his utterance. The city that had captured the whole world was itself captured.

JEROME, *LETTER* 127, AD 412

IN THE COURSE of the 5th century AD occurred that transformation of the Mediterranean world which is commonly termed the 'fall' of Rome. At the start of the century, the Roman empire still stretched from Britain to the Sahara, from Spain to the Middle East. By its end, however, Rome's western provinces were in the hands of barbarian kings, while the empire itself was now limited to the eastern Mediterranean, ruled from Constantinople. The precise reasons for this transformation have vexed scholars for centuries, but a number of trends can be discerned.

Romans and barbarians

From a modern perspective, the most striking aspect of the 'fall' of Rome is the emergence of the barbar-

ian kingdoms in the west. A significant catalyst in this process was the arrival in eastern Europe of the Huns, a nomadic people from central Asia, during the 370s. Their migration into the regions to the north of the Black Sea precipitated the collapse of a number of Gothic kingdoms that had thrived on the lower Danube frontier of the Roman empire since the middle of the 3rd century. In 376, perhaps hoping to recruit numerous Goths into the Roman army, the emperor Valens acquiesced in the transportation of large numbers of Gothic refugees across the Danube into Rome's Balkan provinces. Once within the empire, however, the Goths seem to have suffered maltreatment and extortion at the hands of Roman officials, which pushed them into armed

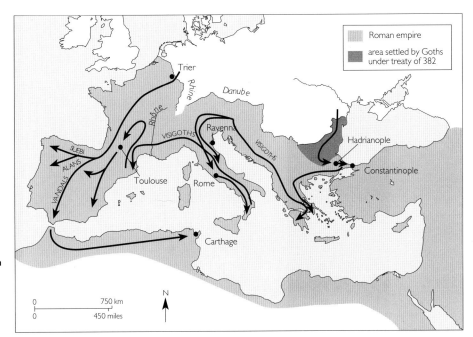

In the early 5th century the Roman empire suffered from major migrations by barbarian peoples, especially in the western provinces, leading to its political dismemberment.

Above **Theodosius I: the emperor who first permitted autonomous communities of barbarians within the empire.**

Roman military hierarchy, but found their ambitions confounded by a combination of imperial vacillation and scheming. In the end, under the leadership of Alaric, the Goths mounted a series of invasions of Italy, culminating in 410 with the sack of Rome: this was the first time in 800 years that the city had fallen to a foreign enemy.

In the course of the 5th century, further migrations of barbarian peoples into the empire – particularly into its western provinces – resulted in its political dismemberment. On New Year's Eve 406, while imperial forces were distracted by the Gothic assault on Italy, a confederation of tribes crossed the Rhine, and made swift progress through the provinces of Gaul and Spain. One of these tribes, the Vandals, crossed the straits of Gibraltar in 429 and, over the next decade, proceeded to conquer the Roman provinces of North Africa. Led by Attila, the Huns broke into the empire anew in the 440s and 450s and wrought considerable destruction in the Balkans, Italy and Gaul. All the while, the Roman authorities conceded power and territory to the barbarians. In the end, even the heart of the empire succumbed. In 476 the uninspiring Romulus Augustulus, the last emperor to rule from Rome, was deposed by barbarian general Odovacer. By the end of the century, Rome and Italy had been incorporated into the realm of the Ostrogothic king Theoderic.

Structural weaknesses of the Roman empire

In seeking to understand why these barbarian polities replaced the empire in the west, it is reasonable to look not only to the military strength of the invading barbarians, but also the reasons why the empire was unable to withstand their onslaught. Much has been made of certain structural weaknesses of the empire, particularly in terms of inadequate military and

Right **Medallion of Theoderic the Ostrogoth: an example of a new barbarian ruler of the west.**

revolt. Having caused widespread disruption in the Balkans, the Goths confronted Valens and the massed forces of the eastern provinces at Hadrianople (modern Edirne in European Turkey) on 9 August, 378. After a bitter battle, Valens himself and almost two-thirds of his army lay dead, leaving the Balkans at the mercy of the Goths. According to the Christian historian Rufinus, writing some 25 years later, the battle of Hadrianople 'was the beginning of evil times for the Roman empire thereafter'.

In the immediate aftermath the empire, under the leadership of Theodosius I, was able to contain the problem, but with a significant concession: although they undertook to provide troops for the Roman army, the Goths were settled in self-governing communities on Roman land. This set a precedent for the establishment of autonomous groups of barbarians within the empire's frontiers. Moreover, the continuing relationship between Goths and Romans was hardly harmonious. Aggrieved at their treatment by Roman commanders, the Gothic leadership made demands for more influential positions in the

Right **The late Roman city with its walls and churches, as depicted in the mosaics of Theoderic the Ostrogoth's church of San Apollinario Nuovo, Ravenna.**

Below **The walls of Rome, built in the 3rd century AD and reinforced in the 5th, were emblematic of the insecurity of the times – but they were not enough to protect the city from Alaric's Goths in 410.**

277

economic resources. In both cases, the survival of the Roman empire in the east provides an instructive series of contrasts with the west. In general, the eastern empire was less prone to attack from beyond its frontiers than was the west. This meant that the military resources of the emperors at Constantinople were under less sustained pressure than were those of their counterparts in the west. Both areas seem to have suffered from a general unwillingness by the empire's inhabitants to provide recruits to the army, but this was bound to have more serious effects on the west, where the exigencies of defence required a more steady supply of manpower.

Similarly, the eastern provinces seem to have been better able to provide revenues than were those in the west. In part, this will have been because agricultural life in the east suffered less disruption by invasion than that in the west, and because the military demands on the eastern treasury were less severe than was the case in the west. Certainly, the archaeological evidence suggests that the cities of the east continued to flourish – itself an indicator of greater economic wherewithal – in marked contrast to the evidence for the shrinking of cities and the disruption of urban life in the west. In general, it seems that an empire based on a primarily agricultural economy was not able to withstand the demands made on it by a protracted period of crisis and disruption.

Matters were not helped by the lack of a united response to the crisis by the different parts of the empire. On the death of Theodosius I in 395, the administration of the empire was divided between east and west, with each half possessing its own imperial court, army and administrative hierarchy. At best this meant that the eastern and western halves of the empire tended to pursue independent policies; at worst, it could lead to open rivalry between the two imperial courts. Alaric's invasions of Italy, for example, exploited a background of bickering and threats between the eastern and western regimes.

Change and continuity

By focusing on the events of the 5th century, it is easy to succumb to the notion that the dismemberment of the Roman empire in the west was some sort of apocalyptic cataclysm. Yet the changes that occurred between the Gothic migration of 376 and the deposition of Romulus Augustulus in 476 can be seen as part of a longer process of cultural, political and social transformation that affected the Mediterranean world between the 3rd and 8th centuries. The

barbarian invasions that seem so precipitous in the 5th century belong to a longer process of tribal migration and ethnic change. Major barbarian attacks on the empire's frontiers began in the 2nd century and continued through the 3rd century. Moreover, new peoples continued to appear on the eastern empire's frontiers throughout the 6th century and beyond, right down to the rise of Islam.

Likewise, imperial society and culture was itself undergoing a slow metamorphosis. The empire's cities provide a good example. In many places, cities continued to flourish. Yet, where once they had been controlled by pagan aristocrats, they came to be dominated between the 4th and 6th centuries by Christian élites led by bishops. This in turn led to physical changes, as the buildings traditionally associated with urban civilization in the Roman world – such as temples, amphitheatres, theatres and baths – fell into disuse and instead the civic landscape came to be dominated by churches. In other words, there were significant changes occurring in the Roman empire independently of those wrought by the advent and invasion of barbarian tribes.

To talk of the 'fall' of Rome is, in a sense, to subscribe to a very narrow view of history that sees things only in terms of what happened to a Roman civilization that is often perceived in idealized and static terms. Roman civilization was dynamic and subject to constant change. In late antiquity, the events associated with the 'fall' of Rome represent a fusion of changes occurring both within the empire and beyond its frontiers.

Map of the Mediterranean world in around 500, showing the new political situation.

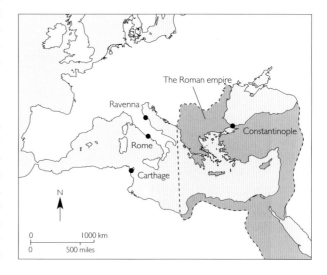

El Niños & the Collapse of Moche Civilization

Time: 8th century AD
Location: north coast of Peru

In Moche society tremendous wealth was concentrated in the hands of a few individuals, who lived in opulence and were surrounded by lesser nobility. Every valley may have had one or two royal courts, each having little direct contact with the common people, yet connected to one another like the royalty of Europe.

WALTER ALVA & CHRISTOPHER DONNAN, 1992

The Moche civilization of Peru's North Coast flourished between AD 100 and 800 under the rule of authoritarian warrior-priests. The Moche lords never ruled vast domains, just a narrow strip of some 400 km (250 miles) between the Lambayeque Valley in the north and the Nepeña Valley in the south. Their subjects dwelt along the Pacific or in dry river valleys that threaded no more than about 100 km (60 miles) inland through one of the driest and most inhospitable environments on earth.

The Moche flourished because of the unique nature of their environment. Their brilliant farming expertise harnessed mountain runoff from the Andes and exploited fertile soils using huge valley irrigation systems capable of producing substantial grain surpluses and acres of cotton with which they created fine textiles. The floodplains of the Lambayeque, Moche and other coastal valleys formed a green patchwork of closely packed irrigated fields nourished by long canals. And close offshore the cold waters of the Humboldt Current in the Pacific caused vigorous upwellings rich in nutrients from the sea bed, which millions of anchovy swarmed to feed on. Moche fisherfolk harvested this bounty from reed canoes and dried their catch or ground it into nutritious fish meal.

(Below left) **The gigantic pyramids of Huaca del Sol, ravaged by conquistadors and El Niños, stand in the Moche river valley.**
(Below right) **Map showing the sites mentioned in the text. The tint shows the area of Moche influence.**

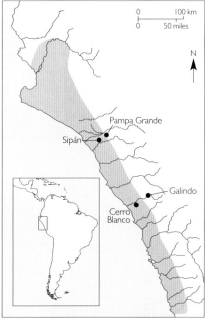

Left **Moche potters were consummate masters of their craft. Here a Moche leader adorned with face paint and ceremonial headdress gazes serenely from a distinctive stirrup-spouted jar.** *Right* **Spectacular burials of Moche lords have been found at Sipán. Here, in a glittering reconstruction, a Lord of Sipán wears his impressive regalia and carries a sceptre as a symbol of his power.**

With such ample food supplies, the Moche prospered, ruled by wealthy lords who lived atop magnificent adobe pyramids. The warrior-priests saw themselves as intermediaries between the living and the forces of the spiritual world. Their lives revolved around warfare, ritual and diplomacy, in an endless round of competition for prestige with their fellow leaders. The Moche were seemingly a prosperous people, ruled by invincible lords. But their civilization faltered, then collapsed suddenly, for reasons that are only now being understood.

Drought cycles

The Quelccaya ice cap in the southern Peruvian Andes has preserved a record of rainfall shifts going back well over 1500 years. The snow record shows how a short drought settled over the Moche region between AD 534 and 540. Between AD 563 and 594, a 30-year drought cycle produced 30 per cent less rainfall, with disastrous results on huge irrigation systems along the North Coast.

The Moche capital at Cerro Blanco sprawled around two enormous adobe huacas, or pyramids, where the warrior-priests had their palaces and performed elaborate rituals. The Huaca del Sol rises 41 m (135 ft) above the plain, two-thirds of the height of the contemporary Pyramid of the Sun at Teotihuacan, Mexico. As the 6th-century droughts intensified, water supplies faltered, water tables in river valleys dropped and crops withered. The lords must have retained firm control by husbanding grain supplies and there was still fish and fishmeal – that is until El Niños struck.

El Niños

El Niño, 'the Christmas Child', is a south-flowing counter-current which appears irregularly off the Peruvian coast as a result of intricate atmospheric-ocean interactions in the southwestern Pacific. The influx of warm water alters the normal flows of currents and the anchovy fishery crashes temporarily. Heavy rains batter the normally arid coast. Torrential floods race down river valleys carrying everything before them. The effects on a weakened Moche state can be imagined.

We do not know the exact years during the long drought when El Niños struck, but when they did Moche civilization was already in a critical state. Grain supplies were low, irrigation systems depleted. As the anchovy vanished, torrential rains swamped the Andes and coastal plains. Surging floods swept everything before them, polluted water supplies and destroyed generations of canals and irrigation works. Muddy water eroded away much of the warrior-priests' pyramids, turning them into crater-sided hills. Typhoid and other epidemics must have swept the valley and wiped out entire communities. Infant mortality soared. Thousands starved, for even a full-strength anchovy harvest could not feed the entire populace.

The Moche lords commissioned new irrigation works, imported more drought-resistant maize strains from neighbours to the east, which appear in archaeological sites dating to soon after the flood. The façades of their magnificent pyramids were rebuilt. For a while the capital regained some of its grandeur. Then a new disaster loomed.

Earthquakes

Periodic earthquakes shook the Moche homeland and could send massive amounts of hillside debris into the river valleys. Strong El Niño floods swept the detritus downstream and deposited it in the Pacific to be washed up in ridges on the beach. Soon marching dunes crept inland, driven by strong onshore winds; they smothered coastal communities, then the capital itself. Between AD 550 and 600, Cerro Blanco's warrior-priests abandoned their city and moved upstream to the strategic neck of the valley, where the Moche river flowed out on to the coastal plain.

Collapse

Nothing in earlier Moche history supplied a precedent for this move, which must have come at a time of crisis, when the people may have lost confidence in their leaders. Fixed in a rigid ideological mind set, the Moche rulers seem to have dismissed any thoughts of more flexible approaches to farming. They now settled close to the intakes to artificial canals that linked one valley with the next and watered the land nearby. Galindo at the top of the Moche valley and Pampa Grande in the Lambayeque became large settlements, the latter housing as many as 10,000 to 12,500 people.

The new locations allowed a more conservative approach to water conservation, which maximized water use in dry years, but made the Moche even more vulnerable to major floods. With the inevitability of a Greek tragedy, an exceptionally strong El Niño event during the 7th century washed away many of the field systems around Galindo and Pampa Grande. Another drought came to the North Coast, which intensified already critical food shortages. A weakened leadership wrestled with social unrest and highland raids. Around AD 700, the Moche abandoned both settlements, perhaps under duress. Whatever the cause of the final abandonment, repeated droughts and El Niño flooding had broken the back of a wealthy and powerful state. Ultimately, the rigid warrior-priests ran out of options and their spectacular civilization collapsed.

Victims sacrificed during an El Niño, buried in the melted walls of an adobe plaza at Huaca de la Luna.

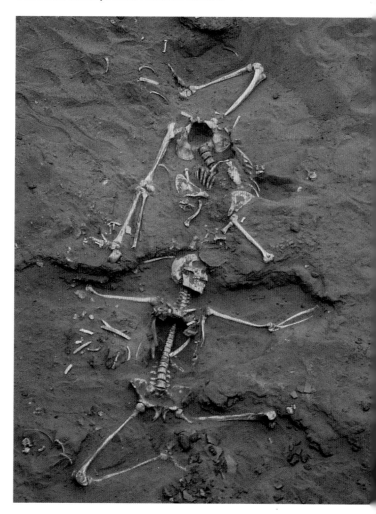

Why Did Maya Civilization Collapse?

Time: c. AD 900
Location: Southern Maya Lowlands of Central America

Such was the scattering of the work, the human design. The people were ground down, overthrown. The mouths and faces of them were destroyed and crushed.

THE POPOL VUH, 16TH CENTURY

THE ANCIENT MAYA of Mesoamerica were among the most flamboyant and longest-lived of all pre-Columbian American civilizations. Once humble village farmers, the Maya transformed their lowlying tropical homeland into a landscape of city-states ruled by powerful lords. Between the last few centuries before Christ and AD 900, Maya civilization flourished in the southern lowlands of Mexico, Guatemala and Honduras. Great dynasties of lords presided over aggressive city-states like Copán, Palenque and Tikal, where they presided as divine

Map of the Maya homeland with the major centres and sites mentioned in the text.

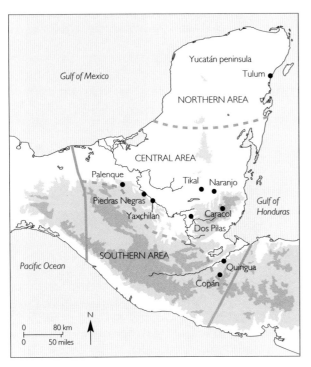

rulers, shamans and intermediaries between the living and the gods and ancestors. They thought of themselves as World Trees, conduits by which humans communicated with the spiritual world. A Maya lord was far more than a secular ruler. He was Maya life, linked to his family and to communities large and small by the sacred institution of kingship and its genealogical ties to the revered ancestors. Unfortunately for the Maya, the form of kingship they espoused depended on an agricultural economy that was unsustainable, given the environment.

Around AD 800, southern lowland Maya civilization abruptly collapsed. The great ceremonial centres of the region were abandoned and huge areas were deserted, never to be reoccupied. In the city of Tikal, the population of 25,000–80,000 (estimates vary) declined to just one-third of that. The survivors clustered in the ruins of the great pyramids and plazas and tried to retain a semblance of their earlier life. Within a few generations, even they were gone. Scholars have long puzzled over the Maya collapse, attributing it to ecological change, social upheaval, political revolution and warfare, among other factors. It remains one of the great mysteries of the past, even if recent palaeoclimatic discoveries have cast drought as one of the major villains.

Everyone who studies the Maya collapse agrees that it was brought on by a combination of ecological, political and social factors. By AD 800, the population density of the southern lowlands was as high as 200 people per square kilometre over an area so large that it was impossible for hungry farmers to move on to uncleared land. There was simply none left. By the time the collapse came, Maya agricultural production had reached its limits, making people extremely vulnerable to drought. A new gen-

Right **Tatiana Proskouriakoff's reconstruction of the central precincts of the Maya city of Copán, in modern Honduras. Archaeologists have been able to unravel the complex architectural history of the site and surveys in the city and its hinterland have documented the collapse of its population in the 8th to 9th centuries.**

Below **The Hero Twin Hunahpu, patron of scribes, features in Maya creation myths, as recorded in the Popol Vuh. The hieroglyph of his father, the Maize God, appears on the rim of the vessel. In Maya myth humankind was fashioned from maize and the crop was essential to the Maya.**

eration of theories places much of the blame on short-term climatic change.

Maya agriculture

The Maya lowlands are quite unlike the fertile Nile Valley or the densely irrigated Moche homeland in Peru (p. 279). The Petén-Yucatán peninsula is a vast limestone shelf with poor drainage and few permanent rivers. The hot and humid lowlands enjoy irregular rainfall but support dense forest in their primordial state, all of which was cleared by the Maya. The greenery we see today is regenerated forest. This unforgiving environment had relatively infertile soils, which could only be cultivated by clearing and burning off the forest. The cleared gardens, called *milpa*, remained fertile for only about two years before they were abandoned to lie fallow for up to seven years. Such fields could not possibly support large cities, let alone a dense concentration of villages, so the Maya drained and canalized swamps, turning agriculturally useless land into highly productive acreage – as long as there was ample groundwater. They also grew crops on terraced hillsides, squeezing as much as they could from every acre planted.

The Maya farmed complex mosaics of landscapes, but long before the collapse came their agricultural production was approaching its limits. In the short term, their intensification of farming had worked at the local level, especially when a growing class of rulers and nobles may have exercised close control over production and crop yields through tribute assessments. But they could never standardize agricultural production over wide areas like the Egyptians or the Moche, where large-scale irrigation works made standardization feasible. The Maya environment was highly diverse, with fragile, easily exhausted tropical soils, and highly unpredictable

rainfall. The farmers faced escalating production demands from their masters at a time when soils were becoming exhausted, torrential rain falling on cleared land had caused widespread sheet erosion, and firewood was chronically short. A major drought cycle was the knockout blow.

Droughts

An accurate record of changing climatic conditions is preserved in the accumulated layers of sediments at the bottom of the region's lakes. Lake Chichancanab in the Yucatán was first filled in about 6200 BC at a time when Caribbean sea levels and the local water table rose sharply. Core samples from the lake's sediments show how conditions remained relatively wet until about 1000 BC, when the climate became drier. Drying continued until it peaked between AD 800 and 1000 – the time of the Maya collapse. The drought cycle of these two centuries was the most arid period of the past 8000 years.

Lake Punta Láguna in the Quintana Roo area has rapidly accumulating sediments, so much so that a core boring yielded a chronology of wet and dry years as accurate as a tree-ring sequence. There were frequent and severe dry spells in AD 585, coinciding with a major drought recorded in the Quelccaya ice core from the Andes that affected the Moche civilization. This drought seems to have caused some disruption to Maya life, but two centuries of abundant rainfall and rapid growth ensued. Then a prolonged dry spell settled over the region between AD 725 and 1020, peaking in 862 and 986. The drought ended abruptly in 1020. Within a century the lake experienced some of the wettest conditions in 8000 years.

The collapse

When the great droughts of the 8th and 9th centuries came, Maya civilization was already under increasing stress. The rapidly growing cities were top-heavy with nobility and riven by factionalism. They were importing food from considerable distances away. Competition for military supremacy and prestige placed ever-heavier demands on their inhabitants. The droughts were the final straw. Crop yields and tribute payments dwindled rapidly. Powerful lords found their spiritual and secular authority withering in the face of a restless and hungry populace.

The combination of drought and environmental damage was beyond the capability of any ruler to endure. As thousands starved, the survivors abandoned the great cities and dispersed into small

Left **Tikal was one of the greatest of Maya city-states, located at the centre of strategic trade routes and its lords presided over several cities. After** AD **800 this powerful ceremonial centre rapidly declined.** *Right* **The Maya were superb craftsmen and artists – this jade mosaic vase with a portrait head of the Maize God comes from a Late Classic burial at Tikal.**

The collapse did not come without turmoil and war. To give one example, in AD 645, the rulers of Dos Pilas in present-day northern Guatemala embarked on ambitious military campaigns to expand their territory. Dos Pilas became a wealthy trade centre until 761, when its rulers overextended themselves. Nearby Tamarindito attacked its once-powerful neighbour and killed the ruler. The surviving nobles fled and built a heavily fortified centre atop a craggy hill at Aguateca. Attacked repeatedly, they held on for another half century before intensive warfare drove them into scattered settlements, which they again fortified. Within their defended areas, with only parched acreage to farm, crop yields must have fallen rapidly. In one last desperate stand, the surviving Aguatecans created an island fortress on a peninsula on Lake Petexbatun by digging three moats across the neck. Even this outpost was abandoned at the height of the drought in the 800s.

The effects of the long dry spells rippled across the Maya world. Southern lowland civilization collapsed almost completely and the centre of Maya life shifted to the northern Yucatán where the water table was closer to the surface. In the south, kingship faltered in the face of drought and rebellious commoners. The elaborate structure of Maya city-states collapsed like a deck of cards within a few generations.

hamlets. Surveys in the hinterland of the city of Copán document the population collapse. Between AD 700 and 850, 20,000 and 25,000 people lived close to, or in, the city, with the population doubling every 80 to 100 years. After 850, the urban core lost half its inhabitants, while the rural population increased by almost 20 per cent. After 1150, the population of the Copán Valley was a mere 2000 to 5000 people.

Below **The small fortified Maya town at Tulum perches on a low cliff above the Caribbean coast of the northern Yucatán. Maya civilization endured and even prospered in the northern lowlands until the Spanish Conquest.**

What Happened to the Anasazi?

Time: 13th century AD
Location: North American Southwest

People have moved from place to place and have joined and separated again throughout our past, and we have incorporated it into our songs, stories, and myths because we must continually remember that, without movement, there is no life.

TESSIE NARANJO, 1995

THE ANASAZI were a prehistoric farming people who inhabited the Colorado Plateau and the northern Rio Grande region of the American Southwest between 800 BC and AD 1600. The name 'Anasazi' is an anglicized Navajo word adopted by early archaeologists. It means 'ancient ones' or 'enemy ancestor'. Enemy, in this case, simply means, 'people who are not ourselves'. Puebloan peoples, the descendants of these early farmers, prefer the term Ancestral Puebloan people. They are famous for the spectacular cliff dwellings, multi-storey stone architecture and rock art that they left behind in places like Canyon de Chelly, Mesa Verde, Chaco Canyon, Canyonlands and Bandelier, many of which are now preserved in national parks and monuments in the Four Corners Area – Arizona, New Mexico, Colorado and Utah. However, these architectural examples represent only the most visible remains of these highly adaptable peoples who, for the most part, lived in small, dispersed settlements, tending their gardens of maize, beans and squash, and foraging for wild game and native plants.

Subregional differences in geography, ecological resources, climate and cultural preferences resulted in the evolution of distinct Anasazi subtraditions, each with its own customs of pottery decoration, masonry styles and architectural forms. Among these subtraditions of the Anasazi are the Virgin, Kayenta, Mesa Verde, Chaco and Rio Grande branches. At their peak size and distribution in the late 11th century, the combined branches inhabited a vast territory stretching from southern Nevada to central New Mexico and northern Arizona to southern Utah. The Chacoans, whose awe-inspiring community centres were in the San Juan Basin of northwestern New Mexico, were the first of the branches to abandon their ancestral territory in the middle of the 12th century for reasons that still being debated. But by the end of the 13th century, the

Right **Betatakin Ruin: this cliff dwelling contains 120 rooms and 3 kivas. It was occupied by people of the Kayenta branch of the Anasazi culture from AD 1250 to 1300.**

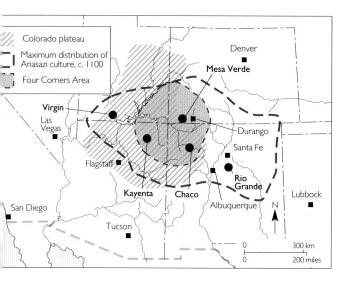

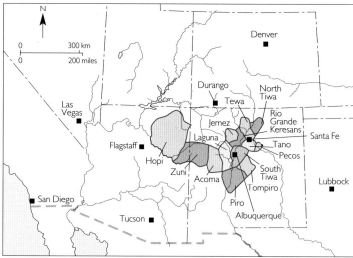

Above left **Map of the traditional homeland of the Anasazi, the maximum distribution of the Anasazi culture, c. 1100 and the five major subtraditions.** *Above* **Locations of the 13 historic pueblos c. 1600.**

Virgin, Kayenta and Mesa Verde branch populations abandoned their Four Corners area homes for destinations south and east. Only the Rio Grande branch and isolated communities on the southern margins of the Colorado Plateau continued. By AD 1600, if not by 1450, these Anasazi descendants are known to us as the ancestral Hopi-, Zuni-, Keres-, Tewa-, Tiwa- and Towa-speaking Pueblo Indians of contemporary Arizona and New Mexico. The history, movement and survival of these resilient peoples has fascinated observers for more than 100 years.

Archaeologists and Native Americans have different but complementary theories about what encouraged the ancestral Puebloans to leave their homes. Many archaeologists think that environmental problems drove people from the area. They argue that unfavourable climatic conditions made it impossible to grow enough food for people to survive. Other archaeologists think that social problems forced people to leave. These researchers argue that internal conflict, warfare and fear of violence caused people first to build their homes in large aggregated villages or high in the cliffs where they could defend themselves and later to abandon their homes for more secure places. Yet other archaeologists think a variety of factors, including new religion, increased safety and a better climate for growing crops, actually attracted people away from the Four Corners area. In short, some archaeologists believe that the Anasazi were 'pushed' from the area by difficult conditions, other archaeologists believe that people were 'pulled' to other areas by attractive conditions, but today most believe that a combination of environmental and social factors, rather than any single factor, was

responsible for the 13th-century Anasazi abandonment of the Four Corners area.

Environmental and social 'pushes'

Environmental problems that would have caused crop failure have been discovered through the study of tree-ring growth, ancient plant remains and floodplain stratigraphy. Among these are a 24-year drought at the end of the 13th century, referred to as the 'Great Drought' of AD 1276 to 1299; closely spaced intervals of cold weather in the early to middle 1200s that would have seriously shortened the length of the growing season; a period after AD 1250 when the rains came too late to help the crops grow;

Trends in rainfall in the Mesa Verde region, 1200–1300. Note the 24-year period of below average rainfall beginning 1276.

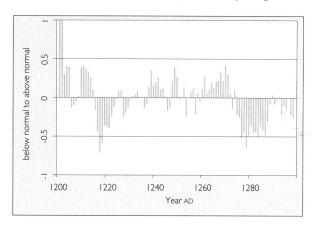

and falling water tables at the end of the 1200s. The combination of these factors would have made dry-land and floodplain farming risky if not impossible.

Social problems may have come about due to difficult environmental conditions. These may have included violent competition for the best farmland; raiding for food by people who lacked stored crops; and starvation, illness and death.

Environmental and social 'pulls'

During the 13th and 14th centuries, places south and east of the Four Corners area had more reliable snow and rainfall patterns than areas to the north and west. These differences may have contributed to planned migration towards places of higher security where friends and relatives were located and where arable land was still available.

New religious and social movements have been documented south of the Four Corners area during the 14th century. These include ceremonial and religious organizations and societies; medicine (curing) and warfare societies; and new town-sized villages that contained different forms of public architecture and community space. It is likely that these developments began in the 13th century and may have attracted ancient Pueblo peoples away from their former homelands.

Puebloan view

Puebloan peoples generally do not dispute archaeological explanations. They see the depopulation not as abandonment, however, but rather as another migration in a continual series of migratory movements that define Pueblo history. According to some oral traditions, the Four Corners area continues to be inhabited by the ancestors. In addition, the Four Corners area is still visited and used by contemporary Pueblo people for a variety of purposes.

Environmental and social factors worked together to move people from a less productive and predictable area to an area with greater security and promise. The Anasazi peoples responded to the physical and social environments around them. When conditions changed, they moved on.

Left above **Pueblo Bonito was a large community that at its peak stood 4 to 5 storeys high; by its abandonment it is estimated that it contained around 600 rooms and 40 kivas. It was occupied by people of the Chaco branch of the Anasazi culture.** *Left* **Cliff Palace, Mesa Verde, contains some 220 rooms and 23 kivas. It was occupied from AD 1250 to 1280 by people of the Mesa Verde branch of the Anasazi culture.**

Catastrophic Impacts from Outer Space?

Time: the past 5000 years
Location: the world

And the third angel sounded, and there fell a great star from Heaven, burning as it were a lamp, and it fell upon a third of the rivers, and upon the foundation of waters.

BOOK OF REVELATION 8: 10

FIRE AND BRIMSTONE, pestilence, Sodom and Gomorrah (pp. 34–7), the seven years of Egyptian famine and the biblical Flood – there are many stories of the Lord's vengeance bringing down grief and destruction on those who offended him. Generations of archaeologists and biblical scholars have argued over the historical validity of these disasters, which may, in truth, be more symbolic than real. Then there are the documented natural cataclysms of the past, such as the massive Thera eruption of the 2nd millennium BC (pp. 271–4), the great earthquake which overwhelmed the Roman town of Kourion in Cyprus in AD 265, and the Mount Tambora eruption of 1815 in Indonesia, which released so much volcanic dust into the atmosphere that 12 months later Europe shivered under the famous 'year without a summer'. Although scientists and historians may argue over the ultimate effects of such disasters, there is no doubt of their existence. Yet some scholars are now posing a new question: were there, in fact, hitherto undocumented natural catastrophes which changed the course of history?

In 1950, Immanuel Velikovsky published his famous *Worlds in Collision*, in which he argued that the ancient world had suffered from many environmental changes caused by comets hitting earth. He carried his arguments still further and claimed that the planets Venus and Mars had also caused havoc on earth during the 2nd and 1st millennia BC. Velikovsky's theories raised such impassioned opposition among scientists that some even tried to have his book banned. His ideas are nonsense, but he did give an accurate description of the destructive meteorite rain which might bombard earth when a comet passed nearby. Half a century after *Worlds in Collision*, comets are back in the archaeological news,

this time as a result of major advances in the study of ancient climate change.

Tree-rings, volcanoes and comets

Palaeoecologist Michael Baillie is an expert in tree-rings and the climate changes revealed by them over the past 5000 years. He points to a particular series of climatic traumas recorded as narrow bands of tree-rings in the ancient Irish oaks he studied, but

Below **Tree rings record the annual growth of the trees and thus reflect climatic conditions at the time. The first section shows rings around the AD 540 event; below is the 1159–1141 BC event showing up in four sections from different trees.**

also found in trees from elsewhere around the world. These can be dated to between 2354 and 2345 BC, 1628 and 1623 BC, 1159 and 1141 BC, 208 and 204 BC and AD 526 and 545. Until recently, such anomalies were all thought to result from major volcanic eruptions releasing ash into the atmosphere – just as the Tambora event did – thus reducing solar radiation and hence causing climatic deterioration and poor tree growth. Volcanic eruptions also leave traces as peaks of acidity in ice-cores, which are a record of the annual build up of layers of compressed snow-fall. These layers can be counted and dated, though linking acidity peaks to particular volcanoes is not always certain. Interestingly, no trace of the early 6th-century AD episode, clearly marked in the tree-rings, has yet been found as an acidity peak.

Having identified such environmental downturns in the tree-rings, Baillie enters a complex maze of archaeology, historical records and folklore. He looks at the tree-ring evidence in relation to a series of major historical and traditional events: the biblical Flood of Genesis, the disasters that befell Egypt at the Exodus and the famines at the end of King David's reign, a famine in China that ended the Qin dynasty, and finally the tales of Merlin and Arthur and the onset of the 'Dark Ages' in Britain. But could volcanic eruptions alone be responsible for such large-scale and dramatic events? As Baillie asks: 'is it possible that there is something else in the equation?' From descriptions in traditional literature from all over the world, Baillie is led to the conclusion that this 'something' might be cometary impacts or cosmic swarms of cometary debris.

The Thera eruption and the Exodus

The 1628 BC anomaly is thought by some to coincide with the Thera eruption in the Aegean. Baillie believes that this in turn could be linked with the breakdown of the Middle Kingdom in Egypt and the Hyksos incursion into the Nile Valley, as well as the biblical Exodus – an event conventionally dated to around 1250 BC. He quotes another author, Ian Wilson, who theorizes that the 'pillar of cloud by day and fire by night' which guided the Israelites was the eruption column from Thera, 800 km (500 miles) away. Could this, as Baillie suggests, be an eyewitness account of the Thera eruption in 1628 BC? He is skating on thin archaeological ice. Not all archaeologists agree with the 1628 BC date for the Thera eruption: long-standing archaeological chronologies based on cross-dates from historical

contexts in Egypt place the disaster at around 1500 BC. But Baillie in addition ties in events in other parts of the world as distant as Ireland and China to this 1628 BC episode, again suggesting that circumstantial evidence points to extraterrestrial, cometary causes which may also have triggered volcanic and other seismic activity.

According to the Bible, 480 years separated the Exodus and the building of King Solomon's temple, when 'a cloud filled the house of the Lord', and Psalm 18 records the earth shaking and trembling at a time when the 'foundations of the hills moved and were shaken ... the foundations of the earth were discovered ... at the blast of the breath of thy nostrils'. Coincidentally, this 480-year gap is very close to the interval between two of Baillie's tree-ring events (1628 and 1159–1141 BC). Baillie believes that the Bible thus records catastrophic and highly significant cometary events which caused sharp downturns in the eastern Mediterranean world.

Baillie takes this further, and points out that cometary impacts could have occurred thousands of times during the earth's existence, but many of them would have been airbursts which would leave no trace in the form of impact craters. Such was the case with the piece of cometary debris which exploded in 1908 about 10 km (6 miles) above Tunguska, in Siberia, with a force of between 12 and 30 megatons, flattening a huge area of forest. Vague

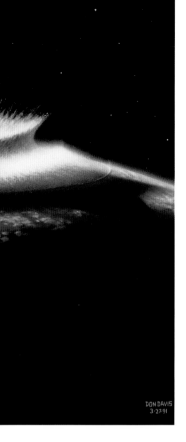

Left **An artist's impression of what the super-impact of an asteroid around 800 km (500 miles) in diameter would look like from space.** *Right* **Meteor Crater in northeast Arizona, United States: caused by a meteor impact around 50,000 years ago, it measures approximately 200 m (650 ft) deep and 800 m (2625 ft) across. It is only relatively recently that it has been recognized as a meteor crater. Not all potentially catastrophic impacts may lave left such dramatic evidence.**

accounts circulated of mysterious sights and sounds but these might have been dismissed or forgotten had not a curious Russian scientist named Leonid Kulik travelled in search of the location of the explosion and recorded its effects. The disaster left no crater and no trace of this impact has been detected in ice-cores, even though we know where to look.

Recent researches using infrasound have revealed the size and frequency of explosions in the atmosphere; results suggest that the earth must have been hit by a comet several hundred metres across or by clusters of smaller fragments at least once, probably several times, over the past 5000 years. These impacts may not have left visible traces, but Baillie believes some may have wreaked havoc in increasingly densely populated areas.

The calamitous 6th century

Tree-rings reveal a major dust-veil event in AD 540, which was apparently not the result of a volcanic eruption. Baillie hypothesizes that a comet may have bombarded earth during the 6th century and triggered a range of natural catastrophes, among them earthquakes, widespread famines, exceptionally cold weather, floods and an outbreak of plague. These unusual happenings survived in folk histories for many centuries.

Journalist David Keys pinpoints the year AD 535/536 as the crisis point when a catastrophic

natural disaster blotted out much solar heat for 18 months and caused climatic anomalies around the world. Unusually heavy rainfall in tropical Africa led to higher rat and flea populations, and thence bubonic plague, which spread across the Mediterranean world and Europe in the 6th century, decimating Constantinople. In AD 537 and 538, a severe drought killed numerous Chinese and affected wide areas of the Mongolian steppe, causing widespread population movements across Eurasia, and ultimately the creation of an Avar empire in eastern Europe and the western Ukraine. The Avars ultimately came into conflict with the Roman empire, which was suffering because of money shortages, the occupation of the Balkans by Avars and Slavs, the Persian occupation of much of the east, plague, and religious dissension. Keys believes these problems are linked either directly or indirectly to well-documented climatic evidence for abnormally unstable weather in western Europe between 535 and 555.

Keys argues that a domino effect, triggered by the climatic and epidemiological events of the 6th century, led to the expansion of Anglo-Saxon England, to widespread drought and famine. Across the Atlantic, 6th-century drought contributed to the collapse of the great city of Teotihuacan and had major political effects in the Maya lowlands, where the Tikal city-state went into temporary decline. In the Andes, ice cores from the Quelccaya glacier document 6th-century droughts and El Niño events that decimated Moche civilization along Peru's North Coast and helped Tiwanaku by Lake Titicaca in the highlands (pp. 202–4) rise to prominence. Keys

Comets were traditionally thought to accompany great disasters. The Bayeux Tapestry records the appearance of Halley's Comet at the time of the Battle of Hastings and the death of Harold, king of England.

thinks all these developments resulted from a massive volcanic eruption in 535 in the Sunda Strait between Java and Sumatra, carrying ash and debris as much as 48 km (30 miles) into the stratosphere, and destabilizing human societies around the world. Here he disagrees with Baillie, who places the blame on cometary bombardment.

According to Baillie, the debris associated with close-passing comets was a major factor in the course of human history. His combination of climatological data, archaeological evidence, historical records and folklore is at present a purely hypothetical scenario. Unfortunately, scientific proof will be hard to find, for many climatic events leave few traces behind them. But the Baillie hypothesis reminds us that we have much to learn about climatic and natural phenomena which have affected life on earth and may affect it again in the future.

A contemporary photograph of the devastation caused by the explosion of a piece of cometary debris over Tunguska, Siberia, in 1908. There was no impact crater and so once the trees had recovered, there would be very little evidence on the ground of this disaster. How many times could such an event have occurred in the past, bringing calamity to human societies but leaving no lasting physical record?

Further Reading

Myths & Legends: Hidden Truths?

1 The Garden of Eden
Koldewey, R., *The Excavations at Babylon* (London, 1914)
Reade, J., 'The Hanging Gardens of Babylon' in Scarre, C. (ed.), *The Seventy Wonders of the Ancient World* (London & New York, 1999), 27–9
Wiseman, D.J., *Nebuchadrezzar and Babylon: The Schweich Lectures of the British Academy 1983* (Oxford, 1985)

2 The Biblical Flood & Noah's Ark
Bright, J., 'Has Archaeology found evidence of the Flood?' in Wright, G.E. & Freedman, D.N. (eds), *Biblical Archaeologist Reader*, I, ASOR (1964), 32–40
Ryan W. & Pitman W., *Noah's Flood* (New York, 1999)
www.nationalgeographic.com/blacksea

3 Moses & the Exodus
Davies, P., 'What Separates a Minimalist from a Maximalist? Not Much', *Biblical Archaeology Review*, 26, no. 2 (2000)
Dever, W.G., 'Save us from Postmodern Malarkey' *Biblical Archaeology Review*, 26, no. 2 (2000)
Sarna, N.A., 'Israel in Egypt', in Shanks, H. (ed.), *Ancient Israel* (Eaglewood Cliffs, 1989)
Millard, A., 'How Reliable is Exodus?' *Biblical Archaeology Review*, 26, no. 4 (2000)

4 The Lost Cities of Sodom & Gomorrah
Harris, G.M. & Beardow, A.P., 'The destruction of Sodom and Gomorrah: a geotechnical perspective', *Quarterly Journal of Engineering Geology*, 28 (1995), 349–62
van Hattem, W.C., 'Once Again: Sodom and Gomorrah', *Biblical Archaeologist*, 44, no. 2 (1981), 87–92
Politis, K.D. et al., *Excavations at the Sanctuary of Lot at Deir 'Ain 'Abata, Jordan* (London, 2001)
Schaub, R.T. & Rast,W.E., *Reports of the Expedition to the Dead Sea Plain, Jordan, Vol. I. Bab edh-Drah: Excavations in the Cemetery Directed by Paul W. Lapp (1965–67)*, ASOR (Winona Lake, 1983)
Neev, D. & Emery, K.O., *The Destruction of Sodom, Gomorrah, and Jericho. Coordination of Biblical and Scientific Information* (New York, 1995)

5 Atlantis: Fact or Fiction?
Castleden, R., *Atlantis Destroyed* (London & New York, 1998)
de Camp, L. Sprague, *Lost Continents: The Atlantis Theme in History, Science, and Literature* (New York, 1970)
Donnelly, I., *Atlantis: The Antediluvian World* (New York, 1971 [1881])
Galanopoulos, A.G. & Bacon, E., *Atlantis: The Truth Behind the Legend* (Indianapolis, 1969)
Luce, J.V., *The End of Atlantis: New Light on an Old Legend* (London & New York, 1969)
Pelligrino, C., *Unearthing Atlantis: An Archaeological Odyssey* (New York, 1991)

6 The Trojan War
Fitton, J.L., *The Discovery of the Greek Bronze Age* (London & Cambridge, Mass., 1996)
Homer, *The Iliad*, trans. R. Fitzgerald (London, 1992)
Johnston, I., 'The Legend of the Trojan War'
www.mala.bc.ca/~johnstoi/clas101/troy.htm
Rutter, J.B., 'Troy VII and the Historicity of the Trojan War'
http://tenaya.cs.dartmouth.edu/history/bronze_age/lessons/27.html.
Wood, M., *In Search of the Trojan War* (London & Berkeley, 1996)

7 Theseus & the Minotaur
Castleden, R., *The Knossos Labyrinth: A New View of the 'Palace of Minos' at Knossos* (London & New York, 1990)
Castleden, R., *Minoans: Life in Bronze Age Crete* (London & New York, 1993)
Fitton, J.L., *The Discovery of the Greek Bronze Age* (London & Cambridge, Mass., 1996)
Frazer, Sir J.G. (trans.), *Apollodorus, The Library* (Cambridge, Mass., 1960)

8 Jason & the Argonauts
Apollonius Rhodius, *Jason and the Golden Fleece: The Argonautica*. Trans. R. Hunter (Oxford & New York, 1993)
Haskas, V., 1996 'Jason and the Argonauts'
http://www.greece.org/poseidon/work/argonautika/argo.html
Mertz, H., *The Wine Dark Sea* (Chicago, 1964)

9 The Ten Lost Tribes of Israel
Parfitt, T., *Journey to a Vanished City: The Search for a Lost Tribe of Israel*. (Phoenix, 1997)

10 The Quest for the Ark of the Covenant
Grierson, R. & Munro-Hay, S., *The Ark of the Covenant* (Phoenix, 2000)

11 The Star of Bethlehem
Brown, R.E., *The Birth of the Messiah: A Commentary on the Infancy Narratives in the Gospels of Matthew and Luke* (New York, 1993)
Cramer, F.H., *Astrology in Roman Law and Politics* (Chicago, 1996)
Freitag, R.S., *The Star of Bethlehem: A List of References* (Washington, 1979)
Lindsay, J., *Origins of Astrology* (New York, 1971)
Molnar, M.R., *The Star of Bethlehem: The Legacy of the Magi* (New Brunswick & London, 1999)

12 King Arthur & the Holy Grail
Alcock, L., *Arthur's Britain* (Harmondsworth, 1971)
Ashe, G. (ed.), *The Quest for Arthur's Britain* (London, 1971)
Lacy, N.J. (ed.), *The New Arthurian Encyclopedia* (New York, 1991)
Lacy, N.J., Ashe, G. & Mancoff, D.N., *The Arthurian Handbook* (New York, 2nd ed., 1997)
Snyder, C., *Exploring the World of King Arthur* (London & New York, 2000)
White, R. (ed.), *King Arthur in Legend and History* (London, 1998)

13 The Turin Shroud
Iannone, J.C., *The Mystery of the Shroud of Turin* (New York, 1998)
Meachem, W., 'The Authentication of the Turin Shroud: An Issue in Archaeological Epistemology', *Current Anthropology* 24 (June 1983)
Scavone, D.C., *The Shroud of Turin* (San Diego, 1989)
Scavone, D.C., 'The Historian and the Shroud', in the *Proceedings of the Symposium History, Science, Theology and the Shroud*, June 22–23, 1991 (St Louis, 1991)
Stevenson, K. & Habermas, G., *The Shroud and the Controversy*, (Nashville, 1990)

14 Maya Myth: Will the World End in 2012
Friedel, D., Schele, L. & Parker, J., *Maya Cosmos: A Thousand Years on the Shaman's Path* (New York, 1993)
Taube, K., *Aztec and Maya Myths* (London, 1993)
Tedlock, D., *The Popol Vuh: The Definitive Edition of the Mayan Book of the Dawn of Life and the Glories of Gods and Kings* (New York, 1985)

15 Aztlán & the Myth of the Aztec Migration
Boone, E.H., 'Migration Histories as Ritual Performance' in D. Carrasco (ed.), *To Change Place: Aztec Ceremonial Landscapes* (Boulder, 1991)
Durán, Fray Diego, *The History of the Indies of New Spain*. Trans. D. Heyden (Norman & London, 1994)
Matos Moctezuma, E., *The Great Temple of the Aztecs* (London & New York, 1988)
Paz, O., *In Search of the Present* (New York, 1991)
Sahagún, Bernardino de, *Florentine Codex: General History of the Things of New Spain*, Book 3, 'The Origin of the Gods', trans. Anderson and Dibble (Santa Fe, 1952)
Thomas, H., *Conquest: Montezuma, Cortes and the Fall of Old Mexico* (New York, 1993)
Townsend, R.F. *The Aztecs* (London & New York, new ed., 2000)

16 Memories of the Dreamtime
Chaloupka, G., *Journey in Time: the World's Longest Continuing Art Tradition* (Chatswood (NSW), 1993)
Flood, J., *Rock Art of the Dreamtime: Images of Ancient Australia* (Sydney, 1997)
Flood, J., *Archaeology of the Dreamtime: the Story of Prehistoric Australia and its People* (Sydney, 2000 [1st ed. 1983])

Mysteries of the Stone Age
17 The Puzzle of Human Origins
Aiello, L. & Wheeler, P., 'The expensive-tissue hypothesis' *Current Anthropology* 36 (1995) 199–221
Boyd, R. & Silk, J.B., *How Humans Evolved* (New York & London, 2nd ed., 2000)
Johanson, D. & Edgar, B., *From Lucy to Language* (London, 1996)
Lahr, M.M. & Foley, R.A., 'Towards a theory of modern human origins: geography, demography, and diversity in recent human evolution' *Yearbook of Physical Anthropology* 41 (1998), 137–76

18 How Did Language Evolve?
Dunbar, R., *Grooming, Gossip and the Evolution of Language* (London, 1996)
Mithen, S., *The Prehistory of the Mind* (London & New York, 1996)
Pinker, S., *The Language Instinct* (New York & London, 1994)
Pinker, S. & Bloom, P., 'Natural language and natural selection' *Behavioral and Brain Sciences* 13 (1990), 707–84

19 What Happened to the Neanderthals?
Mithen, S., *The Prehistory of the Mind* (London & New York, 1996)
Stringer, C. & Gamble, C., *In Search of the Neanderthals* (London & New York, 1993)
Stringer, C. & McKie, R., *African Exodus* (London, 1996)

20 The Enigma of Palaeolithic Cave Art
Chauvet, J.-M., Brunel Deschamps, E. & Hillaire, C., *Chauvet Cave: The Discovery of the World's Oldest Paintings* (London & New York, 1996)
Clottes, J. & Courtin, J., *The Cave Beneath the Sea: Palaeolithic Images at Cosquer* (New York, 1996)
Clottes, J. & Lewis-Williams, J. D., *The Shamans of Prehistory: Trance and Magic in the Painted Caves* (New York, 1998)
Leroi-Gourhan, A., *The Art of Prehistoric Man in Western Europe* (London, 1968)
Ruspoli, M., *The Cave of Lascaux: The Final Photographic Record* (London, 1987)

21 Who Were the First Australians?
Allen, J., Golson, J. & Jones, R. (eds), *Sunda and Sahul. Prehistoric Studies in Southeast Asia, Melanesia and Australia* (London, 1977)
Flood, J., *Archaeology of the Dreamtime: the Story of Prehistoric Australia and its People* (Sydney, 2000 [1st ed. 1983])

22 The First Americans and Kennewick Man
Chatters, J., 'The Recovery and Analysis of an Early Holocene Human Skeleton from Kennewick, Washington', *American Antiquity* 65(2) (2000), 291–316

Dillehay, T., *The First Settlement of the Americas: A New Prehistory* (New York, 2000)
Dillehay, T. & Meltzer, D. (eds), *The First Americans: Search and Research* (Boston, 1991)
Dixon, J., *Bones, Boats, and Bison: Archaeology and the First Colonization of Western North America* (Albuquerque, 1998)
Fagan, B.M., *The Great Journey* (London & New York, 1987)
Meltzer, D., 'The Discovery of Deep Time: A History of Views of the Peopling of the Americas' in Bonnichsen, R. & Steele, D.G. (eds), *Method and Theory for Investigating the Peopling of the Americas* (Corvallis, 1994), 7–26
Thomas, D.H., *Skull Wars* (New York, 2000)

23 What Wiped Out the Big Game Animals?
'The Mammoth's Demise', *Discovering Archaeology* Sept/Oct (1999), 31–61
Bahn, P. & Lister, A., *Mammoths* (London, 1995)
Haynes, G., *Mammoths, Mastodonts and Elephants* (Cambridge, 1991)
Martin, P.S. & Klein, R.G. (eds), *Quaternary Extinctions, A Prehistoric Revolution* (Tucson, 1984)
Stuart, A.J., 'Mammalian extinctions in the late Pleistocene of Northern Eurasia and North America, *Biological Review* 66 (1991), 453–562

24 How Did Farming Begin?
Anderson. P., *Prehistory of Agriculture: New Experimental and Ethnographic Approaches*, Institute of Archaeology, University of California, Monograph no. 40 (Los Angeles, 1999)
Bar-Yosef, O., 'The Natufian Culture in the Levant, threshold to the origins of agriculture' *Evolutionary Anthropology* (1998), 159–77
Smith, B., *The Emergence of Agriculture* (Washington DC, 1997)

25 The Mysteries of Rock Art
Bahn, P.G., *The Cambridge Illustrated History of Prehistoric Art* (Cambridge & New York, 1998)
Chippindale, C. & Taçon, P.S.C. (eds), *The Archaeology of Rock-Art* (Cambridge & New York, 1998)
Lewis-Williams, J.D. & Dowson, T.A., *Images of Power: Understanding Bushman Rock Art* (Johannesburg, 1989)

26 The Meaning of the Megaliths
Burl, A. & Milligan, M., *Circles of Stone: The Prehistoric Rings of Britain & Ireland* (London, 1999)
Joussaume, R., *Dolmens for the Dead: Megalith-Building Around the World* (London, 1987)
Renfrew, C. (ed.), *The Megalithic Monuments of Western Europe* (London & New York, 1983)

27 Was There a Mother Goddess Cult?
Ehrenberg, M., *Women in Prehistory* (London, 1989)
Gimbutas, M., *The Living Goddesses* (Berkeley, 1999)
Goodison, L. & Morris, C. (eds), *Ancient Goddesses* (London & Madison, 1998)

28 The Iceman: Shepherd or Shaman?
Barfield, L., 'The Iceman Reviewed', *Antiquity* 68 (1994), 10–26
Fowler, B., *Iceman: Uncovering the Life and Times of a Prehistoric Man Found in an Alpine Glacier* (New York, 2000)
Spindler, K., *The Man in the Ice* (London, 1994)

29 How Did They Build Stonehenge?
Chippindale, C., *Stonehenge Complete* (London & New York, 2nd ed., 1994)
Fitchen, J., *Building Construction before Mechanization* (Cambridge, Mass., 1986)
Richards, J. & Whitby, M., 'The engineering of Stonehenge', in Cunliffe, B. & Renfrew, C. (eds), *Science and Stonehenge*, Oxford, Proceedings of the British Academy 92 (1997), 231–56

30 Where Did the Indo-Europeans Come From?
Anthony, D.W., 'The archaeology of Indo-European origins' *Journal of Indo-European Studies* 19 (1991), 193–222

Gimbutas, M., 'The fall and transformation of Old Europe: Recapitulation' in Dexter, M.R. & Jones-Bley, K. (eds), *The Kurgan Culture and the Indo-Europeanization of Europe* , Journal of Indo-European Studies Monograph No. 18 (Washington DC, 1997) 351–72

Mallory, J.P., *In Search of the Indo-Europeans* (London & New York, 1989)

Mallory, J.P. 'The homelands of the Indo-Europeans' in Blench, R. & Spriggs, M. (eds), *Archaeology and Language I* (London & New York, 1997), 93–121

Mallory, J.P. & Adams, D.Q., *Encyclopedia of Indo-European Culture* (London, 1997)

Nichols, J., 'The epicentre of the Indo-European linguistic spread' in Blench, R. & Spriggs, M. (eds) *Archaeology and Language I* (London & New York, 1997), 122–48

Renfrew, C., *Archaeology and Language* (London, 1987)

Ancient Civilizations

31 Were the Ancient Egyptians Black Africans?

Bernal, M., *Black Athena: The Afro-Asiatic Roots of Classical Civilization*, 2 vols (New Brunswick, 1987–91)

Brothwell, D.R. & Chiarelli, B.A. (eds), *Population Biology of the Ancient Egyptians* (New York, 1973)

Celenko, T. (ed.), *Egypt in Africa* (Bloomington, 1996)

Derry, D.E., 'The dynastic race in Egypt', *Journal of Egyptian Archaeology* 42 (1956), 80–5

Diop, C.A., *The African Origin of Civilization: Myth or Reality?* (New York, 1974)

Trigger, B.G., 'Nubian, Negro, Black, Nilotic?', in Hochfield, S. & Riefstahl, E. (eds), *Africa in Antiquity: The Arts of Ancient Nubia and the Sudan I* (Brooklyn, 1978), 26–35

32 How Did They Erect Pyramids and Obelisks?

Arnold, D., *Building in Egypt: Pharaonic Stone Masonry* (Oxford & New York, 1991)

Dibner, B., *Moving the Obelisks* (Cambridge, Mass., 1970)

Edwards, I.E.S., *The Pyramids of Egypt* (Harmondsworth, 5th ed., 1993)

Engelbach, R., *The Problem of the Obelisks* (New York, 1923)

Fisher, M.J. & Fisher, D.E., *Mysteries of Lost Empires* (London, 2000)

Habachi, L., *The Obelisks of Egypt: Skyscrapers of the Past* (Cairo, 1984)

Lehner, M., *The Complete Pyramids* (London & New York, 1997)

33 The Riddle of the Sphinx

Dessenne, A., *Le Sphinx: étude iconographique* (Paris, 1957)

Demisch, H., *Die Sphinx* (Stuttgart, 1977)

de Wit, C., *Le rôle et le sens du lion dans l'Egypte ancienne* (Leiden, 1951)

Hassan, S., *The Sphinx: Its History in Light of Recent Excavations* (Cairo, 1949)

Jordan, P. & Ross, J.G., *Riddles of the Sphinx* (London & New York, 1998)

Lehner, M., 'Reconstructing the Sphinx', *Cambridge Archaeological Journal* 2/1 (1992), 3–26

34 Where Was the Land of Punt?

Bradbury, L., 'Kpn-boats, Punt trade, and a lost emporium', *Journal of the American Research Center in Egypt* 33 (1996), 37–60

Fattovich, R., 'Punt: the archaeological perspective', in *Sesto Congresso Internazionale di Egittologia, Atti II* (Turin, 1993), 399–405

Herzog, R., *Pount* (Glückstadt, 1968)

Kitchen, K.A., 'Punt and how to get there', *Orientalia* 40 (1971), 184–207

Kitchen, K.A., 'The land of Punt', in T. Shaw et al. (eds), *The Archaeology of Africa* (London, 1993), 587–608

Stevenson Smith, W., 'The land of Punt', *Journal of the American Research Center in Egypt* 1 (1962), 59–60

35 Was Tutankhamun Murdered?

Brier, B., *The Murder of Tutankhamen: a True Story* (New York & London, 1998)

Forbes, D.C., 'Abusing Pharaoh', *KMT: a Modern Journal of Egyptology* 3:1 (1992), 58–67

Harrison, R.G. & Abdalla, A.B., 'The Remains of Tutankhamun', *Antiquity* 46 (1972), 8–14

Leek, F. Filce, *The Human Remains from the Tomb of Tut'ankhamun* (Oxford, 1972)

Reeves, N., *The Complete Tutankhamun* (London & New York, 1990)

36 The Tarim Mummies: Who Were They?

Barber, E.W., *The Mummies of Ürümchi* (New York & London, 1999)

Mallory, J.P. & Mair, V.H., *The Tarim Mummies: Ancient China and the Mystery of the Earliest Peoples from the West* (London & New York, 2000)

37 Were the Olmecs African?

Coe, M.D., *America's First Civilization: Discovering the Olmec* (New York, 1968)

Diehl, R.A., 'The Olmec World', in Benson, E.P. & de la Fuente, B. (eds), *Olmec Art of Ancient Mexico* (Washington DC, 1996), 29–34

Haslip-Viera, G., Ortiz de Montellano, B. & Barbour, W., 'Robbing Native American Cultures: Van Sertima's Afrocentricity and the Olmecs', *Current Anthropology* 38:3 (1997), 419–41

Ortiz de Montellano, B., Haslip-Viera, G. & Barbour, W., 'They Were NOT Here before Columbus: Afrocentric Hyperdiffusionism in the 1990s', *Ethnohistory* 44:2 (1997), 199–234

Van Sertima, I., *They Came Before Columbus: The African Presence in Ancient America* (New York, 1976)

38 Why Did the Carthaginians Sacrifice Children?

Brown, S., *Late Carthagininan Child Sacrifice and Sacrificial Monuments in their Mediterranean Context* (Sheffield, 1991)

Hurst, H., 'Child sacrifice at Carthage', *Journal of Roman Archaeology* 7 (1994), 325–8

Hurst, H., *The Sanctuary of Tanit at Carthage in the Roman Period Journal of Roman Archaeology* Supp. Series 30 (Portsmouth, R.I., 1999)

Lancel, S., *Carthage, a History* (Oxford, 1995), 227–56

Moscati, S., *Gli adoratori de Moloch: indagine su un celebre rito cartaginese* (Milan, 1991)

Stager, L.E., 'The rite of child sacrifice at Carthage', in Pedley, J.G. (ed.), *New Light on Ancient Carthage* (Ann Arbor, 1980), 1–11

39 Ancient Oracles: Prophets or Profiteers?

Fontenrose, J., *The Delphic Oracle: Its Responses and Operations with a Catalogue of Responses* (Berkeley, 1978)

Maurizio, L., 'Anthropology and Spirit Possession: A Reconsideration of the Pythia's Role at Delphi', *Journal of Hellenic Studies* 115 (1995)

Morgan, C., *Athletes and Oracles* (Cambridge, 1985)

Parke, H.W.A., *History of the Delphic Oracle* (Oxford, 1939)

Price, S., 'Delphi and Divination', in Easterling, P.E. & Muir, J.V. (eds), *Greek Religion and Society* (Cambridge, 1985)

40 Who Were the Celts?

Chapman, M., *The Celts: the Construction of a Myth* (Basingstoke & London, 1992)

Cunliffe, B., *The Ancient Celts* (Oxford, 1997)

Green, M.J. (ed.), *The Celtic World* (London, 1995)

Haywood, J. *The Historical Atlas of the Celtic World* (London & New York, 2001)

James, S., *Exploring the World of the Celts* (London & New York, 1993)

James, S., *The Atlantic Celts: Ancient People or Modern Invention?* (London, 1999)

Kruta, V. (ed.), *The Celts* (London & New York, 1991)

41 Bog Bodies: Murder Victims or Sacrifices?

Glob, P.V., *The Bog People. Iron Age Man Preserved* (London, 1969)

van der Sanden, W., *Through Nature to Eternity. The Bog Bodies of Northwest Europe* (Amsterdam, 1996)

Turner, R.C. & Scaife, R.G. (eds), *Bog Bodies. New Discoveries and New Perspectives* (London, 1995)

42 The Lost Legions of Rome

Birley, E., 'The end of the Ninth Legion', in Butler, R.M. (ed.), *Soldier and Civilian in Roman Yorkshire* (Leicester, 1971)

Keppie, L., 'Legio VIIII in Britain: the beginning and the end', in Brewer, R. (ed.), *Roman Fortresses and their Legions* (London, 2000), 83–100

Keppie, L., *The Making of the Roman Army: from Republic to Empire* (London, new ed., 1998)

Webster, G., *The Roman Imperial Army* (London, new ed., 1998)

43 The Mysteries of Mithraism

Beard, M., North, J. & Price, S., *Religions of Rome*, Vol. 2 (Cambridge, 1998), 88–91, 305–19

Beck, R., 'Mithraism since Franz Cumont', in *Aufstieg und Niedergang der römischen Welt* II.17.4 (Berlin & New York, 1984), 2002–15

Beck, R., 'The mysteries of Mithras', in Klappenborg, J.S. & Wilson, S.G. (eds), *Voluntary Associations in the Graeco-Roman World* (London, 1996), 176–85

Turcan, R., *The Cults of the Roman Empire* (Oxford, 1996), 195–247

Ulansey, D., *The Origins of the Mithraic Mysteries* (New York, 1989)

Vermaseren, M.J., *Corpus inscriptionum et monumentorum religionis Mithraicae*, 2 vols (The Hague, 1956 and 1960)

Vermaseren, M.J., *Mithras, the Secret God* (London, 1963)

44 Lost City of the Maya: The Hunt for Site Q

Graham, I., 'Mission to La Corona', *Archaeology* 50(5) (1997), 46

Marcus, J., *Emblem and State in the Classic Maya Lowlands: An Epigraphic Approach to Territorial Organization* (Washington DC, 1976)

Martin, S. & Grube, N., *Chronicle of the Maya Kings and Queens: Deciphering the Dynasties of the Ancient Maya* (London & New York, 2000)

Schuster, A., 1997 'The Search for Site Q' *Archaeology* 50(5) (1997), 42–5

Stuart, D. & Houston, S.D., *Classic Maya Place Names*, Studies in Pre-Columbian Art and Archaeology No.33 (Washington DC, 1994)

45 The Mystery of the Nazca Lines

Aveni, A. (ed.), *The Lines of Nazca* (Philadelphia, 1990)

Aveni, A., 'Solving the Mystery of the Nasca Lines', *Archaeology* 53(3) (2000) 26–35

Aveni, A., *Nasca. Eighth Wonder of the World?* (London, 2000)

von Hagen, A. & Morris, C., *The Cities of the Ancient Andes* (London & New York, 1999)

Moseley, M., *The Incas and Their Ancestors* (London & New York, new ed., 2001)

Silverman, H., 'The Early Nasca Pilgrimage Center of Cahuachi and the Nasca Lines: Anthropological and Archaeological perspectives' in Aveni, A. (ed.), *The Lines of Nazca* (Philadelphia, 1990), 209–44

46 Who Built Tiwanaku?

Bauer, B. & Stanish, C., *Ritual and Pilgrimage in the Ancient Andes* (Austin, 2001)

Goldstein, P., 'Tiwanaku temples and state expansion: a Tiwanaku sunken-court temple in Moquegua, Peru' *Latin American Antiquity* 4(1) (1993) 22–47

Janusek, J.W., 'Craft and local power: embedded specialization in Tiwanaku cities' *Latin American Antiquity* 10(2) (1999) 107–31

Kolata, A., *The Tiwanaku* (London, 1993)

Moseley, M., *The Incas and their Ancestors* (London & New York, new ed., 2001)

47 Why Did the Incas Sacrifice Children?

Bauer, B., *The Sacred Landscape of the Inca. The Cusco Ceque System* (Austin, 1998)

Cobo, B., *Inca Religion and Customs.* Trans. & ed. R. Hamilton (Austin, 1990 [1653])

McEwan, C. & van de Guchte, M., 'Ancestral Time and Sacred Space in Inca State Ritual' in Townsend, R. (ed.), *The Ancient Americas: Art from Sacred Landscapes* (Chicago & London, 1992), 359–71

Reinhard, J., 'Llullaillaco: An Investigation of the World's Highest Archaeological Site' *Latin American Indian Literatures Journal* 9(1) (1993) 32–65

Reinhard, J., 'Frozen in Time' *National Geographic Magazine* (November 1999) 36–55

48 How Did the Polynesians Find their Homeland?

Beaglehole, J., *The Life of Captain James Cook* (Palo Alto, 1974)

Bellwood, P., *The Polynesians* (London & New York, 1987)

Finney, B., *Voyage of Rediscovery* (Berkeley, 1994)

Irwin, G., *The Prehistoric Exploration and Colonization of the Pacific* (Cambridge, 1992)

49 Statues and Survival on Easter Island

Diamond, J., *Guns, Germs and Steel* (New York & London, 1997)

Finney, B., *Voyage of Rediscovery* (Berkeley, Los Angeles, London, 1994)

Heyerdahl, T. & Ferdon, E.N. Jr. (eds), *Archaeology of Easter Island* (Santa Fe, 1961)

Kirch, P.V., *On the Road of the Winds* (Berkeley, Los Angeles, London, 2000)

Metraux, A., *Ethnology of Easter Island*, Bernice P. Bishop Museum Bulletin 140 (Honolulu, 1940)

Routledge, K., *Mystery of Easter Island* (London, 1919)

Van Tilburg, J. *Easter Island Archaeology, Ecology and Culture* (London & Washington DC, 1994)

Tombs and Lost Treasures
50 The Puzzle of Tomb 55

Bell, M., 'An Armchair Excavation of KV 55', *Journal of the American Research Center in Egypt* 27 (1990), 97–137

Brock, L.P., 'Theodore Davis and the Rediscovery of Tomb 55', in Wilkinson, R.H. (ed.), *Valley of the Sun Kings: New Explorations in the Tombs of the Pharaohs* (Tucson, 1995), 34–46

Dodson, A., 'Kings' Valley Tomb 55 and the Fates of the Amarna Kings', *Amarna Letters* 3 (1994), 92–103

Dodson, A., *The Coffins and Canopic Equipment from the Tomb of Tutankhamun* (Oxford, in preparation)

Forbes, D.C., 'The "Missing" Coffin Trough from KV55', *KMT: a Modern Journal of Egyptology* 10/3 (1999), 18–19

Harrison, R.G., 'An Anatomical Examination of the Pharaonic Remains Purported to be Akhenaten' *Journal of Egyptian Archaeology* 52 (1966), 95–119

Reeves, C.N., 'A Reappraisal of Tomb 55 in the Valley of the Kings', *Journal of Egyptian Archaeology* 67 (1981), 48–55

51 The Lost Tomb of Alexander the Great

Adriani, A., *La tomba di Alessandro: realtà, ipotesi e fantasie* (Rome, 2000)

Colvin, H.M., *Architecture and the After-Life* (New Haven & London, 1991), 42

Fraser, P.M., *Ptolemaic Alexandria* (Oxford, 1972), I. 14–17 & II. 31–3 (n. 79) & 35 (n. 83)

Fedak, J., *Monumental Tombs of the Hellenistic Age* (Toronto, 1990)

Grimm, G., *Alexandria. Die erste Königsstadt der hellenistischen Welt*, (Mainz, 1998), 66–9

52 The Tomb of China's First Emperor

Cotterell, A., *The First Emperor of China* (London, 1981)

Li Xueqin, *Eastern Zhou and Qin Civilizations* (New Haven, 1985)

Loewe, M. & O'Shaughnessy, E.L. (eds), *The Cambridge History of Ancient China* (Cambridge, 1999)

Pirazzoli-t'Serstevens, M., *The Han Dynasty* (New York, 1982)

53 The Hidden Treasure of the Dead Sea

Kyle McCarter Jr, P., 'The mystery of the Copper Scroll after 40 years' in Shanks, H. (ed), *The Dead Sea Scrolls*, BAS (1992)

Vermes, G., *Introduction to the Complete Dead Sea Scrolls* (London, 1999)

Wolters, W., *The Copper Scroll, Overview, Text and Translation* (Sheffield, 1996)

54 The Tomb of Christ

Biddle, M., *The Tomb of Christ* (Stroud, 1999)

Murphy-O'Connor, J., *The Holy Land* (Oxford, 4th ed., 1998)

Ancient and Undeciphered Scripts
55 The Origins of Writing
Englund, R.K., 'The origins of script', *Science*, 11 June 1993
Claiborne, R., *The Birth of Writing* (New York, 1974)
Harris, R., *The Origin of Writing* (London, 1986)
Marshack, A., *The Roots of Civilization* (New York, 2nd ed., 1991)
Robinson, A., *The Story of Writing* (London & New York, 1995)
Schmandt-Besserat, D., *How Writing Came About* (Austin, 1996)

56 The Proto-Elamite Script
Nissen, H.J., Damerow, P. & Englund, R.K., *Archaic Bookkeeping* (Chicago, 1993)
Potts, D.T., *The Archaeology of Elam* (Cambridge, 1999)
Walker, C.B.F., *Cuneiform* (London, 1987)

57 The Indus Script
Jansen, M., Mulloy, M. & Urban, G. (eds), *Forgotten Cities on the Indus* (Mainz, 1991)
Kenoyer, J.M., *Ancient Cities of the Indus Valley Civilization* (Karachi, 1998)
Parpola, A., *Deciphering the Indus Script* (Cambridge, 1994)
Possehl, G.L., *Indus Age: The Writing System* (Philadelphia, 1996)
http://www.harappa.com

58 Linear A & the Phaistos Disc
Chadwick, J., *Linear B and Related Scripts* (London, 1987)
Duhoux, Y., *Le Disque de Phaistos* (Louvain, 1977)
Pope, M. & Raison, J., 'Linear A: changing perspectives', in Duhoux, Y. (ed.), *Études Minoennes I: Le Linéaire A* (Louvain, 1978)
http://www.math.leidenuniv.nl/%7Elipi/archaeology/phaistos.html

59 The Origins of the Alphabet
Gardiner, A.H., 'The Egyptian origin of the Semitic alphabet', *Journal of Egyptian Archaeology*, 3 (1916)
Healey, J.F., *The Early Alphabet* (London, 1990)
King, C., *The Twenty-Two Letters* (London, 1966)
Naveh, J., *Origins of the Alphabet* (London, 1975)
Powell, B.B., *Homer and the Origin of the Greek Alphabet* (Cambridge, 1991)
Sassoon, J., 'Who on earth invented the alphabet?', *Visible Language*, Spring (1990)

60 The Etruscan Alphabet
Bonfante, G. & Bonfante, L., *The Etruscan Language* (Manchester, 1983)
Bonfante, L., *Etruscan* (London, 1990)
Pallottino, M., *The Etruscans* (London, rev. ed., 1975)
Spivey, N., *Etruscan Art* (London & New York, 1997)

61 The Meroitic Script
Griffith, F. Ll., 'Meroitic inscriptions', in Randall Maciver, D. & Woolley, C.L., *Areika* (Oxford, 1909)
Shinnie, P.L., *Meroe: A Civilisation of the Sudan* (London, 1967)
Welsby, D.A., *The Kingdom of Kush* (London, 1996)

62 The Zapotec & Isthmian Scripts
Coe, M.D., *Mexico* (London & New York, 4th ed., 1994)
Justeson, J.S. & Kaufman, T., 'A decipherment of epi-Olmec hieroglyphic writing', *Science*, 259, 19 March (1993)
Macri, M.J., 'Maya and other Mesoamerican scripts', in Daniels, P.T. & Bright, W. (eds), *The World's Writing Systems* (New York, 1996)
Urcid, J., 'Codices on stone: the genesis of writing in ancient Oaxaca', *Indiana Journal of Hispanic Literatures*, 13 (1998)

63 Runes & Pictish Symbol Stones
Cummins, W.A., *The Age of the Picts* (Stroud, 1995)
Elliott, R.W.V., 'The Runic script', in Daniels, P.T. & Bright, W. (eds), *The World's Writing Systems* (New York, 1996)
Page, R.I., *Runes* (London, 1987)
Sutherland, E., *The Pictish Guide* (Edinburgh, 1997)

64 Rongorongo
Bahn, P. & Flenley, J., *Easter Island, Earth Island* (London & New York, 1992)
Fischer, S.R., *Rongorongo: The Easter Island Script* (Oxford, 1997)
http://www.rongorongo.org

The Fall of Civilizations
65 The Thera Eruption & the Fall of the Minoans
Dickinson, O., *The Aegean Bronze Age* (Cambridge & New York,1994)
Hood, S., *The Minoans* (London & New York, 1971)
Friedrich, W.L., *Fire in the Sea: The Santorini Volcano, Natural History and the Legend of Atlantis* (Cambridge, 2000)
Luce, J.V., *The End of Atlantis: New Light on an Old Legend* (London & New York 1969)
Manning, S., 1988. 'The Bronze Age Eruption of Thera', *Journal of Mediterranean Archaeology* 1(1) (1988) 17–82
Manning, S., *Absolute Chronology of the Aegean Bronze Age* (Sheffield, 1995)

66 The Fall of Rome
Bowersock, G.W., Brown, P. & Grabar, O., *Late Antiquity. A Guide to the Postclassical World* (Cambridge, Mass. & London, 1999)
Brown, P., *The World of Late Antiquity. From Marcus Aurelius to Mohammed* (London, 1971)
Gibbon, E., *The History of the Decline and Fall of the Roman Empire*, 6 vols (London 1776–88; new ed. by D. Womersley, 3 vols, London, 1994)
Jones, A.H.M., *The Later Roman Empire, 284–602. A Social, Economic, and Administrative Survey*, 3 vols. (Oxford, 1964)
Webster, L. & Brown, M. (eds), *The Transformation of the Roman World AD 400–900* (London, 1997)

67 El Niños & the Collapse of Moche Civilization
Alva, W. & Donnan, C., *The Royal Tombs of Sipán* (Los Angeles, 1992)
Donnan, C., *Moche Art and Iconography* (Los Angeles, 1978).
Fagan, B.M., *Floods, Famines, and Emperors: El Niño and the Collapse of Civilizations* (New York, 1999)
Moseley, M., *The Incas and Their Ancestors.* (London & New York, new ed., 2001)
Shimada, I., *Pampa Grande and the Mochica Culture* (Austin, 1994)

68 Why Did Maya Civilization Collapse?
Coe, M., *The Maya* (London & New York, 6th ed., 1999)
Culbert, P., (ed.), *The Ancient Maya Collapse* (Albuquerque, 1973)
Culbert, P., 'The Collapse of Classic Maya Civilization' in Yoffee, N. & Cowgill, G. (eds), *The Collapse of Ancient States and Civilizations* (Tucson, 1988), 232–54
Sabloff, J.A., *The Cities of Ancient Mexico* (London & New York, 1997).
Schele, L. & Freidel, D., *A Forest of Kings* (New York, 1990)

69 What Happened to the Anasazi?
Cordell, L., *Archaeology of the Southwest* (San Diego, 2nd ed., 1997)
Ferguson, W.M. & Rohn, A.H., *Anasazi Ruins of the Southwest in Color* (Albuquerque, 1987)
Plog, S., *Ancient Peoples of the American Southwest* (London & New York, 1997)
Roberts, D., *In Search of the Old Ones: Exploring the Anasazi World of the Southwest* (New York, 1996)
Stewart, D., *Anasazi America* (Albuquerque, 2000)

70 Catastrophic Impacts from Outer Space?
Baillie, M., *A Slice Through Time: Dendrochronology and Precision Dating* (London, 1995)
Baillie, M., *Exodus to Arthur* (London, 1999)
Drews, R., *The End of the Bronze Age: Changes in Warfare and the Catastrophe ca. 1200 B.C.* (Princeton, 1993)
Keys, D., *Catastrophe: An Investigation into the Origins of the Modern World* (London, 1999)
Levy, D.H., *The Quest for Comets* (Oxford, 1995)
Velikovsky, I., *Worlds in Collision* (London, 1950)

Sources of Illustrations

t = top; a = above; l = left; r = right; c = centre; b = bottom

1 Heraklion Archaeological Museum. 2–3 © N. J. Saunders. 5l Z. Radovan, Jerusalem. 5r © Mick Sharp. 6l Robert Harding Picture Library. 6r © Daniel Schwartz/Lookat, Zürich. 7l © British Museum, 2001. 7r Louvre, Paris. 10–11 Courtesy of the French Ministry of Culture and Communication, Regional Direction for Cultural Affairs – Rhône-Alpes, Regional Department of Archaeology. 12 Louvre, Paris. Photo AKG, London/Erich Lessing. 13t © British Museum, 2001. 13b Elizabeth Pendleton. 14t © Christopher Chippindale. 14b © Johan Reinhard. 15 Z. Radovan, Jerusalem. 16t, 16–17 © Tony Morrison/South American Pictures. 16b Museum of Antiquities, University of Newcastle upon Tyne. 17 Museo Archeologico, Florence. Photo Gabinetto Fotografico, Florence. 18–19 © The National Gallery, London. 20 MS Fr 112, Bibliothèque nationale, Paris. 21 Bibliothèque Royale de Belgique, Brussels, Belgium/Bridgeman Art Library. 22l Collection Kofler Truniger, Lucerne. Photo Eileen Tweedy. 22r British Museum. Photo Eileen Tweedy. 23t © British Museum, 2001. 23b Pergamonmuseum, Berlin. Photo AKG London/Erich Lessing. 24l S. Maria del Carmine, Brancacci Chapel, Florence. 24r © British Museum, 2001. 25 Z. Radovan, Jerusalem. 26 © British Museum, 2001. 27 Werner Forman Archive. 28 Department of Western Asiatic Antiquities, British Museum, London. 29t Photo Sean Markey/ nationalgeographic.com © 2001 National Geographic Society. All rights reserved. 29b P. Winton. 30, 31t Z. Radovan, Jerusalem. 31b Palacio de Liria, Madrid. 32 Ashmolean Museum, Oxford. 33t P. Winton. 33b Photo © Jürgen Liepe. 34 Glasgow Museums: The Burrell Collection. 35t P. Winton. 35b Z. Radovan, Jerusalem. 36, 36–7, 37 © K. D. Politis. 38 Holkham Hall, Norfolk. 39t Photo Hirmer. 39b A. Kircher, *Mundus Subterraneus*, 1678. 40 AKG London/Erich Lessing. 40–1 © Peter Clayton. 41 Heraklion Archaeological Museum . Photo Agenzia Fotografica Luisa Ricciarini. 42t I. Donnelly, *Atlantis: The Antediluvian World*, 1882. 42b Museo del Prado, Madrid. Photo AKG London. 43 © The National Gallery, London. 44–5 Drawing by Lloyd Townsend. 45c P. Winton after Dörpfeld, revised M. Korfmann. 45bl © Peter Clayton. 45r Photo AKG London. 46t Courtesy Troia Project, Eberhard-Karls-University, Tübingen. 46bl Mansell Collection. 46br Pushkin Museum, Moscow. 47 Mykonos Museum. Photo German Archaeological Institute, Athens. 48 © Tate Gallery, London 2000. 49t Vienna Kunsthistorisches Museum. Photo AKG London. 49b Victoria & Albert Museum, London, UK/Bridgeman Art Library. 50 Heraklion Archaeological Museum. Photo AKG London. 51tl © Peter Clayton. 51r Heraklion Archaeological Museum. Photo AKG/Erich Lessing. 51bl After Dr Stylianos Alexiou (*Minoikos Politismos*). 52 The Metropolitan Museum of Art, Harris Brisbane Dick Fund, 1934. 53t Photo John Egan/Severin Archive. 53b The State Hermitage Museum, St Petersburg. 54t Mary Evans Picture Library. 54b, 55l, 55r P. Winton. 56 © Jewish National and University Library, Jerusalem. Beth Hatefutsoth Photo Archive, Tel Aviv. 57t © Jerusalem, Amishav – on behalf of the dispersed of Israel. Beth Hatefutsoth Photo Archive, Tel Aviv. 57b © British Museum, 2001. Photo AKG London/ Erich Lessing. 58t P. Winton. 58r From *Illustrations to the Epitome of the Ancient History of Japan*, by N. Mckeod, Kyoto, 1877. © Jewish National and University Library, Jerusalem. Beth Hatefutsoth Photo Archive, Tel Aviv. 58 © Tudor Parfitt. 60 Bibliothèque Nationale, Paris. 61t, 61b, 62t Z. Radovan, Jerusalem. 62b Palestine Archaeological Museum. 63 Michael Molnar after Raffaele Garrucci, *Storia dell arte cristina nei primi otto della chiesa* (Prato, G. Guasti, 1881), vol. 6, pl. 485. 64t Photo AKG London/Erich Lessing. 64l, 64r Molnar Collection. Photo Michael Molnar. 65 Photo AKG London/Cameraphoto. 66tl, 66tr Michael Molnar. 66b Photo David Silverman © 2000. 67 © David Lyons/Event Horizons. 68t © Crown Copyright NMR. 68b Photo courtesy Department of Archaeology, Glasgow University. 69t © English Heritage Photo Library/Jonathan Bailey. 69b © Hampshire City Council. 70 National Museum of Ireland, Dublin. 71l By permission of the Holy Shroud Guild. 71c By permission of Father Damianos, the Sacred Council, and the Monks of St. Catherine's Monastery. 71r Fortean Picture Library. 72l, 72r © 1978 Barrie Schwortz. 73t © 1978 Mark Evans. 73c © 1997 Barrie Schwortz. 73b Fortean Picture Library. 74 © Justin Kerr. 75tl, 75tr From Alfred Percival Maudslay *Archaeology*, R. H. Porter and Dulau London, 1889–1902. 75b Codex Dresdensis, p74. 76l, 76r Richard Townsend. 77t Museo del Templo Mayor, Mexico City. 77b Bodleian Library, Oxford, MS. Arch. Selden. A. I, f. 2r. 78t P. Winton. 78b Museo Nacional de Antropología, Mexico City. Photo Richard

Townsend. 79 © Christopher Chippindale. 80t © Ken Wilson, Robert Harding Picture Library. 80b © Christopher Chippindale. 81tl Private Collection, New York. Werner Forman Archive. 81tr © Christopher Chippindale. 81b Bruce Nabegeyo, *Ngalyod – Rainbow Serpent*, 1995. Reproduced by permission of the artist/Injalak Arts & Crafts Association. Photo © Christopher Chippindale. 82–3 © Jean Williamson/Mick Sharp. 84 Photo Jean Vertut. 85t Photo Michael Day. 85b P. Winton. 86 © 2001, The Natural History Museum, London. 86–7 Photo Michael Day. 87 Courtesy of the National Museums of Kenya. 89 Photo Anna Klopet. 90 Photo by Robert I. M. Campbell. Courtesy of the National Museums of Kenya. 91t P. Winton. 91c Sackler School of Medicine, Tel Aviv University. 91b Volker Steger/Nordstar – 4 Million Years of Man/Science Photo Library. 92 T. Huxley *Man's Place in Nature*, 1863. 93t Giovanni Casselli. 93b P. Winton/ A. Petersen. 94t Photo courtesy Jean-Jacques Hublin. 94 John Reader/ Science Photo Library. 95l © Instituto Portuguès de Arqueologia, Lisbon. 95r © Stephen Morley. Reproduced by permission of Channel Four Books. 96 Photo A. B. Weiden. 97t Musée des Antiquités Nationales, St. Germain-en-Laye. 97b Courtesy of the French Ministry of Culture & Communication, Regional Direction for Cultural Affairs – Rhône-Alpes, Regional Department of Archaeology. 98, 98–9 Photo M. O. & J. Plassard. 99 Photo A. B. Weiden. 100 Photo Laborie, Bergerac. 101 P. Winton. 102 © Stephen L. Davis. 103tl, bl © 2001, The Natural History Museum, London. 103r © Alan Thorne. 104 Photo J. L. Shellshear Museum. 105 Photo courtesy J. M. Adovasio, University of Pittsburgh. 106l Denver Museum of Natural History. 106r Montana Historical Society Collection, gift of Faye Case in memory of Ben Hargis. Photo Peter A. Bostrom. 106–7 Photo Tom Dillehay. 107t, 107b Photo © James C. Chatters. 108 P. Winton. 109 Photo Eileen Tweedy. 110 Drawing Andrew Farmer, A. Lister & P. Bahn *Mammoths*, Marshall Editions, 1994. 111t N.K. Vereshchagin. 111b Denver Museum of Natural History. 112 G. Penna. 112–13 G. Penna after Ann Winterbotham, A. Lister & P. Bahn *Mammoths*, Marshall Editions, 1994. 113 Photo by Denis Fennin/ American Natural History Museum, NYC. 114 Z. Radovan, Jerusalem. 115tl Collection of the Israel Antiquities Authority. Photo © The Israel Museum, Jerusalem. 115cr, b © Andrew Moore. 116 P. Winton. 117 © Andrew Moore. 118, 119t © Christopher Chippindale. 119b, 120t © Christopher Chippindale. 120b, 121tr Alison Gascoigne. 121c Rock Art Research Institute, University of Witwatersrand. 121b © 1982 Centro Camuno di Studi Preistorici, 25044 Capo di Monte, Italy. 122 © Paul Bahn. 123, 124t © Mick Sharp. 124b George Eogan. 125t Picardt, from *Korte Beschryvinge von England, Scotlande ende Irland*. 125b M. Jos le Doare, Chateaulin (Finistère). 126 © David Lyons/Event Horizons. 127 © Skyscan Balloon Photography. English Heritage Photo Library. 128 Photo AKG London/Erich Lessing. 129t Photo C. M. Dixon. 129b Photo AKG London/ Erich Lessing. 130t Photo © Peter Clayton. 131 Dúchas, The Heritage Service, Dublin. 132 © Frank Spooner Pictures. Photo Hanny Paul. 133l Christin Beeck, Romisch-Germanisches Zentralmuseum, Mainz. 133r South Tyrol Museum of Archaeology, Museumstr. 43, I-39100 Bozen, www.iceman.it. Photo Augustin Ochsenreiter. 134l © Frank Spooner Pictures. 134r Christin Beeck, Romisch-Germanisches Zentralmuseum, Mainz. 135 © Frank Spooner Pictures. Photo G. Hinterleitner. 136–7 © English Heritage Photo Library. 137 © Wendy George, 1999. 138 © Mick Sharp. 139 Photo © Phil Rees. Dragon News & Picture Agency. 140t P. Winton after Richards, J. & Whitby, M., in Cunliffe, B. & Renfrew, C. (eds), *Science and Stonehenge* (1997). 140b Photo Julian Richards. 141 Historisches Bezirkmuseum, Lowetsch. Photo AKG London/Erich Lessing. 142t, 142bl, 142br 143t 143bl, 143br P. Winton after J. P. Mallory and V. H. Mair, *Tarim Mummies*, Thames & Hudson, 2000. 144–5 © Peter Clayton. 146 Photo Heidi Grassley © Thames & Hudson Ltd. 147l, 147r Museum of Fine Arts, Boston. 148t, 148b, 149 Cairo Museum. Photo © Jürgen Liepe. 150 I. Rosellini, *Monumenti dell'Egitto*, 1834. 151l Mark Lehner. 151r Metropolitan Museum of Art, New York. 152–3 Courtesy Czech Institute of Egyptology, Prague. Photo Kamil Vodera. 153, 154t Lesley & Roy Adkins Picture Library. 154b P. Winton after M. Prendergast, in M.J. Fisher and D.E. Fisher *Mysteries of Lost Empires*, Channel Four Books, 2000. 155 Mark Lehner. 156 Photo Heidi Grassley © Thames & Hudson Ltd. 157tl Photo © Jürgen Liepe. 157tr © John Ross. 157b © Simon Harris. Robert Harding Picture Library. 158 *La Description de l'Égypte*, Paris 1809. 159 Mark Lehner. 160t A. Kircher, *Turris Babel*, 1679. 160b Mark Lehner. 161l, 161r Cairo Museum. Photo © Jürgen Liepe. 162t Photo © F. Jackson, Robert Harding Picture Library. 162b A. Mariette, *Deir-el-Bahari*, 1877. 163t P. Winton. 163b Photo © Ullstein. 164l © John Ross. 164r Griffith

Institute, Ashmolean Museum, Oxford. 165t Cairo Museum. 165b © John Ross. 166l Griffith Institute, Ashmolean Museum, Oxford. 166r From Harrison and Abdalla, *Antiquity*, 46/181, 1972. 167, 168 Jeffery Newbury, *Discover Magazine*. 169 Photo He Duxiu. 170tl After Albert von Le Coq, *Chotscho*, Berlin, 1913, D. Reimer, 21. 170tr, 170b P. Winton after J.P. Mallory and V.H. Mair *Tarim Mummies*, Thames & Hudson, 2000.171 Richard Stewart/NGS Image Collection. 172 Photo © Rafael Doniz. 173 Roger Wilson. 174 T. Wellman. 174–5, 175tr Roger Wilson. 175bl Bardo Museum, Tunis. 176 Roger Wilson. 177 Antikenmuseum, Staatliche Museen Preussischer Kulturbesitz, Berlin. 178t Photo © Tony Gervis. Robert Harding Picture Library. 178b Courtesy École Francaise D'Athènes. 179t © G. Dagli Orti. 179b Photo Heidi Grassley © Thames & Hudson Ltd. 180–1 Delphi Museum. 181 Delphi Museum. Photo Hirmer. 182 © Landesamt für Denkmalpflege Hessen. Photo Ursula Seitz-Gray. 183 © David Lyons/Event Horizons. 184 Museo Nazionale delle Terme, Rome. Photo Hirmer. 185 Rheinisches Landesmuseum, Trier. 186 © Silkeborg Museum, Denmark. 187l Archäologisches Landesmuseum Christian-Albrechts-Universität, Schleswig. 187r, 188 National Museum of Denmark, Copenhagen. 189l Rheinisches Landesmuseum, Bonn. 189c, 189r Hunter Coin Cabinet, The Hunterian Museum, University of Glasgow. 190t © National Museum of Wales, Cardiff. 190b, 191t Courtesy of the Yorkshire Museum. 191b Photo courtesy of The Ermine Street Guard. 192t P. Winton. 192b © Reading Museum Service (Reading Borough Council). All rights reserved. 193 Courtesy of the Smithsonian Institution, Freer Gallery of Art, Washington DC. 194 British Museum. Photo Roger Wilson. 195t Kurpfälzisches Museum, Heidelberg. Photo Roger Wilson. 195b Roger Wilson. 196tl Werner Forman Archive. 196tr, 196b Roger Wilson. 197l P. Winton. 197r Simon Martin. 198t © Justin Kerr. 198b Simon Martin. 199 © Tony Morrison/ South American Pictures. 200l P. Winton. 200r Archivio Whitestar. 201t University Museum of Archaeology and Ethnology, Cambridge. 201b Courtesy Helaine Silverman, Dept. of Anthropology, University of Illinois, Urbana-Champaign. 202l Museo de Metales Preciosos Precolombinos, La Paz. Photo Dirk Bakker. 202r Michael Glavin after Alan Kolata. 203t Robert Harding Picture Library. 203b Photo Robert Frerck © Robert Harding Picture Library. 204 Photo Charles Stanish. 205l © Johan Reinhard. 205r Photo Loren McIntyre. 206l © Johan Reinhard. 206r, 207 Photo Loren McIntyre. 208 P. Winton. 209t Photo © Derek Bayes. Aspect Picture Library. 209b © David Hiser/Photographers Aspen Inc. 210 © Patrick Short. 211 Duché de Vancy,1786. 212l © Corson Hirschfeld. 212tr Drawings by Cristián Arévalo Pakarati. 212–13 © Geoff Renner. Robert Harding Picture Library. 213 © Jo Anne Van Tilburg. 214 Photo Elizabeth Pendleton. 214–15, 215tl, 215tr © Jo Anne Van Tilburg. 216–17 © Daniel Schwartz/Lookat, Zürich. 218 Z. Radovan, Jerusalem. 219l Dublin Historical Society, Dublin, New Hampshire. Gift of Jessie Taylor Hale. 219r © 1985 H. Parkinson and Richard B. Parkinson. 220t © Jürgen Liepe. 220b © 1985 H. Parkinson and Richard B. Parkinson. 221 Egyptian Museum, Cairo. 222tl, tr From F. G. Harrison, *Journal of Egyptian Archaeology* 52, 1966, pl. XXVIII (I). 222l Griffith Institute, Ashmolean Museum, Oxford. 223l Photo Othmar Pferschy, Istanbul. 223r Bibliothèque Nationale, Paris. 224 © Michael Pfrommer. 225t P. Winton. 225b H. M. Colvin *Architecture and the After-Life*, Yale University Press, 1991. 226t, 226b Photo Roger Wilson. 227 Photo INDEX/Summerfield. 228t P. Winton. 228b, 229t © Daniel Schwartz/Lookat, Zürich. 229b, 230 Photo INDEX/Summerfield. 231 Photo David Silverman © 2000. 232t Z. Radovan, Jerusalem. 232b, 233 Allegro Photo Archive (Manchester Museum) © Estate of John M. Allegro. 234 Z. Radovan, Jerusalem. 235 Marcello Bertinetti/Archivio Whitestar. 236 Arthaud – Michael Audrain. 237t Photograph John Crook. 237b Luca Rossi/Archivio Whitestar. 238–9, 240 © British Museum. 241 Photo © RMN – Gérard Blot. 242l Photo Jean Vertut. 242tr, 243tl Institute of Graphic Arts for U. S. Department of Transportation. 243tr © 2001 Cordon Art B.V. – Baarn, Holland. All rights reserved. 243cr Photo Albert Shoucair. 244t From G. Palatino *Libro Nuovo*, c.1540. 244b By kind permission of the British Library. 245 P. Winton after Lamberg-Karlovsky. 246t Photo © RMN. 246b T. Wellman after fig. 74 of Hans J. Nissen, Peter Damerow, R. K. Englund *Archaic Bookkeeeping*, University of Chicago Press 1993. 247 Robert Harding Picture Library. 248tl P. Winton. 248tr National Museum, New Delhi. 249tl Photo Jyrki Lyytikkä for the University of Helsinki/Department of Archaeology and Museums, Government of Pakistan. 249tr Photo Jyrki Lyytikkä for the University of Helsinki/Archaeological Survey of India. 249b P. Winton after A. Parpola. 250 Ashmolean Museum, Oxford. 250–1 M. Winch/Axiom. 251 A. Evans *The Palace at Minos*, Vol.IV, 1935. 252l, 252r Heraklion Archaeological Museum. 254 P. Winton after A. Petersen, A. Robinson *Story of Writing*, London 1995. 255t © Michael Jenner. 255b Rudyard Kipling *Just So Stories* 1902. 256t British Museum, London. 256bl William Foxwell Albright's *The Proto-Sinaitic Inscriptions and their Decipherment, Harvard Theological Studies*, vol. 22, 1966. Copyright 1966 by the President and Fellows of Harvard College. 256br, 257l T. Wellman. 257r Photograph by Bruce Zuckerman and Marilyn Lundberg, West Semitic Research. 258r The Metropolitan Museum of Art, Fletcher Fund, 1924. 259l Museo di Villa Giulia, Rome. 260 Derek Welsby. 261r Smithsonian Institution, Washington DC. 262Drawing courtesy George Stuart. 263 Photo Jan Rietz/Tiofoto. 264c T. Wellman. 264b © The Trustees of the National Museums of Scotland 2001. 265l The Sutherland Trust, Dunrobin Castle. Photo David Sim. 265r © The Trustees of the National Museums of Scotland 2001. 267t Peter Bellwood. 268–9 © Tom Till. 270 Photo AKG London. 271 P. Winton. 272r Photo Henri Stierlin. 272b © Jürgen Liepe. 273t, 273b Photo Henri Stierlin. 274 Photo G. Goakimedes. 275 P. Winton. 276t Academia de la Historia, Madrid. Werner Forman Archive. 276b Museo delle Terme, Rome. Photo German Archaeological Institute, Rome. 277t Photo AKG London/Erich Lessing. 277b Photo Mark Humphries. 278 P. Winton. 279l Tony Morrison/South American Pictures. 279r P. Winton. 280l British Museum, London. 280r © UCLA Fowler Museum of Cultural History. Photo Susan Einstein, Los Angeles. 281 Photo Steve Bourget. 282 P. Winton. 283t T. Proskouriakoff. 283b © Justin Kerr. 284 N. Grube 285t © Justin Kerr. 285b Photo Massimo Borchi/Archivio Whitestar. 286 National Park Service, US Dept. of the Interior. Photo by Fred Mung, Jr. 287tl, 287tr P. Winton after Linda Cordell *Archaeology of the Southwest*, Academic Press Inc., 1997. 287b P. Winton after Carol J. Ellick 288t, 288b © Mick Sharp. 289t, 289b Photo Mike Baillie. 290–1 NASA/Science Photo Library. 291 David Parker/Science Photo Library. 292t Musée de la Tapisserie, Bayeux. Photo Giraudon 292b © Novosti (London).

Sources of quotations:
67 Winston Churchill, *A History of the English-Speaking Peoples*, 1956; 79 Wally Carauna, *Aboriginal Art*, 1993; 85 Richard Dawkins, *The Cambridge Encyclopedia of Human Evolution*, 1992; 89 Stephen Pinker, *The Language Instinct*, 1994; 92 Erick Trinkaus and Pat Shipman, *The Neanderthals, Changing the Image of Mankind*, 1992; 96 John Keats, Ode on a Grecian Urn, 1819; 101 James Barripang, in Stephen Davis, *Above Capricorn. Aboriginal Biographies from Northern Australia*, 1994; 105 Tom Dillehay, *The First Settlement of the Americas: A New Prehistory*, 2000; 109 Paul Martin, *Discovering Archaeology*, Sep/Oct 1999; 114 V. Gordon Childe, *Man Makes Himself*, 1936; 118 W.J. Sollas, *Ancient Hunters and their Modern Representatives*, 1911; 123 H.M. Grover, *A Voice from Stonehenge*, 1847; 128 Marija Gimbutas, *The Living Goddesses*, 1999; 132 Konrad Spindler, *The Man in the Ice*, 1994; 141 James Parsons, *Remains of Japhet*, 1767; 147 Émile Amélineau, *Nouvelles fouilles d'Abydos*, 1899; 167 Aurel Stein, quoted in *The Tarim Mummies*, 2000; 171 José Melgar y Serrano, quoted in *Olmec Art of Ancient Mexico*, ed. Elizabeth P. Benson and Beatriz de la Fuente; 182 J.R.R. Tolkien, 'English and Welsh', in *Angles and Britons; the O'Donnell Lectures*, 1963; 189 Rosemary Sutcliff, *The Eagle of the Ninth*, 1954; 193 Rudyard Kipling, 'Pook of Puck's Hill', 1906; 197 John Lloyd Stephens, *Incidents of Travel in Central America, Chiapas and Yucatan*, 1841; 199 Anthony Aveni, 'Solving the Mystery of the Nasca Lines', *Archaeology* 53(3), 2000; 211 Katherine Routledge, unpublished letter, Royal Geographical Society Archives; 219 Gaston Maspero, in J. Lindon Smith, *Temples, Tombs and Ancient Art*, 1956; 231 Kyle McCarter, 'The Mystery of the Copper Scroll' in *The Dead Sea Scrolls After Forty Years*, 1991; 245 Daniel T. Potts, *The Archaeology of Elam*, 1999; 247 Sir Mortimer Wheeler, *The Indus Civilization*, 1953; 250 Yves Duhoux, 'How not to decipher the Phaistos disc', *American Journal of Archaeology*, 104, 2000; 254 Joseph Naveh, *Origins of the Alphabet*, 1975; 258 Massimo Pallottino, *The Etruscans*, 1975; 260 Francis Ll. Griffith, 'Meroitic inscriptions', in D. Randall Maciver and C. Leonard Woolley, *Areika*, 1909; 261 Martha J. Macri, 'Maya and other Mesoamerican scripts', in Peter T. Daniels and William Bright, eds, *The World's Writing Systems*, 1996; 271 S. Marinatos, 'Thera: Key to the Riddle of Minos', *National Geographic*, 1972; 279 Water Alva and Christopher Donnan, *The Royal Tombs of Sipán*, 1992; 286 Tessie Naranjo, 'Thoughts on Migration by Santa Clara Pueblo', *Journal of Anthropological Archaeology* 14(2), 1995.

Index